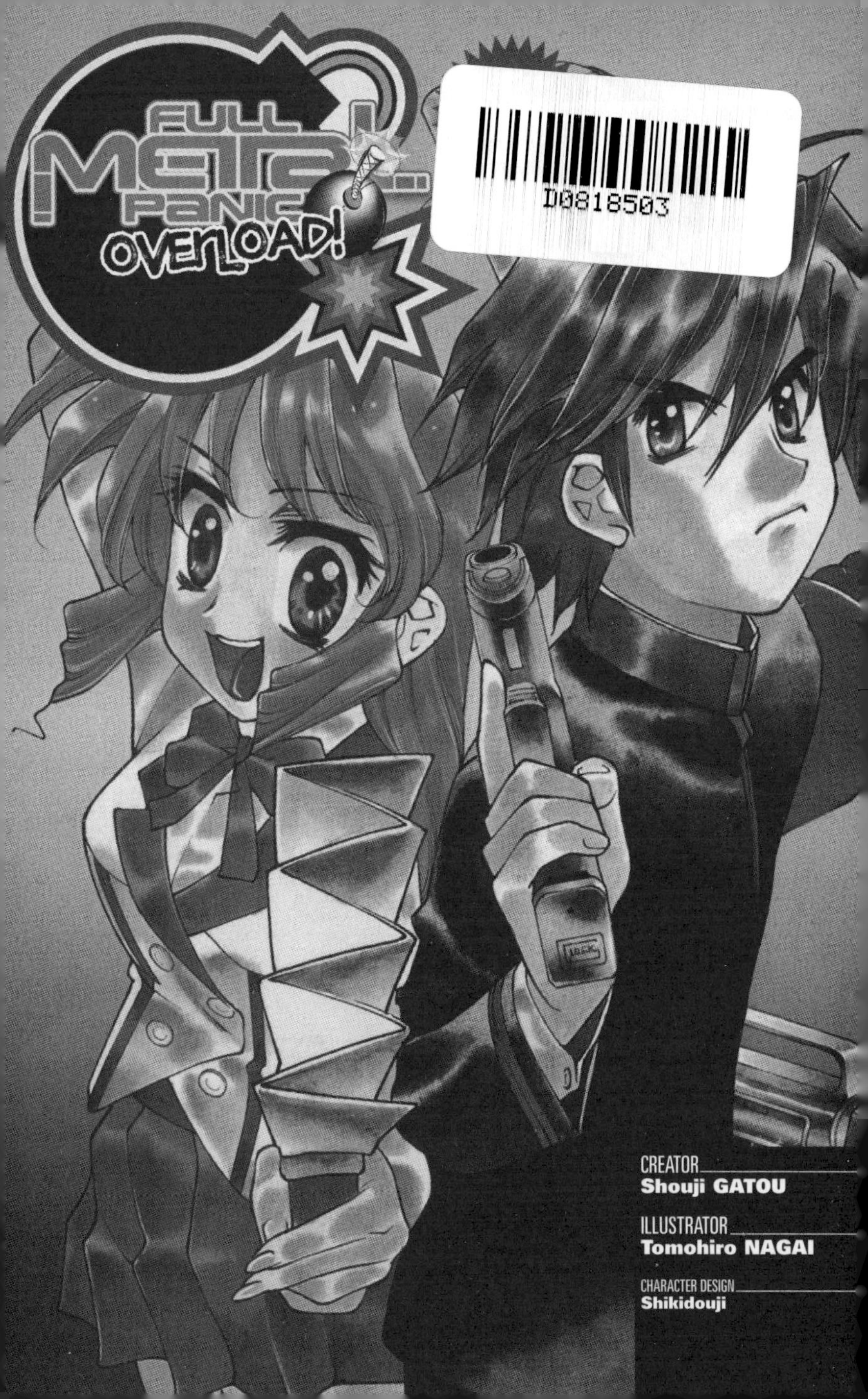
FULL METAL PANIC
OVERLOAD!

CREATOR
Shouji GATOU

ILLUSTRATOR
Tomohiro NAGAI

CHARACTER DESIGN
Shikidouji

CONTENTS

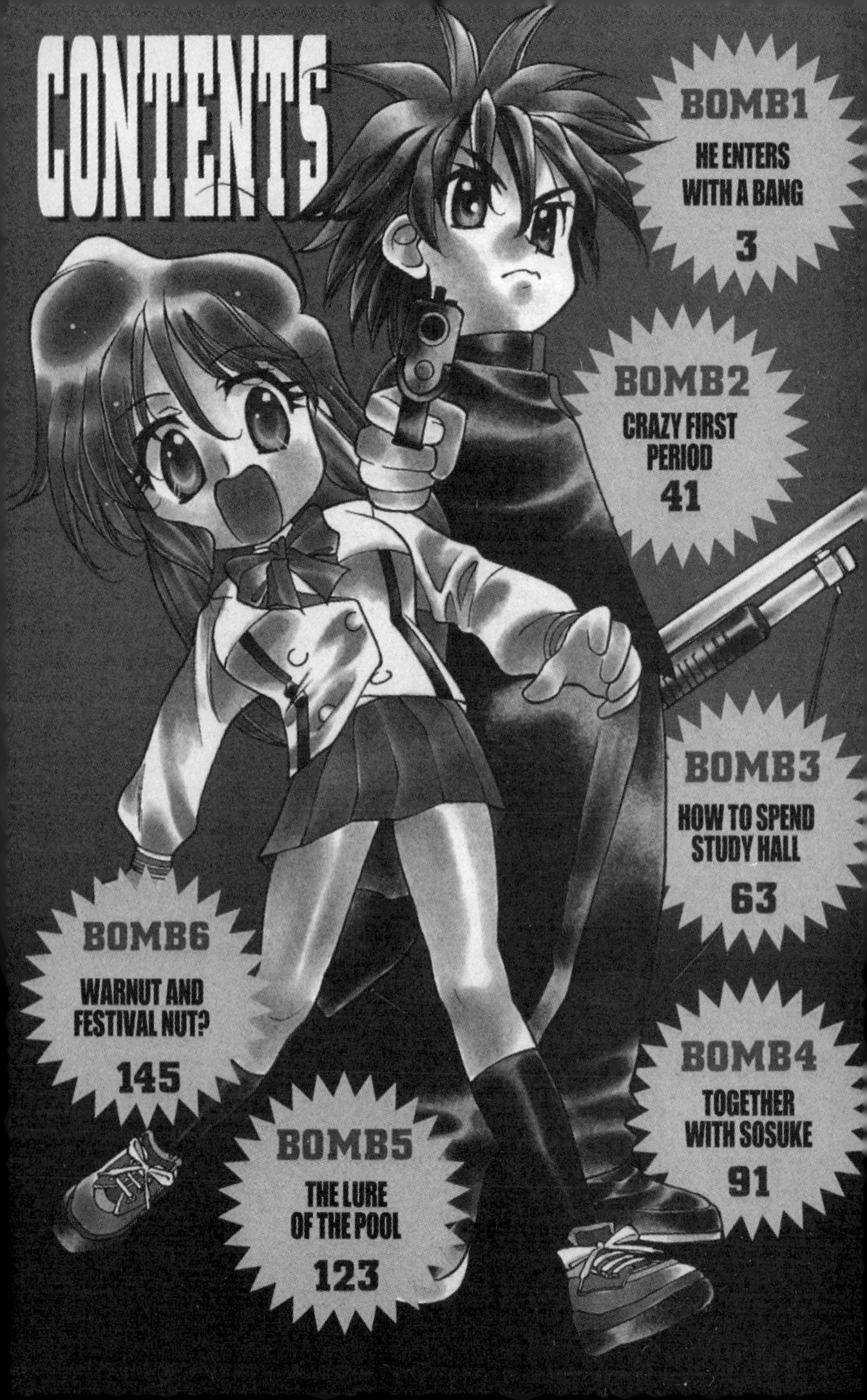

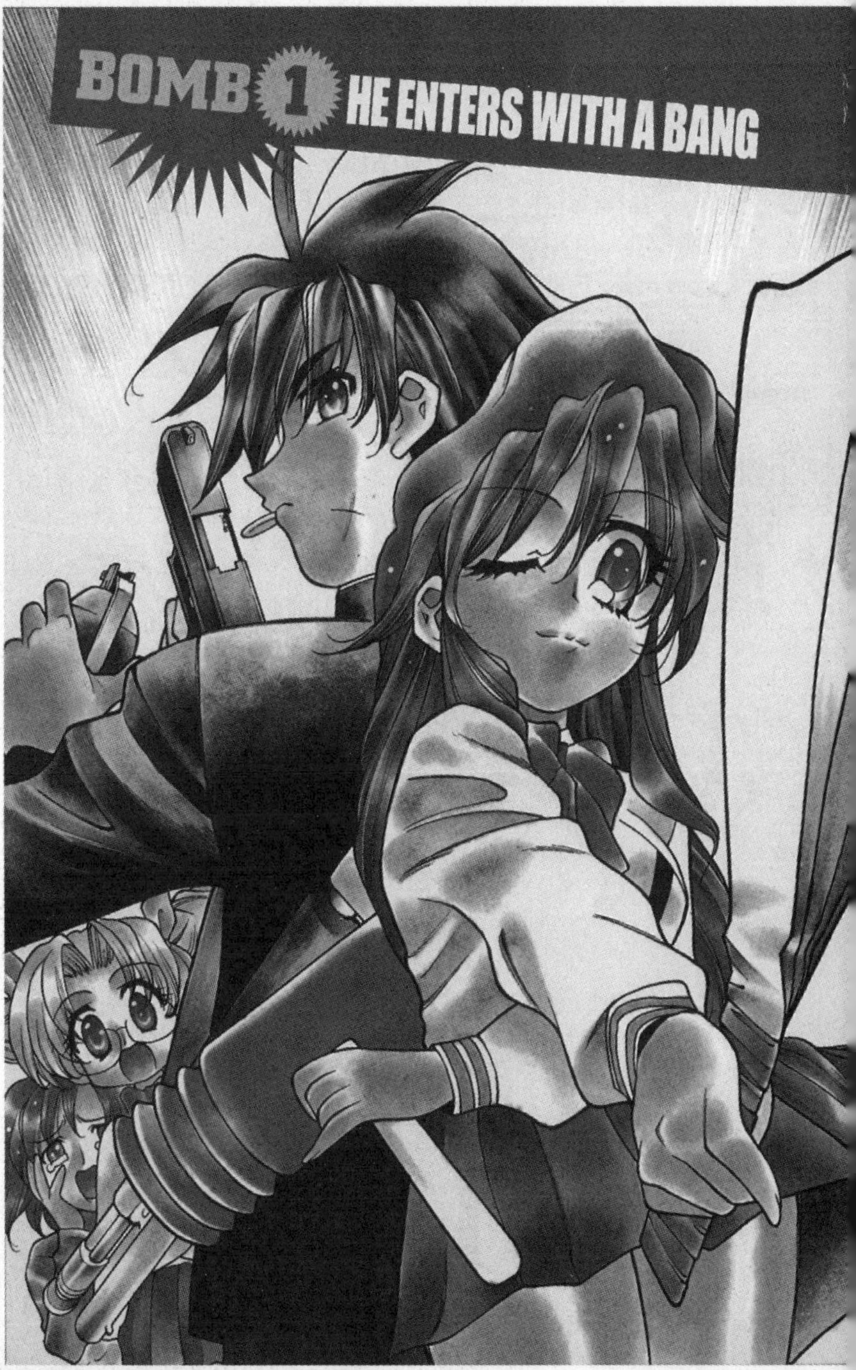
BOMB 1
HE ENTERS WITH A BANG

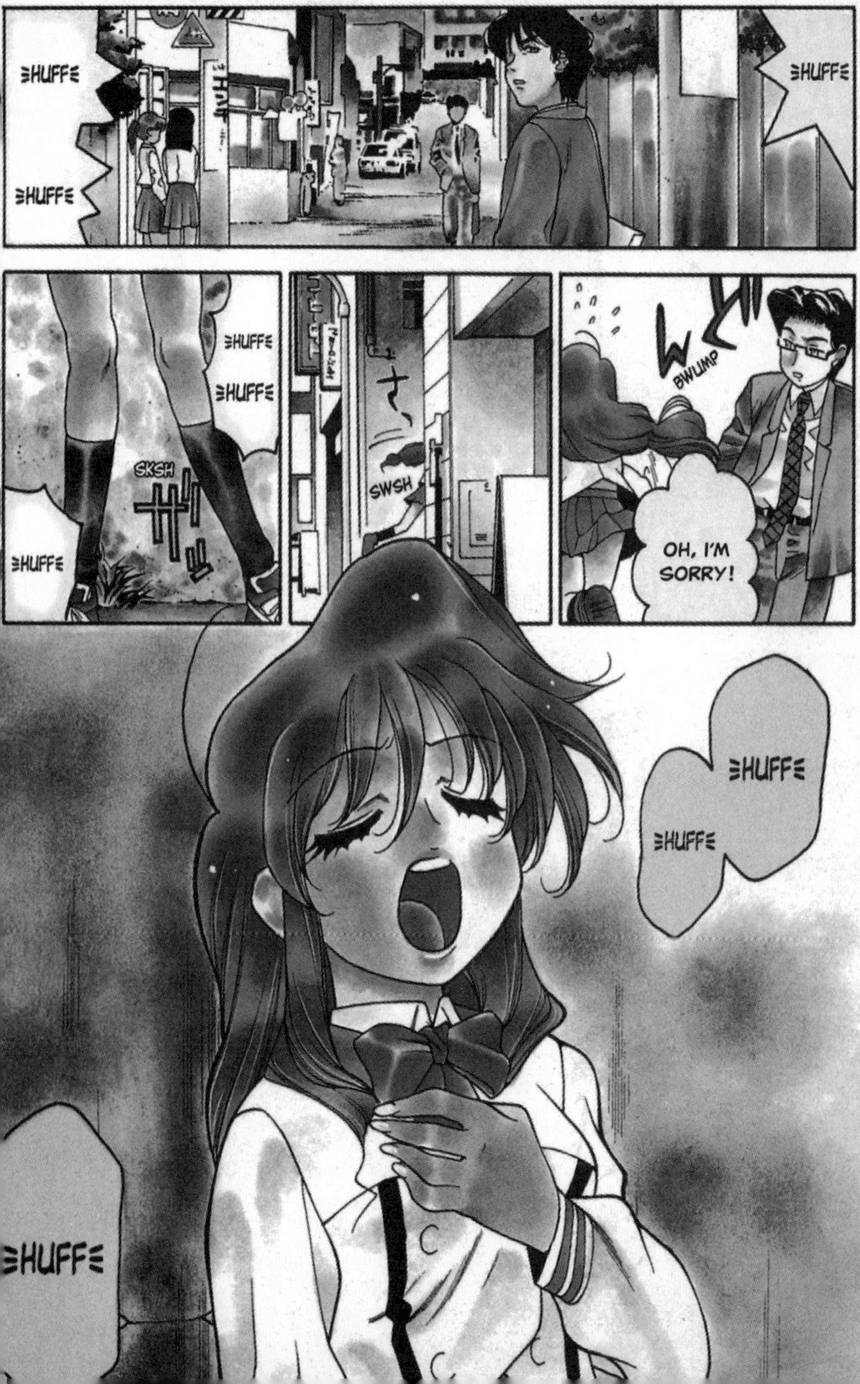

≡HUFF≡
≡HUFF≡
≡HUFF≡
≡HUFF≡
≡HUFF≡
SKSH
≡HUFF≡
SWSH
BWUMP
OH, I'M SORRY!
≡HUFF≡
≡HUFF≡
≡HUFF≡

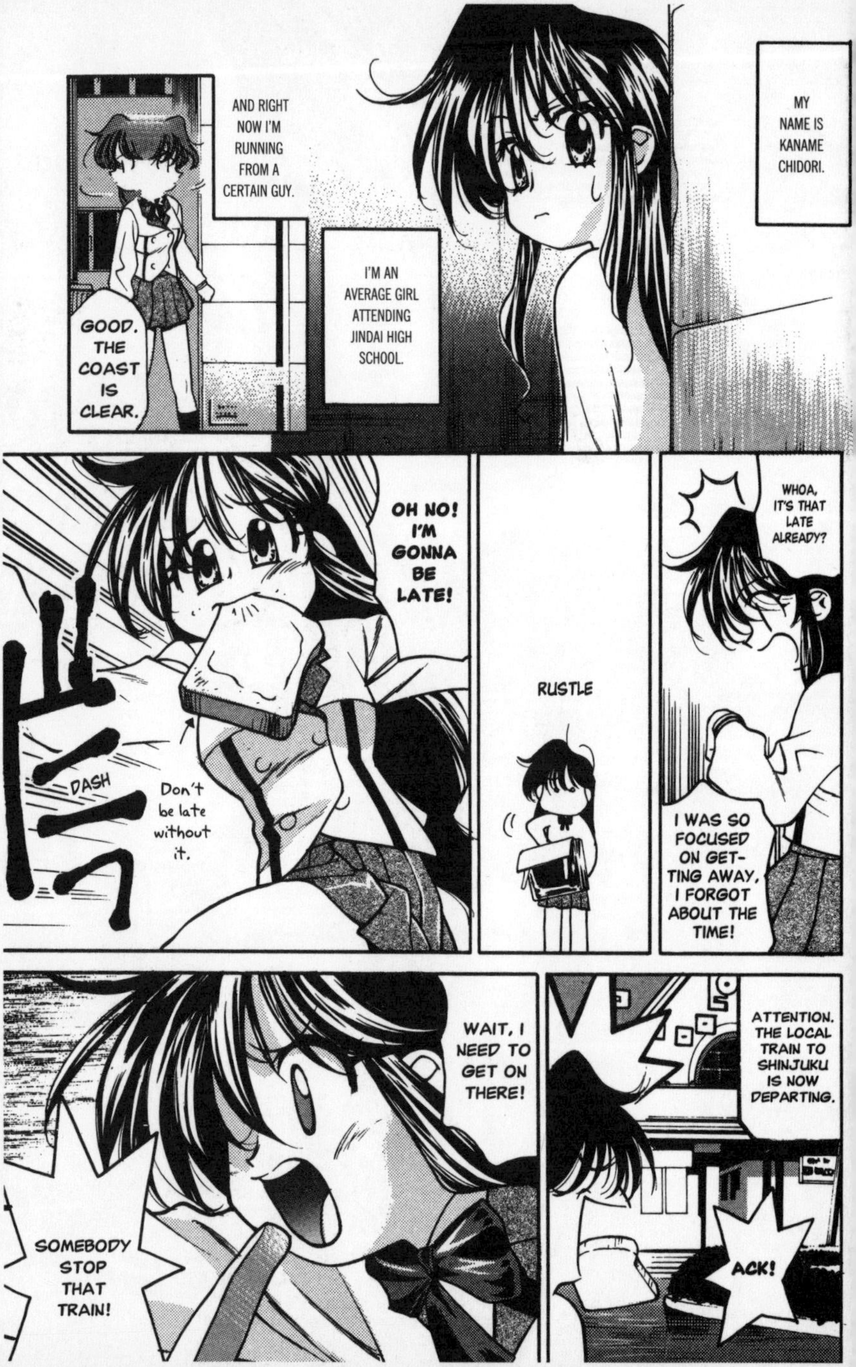
MY NAME IS KANAME CHIDORI.
I'M AN AVERAGE GIRL ATTENDING JINDAI HIGH SCHOOL.
AND RIGHT NOW I'M RUNNING FROM A CERTAIN GUY.
GOOD. THE COAST IS CLEAR.
WHOA, IT'S THAT LATE ALREADY?
I WAS SO FOCUSED ON GET-TING AWAY, I FORGOT ABOUT THE TIME!
RUSTLE
OH NO! I'M GONNA BE LATE!
DASH
Don't be late without it.
ATTENTION. THE LOCAL TRAIN TO SHINJUKU IS NOW DEPARTING.
ACK!
WAIT, I NEED TO GET ON THERE!
SOMEBODY STOP THAT TRAIN!

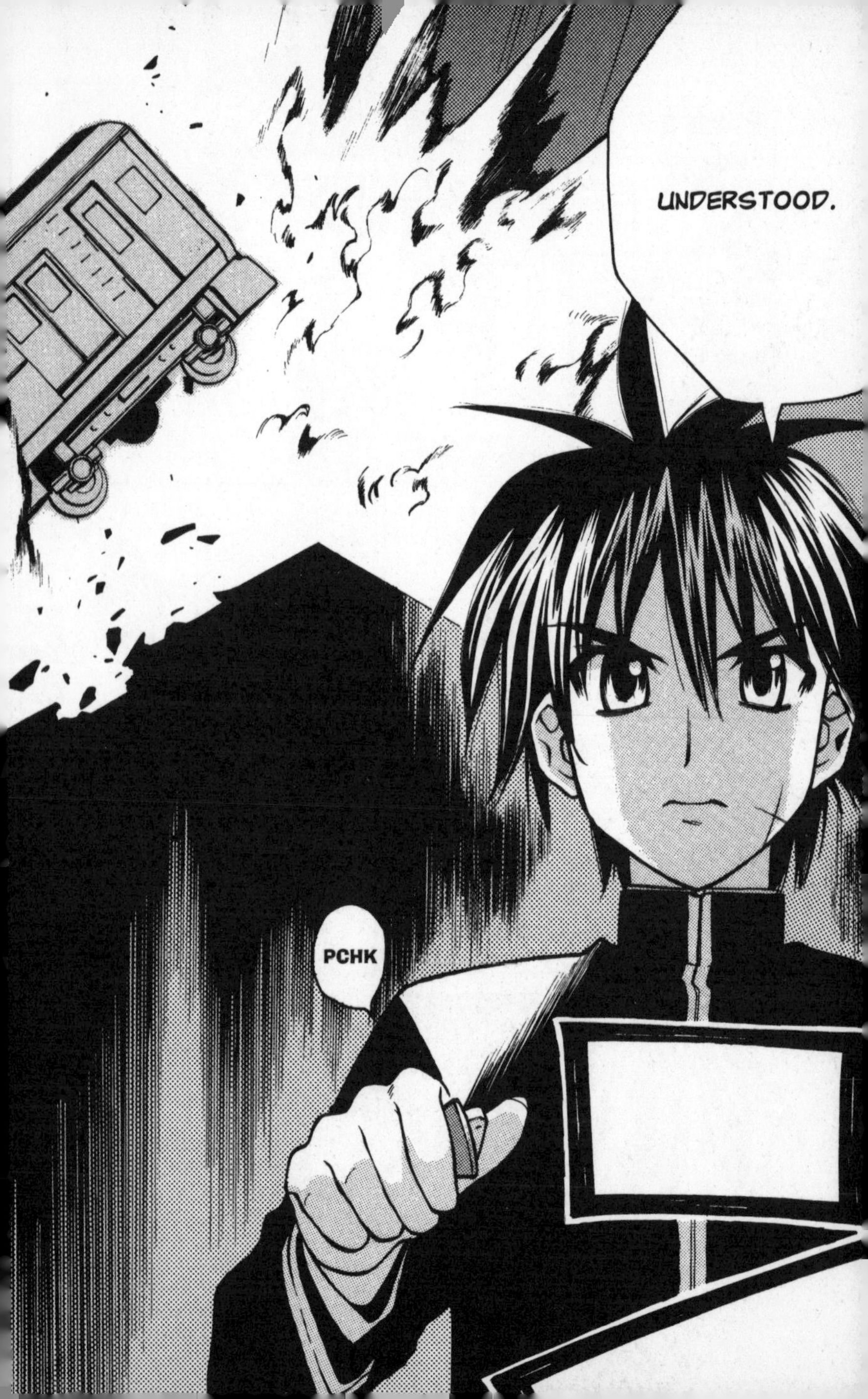
UNDERSTOOD.
PCHK

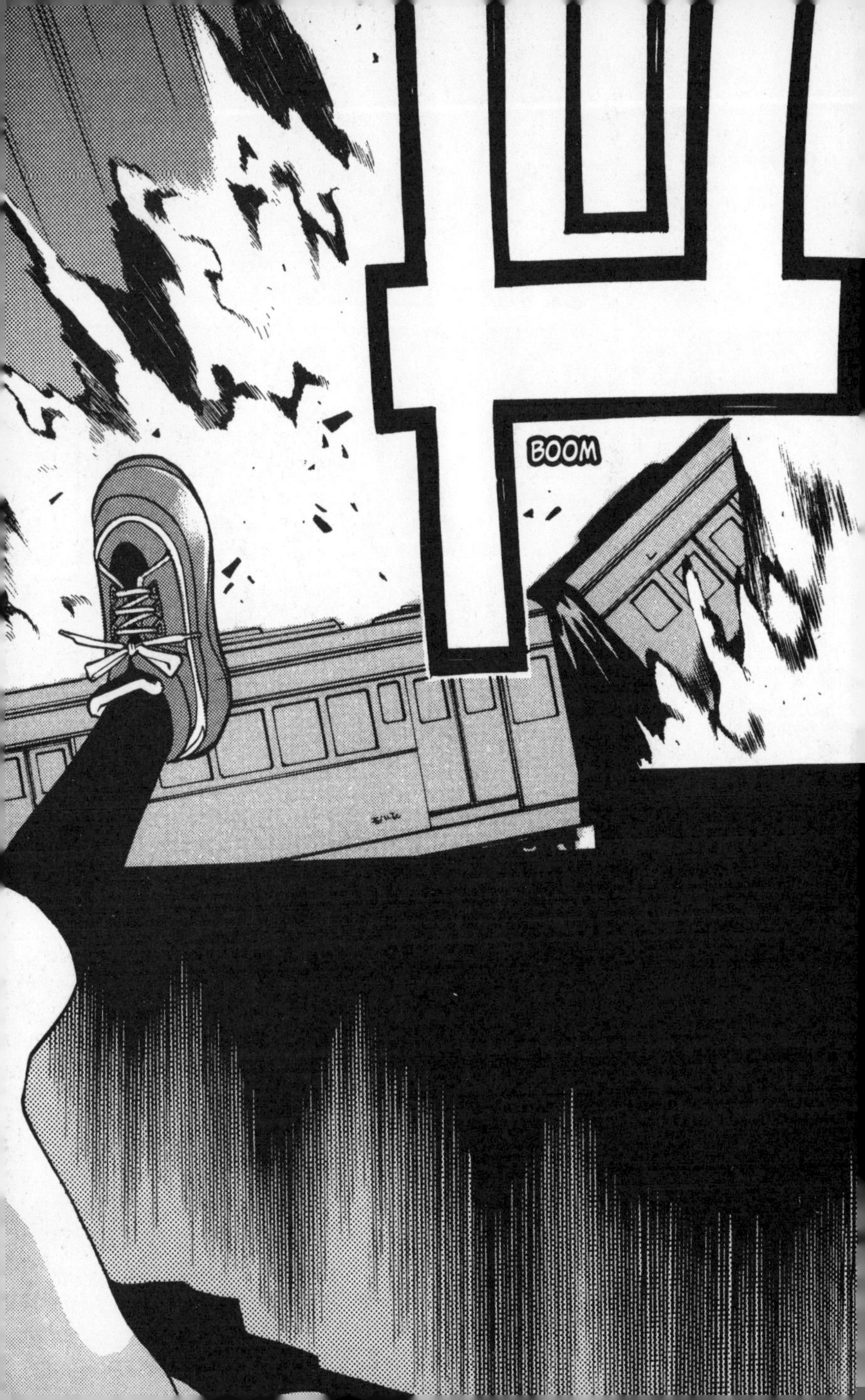
BOOM

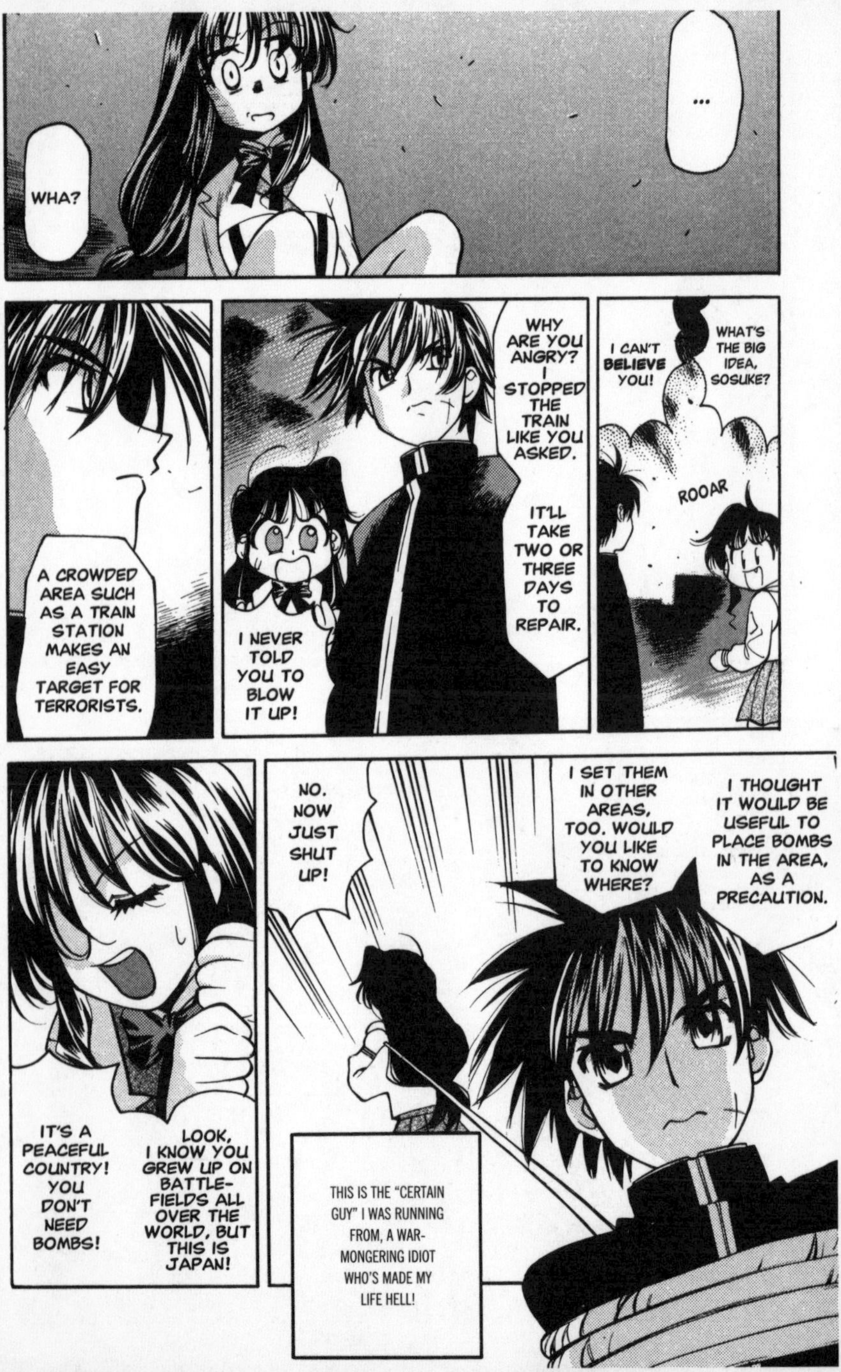
...
WHA?
WHAT'S THE BIG IDEA, SOSUKE?
I CAN'T BELIEVE YOU!
ROOAR
WHY ARE YOU ANGRY? I STOPPED THE TRAIN LIKE YOU ASKED.
IT'LL TAKE TWO OR THREE DAYS TO REPAIR.
I NEVER TOLD YOU TO BLOW IT UP!
A CROWDED AREA SUCH AS A TRAIN STATION MAKES AN EASY TARGET FOR TERRORISTS.
I THOUGHT IT WOULD BE USEFUL TO PLACE BOMBS IN THE AREA, AS A PRECAUTION.
I SET THEM IN OTHER AREAS, TOO. WOULD YOU LIKE TO KNOW WHERE?
NO. NOW JUST SHUT UP!
THIS IS THE "CERTAIN GUY" I WAS RUNNING FROM, A WAR-MONGERING IDIOT WHO'S MADE MY LIFE HELL!
LOOK, I KNOW YOU GREW UP ON BATTLE-FIELDS ALL OVER THE WORLD, BUT THIS IS JAPAN!
IT'S A PEACEFUL COUNTRY! YOU DON'T NEED BOMBS!

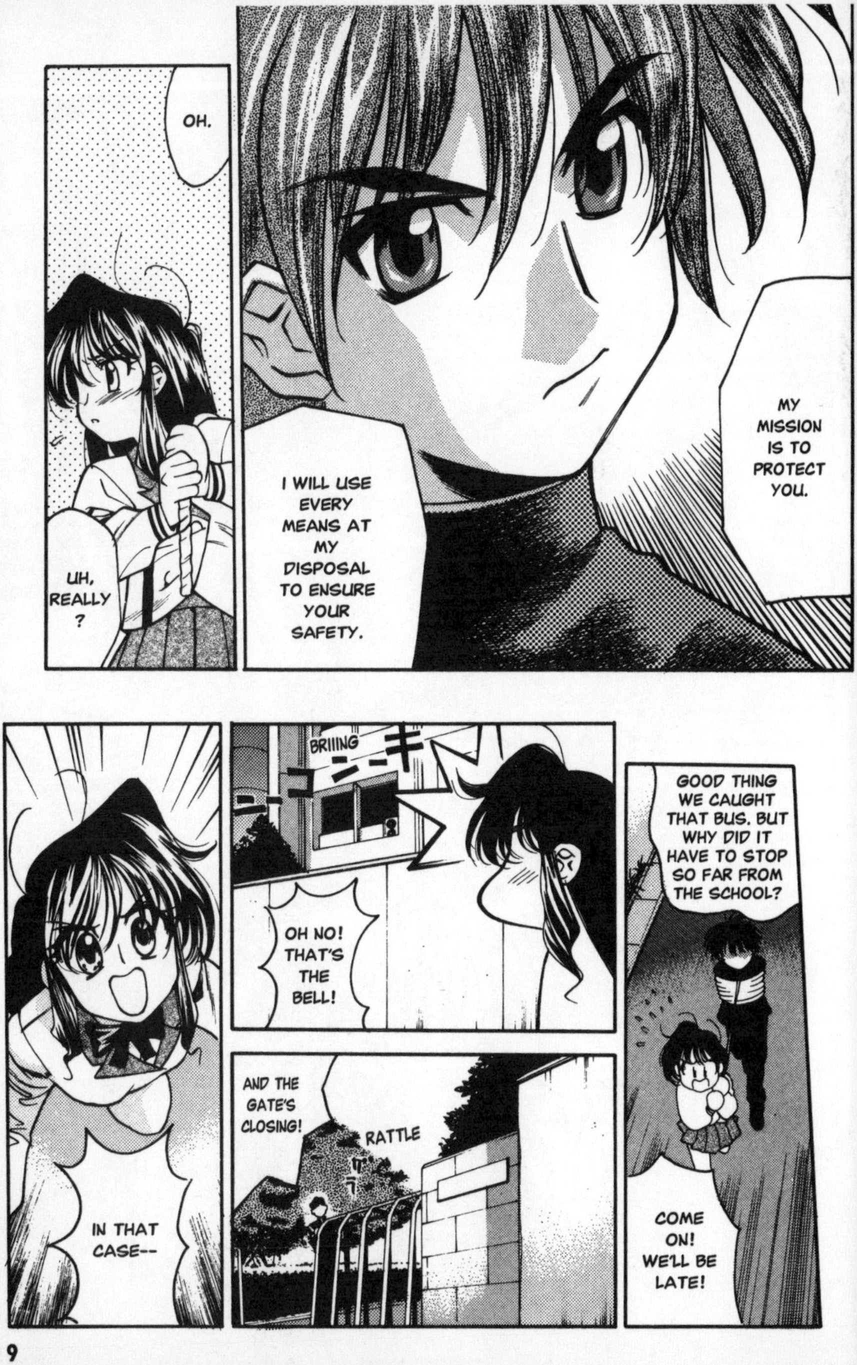
MY MISSION IS TO PROTECT YOU.
I WILL USE EVERY MEANS AT MY DISPOSAL TO ENSURE YOUR SAFETY.
OH.
UH, REALLY?
GOOD THING WE CAUGHT THAT BUS. BUT WHY DID IT HAVE TO STOP SO FAR FROM THE SCHOOL?
COME ON! WE'LL BE LATE!
BRIIING
OH NO! THAT'S THE BELL!
AND THE GATE'S CLOSING!
RATTLE
IN THAT CASE--

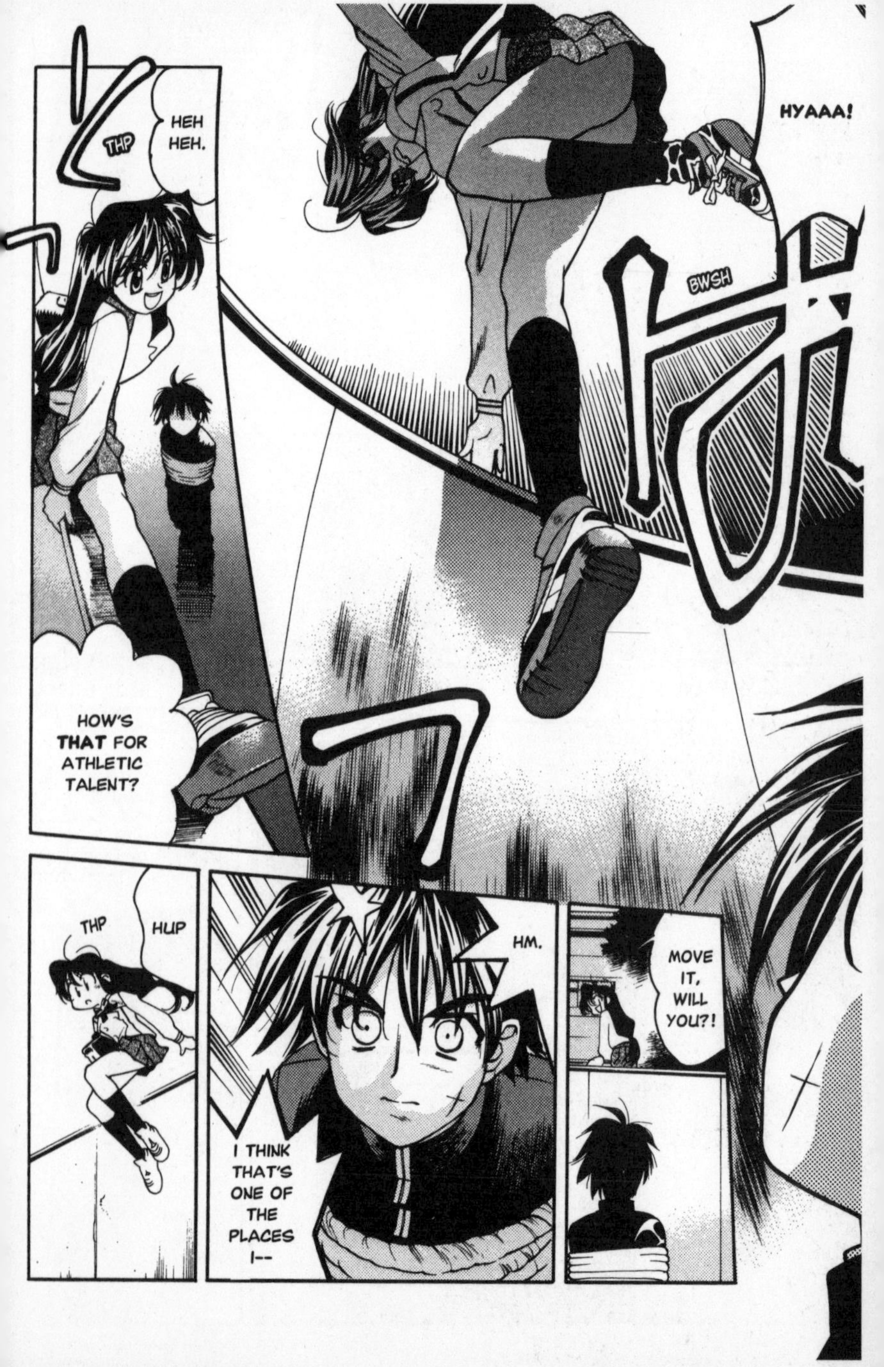
HYAAA!
BWSH
HEH HEH.
THP
HOW'S **THAT** FOR ATHLETIC TALENT?
MOVE IT, WILL YOU?!
HM.
I THINK THAT'S ONE OF THE PLACES I--
HUP
THP

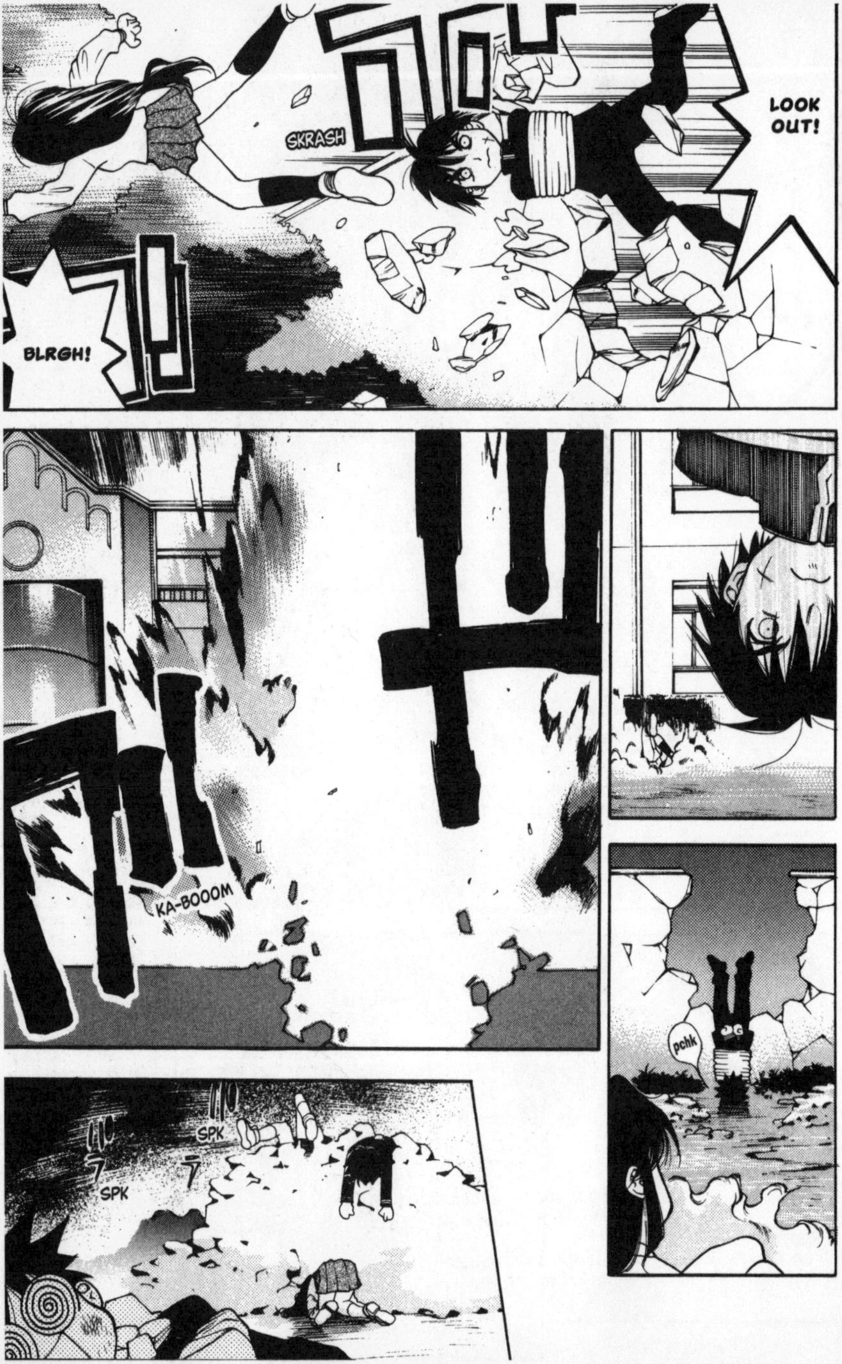
LOOK OUT!
SKRASH
BLRGH!
KA-BOOOM
pchk
SPK
SPK

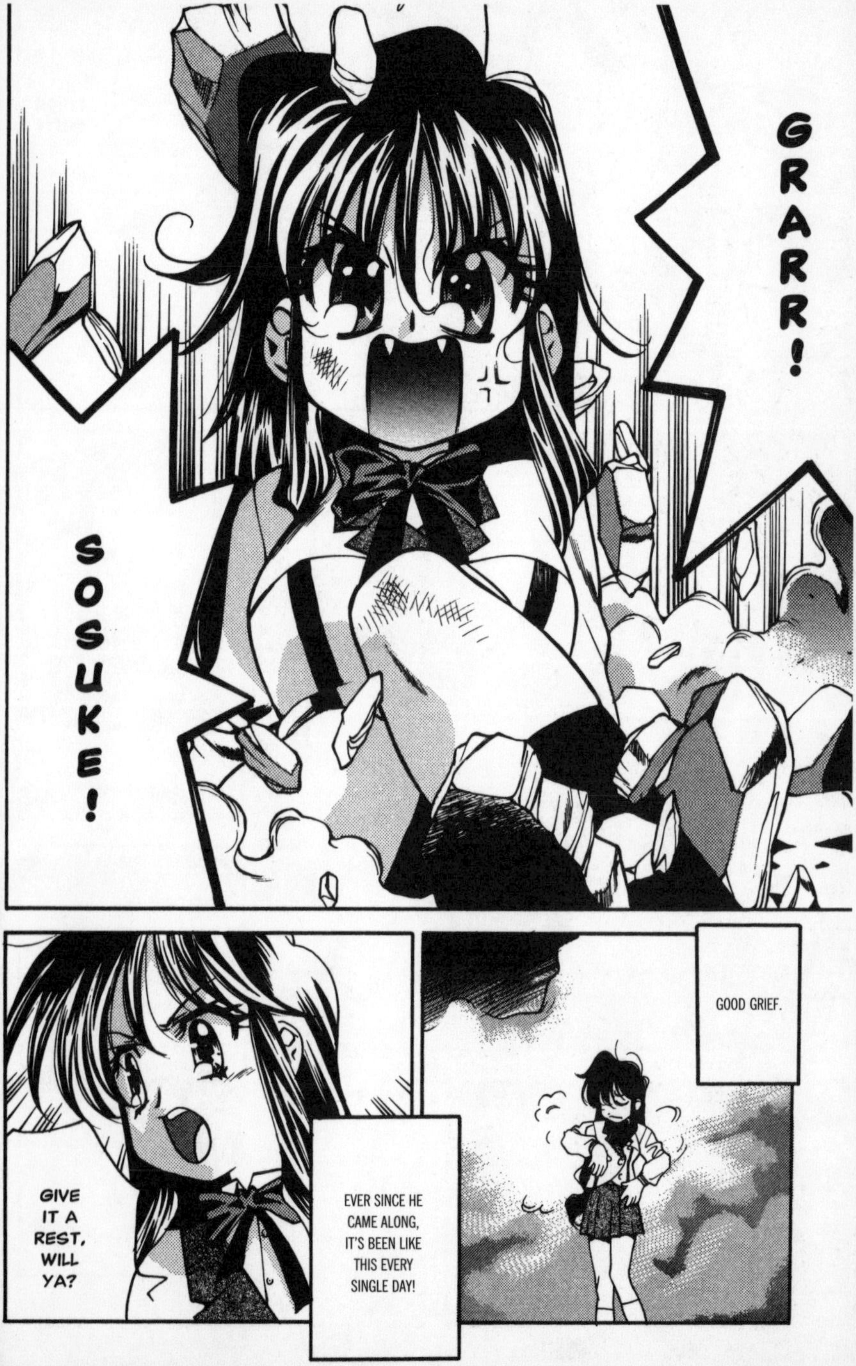
GRARR!
SOSUKE!
GOOD GRIEF.
EVER SINCE HE CAME ALONG, IT'S BEEN LIKE THIS EVERY SINGLE DAY!
GIVE IT A REST, WILL YA?

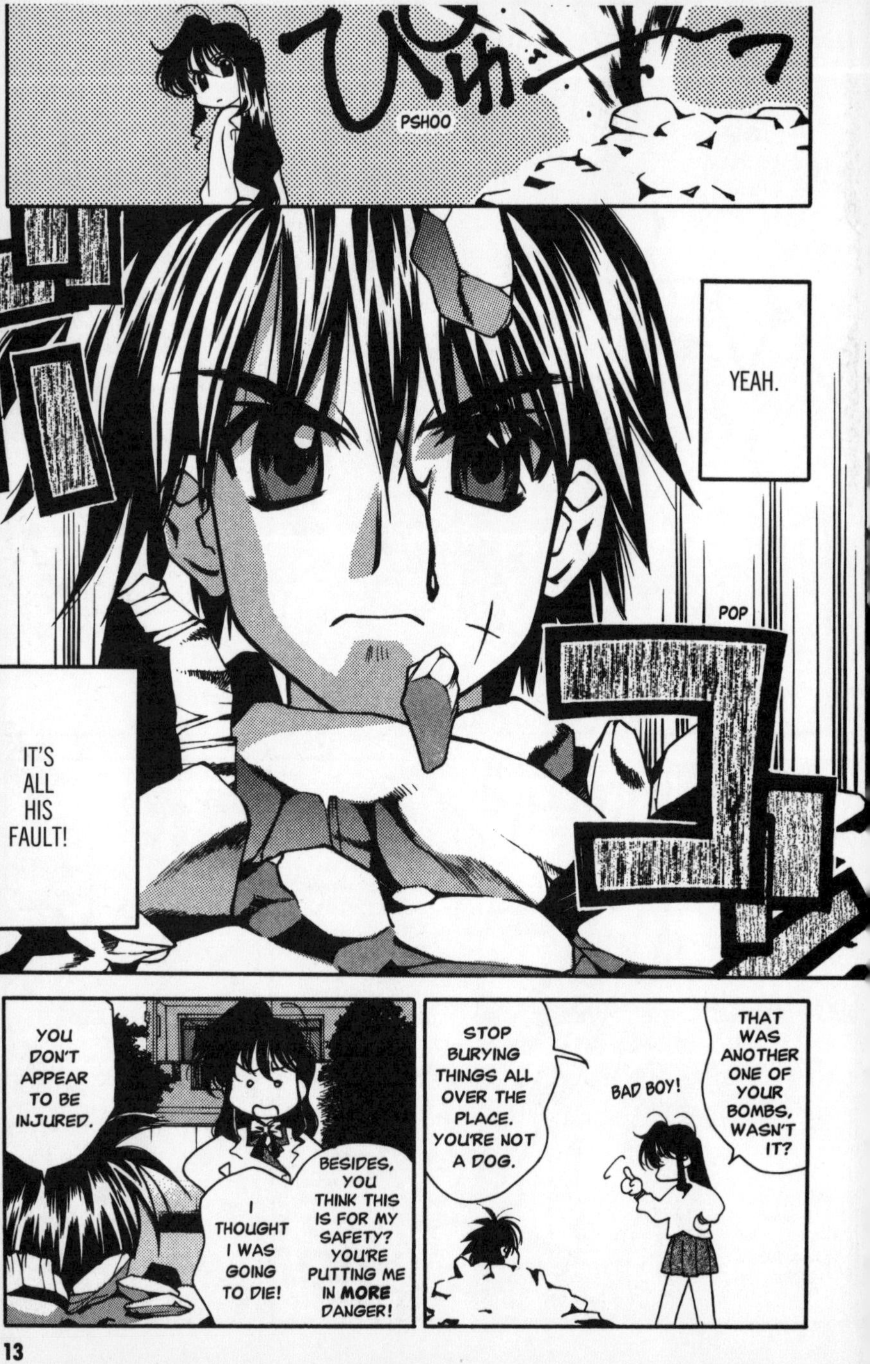
PSHOO
YEAH.
POP
IT'S ALL HIS FAULT!
THAT WAS ANOTHER ONE OF YOUR BOMBS, WASN'T IT?
BAD BOY!
STOP BURYING THINGS ALL OVER THE PLACE. YOU'RE NOT A DOG.
YOU DON'T APPEAR TO BE INJURED.
BESIDES, YOU THINK THIS IS FOR MY SAFETY? YOU'RE PUTTING ME IN **MORE** DANGER!
I THOUGHT I WAS GOING TO DIE!

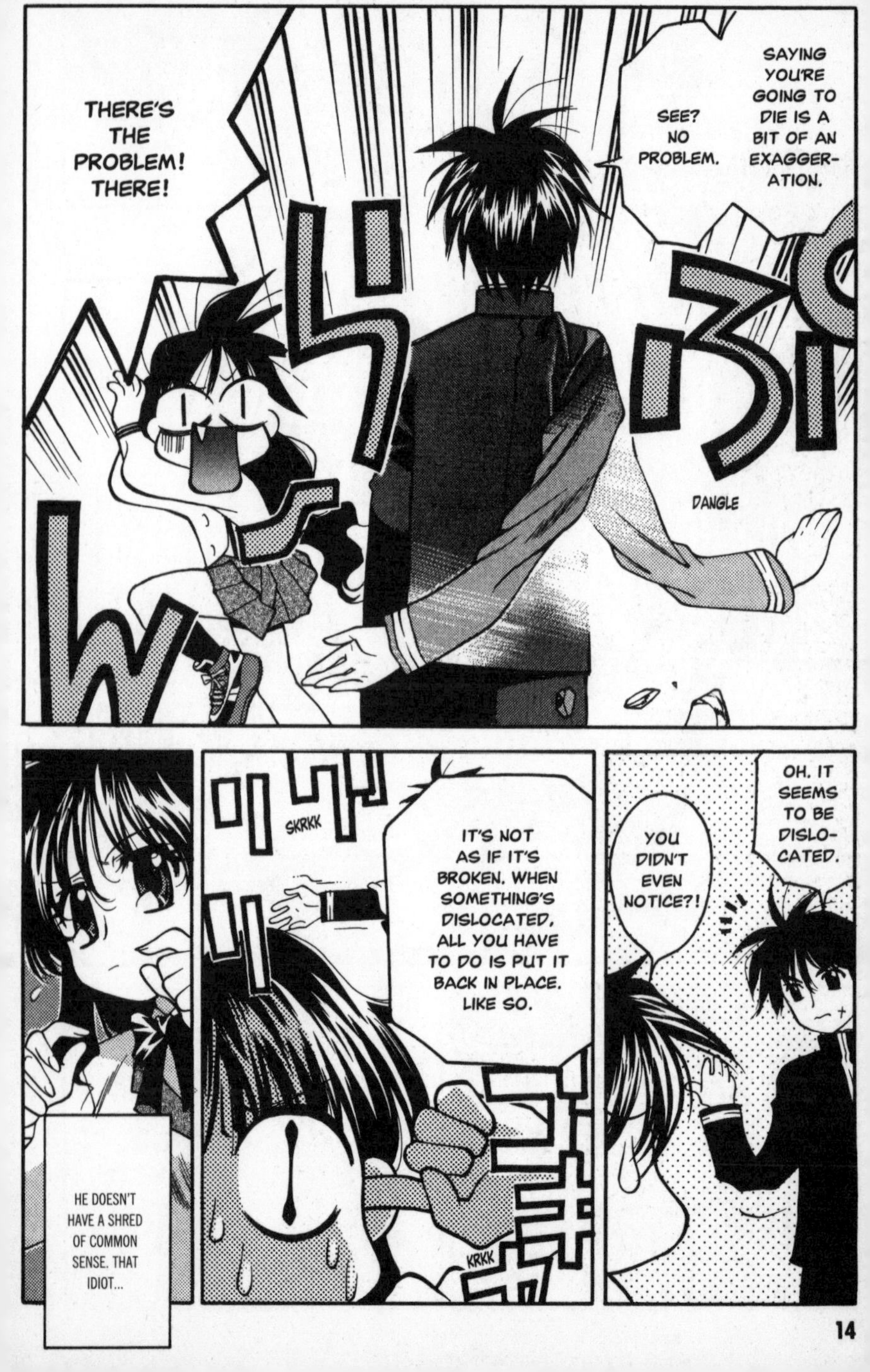
SAYING YOU'RE GOING TO DIE IS A BIT OF AN EXAGGER-ATION.
SEE? NO PROBLEM.
THERE'S THE PROBLEM! THERE!
DANGLE
OH. IT SEEMS TO BE DISLO-CATED.
YOU DIDN'T EVEN NOTICE?!
SKRKK
IT'S NOT AS IF IT'S BROKEN. WHEN SOMETHING'S DISLOCATED, ALL YOU HAVE TO DO IS PUT IT BACK IN PLACE. LIKE SO.
KRKK
HE DOESN'T HAVE A SHRED OF COMMON SENSE. THAT IDIOT...

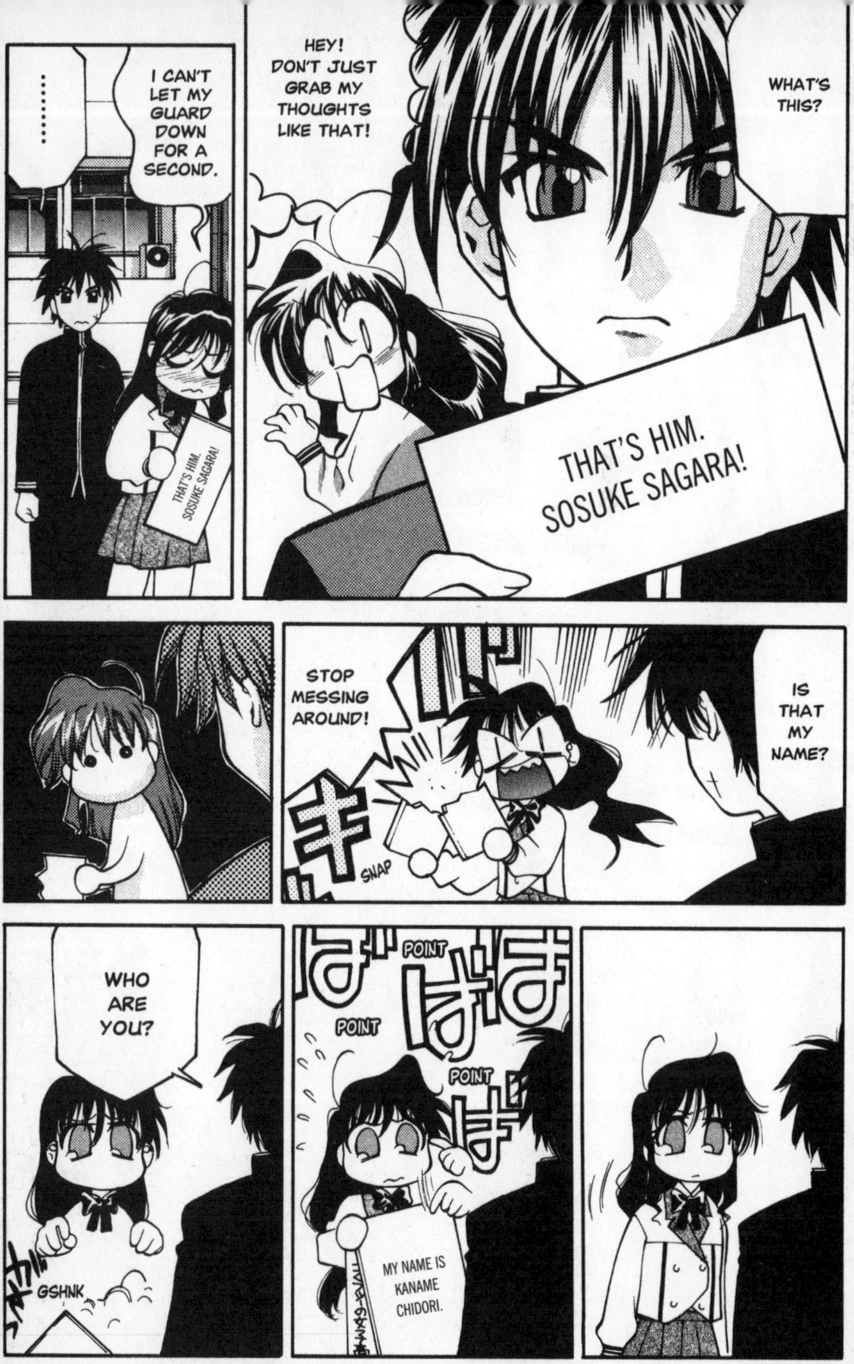
WHAT'S THIS?
THAT'S HIM. SOSUKE SAGARA!
HEY! DON'T JUST GRAB MY THOUGHTS LIKE THAT!
I CAN'T LET MY GUARD DOWN FOR A SECOND.
......
THAT'S HIM. SOSUKE SAGARA!
IS THAT MY NAME?
STOP MESSING AROUND!
SNAP
POINT
POINT
POINT
MY NAME IS KANAME CHIDORI.
WHO ARE YOU?
GSHNK

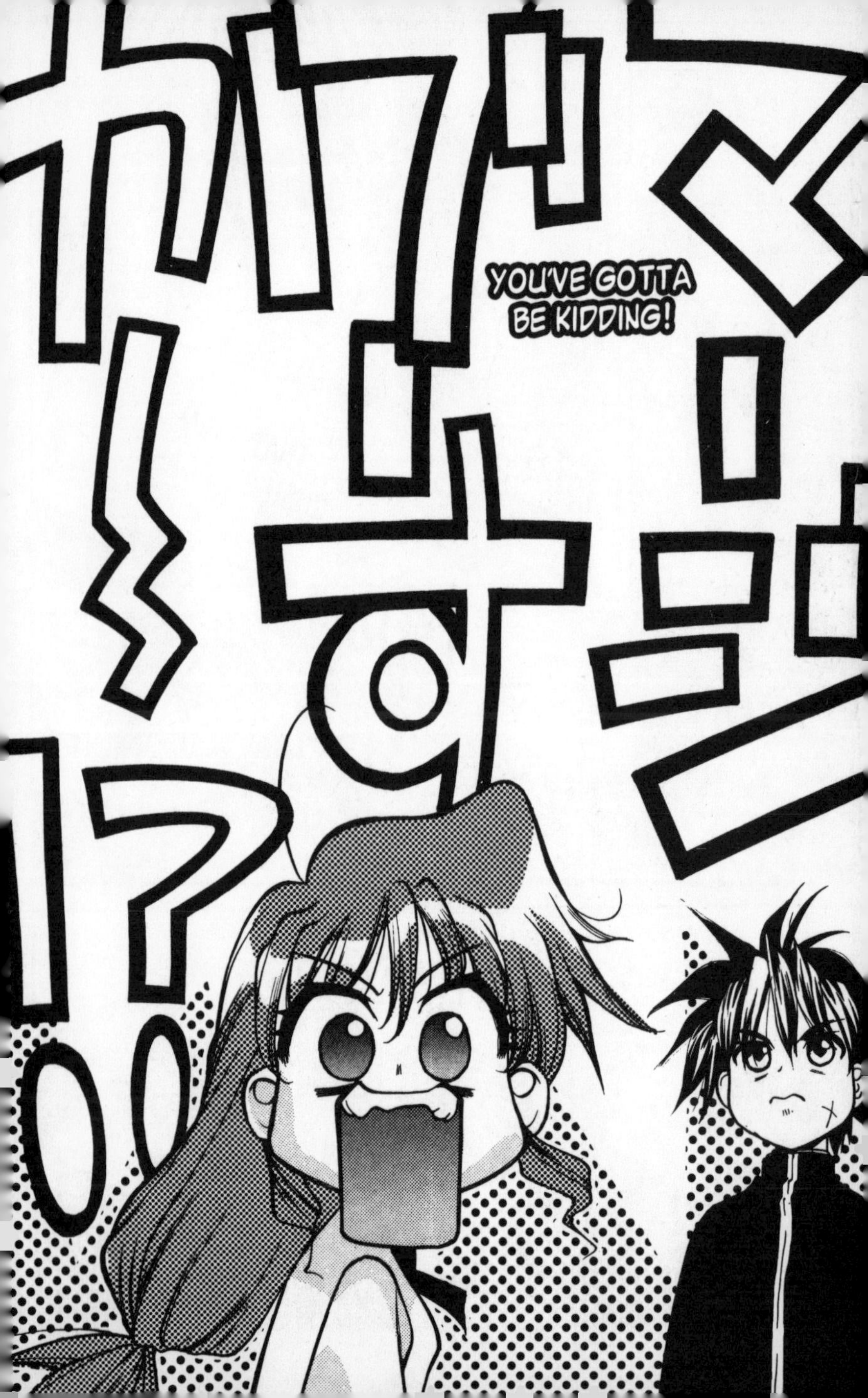
YOU'VE GOTTA BE KIDDING!

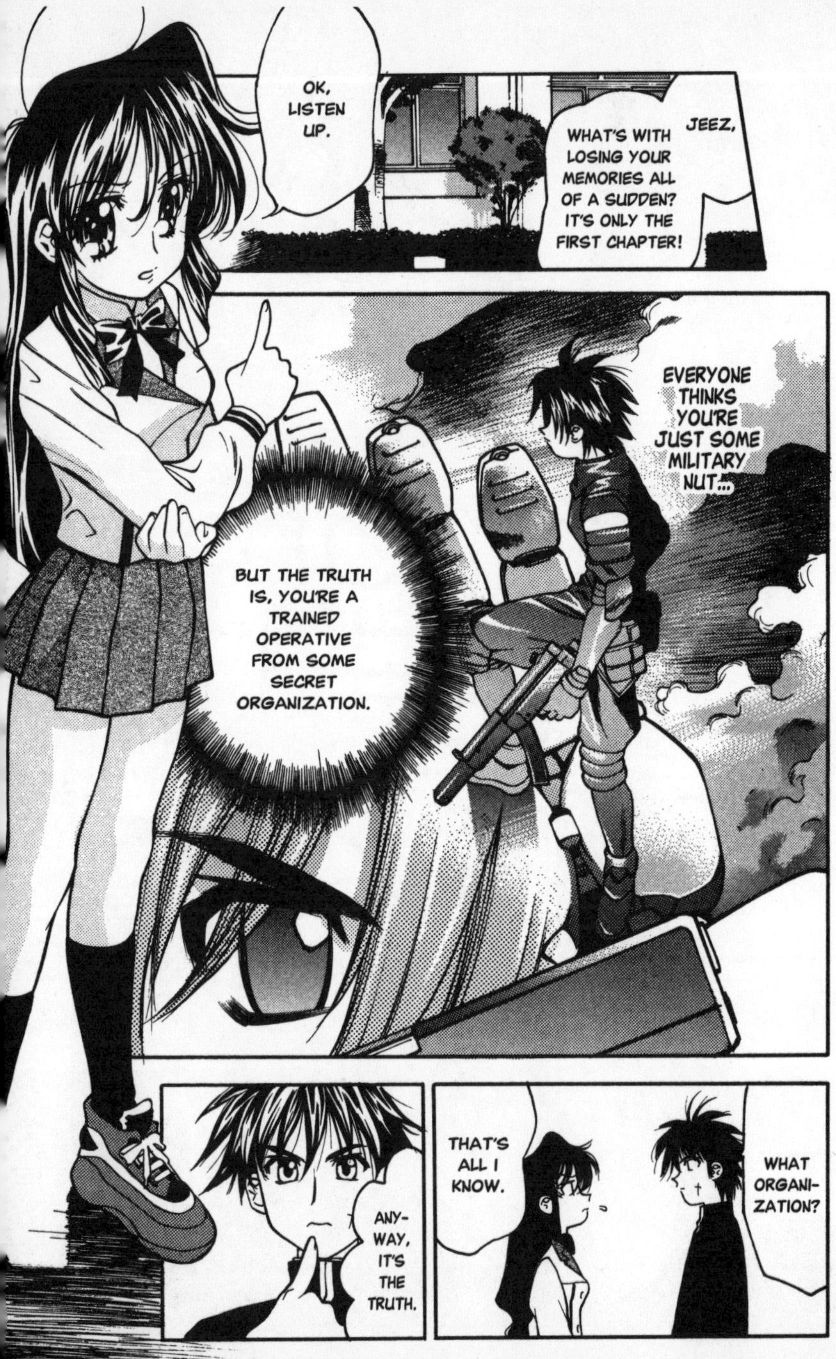
JEEZ,
WHAT'S WITH LOSING YOUR MEMORIES ALL OF A SUDDEN? IT'S ONLY THE FIRST CHAPTER!
OK, LISTEN UP.
EVERYONE THINKS YOU'RE JUST SOME MILITARY NUT...
BUT THE TRUTH IS, YOU'RE A TRAINED OPERATIVE FROM SOME SECRET ORGANIZATION.
WHAT ORGANI-ZATION?
THAT'S ALL I KNOW.
ANY-WAY, IT'S THE TRUTH.

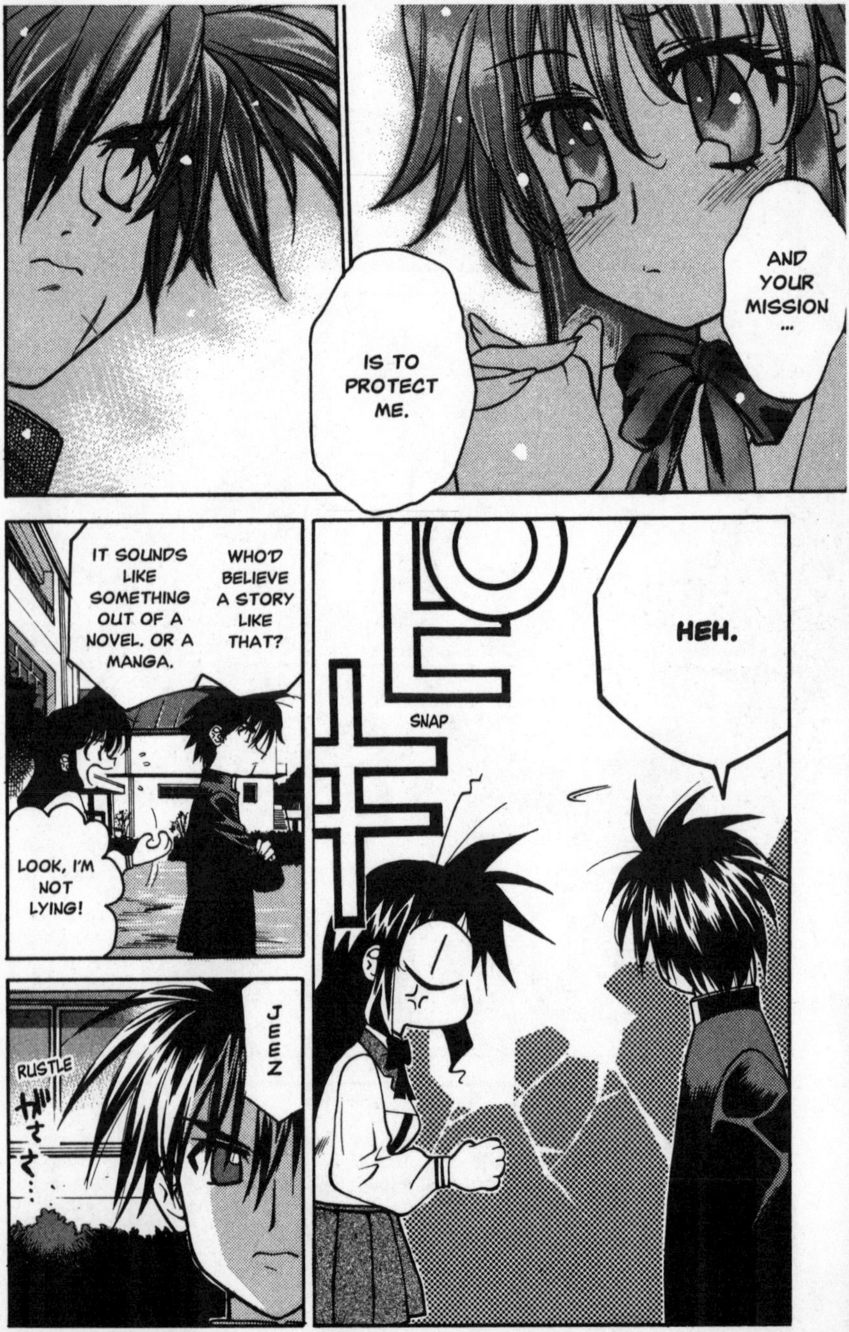
AND YOUR MISSION ...
IS TO PROTECT ME.
WHO'D BELIEVE A STORY LIKE THAT?
IT SOUNDS LIKE SOMETHING OUT OF A NOVEL. OR A MANGA.
LOOK, I'M NOT LYING!
JEEZ
RUSTLE
がささ…
SNAP
HEH.

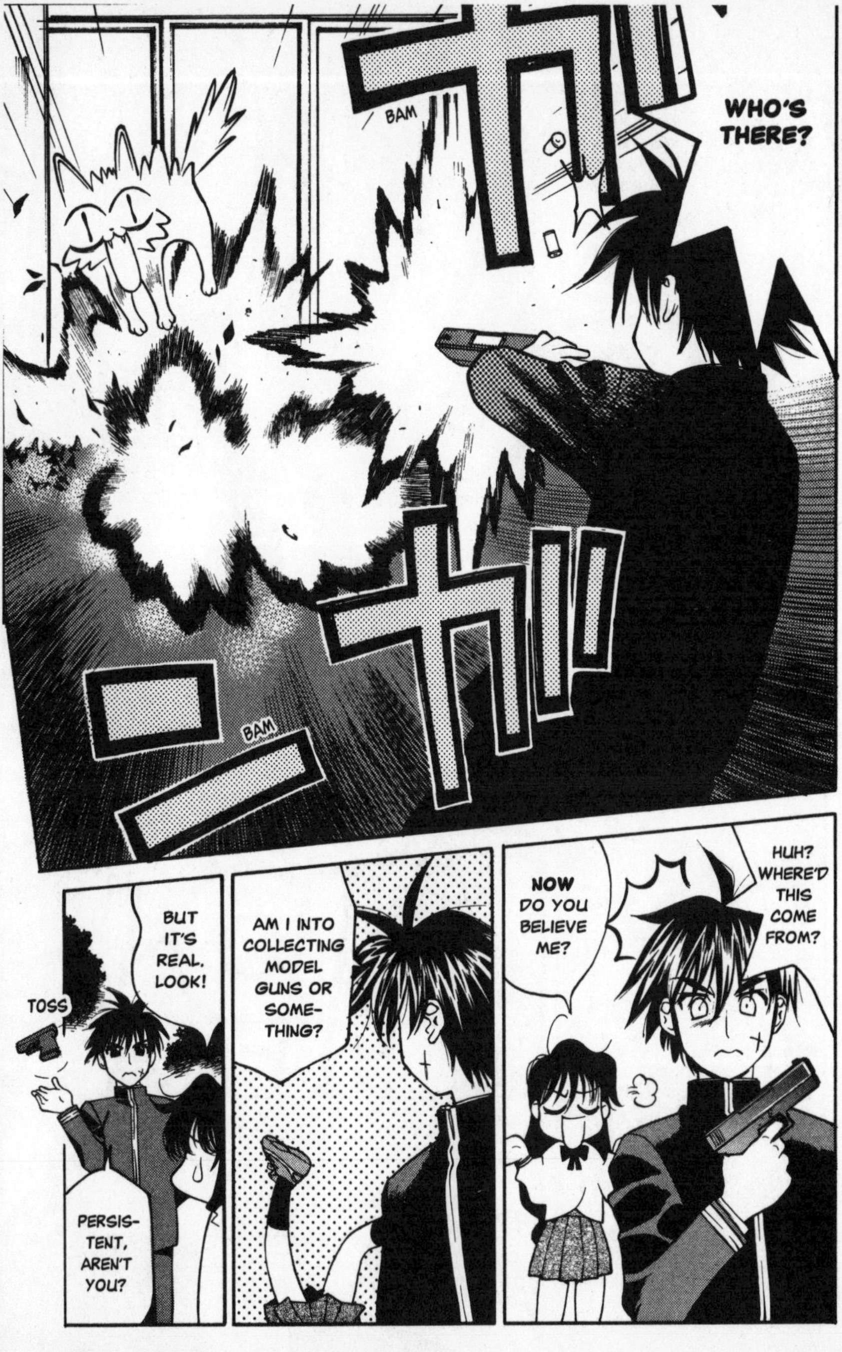
BAM
WHO'S THERE?
BAM
HUH? WHERE'D THIS COME FROM?
NOW DO YOU BELIEVE ME?
AM I INTO COLLECTING MODEL GUNS OR SOME-THING?
BUT IT'S REAL. LOOK!
TOSS
PERSIS-TENT, AREN'T YOU?

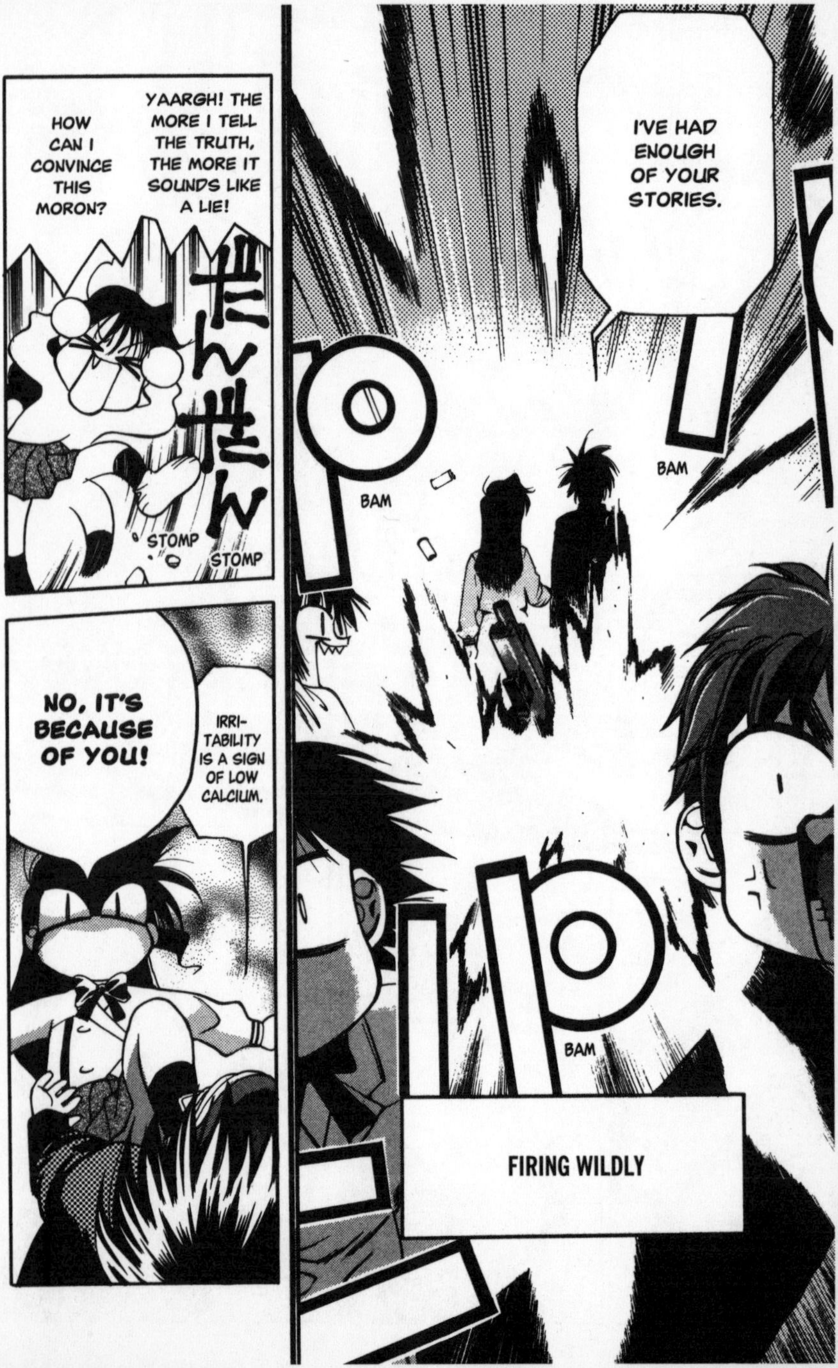

I'VE HAD ENOUGH OF YOUR STORIES.
BAM
BAM
BAM
FIRING WILDLY
YAARGH! THE MORE I TELL THE TRUTH, THE MORE IT SOUNDS LIKE A LIE!
HOW CAN I CONVINCE THIS MORON?
だんだん
STOMP
STOMP
IRRI-TABILITY IS A SIGN OF LOW CALCIUM.
NO, IT'S BECAUSE OF YOU!

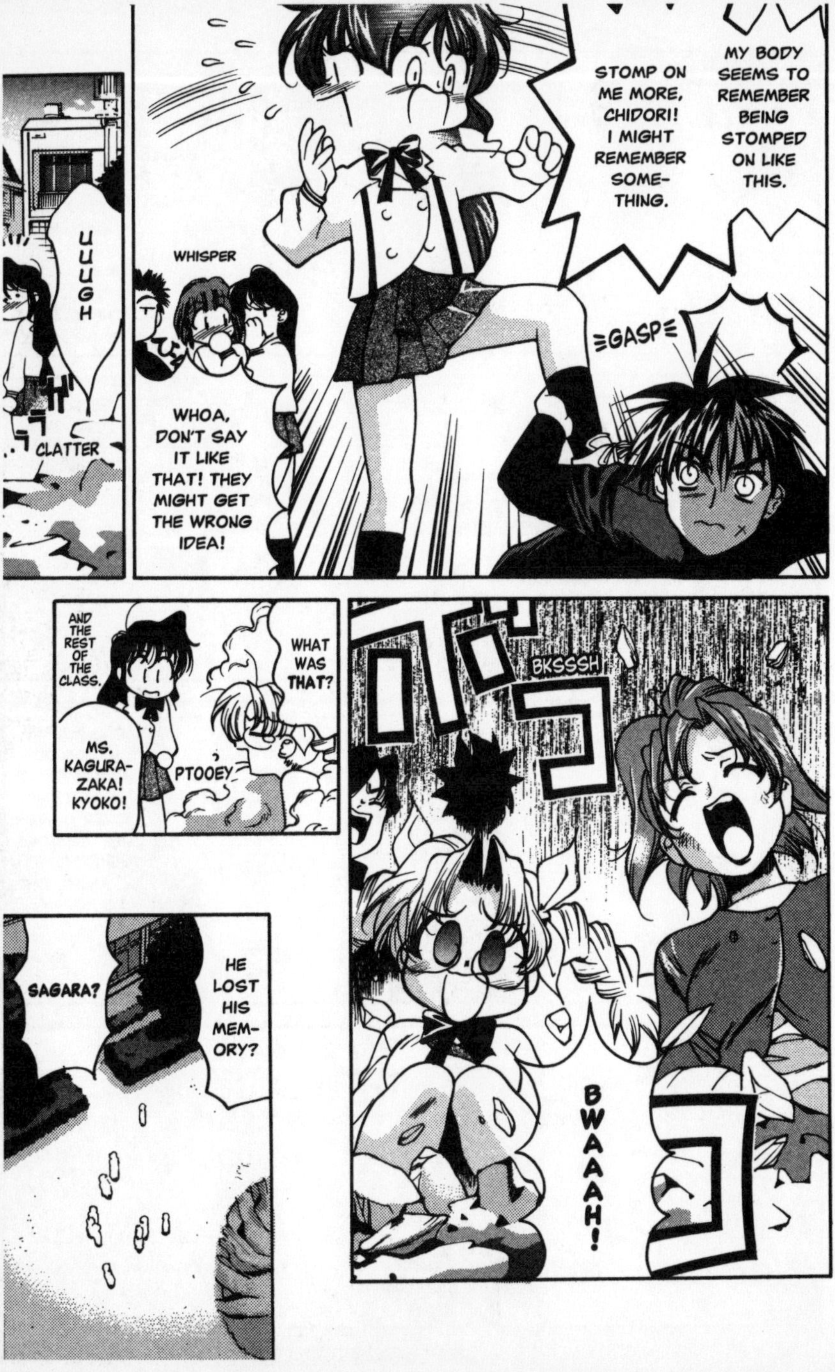
MY BODY SEEMS TO REMEMBER BEING STOMPED ON LIKE THIS.
STOMP ON ME MORE, CHIDORI! I MIGHT REMEMBER SOME-THING.
GASP
WHISPER
WHOA, DON'T SAY IT LIKE THAT! THEY MIGHT GET THE WRONG IDEA!
UUUGH
CLATTER
BKSSSH
BWAAAAH!
WHAT WAS THAT?
PTOOEY
MS. KAGURA-ZAKA! KYOKO!
AND THE REST OF THE CLASS.
HE LOST HIS MEM-ORY?
SAGARA?

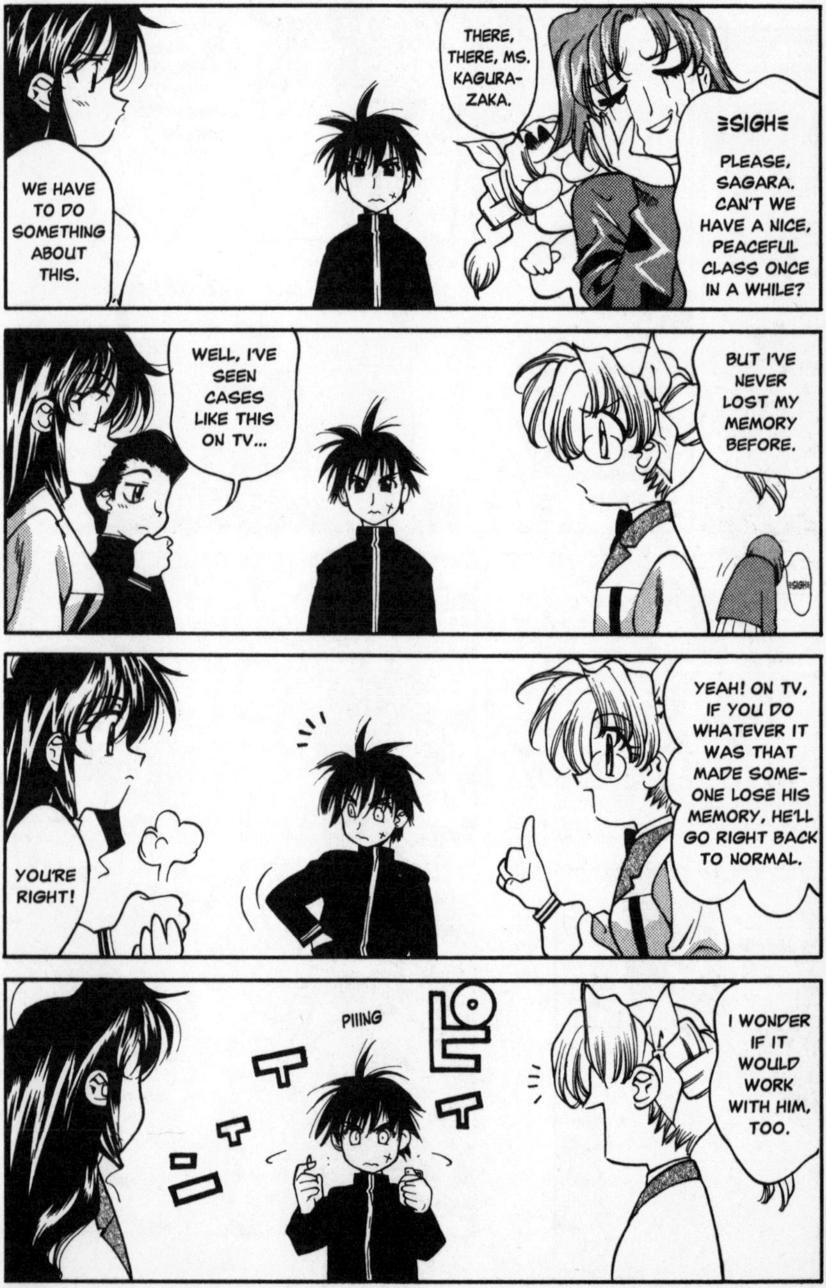

≡SIGH≡
PLEASE, SAGARA. CAN'T WE HAVE A NICE, PEACEFUL CLASS ONCE IN A WHILE?
THERE, THERE, MS. KAGURA-ZAKA.
WE HAVE TO DO SOMETHING ABOUT THIS.
BUT I'VE NEVER LOST MY MEMORY BEFORE.
≡SIGH≡
WELL, I'VE SEEN CASES LIKE THIS ON TV...
YEAH! ON TV, IF YOU DO WHATEVER IT WAS THAT MADE SOME-ONE LOSE HIS MEMORY, HE'LL GO RIGHT BACK TO NORMAL.
YOU'RE RIGHT!
I WONDER IF IT WOULD WORK WITH HIM, TOO.
PIIING

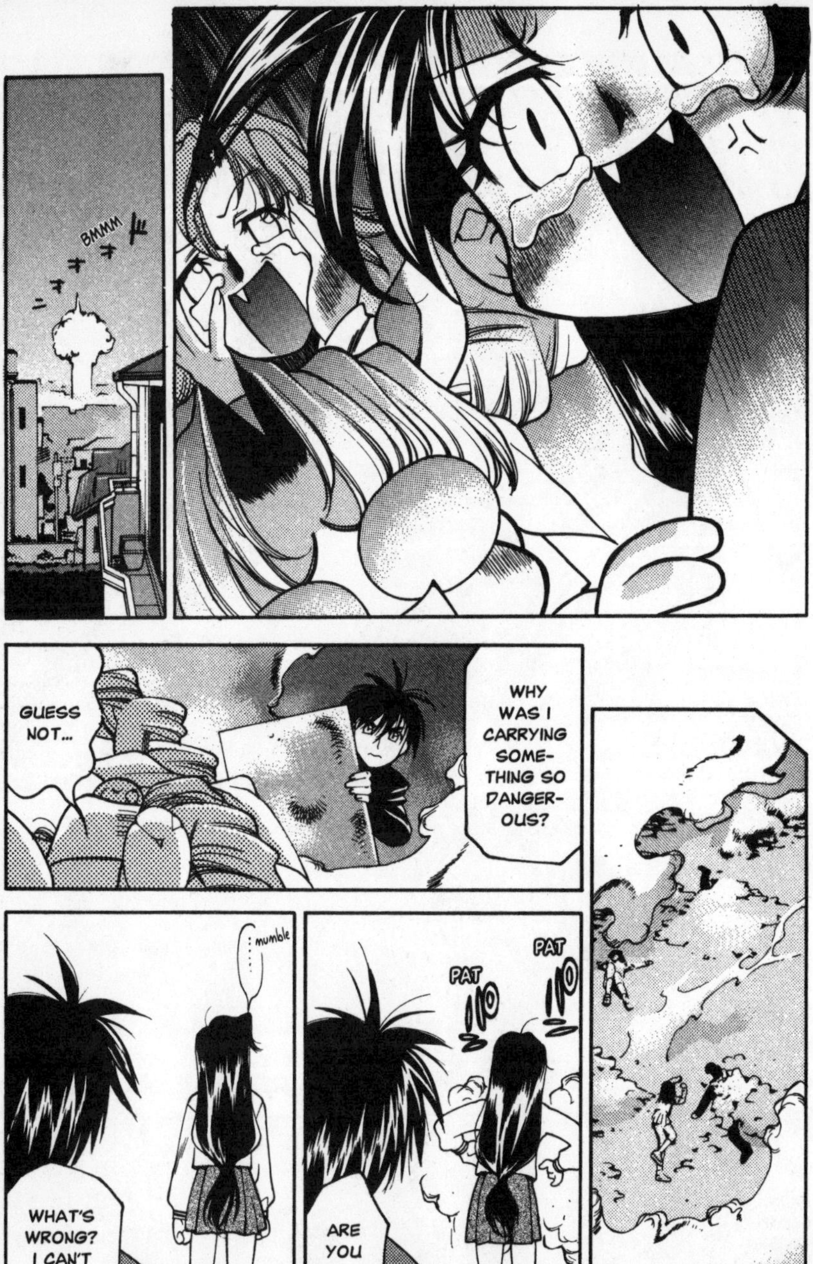
BMMM
WHY WAS I CARRYING SOMETHING SO DANGEROUS?
GUESS NOT...
PAT
PAT
ARE YOU AL-RIGHT?
mumble
WHAT'S WRONG? I CAN'T HEAR YOU.

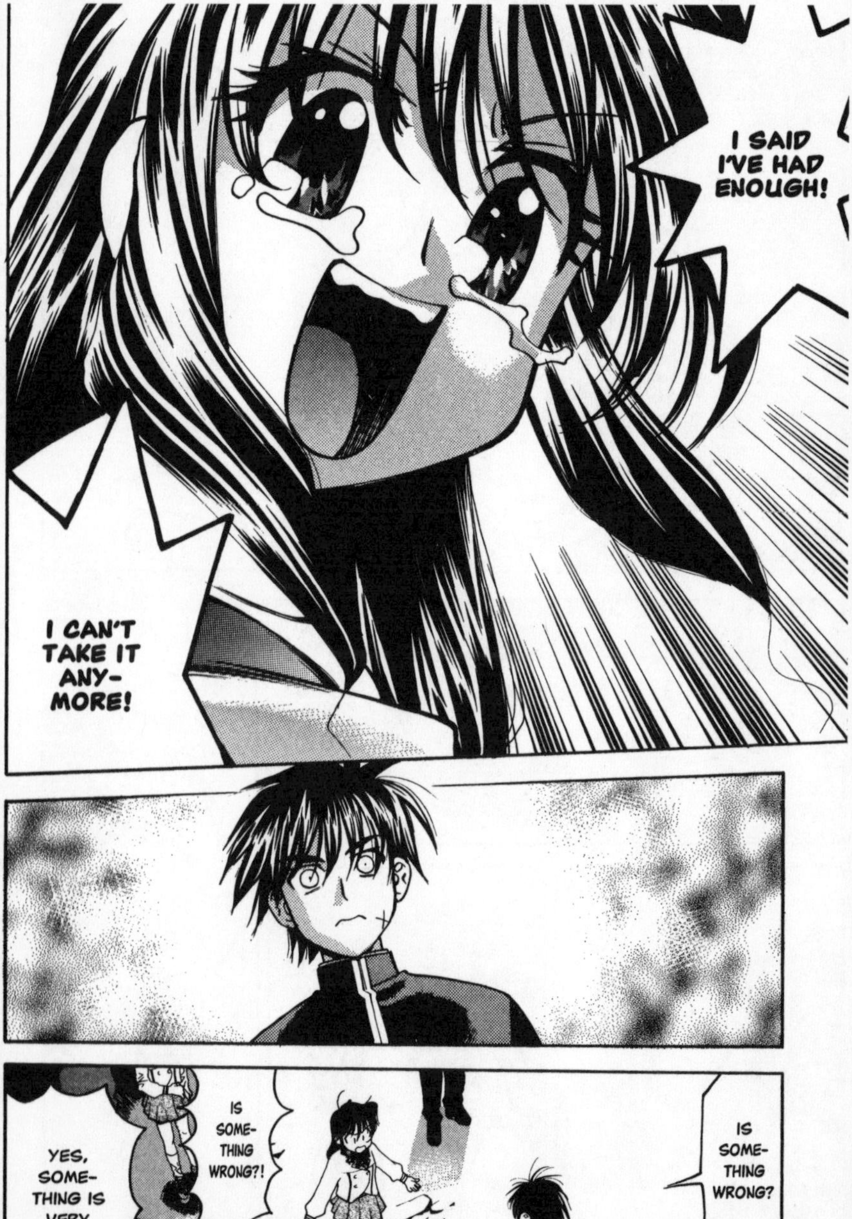
I SAID I'VE HAD ENOUGH!
I CAN'T TAKE IT ANY-MORE!
IS SOME-THING WRONG?
IS SOME-THING WRONG?!
YES, SOME-THING IS VERY WRONG!

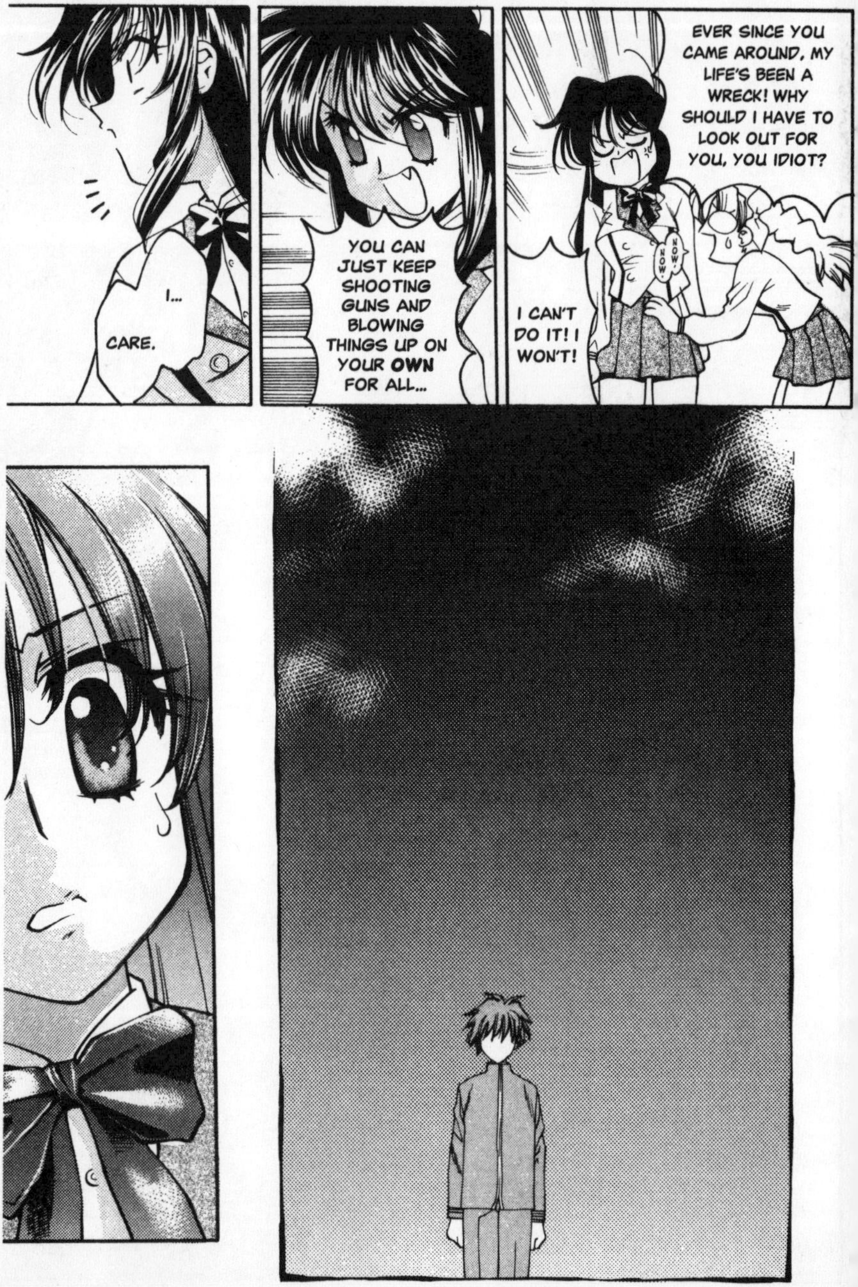
EVER SINCE YOU CAME AROUND, MY LIFE'S BEEN A WRECK! WHY SHOULD I HAVE TO LOOK OUT FOR YOU, YOU IDIOT?
NOW, NOW.
I CAN'T DO IT! I WON'T!
YOU CAN JUST KEEP SHOOTING GUNS AND BLOWING THINGS UP ON YOUR OWN FOR ALL...
I...
CARE.

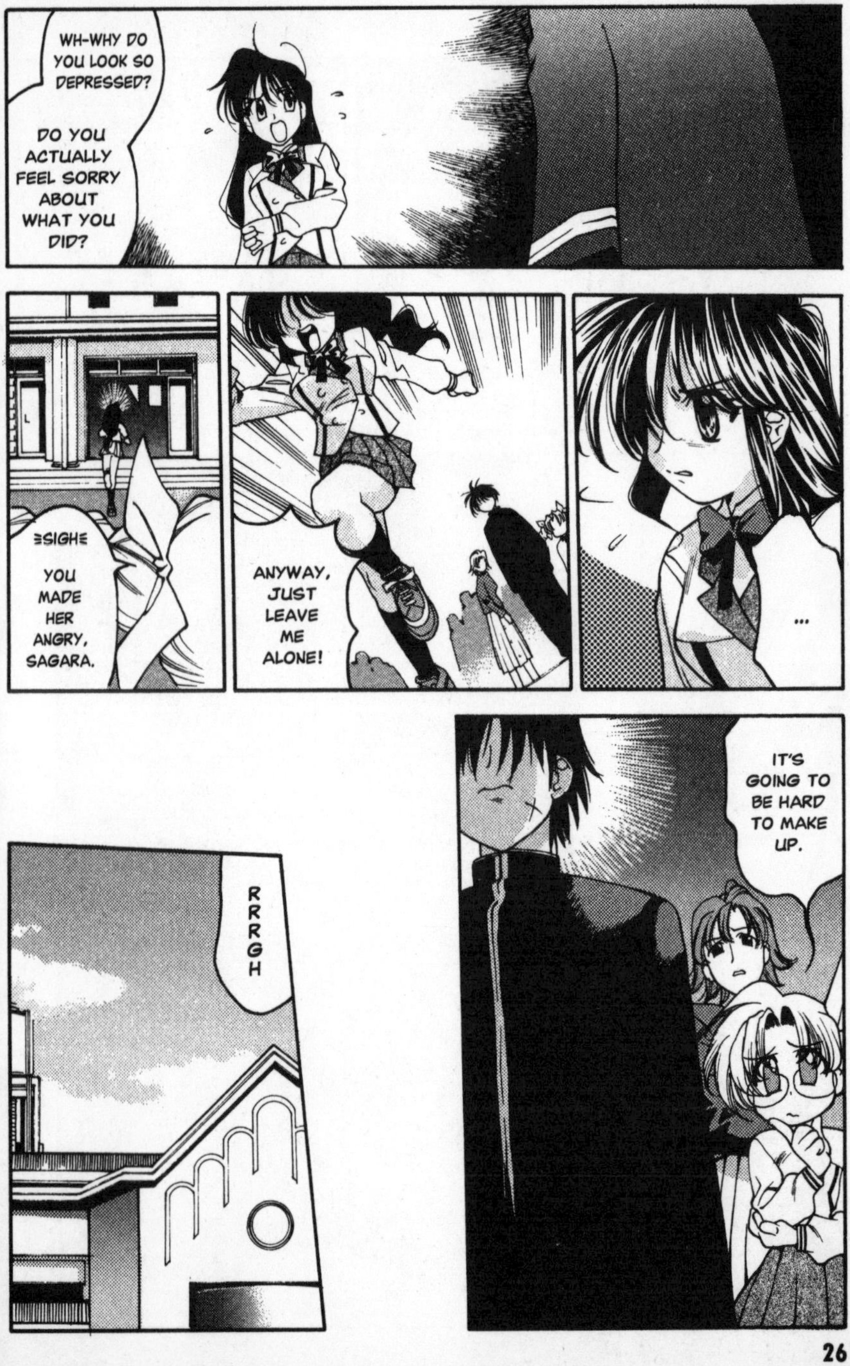
WH-WHY DO YOU LOOK SO DEPRESSED?
DO YOU ACTUALLY FEEL SORRY ABOUT WHAT YOU DID?
...
ANYWAY, JUST LEAVE ME ALONE!
≡SIGH≡
YOU MADE HER ANGRY, SAGARA.
IT'S GOING TO BE HARD TO MAKE UP.
RRRGH

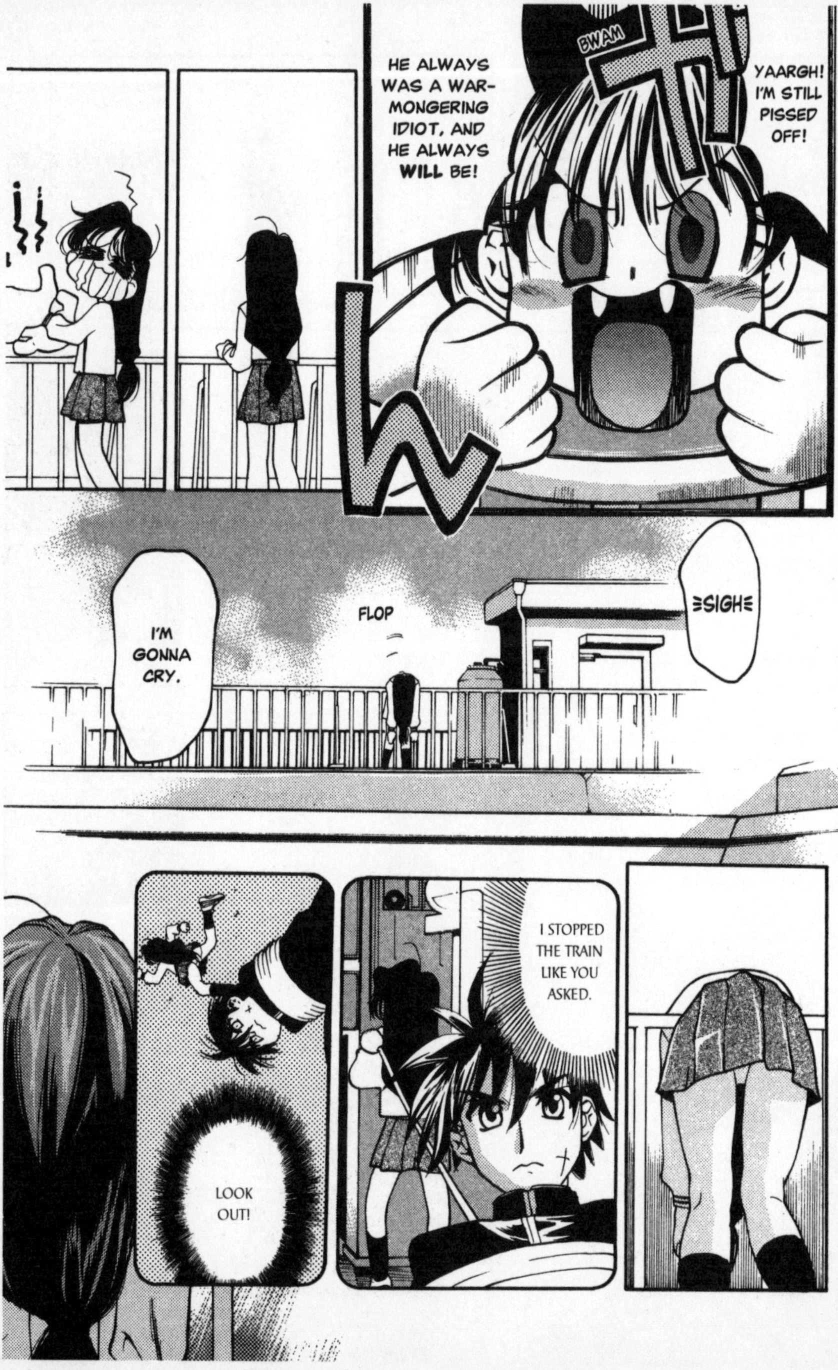
YAARGH! I'M STILL PISSED OFF!
BWAM
HE ALWAYS WAS A WAR-MONGERING IDIOT, AND HE ALWAYS **WILL** BE!
SIGH
FLOP
I'M GONNA CRY.
I STOPPED THE TRAIN LIKE YOU ASKED.
LOOK OUT!

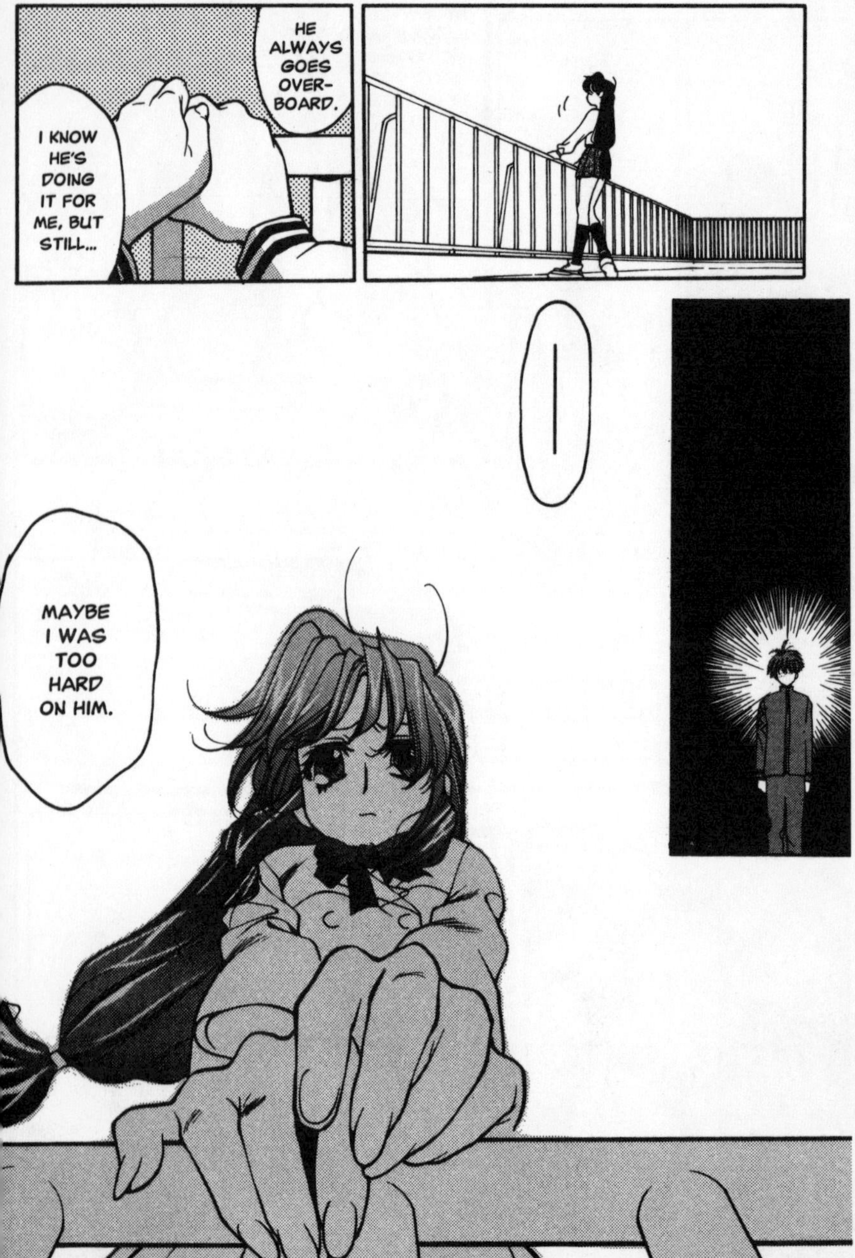
HE ALWAYS GOES OVER-BOARD.
I KNOW HE'S DOING IT FOR ME, BUT STILL...
MAYBE I WAS TOO HARD ON HIM.

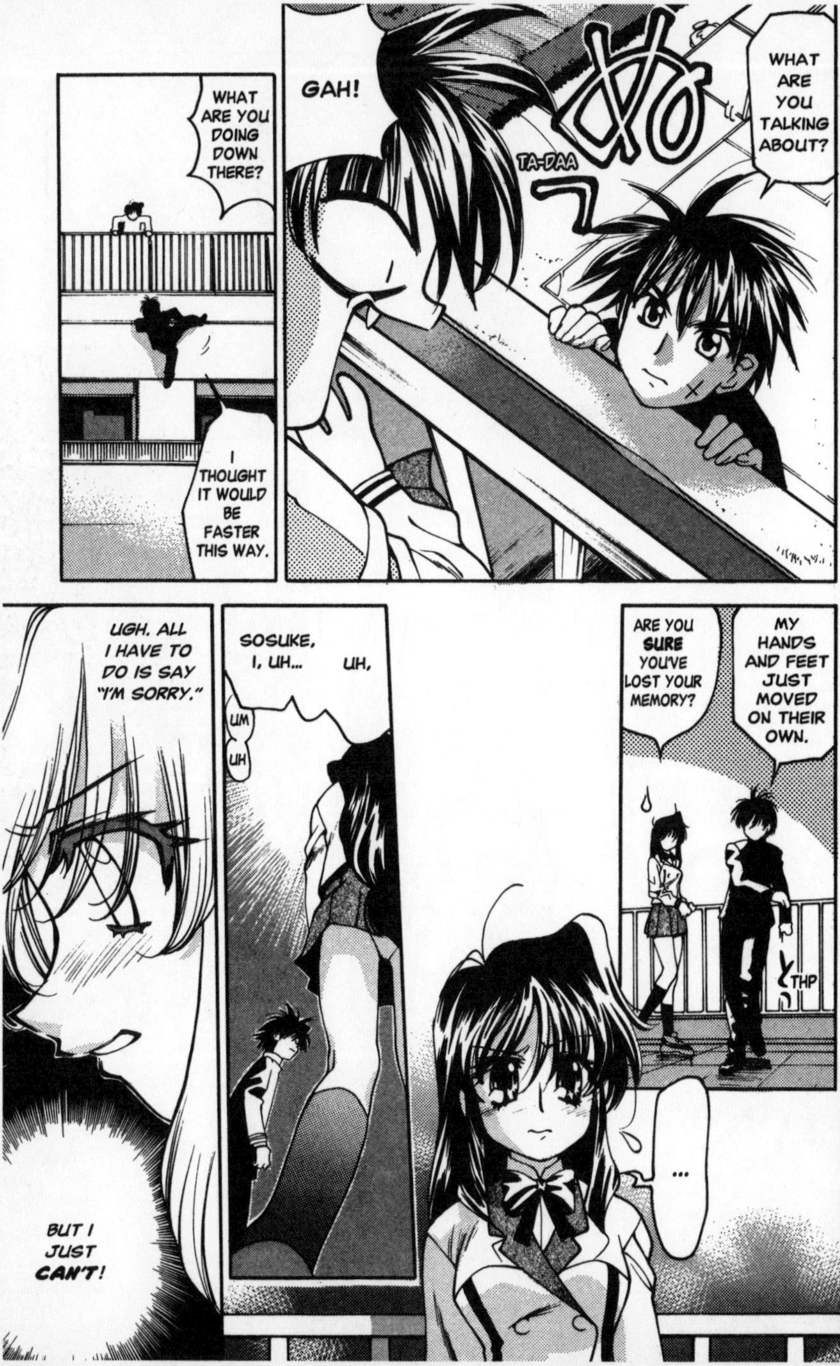
WHAT ARE YOU TALKING ABOUT?
TA-DAA
GAH!
WHAT ARE YOU DOING DOWN THERE?
I THOUGHT IT WOULD BE FASTER THIS WAY.
MY HANDS AND FEET JUST MOVED ON THEIR OWN.
ARE YOU **SURE** YOU'VE LOST YOUR MEMORY?
THP
...
SOSUKE, I, UH... UH,
UM
UH
UGH. ALL I HAVE TO DO IS SAY "I'M SORRY."
BUT I JUST **CAN'T**!

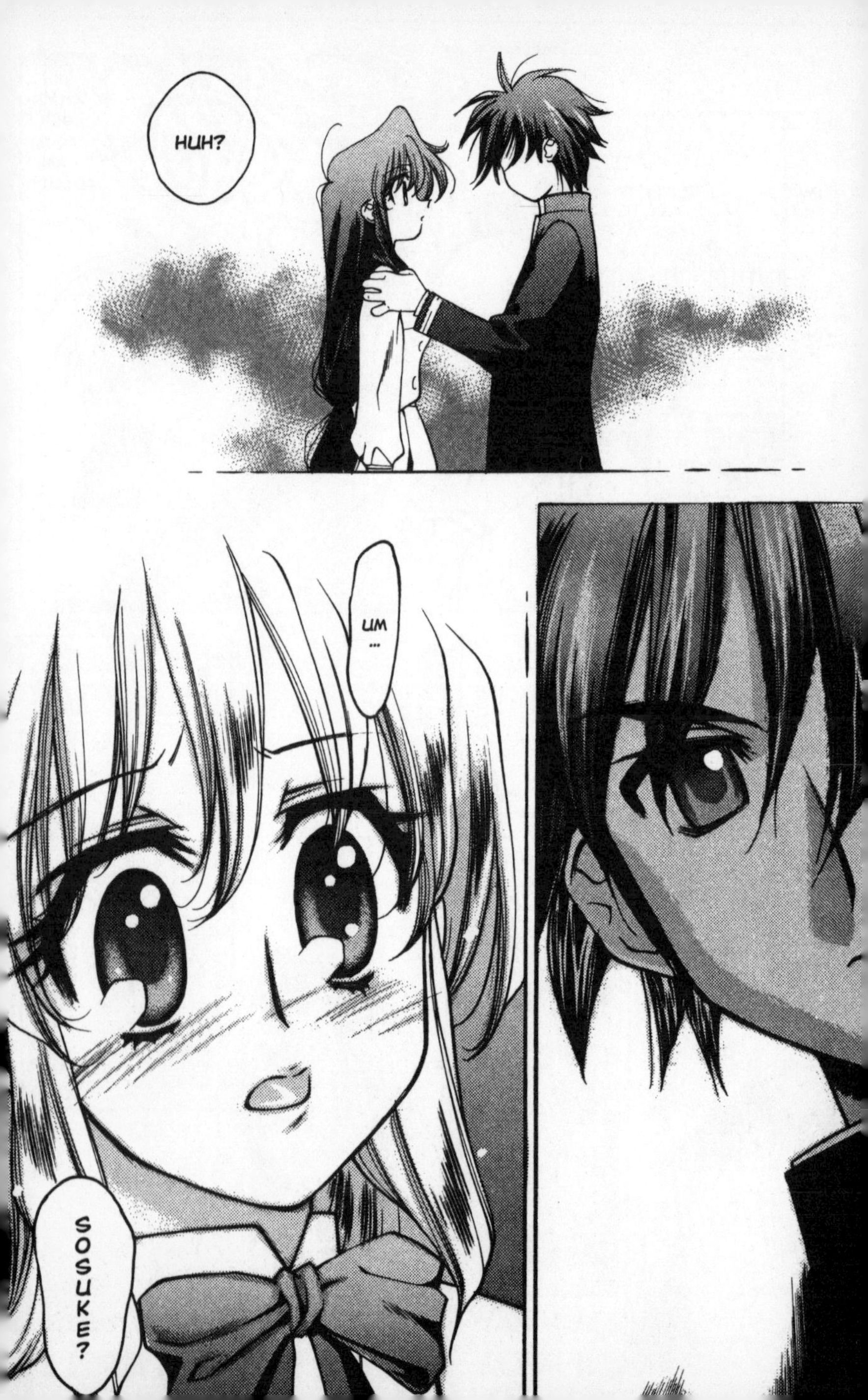
HUH?
UM ...
SOSUKE?

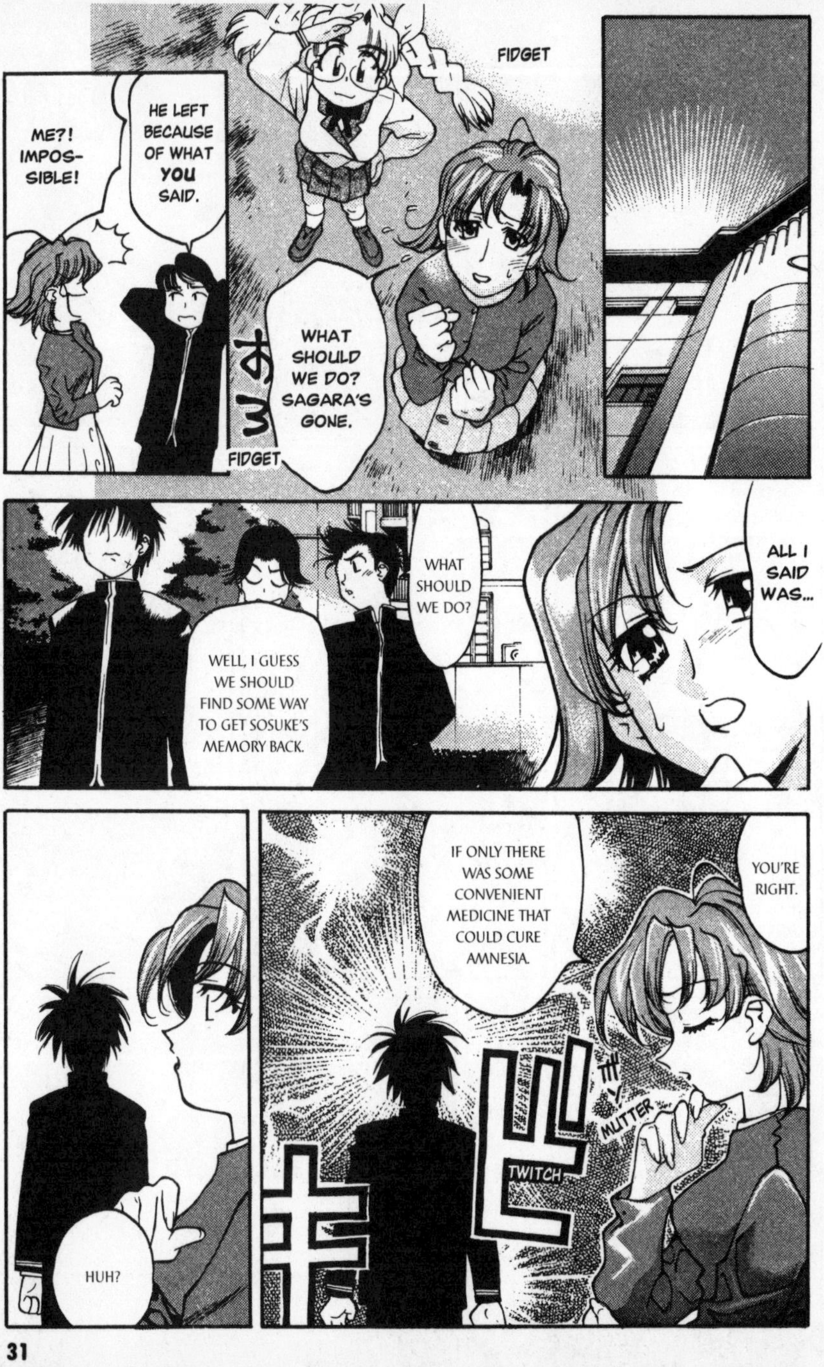
FIDGET
WHAT SHOULD WE DO? SAGARA'S GONE.
FIDGET
HE LEFT BECAUSE OF WHAT YOU SAID.
ME?! IMPOS-SIBLE!
ALL I SAID WAS...
WHAT SHOULD WE DO?
WELL, I GUESS WE SHOULD FIND SOME WAY TO GET SOSUKE'S MEMORY BACK.
YOU'RE RIGHT.
IF ONLY THERE WAS SOME CONVENIENT MEDICINE THAT COULD CURE AMNESIA.
MUTTER
TWITCH
HUH?

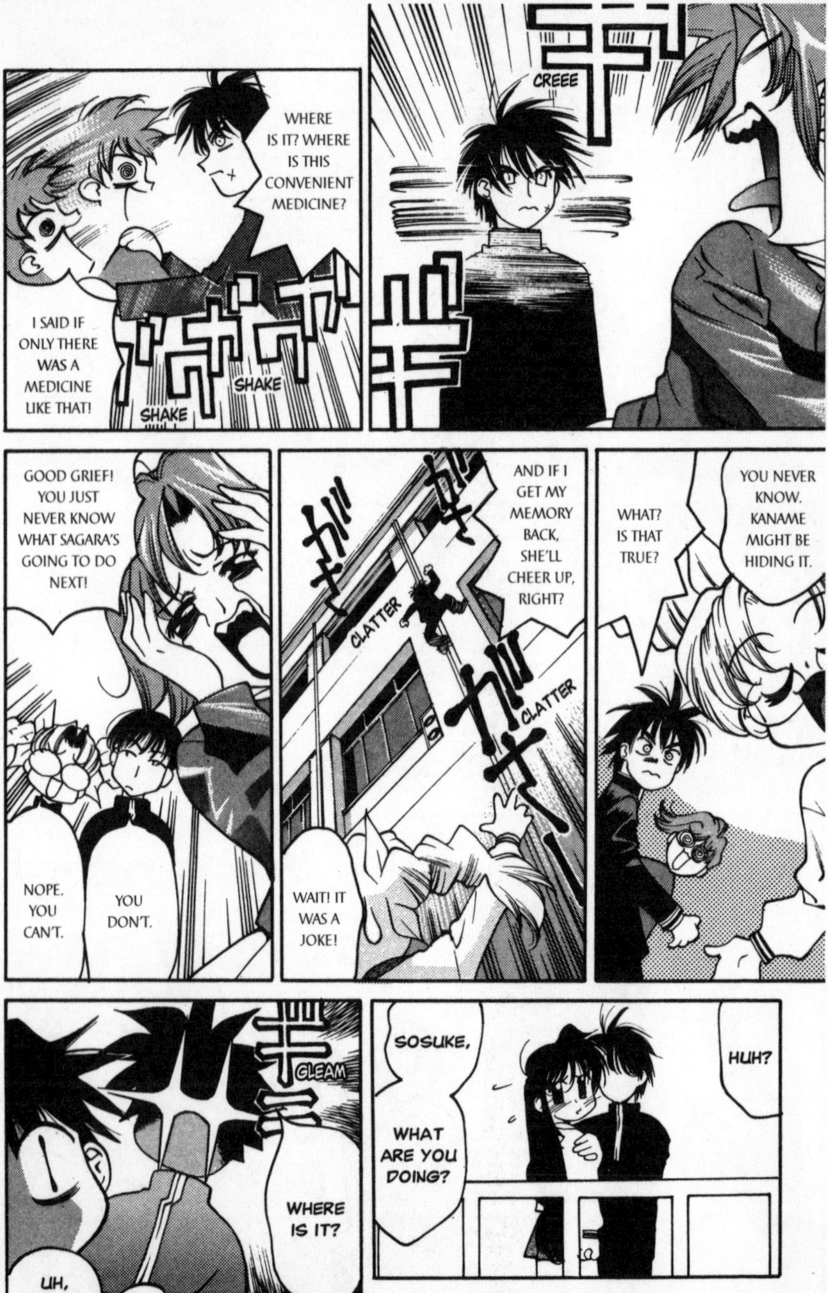
CREEE
WHERE IS IT? WHERE IS THIS CONVENIENT MEDICINE?
I SAID IF ONLY THERE WAS A MEDICINE LIKE THAT!
SHAKE
SHAKE
YOU NEVER KNOW. KANAME MIGHT BE HIDING IT.
WHAT? IS THAT TRUE?
AND IF I GET MY MEMORY BACK, SHE'LL CHEER UP, RIGHT?
CLATTER
CLATTER
WAIT! IT WAS A JOKE!
GOOD GRIEF! YOU JUST NEVER KNOW WHAT SAGARA'S GOING TO DO NEXT!
YOU DON'T.
NOPE. YOU CAN'T.
SOSUKE,
HUH?
WHAT ARE YOU DOING?
GLEAM
WHERE IS IT?
UH, WHAT?

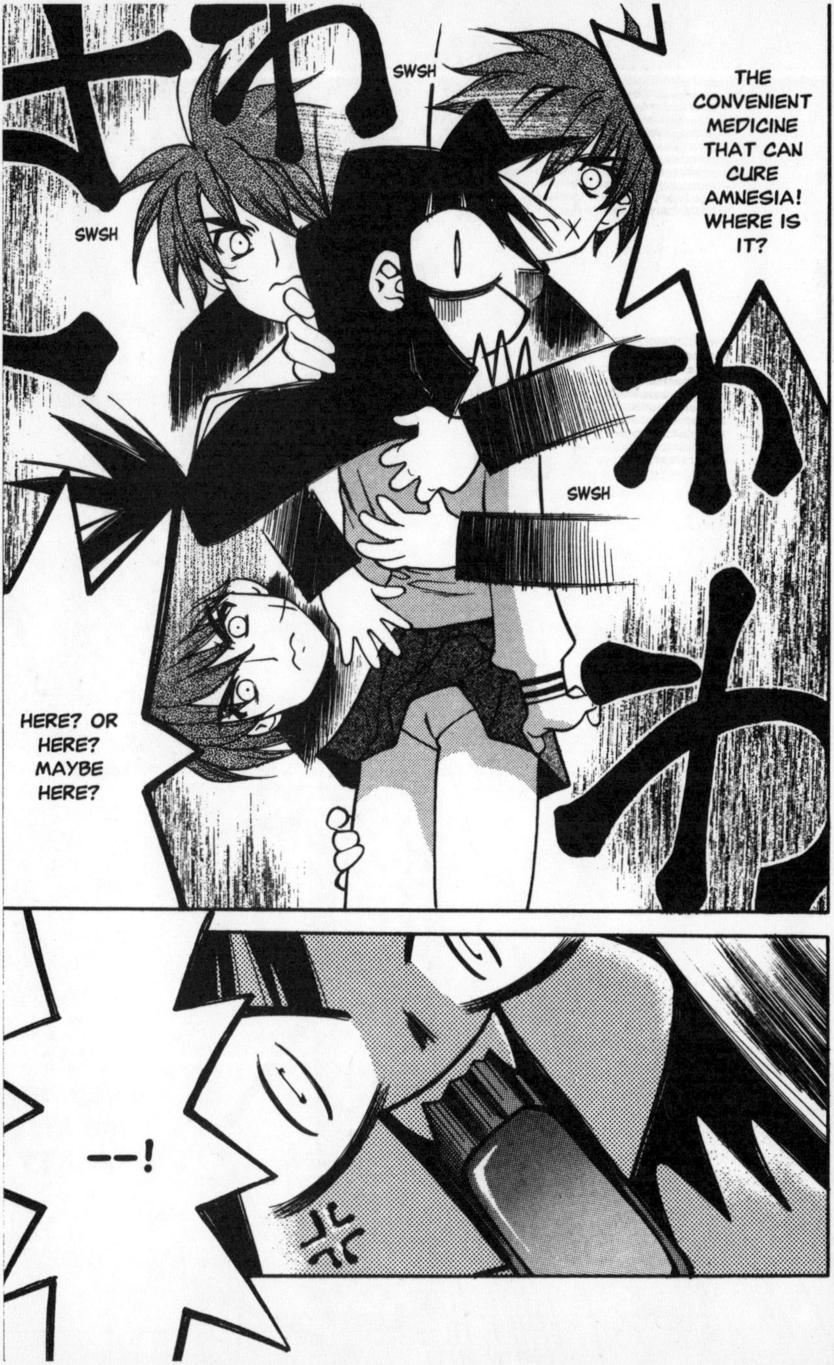
THE CONVENIENT MEDICINE THAT CAN CURE AMNESIA! WHERE IS IT?
SWSH
SWSH
SWSH
HERE? OR HERE? MAYBE HERE?
--!

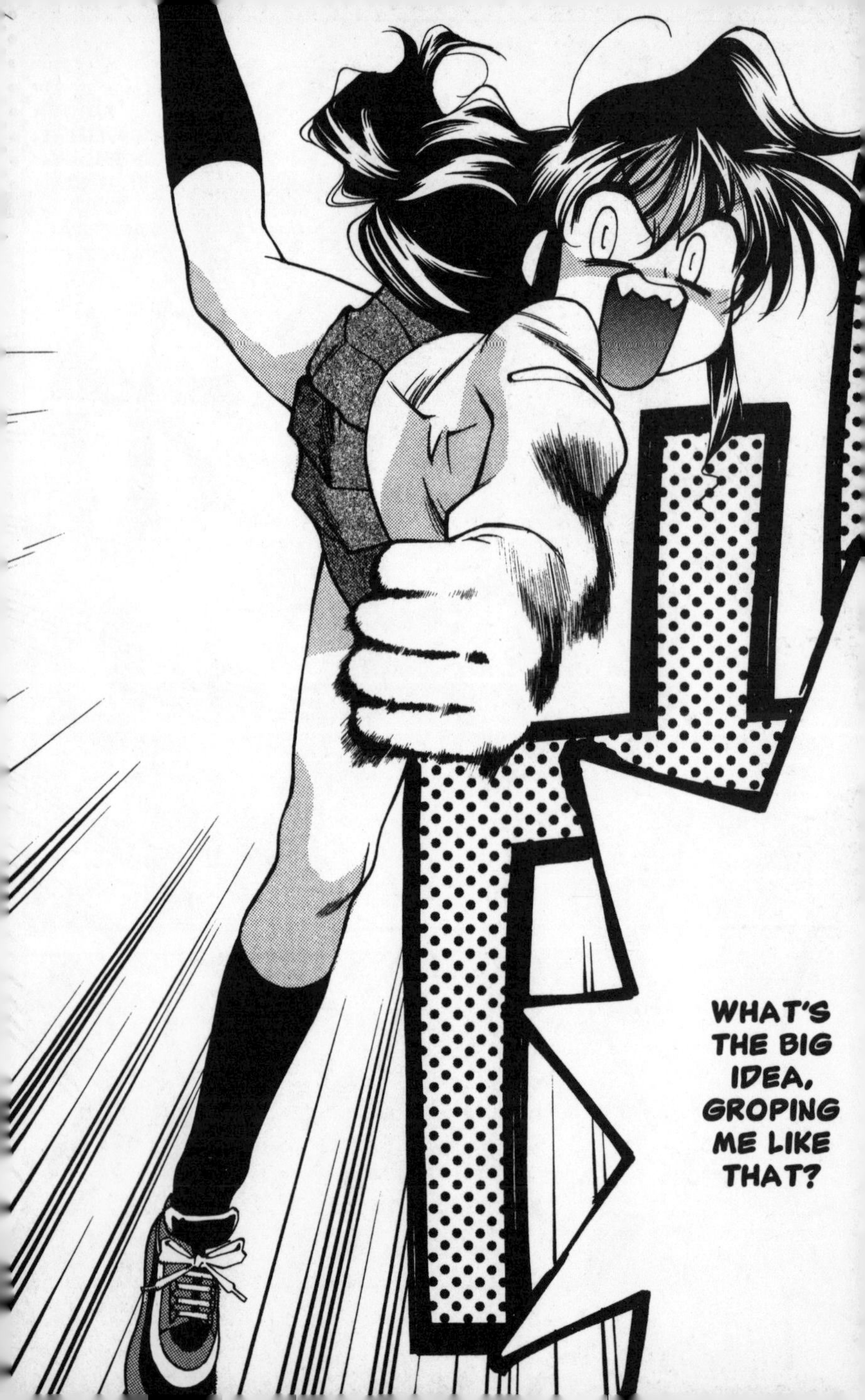
WHAT'S THE BIG IDEA, GROPING ME LIKE THAT?

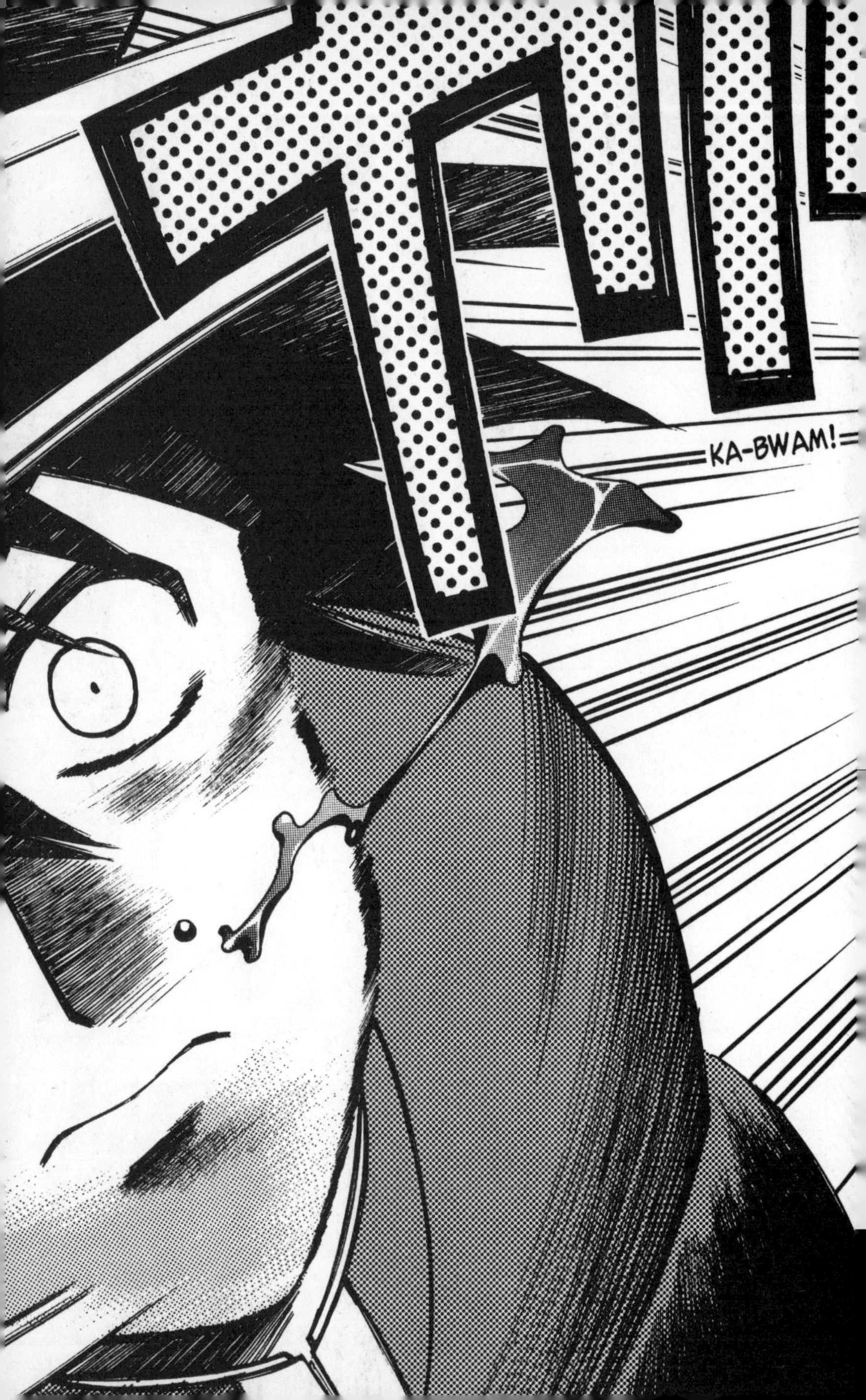
KA-BWAM!

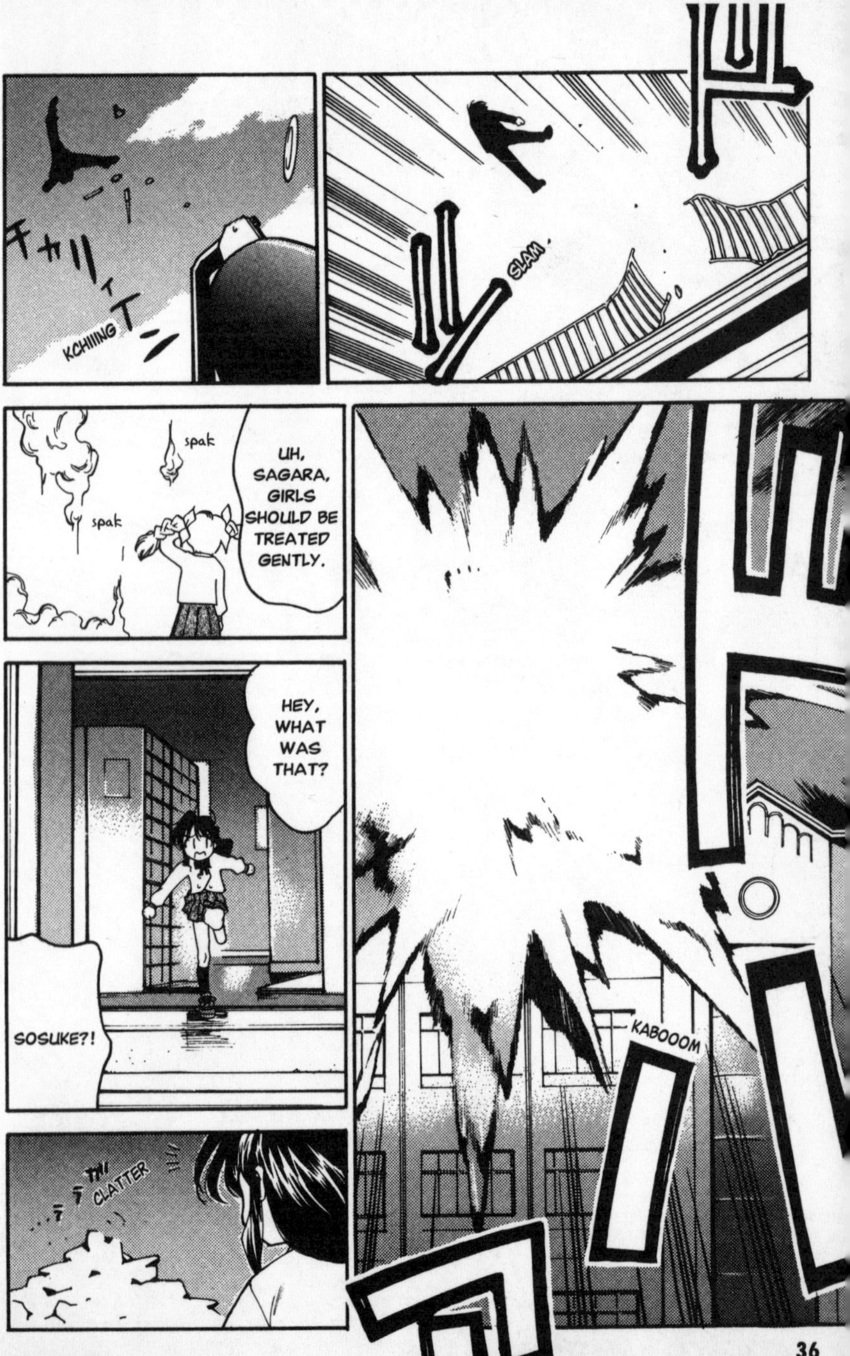
SLAM
KCHIIING
KABOOOM
UH, SAGARA, GIRLS SHOULD BE TREATED GENTLY.
spak
spak
HEY, WHAT WAS THAT?
SOSUKE?!
CLATTER

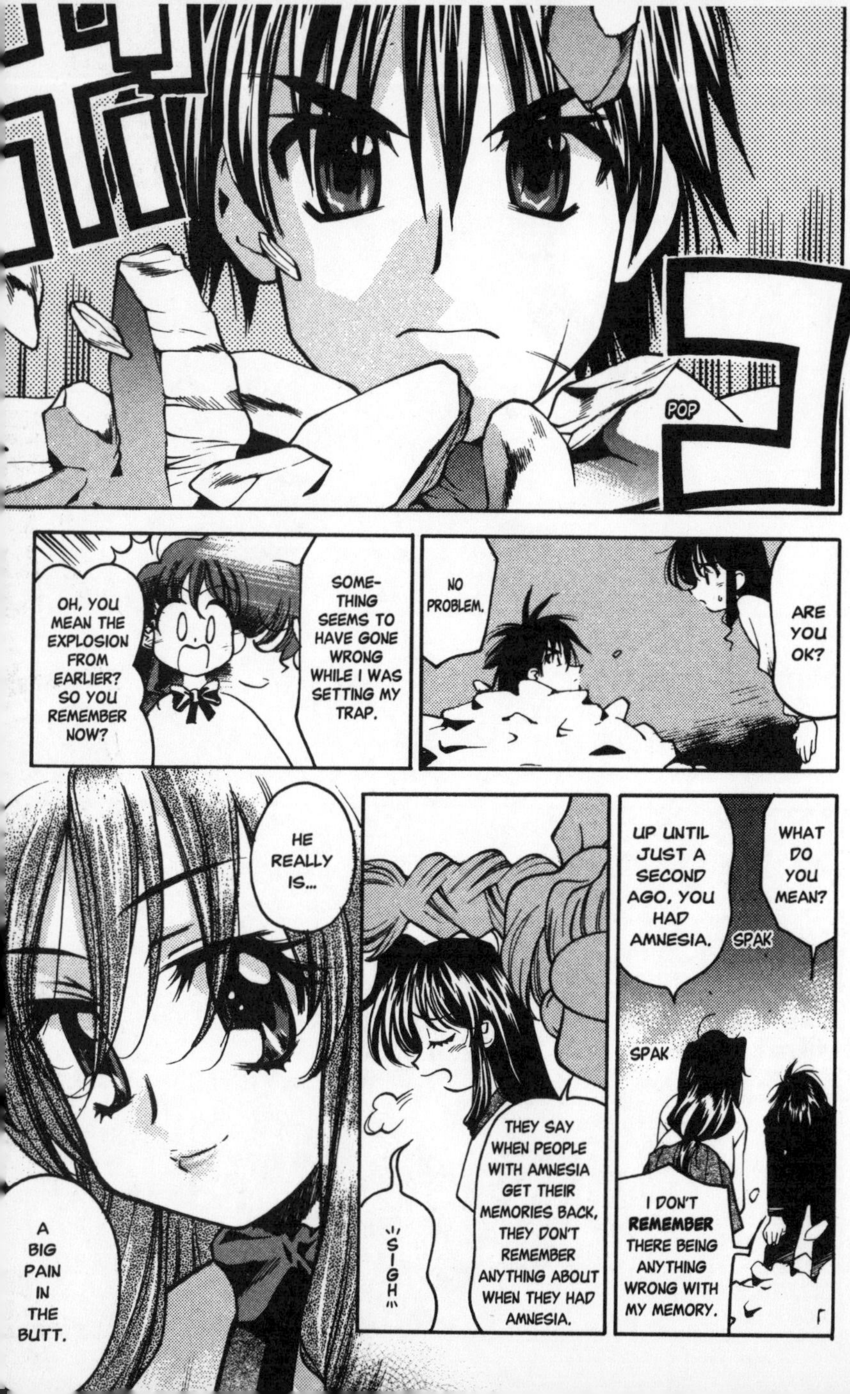
POP
ARE YOU OK?
NO PROBLEM.
SOME-THING SEEMS TO HAVE GONE WRONG WHILE I WAS SETTING MY TRAP.
OH, YOU MEAN THE EXPLOSION FROM EARLIER? SO YOU REMEMBER NOW?
WHAT DO YOU MEAN?
UP UNTIL JUST A SECOND AGO, YOU HAD AMNESIA.
SPAK
SPAK
I DON'T **REMEMBER** THERE BEING ANYTHING WRONG WITH MY MEMORY.
THEY SAY WHEN PEOPLE WITH AMNESIA GET THEIR MEMORIES BACK, THEY DON'T REMEMBER ANYTHING ABOUT WHEN THEY HAD AMNESIA.
SIGH
HE REALLY IS...
A BIG PAIN IN THE BUTT.

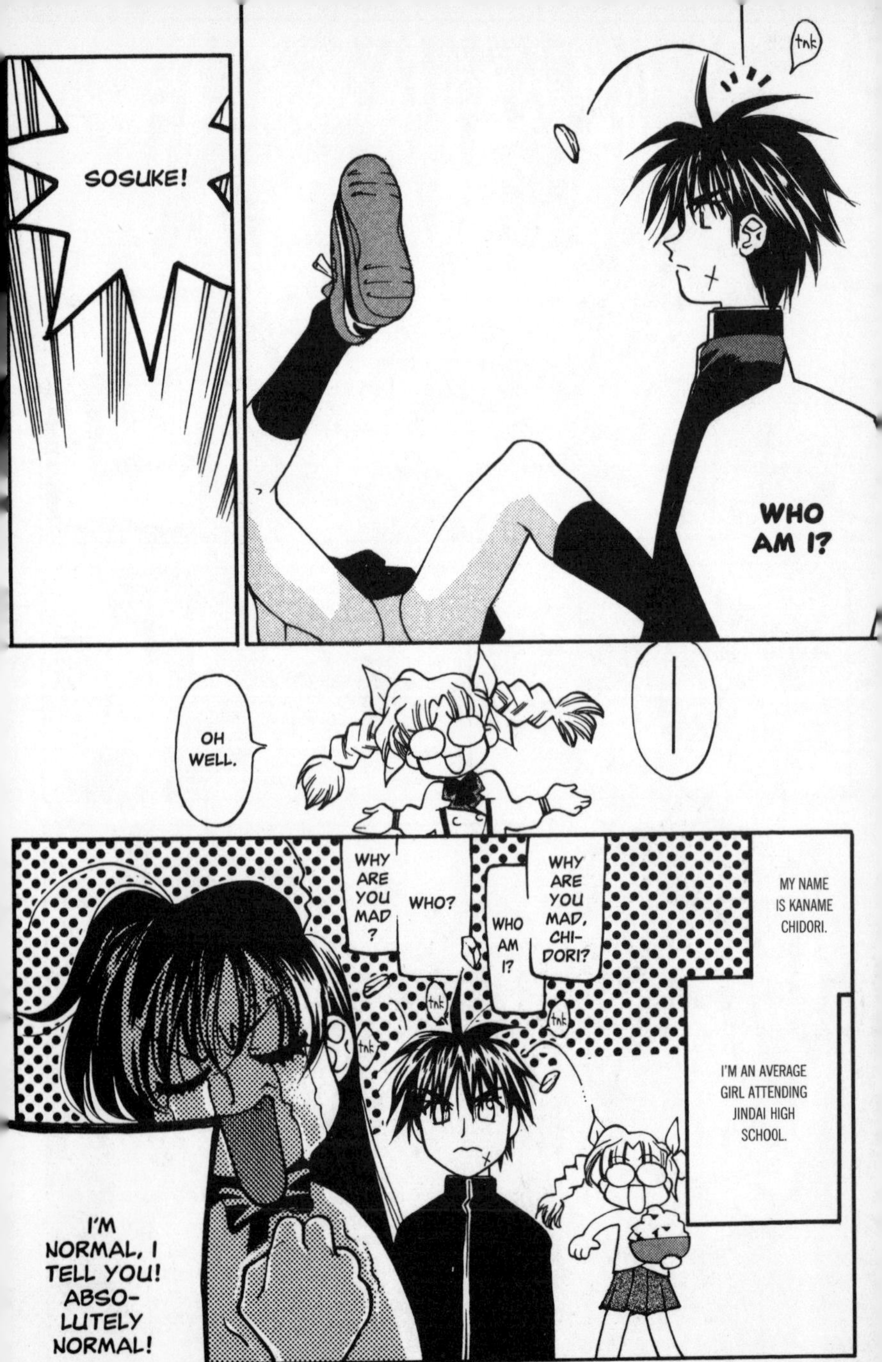
tnk
WHO AM I?
SOSUKE!
OH WELL.
MY NAME IS KANAME CHIDORI.
I'M AN AVERAGE GIRL ATTENDING JINDAI HIGH SCHOOL.
WHY ARE YOU MAD, CHI-DORI?
WHO AM I?
WHO?
WHY ARE YOU MAD?
tnk
tnk
tnk
I'M NORMAL, I TELL YOU! ABSO-LUTELY NORMAL!

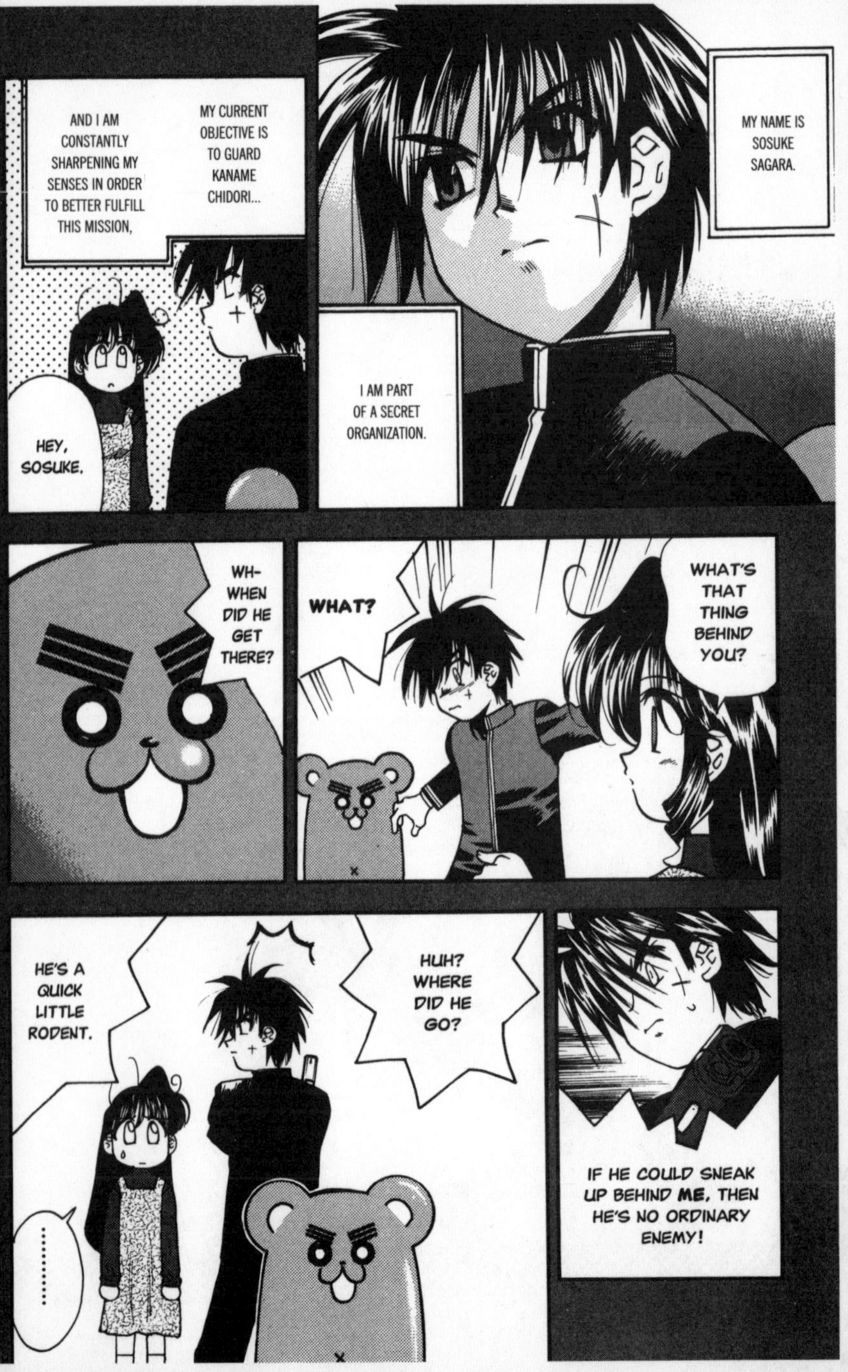
MY NAME IS SOSUKE SAGARA.
I AM PART OF A SECRET ORGANIZATION.
MY CURRENT OBJECTIVE IS TO GUARD KANAME CHIDORI...
AND I AM CONSTANTLY SHARPENING MY SENSES IN ORDER TO BETTER FULFILL THIS MISSION,
HEY, SOSUKE.
WHAT'S THAT THING BEHIND YOU?
WHAT?
WH- WHEN DID HE GET THERE?
IF HE COULD SNEAK UP BEHIND ME, THEN HE'S NO ORDINARY ENEMY!
HUH? WHERE DID HE GO?
HE'S A QUICK LITTLE RODENT.
....

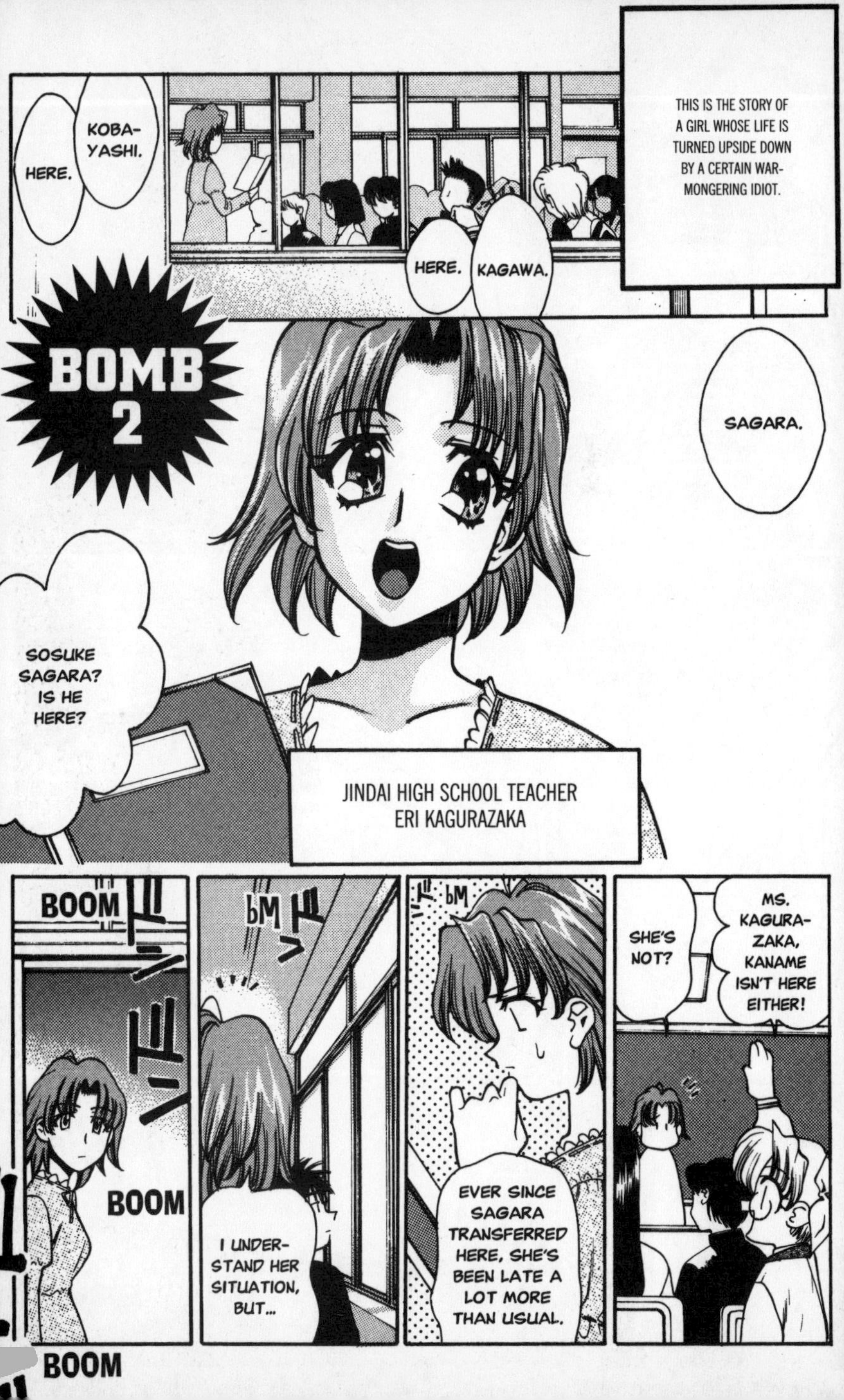
THIS IS THE STORY OF A GIRL WHOSE LIFE IS TURNED UPSIDE DOWN BY A CERTAIN WAR-MONGERING IDIOT.
KAGAWA.
HERE.
KOBA-YASHI.
HERE.
BOMB 2
SAGARA.
SOSUKE SAGARA? IS HE HERE?
JINDAI HIGH SCHOOL TEACHER ERI KAGURAZAKA
MS. KAGURA-ZAKA, KANAME ISN'T HERE EITHER!
SHE'S NOT?
EVER SINCE SAGARA TRANSFERRED HERE, SHE'S BEEN LATE A LOT MORE THAN USUAL.
bM
I UNDER-STAND HER SITUATION, BUT...
bM
BOOM
BOOM
BOOM

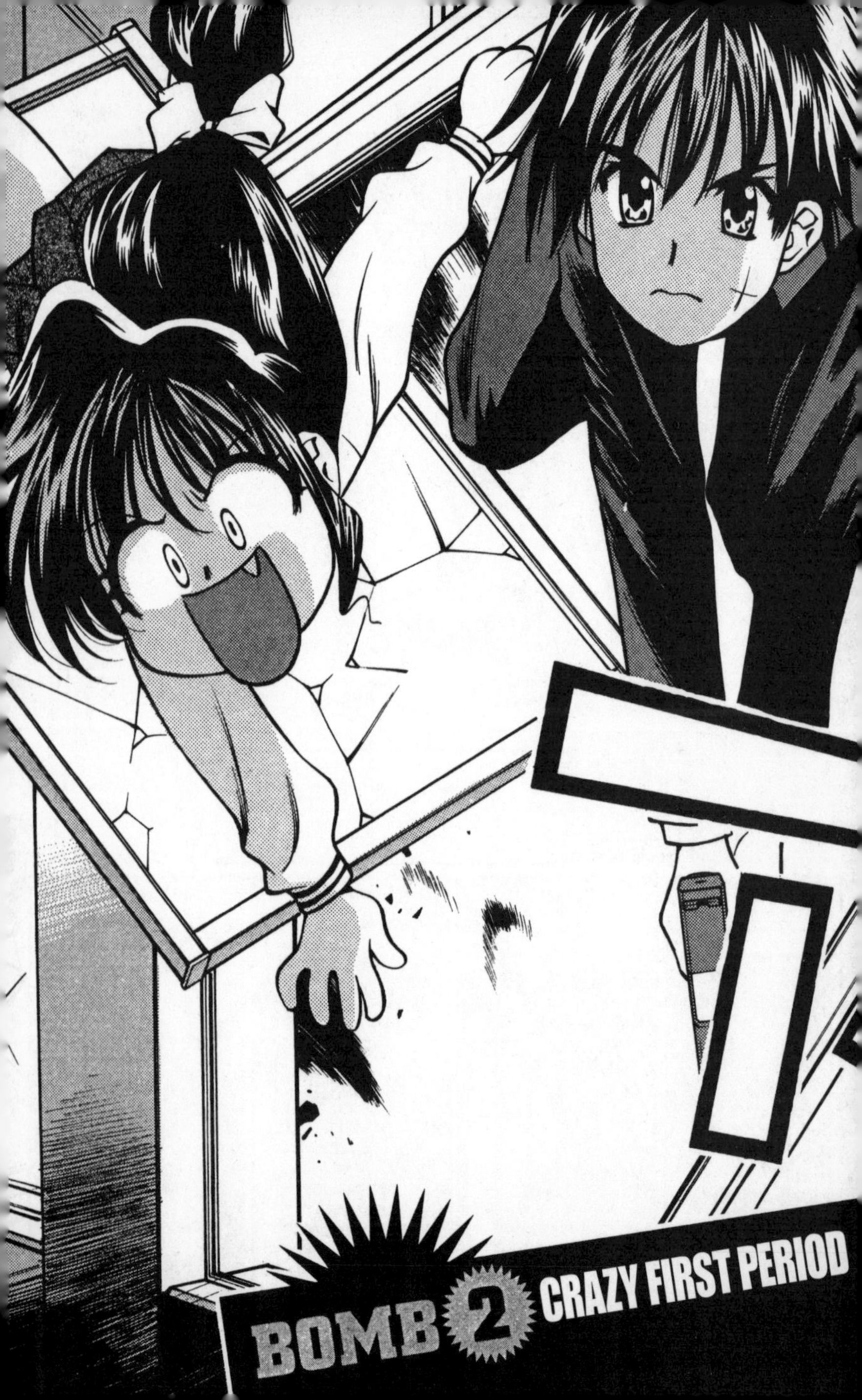

BOMB 2
CRAZY FIRST PERIOD

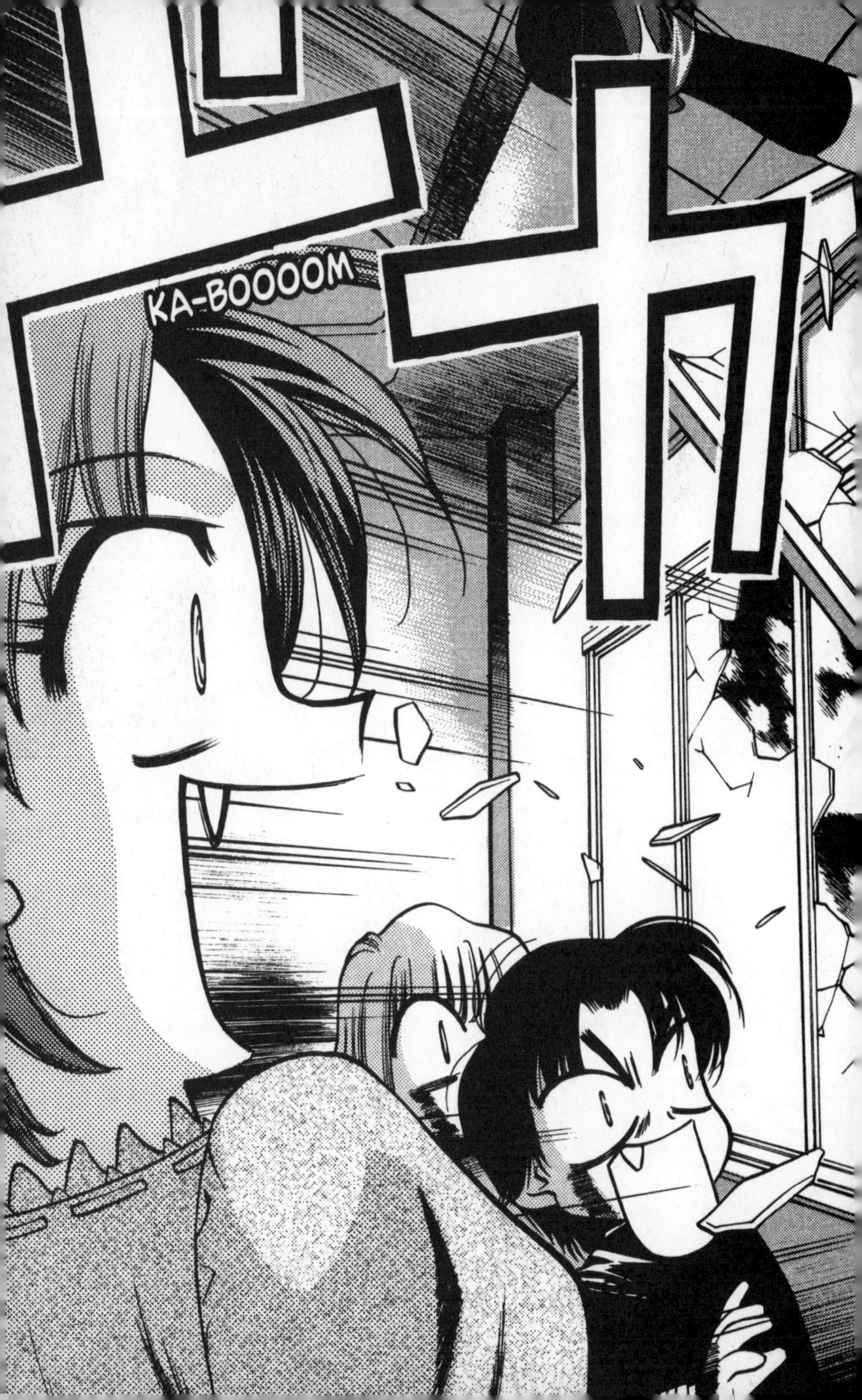
ドカ
KA-BOOOOM

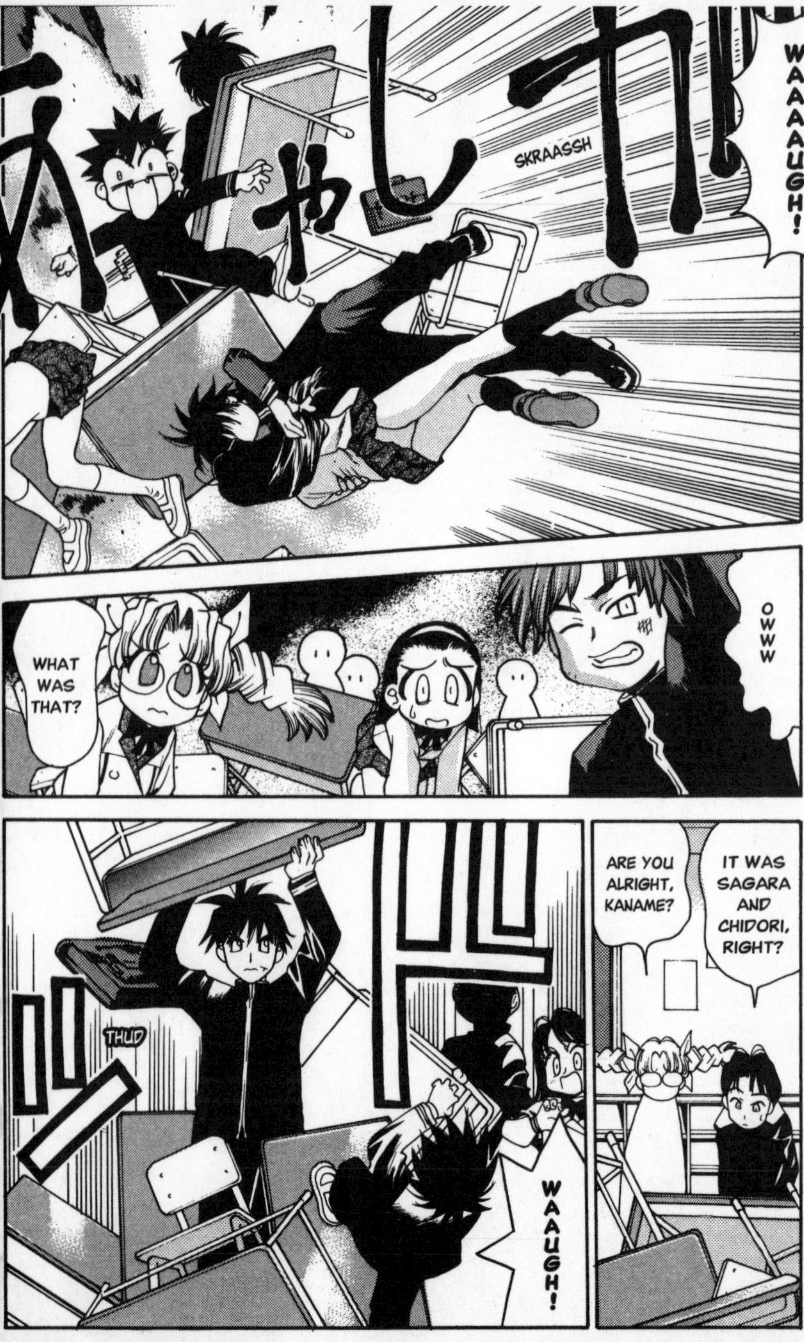

WAAAAAUGH!
SKRAASSH
OWWW
WHAT WAS THAT?
IT WAS SAGARA AND CHIDORI, RIGHT?
ARE YOU ALRIGHT, KANAME?
WAAUGH!
THUD

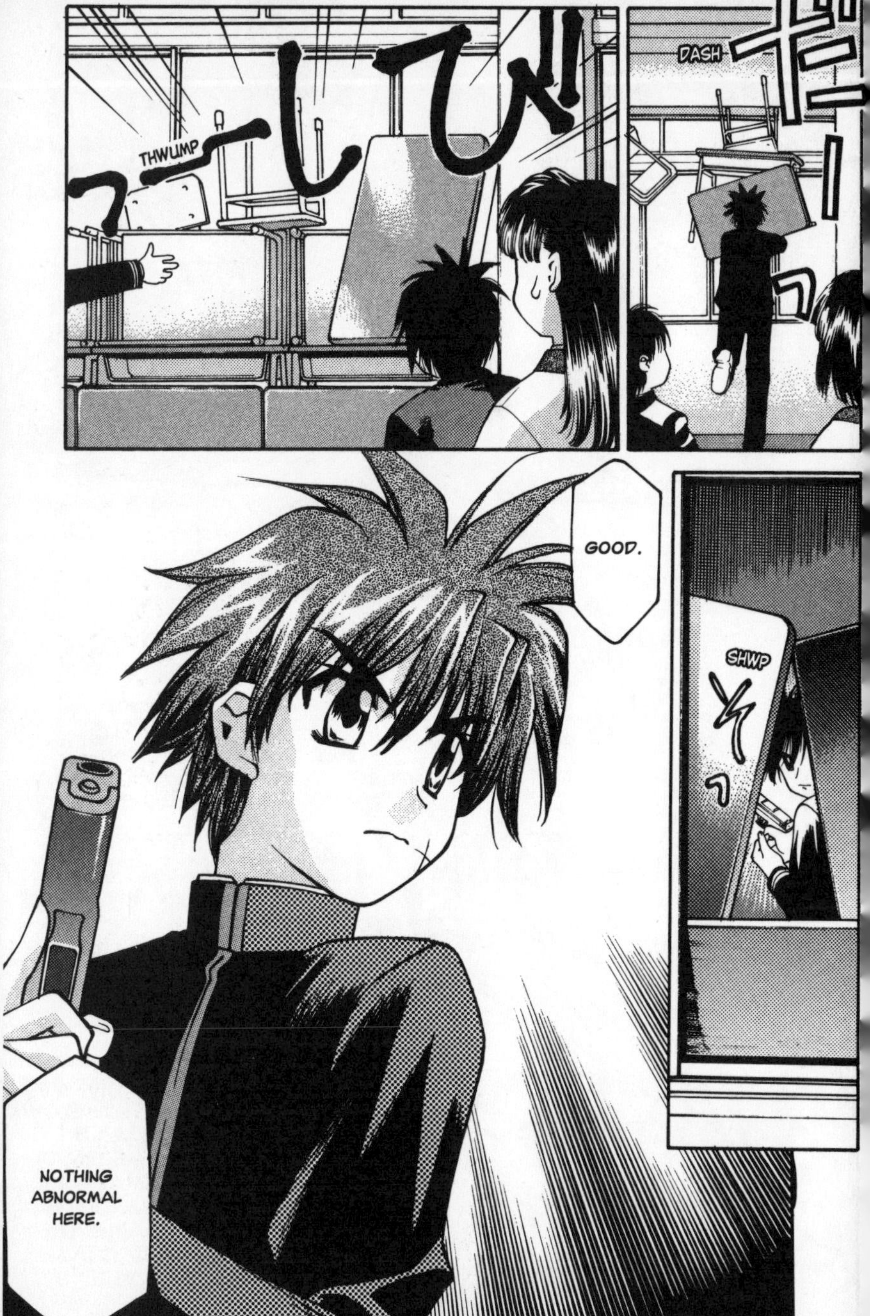

DASH
THWUMP
GOOD.
SHWP
NOTHING ABNORMAL HERE.

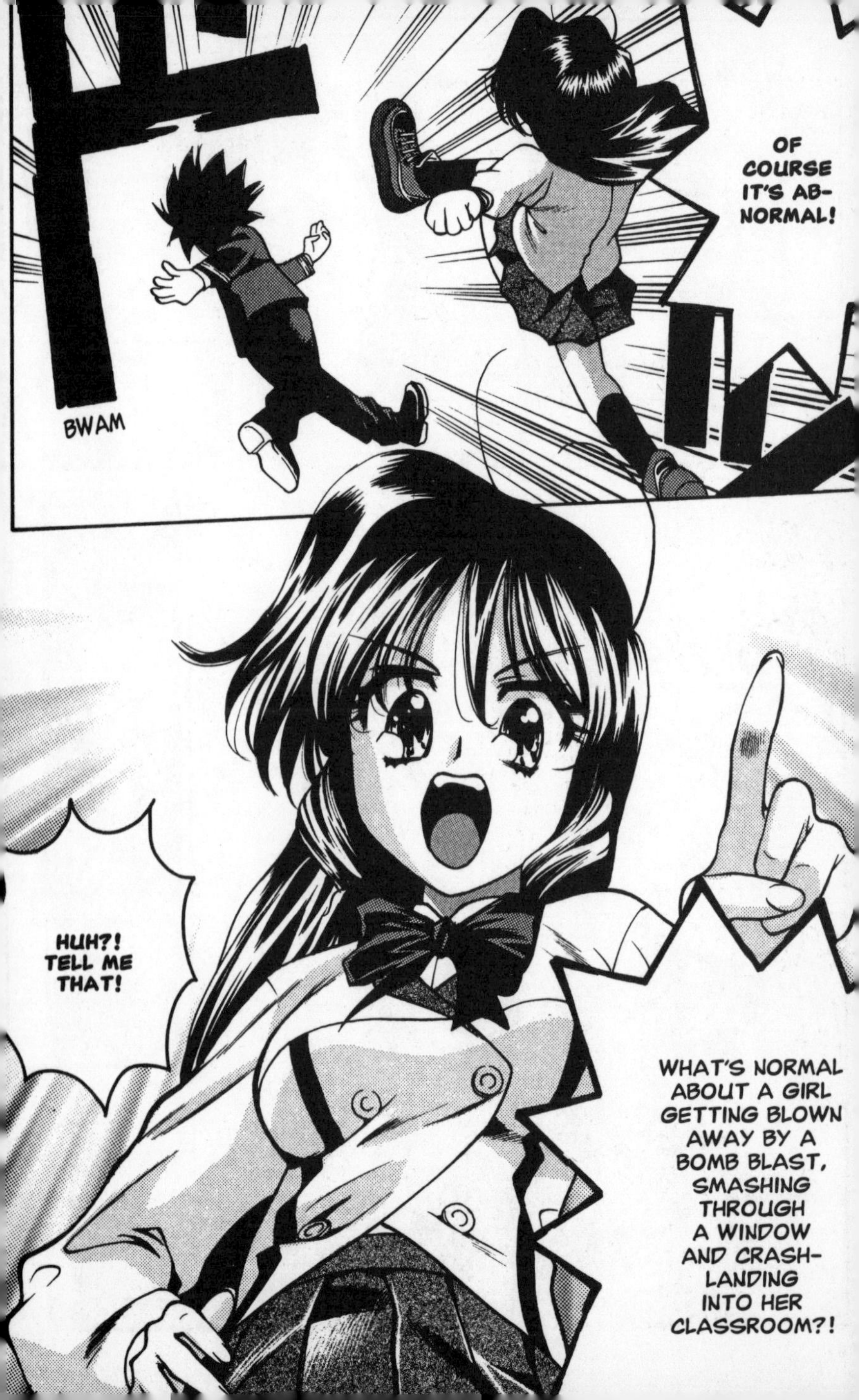
OF COURSE IT'S AB-NORMAL!
BWAM
WHAT'S NORMAL ABOUT A GIRL GETTING BLOWN AWAY BY A BOMB BLAST, SMASHING THROUGH A WINDOW AND CRASH-LANDING INTO HER CLASSROOM?!
HUH?! TELL ME THAT!

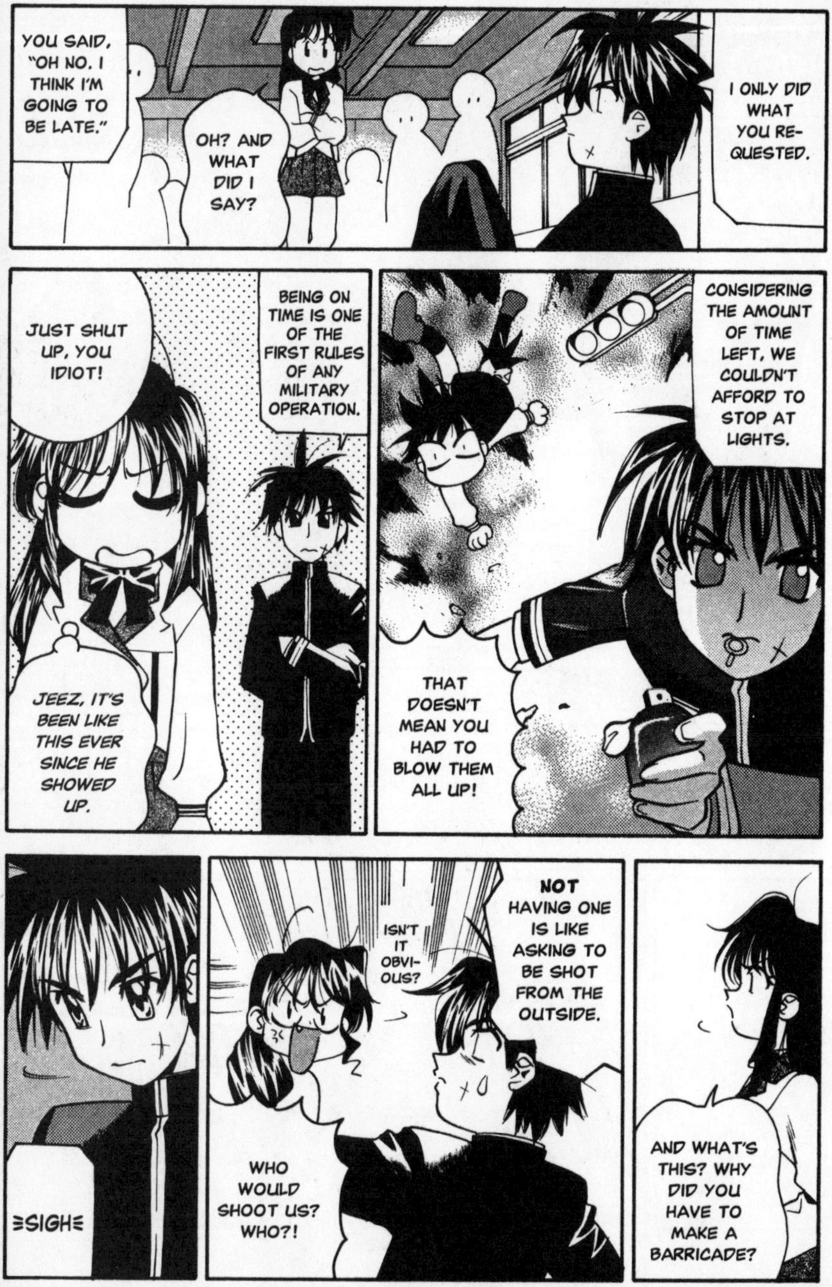
I ONLY DID WHAT YOU RE-QUESTED.
OH? AND WHAT DID I SAY?
YOU SAID, "OH NO. I THINK I'M GOING TO BE LATE."
CONSIDERING THE AMOUNT OF TIME LEFT, WE COULDN'T AFFORD TO STOP AT LIGHTS.
THAT DOESN'T MEAN YOU HAD TO BLOW THEM ALL UP!
BEING ON TIME IS ONE OF THE FIRST RULES OF ANY MILITARY OPERATION.
JUST SHUT UP, YOU IDIOT!
JEEZ, IT'S BEEN LIKE THIS EVER SINCE HE SHOWED UP.
AND WHAT'S THIS? WHY DID YOU HAVE TO MAKE A BARRICADE?
NOT HAVING ONE IS LIKE ASKING TO BE SHOT FROM THE OUTSIDE.
WHO WOULD SHOOT US? WHO?!
ISN'T IT OBVI-OUS?
≡SIGH≡

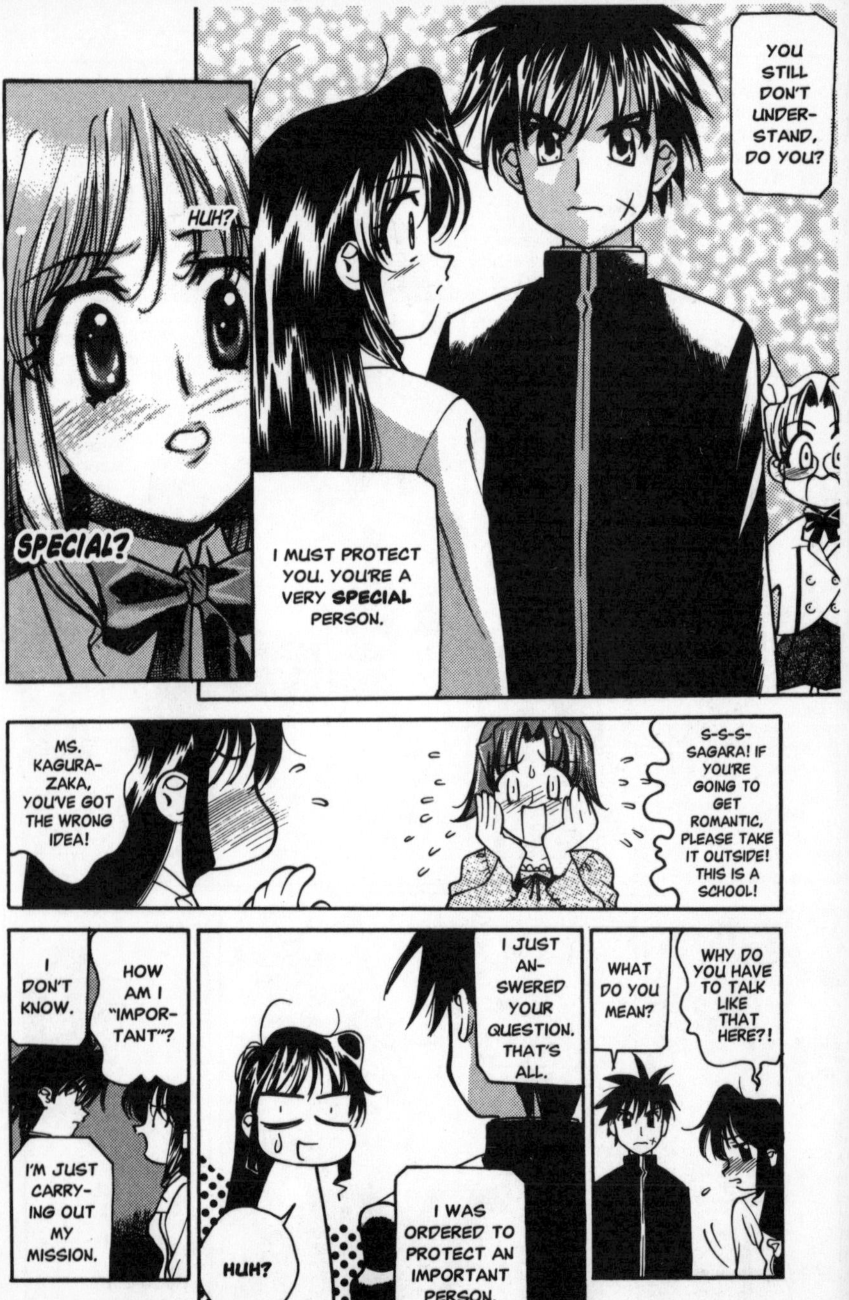
YOU STILL DON'T UNDER-STAND, DO YOU?
I MUST PROTECT YOU. YOU'RE A VERY **SPECIAL** PERSON.
HUH?
SPECIAL?
S-S-S-SAGARA! IF YOU'RE GOING TO GET ROMANTIC, PLEASE TAKE IT OUTSIDE! THIS IS A SCHOOL!
MS. KAGURA-ZAKA, YOU'VE GOT THE WRONG IDEA!
WHY DO YOU HAVE TO TALK LIKE THAT HERE?!
WHAT DO YOU MEAN?
I JUST AN-SWERED YOUR QUESTION. THAT'S ALL.
I WAS ORDERED TO PROTECT AN IMPORTANT PERSON. YOU.
HUH?
HOW AM I "IMPOR-TANT"?
I DON'T KNOW.
I'M JUST CARRY-ING OUT MY MISSION.

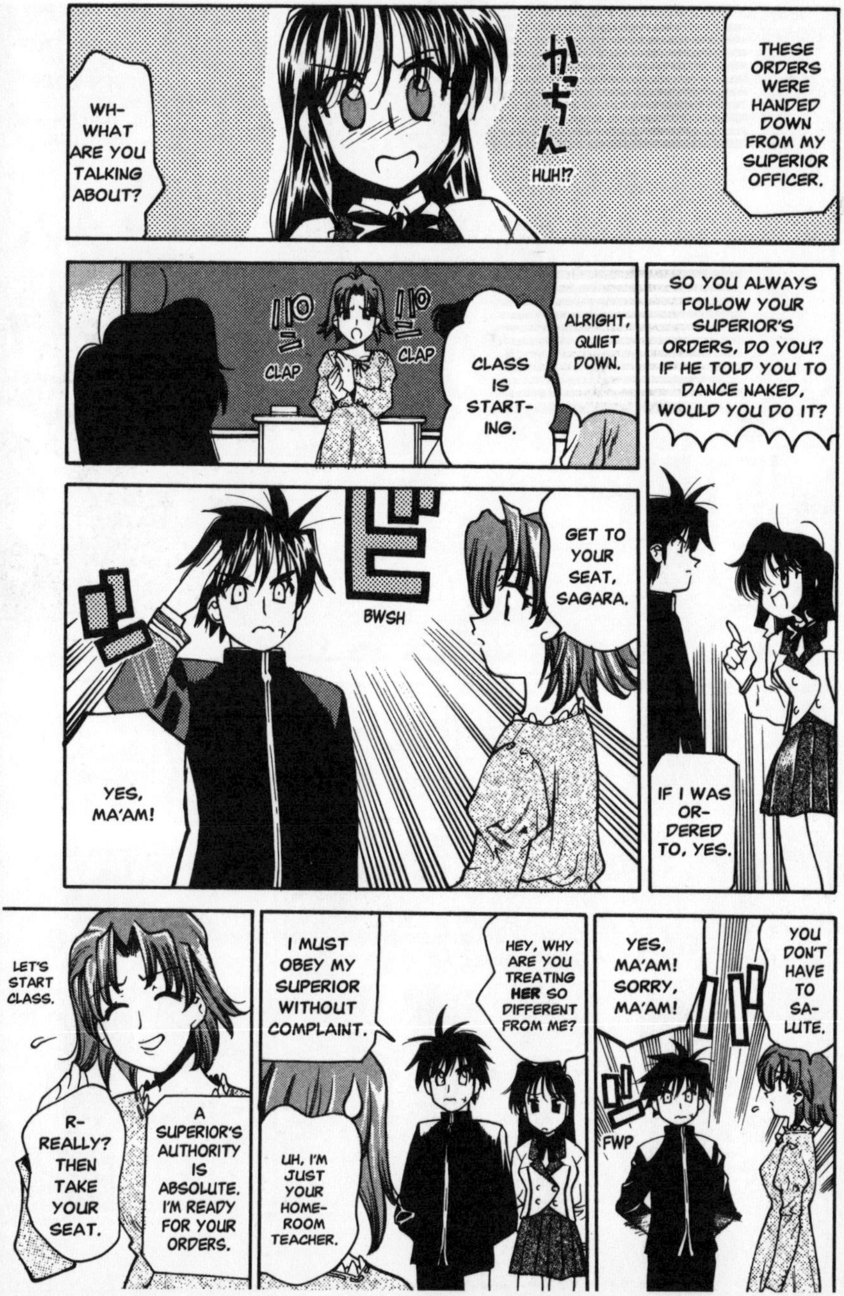

THESE ORDERS WERE HANDED DOWN FROM MY SUPERIOR OFFICER.
かちん
HUH!?
WH-WHAT ARE YOU TALKING ABOUT?
SO YOU ALWAYS FOLLOW YOUR SUPERIOR'S ORDERS, DO YOU? IF HE TOLD YOU TO DANCE NAKED, WOULD YOU DO IT?
IF I WAS OR-DERED TO, YES.
ALRIGHT, QUIET DOWN.
CLASS IS START-ING.
パン
CLAP
パン
CLAP
GET TO YOUR SEAT, SAGARA.
BWSH
YES, MA'AM!
YOU DON'T HAVE TO SA-LUTE.
YES, MA'AM! SORRY, MA'AM!
FWP
HEY, WHY ARE YOU TREATING **HER** SO DIFFERENT FROM ME?
I MUST OBEY MY SUPERIOR WITHOUT COMPLAINT.
UH, I'M JUST YOUR HOME-ROOM TEACHER.
A SUPERIOR'S AUTHORITY IS ABSOLUTE. I'M READY FOR YOUR ORDERS.
R-REALLY? THEN TAKE YOUR SEAT.
LET'S START CLASS.

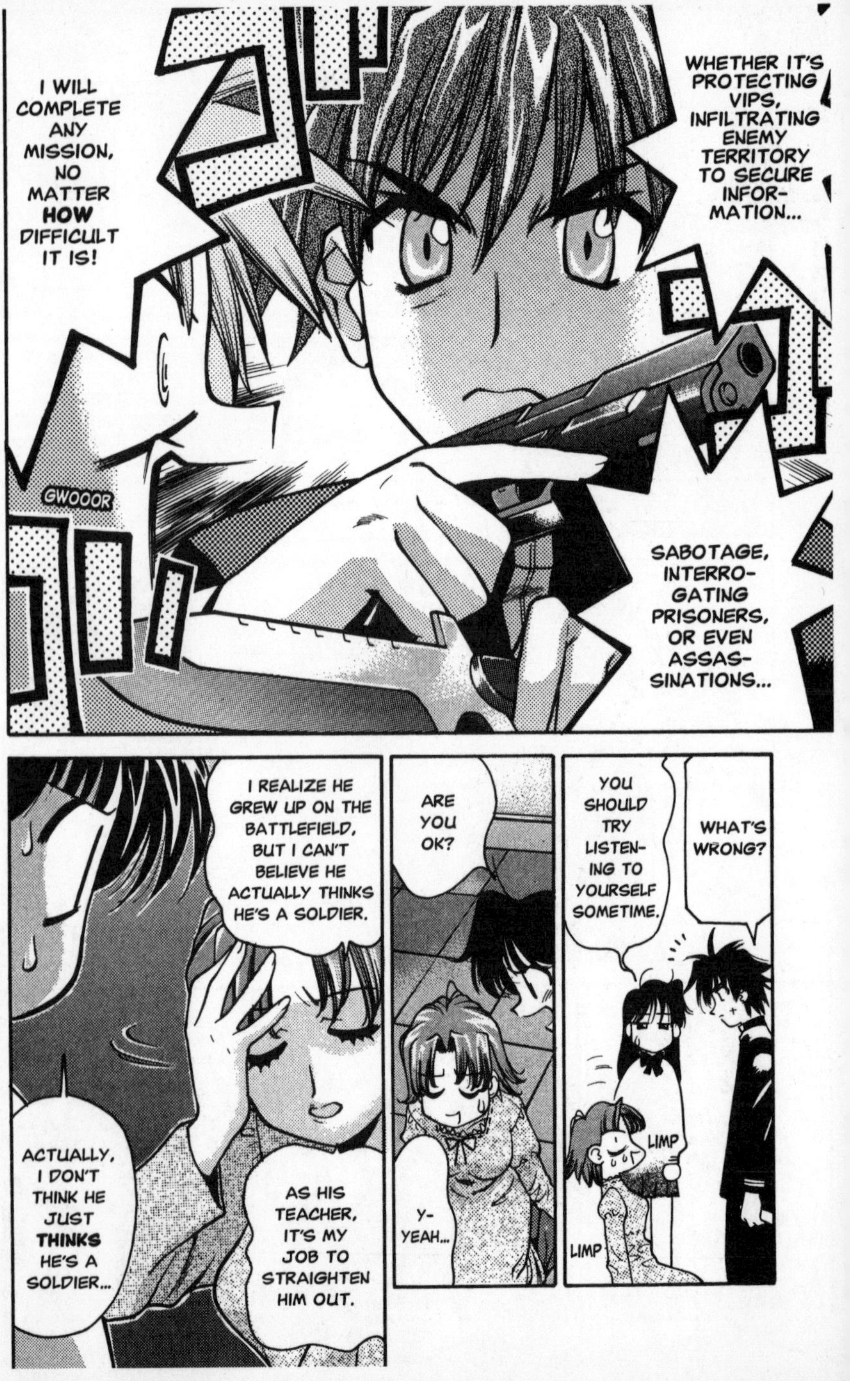
WHETHER IT'S PROTECTING VIPS, INFILTRATING ENEMY TERRITORY TO SECURE INFOR-MATION...
SABOTAGE, INTERRO-GATING PRISONERS, OR EVEN ASSAS-SINATIONS...
I WILL COMPLETE ANY MISSION, NO MATTER **HOW** DIFFICULT IT IS!
GWOOOR
WHAT'S WRONG?
YOU SHOULD TRY LISTEN-ING TO YOURSELF SOMETIME.
LIMP
LIMP
ARE YOU OK?
Y-YEAH...
I REALIZE HE GREW UP ON THE BATTLEFIELD, BUT I CAN'T BELIEVE HE ACTUALLY THINKS HE'S A SOLDIER.
AS HIS TEACHER, IT'S MY JOB TO STRAIGHTEN HIM OUT.
ACTUALLY, I DON'T THINK HE JUST **THINKS** HE'S A SOLDIER...

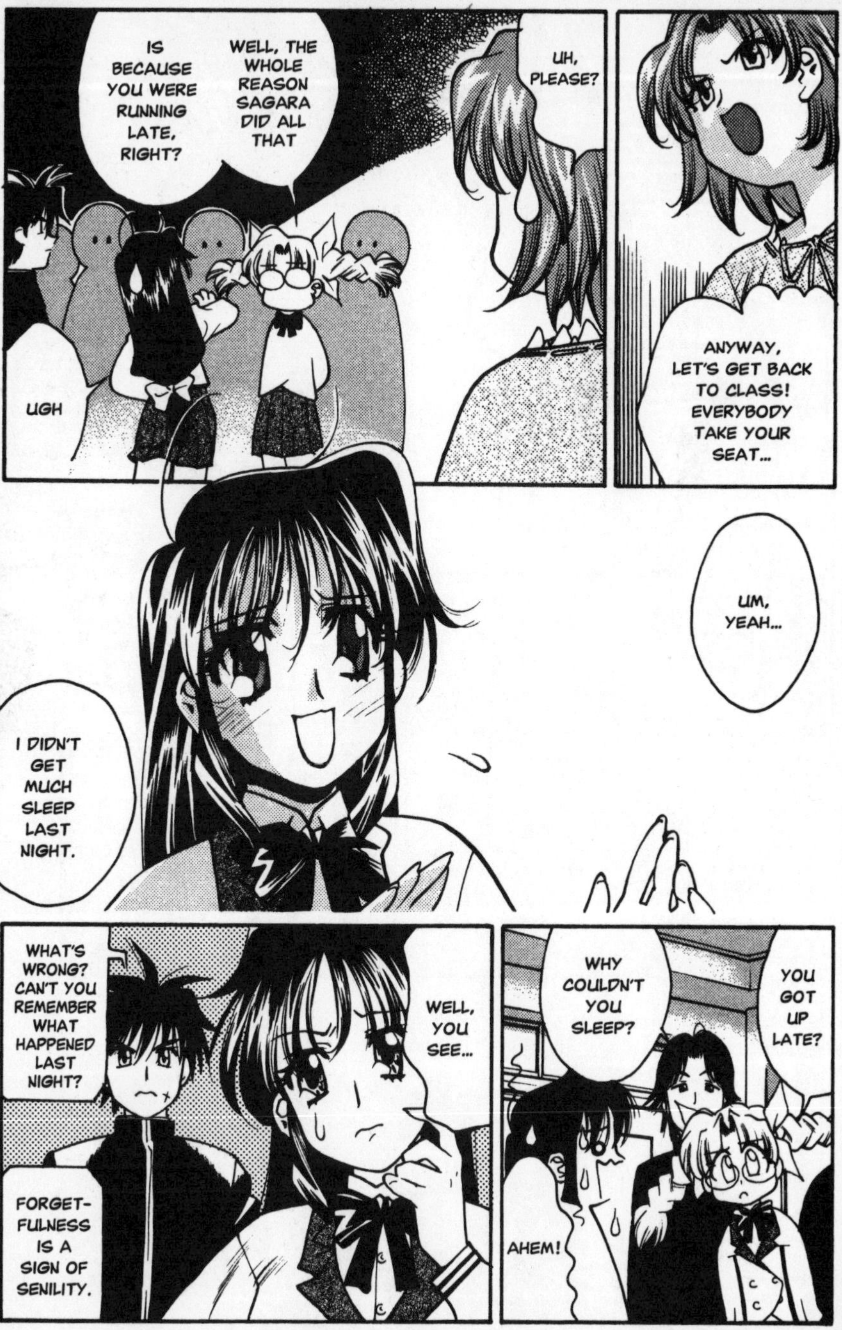
ANYWAY, LET'S GET BACK TO CLASS! EVERYBODY TAKE YOUR SEAT...
UH, PLEASE?
WELL, THE WHOLE REASON SAGARA DID ALL THAT
IS BECAUSE YOU WERE RUNNING LATE, RIGHT?
UGH
UM, YEAH...
I DIDN'T GET MUCH SLEEP LAST NIGHT.
YOU GOT UP LATE?
WHY COULDN'T YOU SLEEP?
AHEM!
WELL, YOU SEE...
WHAT'S WRONG? CAN'T YOU REMEMBER WHAT HAPPENED LAST NIGHT?
FORGET-FULNESS IS A SIGN OF SENILITY.

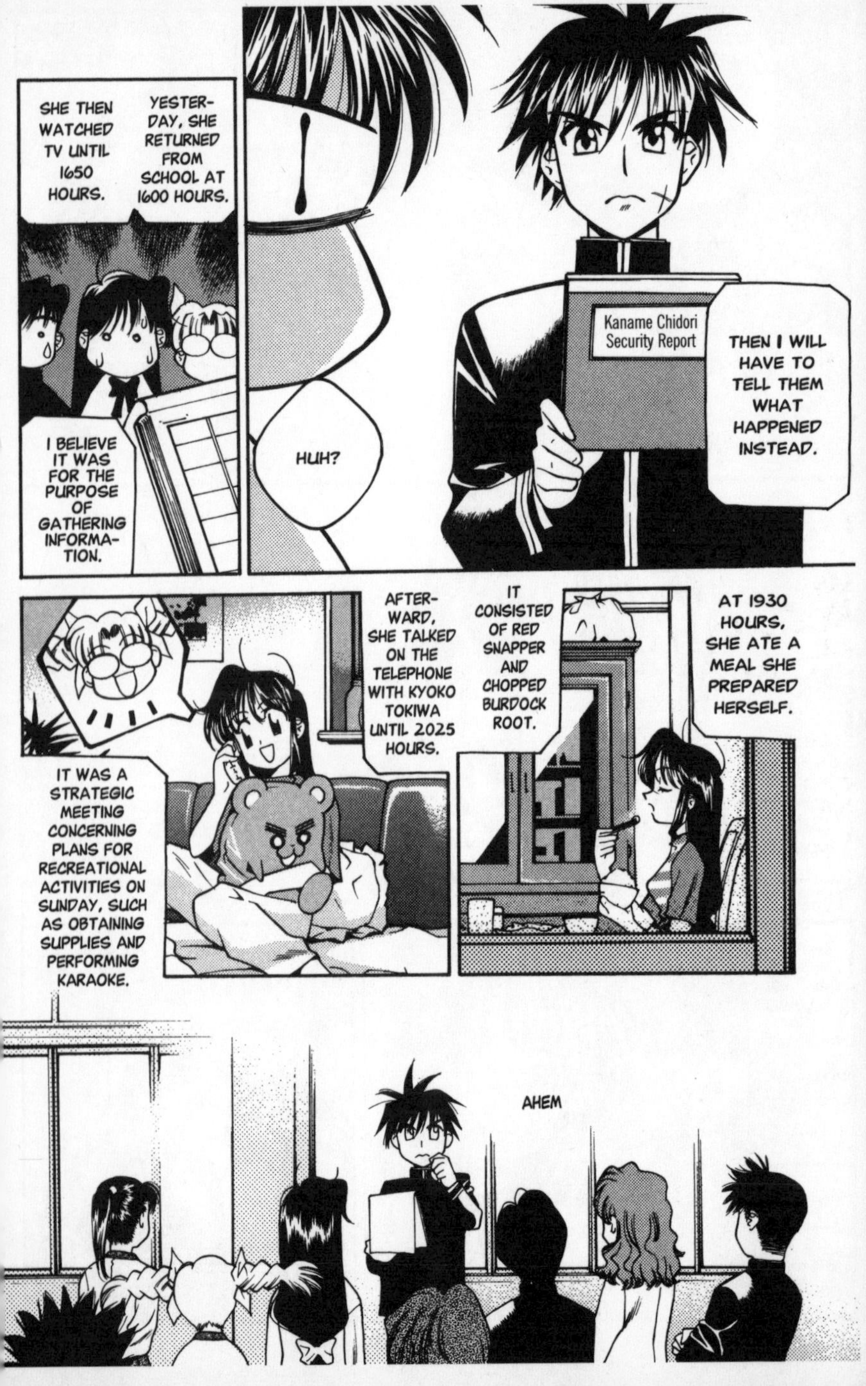
Kaname Chidori Security Report
THEN I WILL HAVE TO TELL THEM WHAT HAPPENED INSTEAD.
HUH?
YESTERDAY, SHE RETURNED FROM SCHOOL AT 1600 HOURS.
SHE THEN WATCHED TV UNTIL 1650 HOURS.
I BELIEVE IT WAS FOR THE PURPOSE OF GATHERING INFORMATION.
AT 1930 HOURS, SHE ATE A MEAL SHE PREPARED HERSELF.
IT CONSISTED OF RED SNAPPER AND CHOPPED BURDOCK ROOT.
AFTERWARD, SHE TALKED ON THE TELEPHONE WITH KYOKO TOKIWA UNTIL 2025 HOURS.
IT WAS A STRATEGIC MEETING CONCERNING PLANS FOR RECREATIONAL ACTIVITIES ON SUNDAY, SUCH AS OBTAINING SUPPLIES AND PERFORMING KARAOKE.
AHEM

AT 2304 HOURS, SHE PREPARED FOR A BATH.

W-WAIT A MINUTE! GET YOUR MIND OUT OF THE GUTTER!

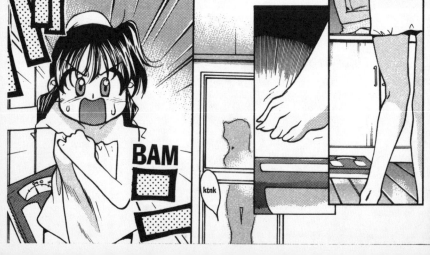

BAM

ktnk

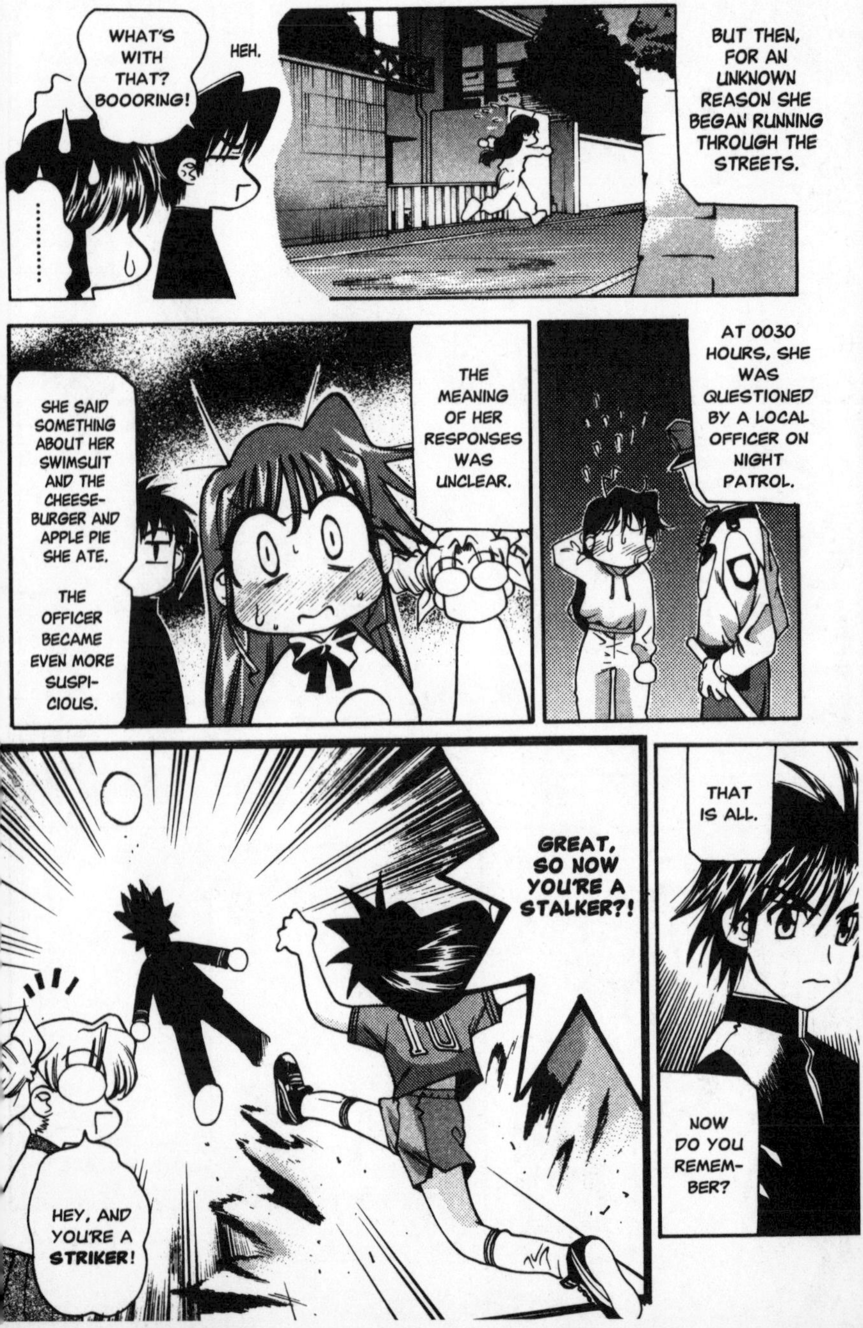
BUT THEN, FOR AN UNKNOWN REASON SHE BEGAN RUNNING THROUGH THE STREETS.
HEH.
WHAT'S WITH THAT? BOOORING!
AT 0030 HOURS, SHE WAS QUESTIONED BY A LOCAL OFFICER ON NIGHT PATROL.
THE MEANING OF HER RESPONSES WAS UNCLEAR.
SHE SAID SOMETHING ABOUT HER SWIMSUIT AND THE CHEESE-BURGER AND APPLE PIE SHE ATE.
THE OFFICER BECAME EVEN MORE SUSPI-CIOUS.
THAT IS ALL.
NOW DO YOU REMEM-BER?
GREAT, SO NOW YOU'RE A STALKER?!
HEY, AND YOU'RE A STRIKER!

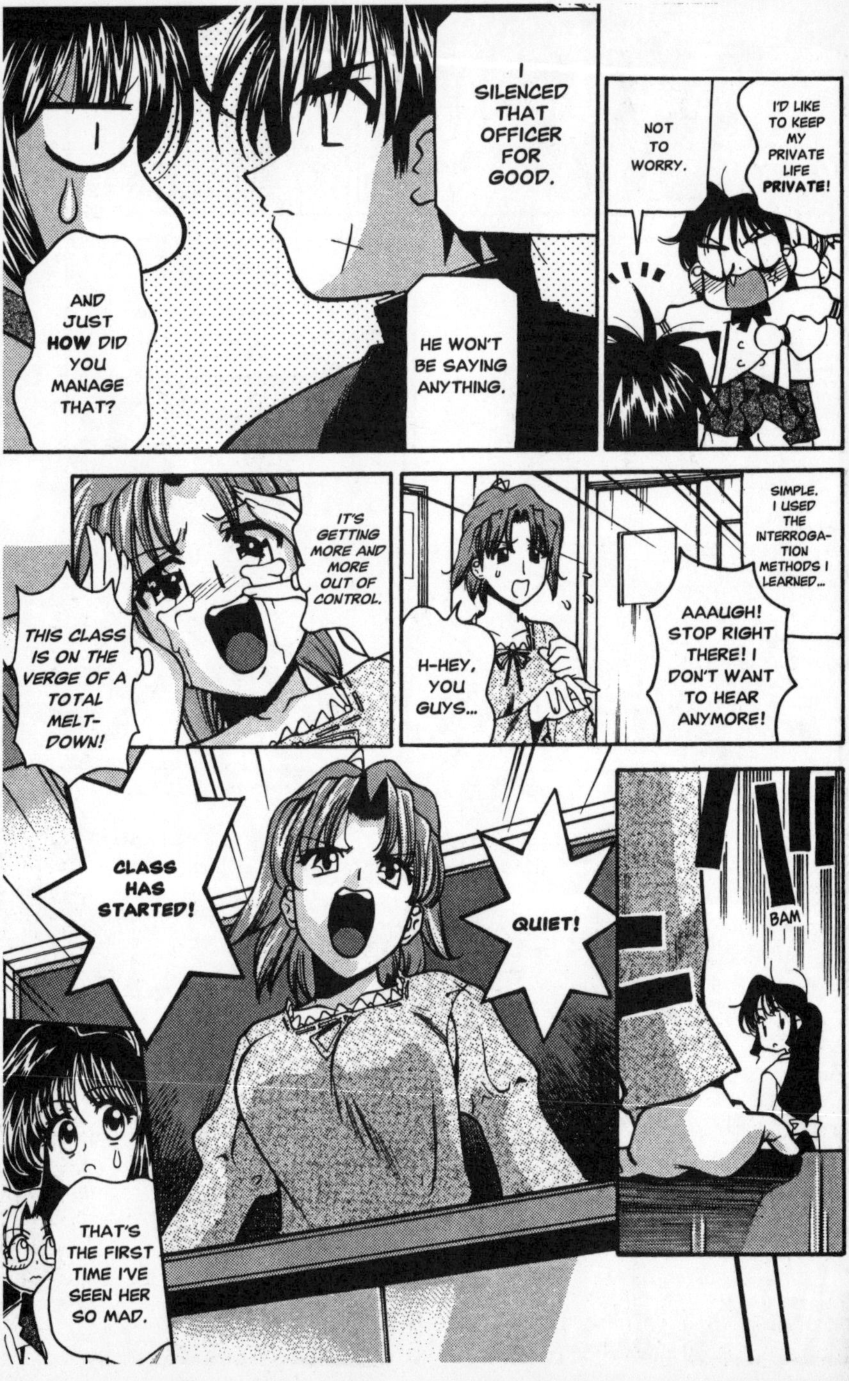
I'D LIKE TO KEEP MY PRIVATE LIFE PRIVATE!
NOT TO WORRY.
I SILENCED THAT OFFICER FOR GOOD.
HE WON'T BE SAYING ANYTHING.
AND JUST HOW DID YOU MANAGE THAT?
SIMPLE. I USED THE INTERROGA-TION METHODS I LEARNED...
AAAUGH! STOP RIGHT THERE! I DON'T WANT TO HEAR ANYMORE!
H-HEY, YOU GUYS...
IT'S GETTING MORE AND MORE OUT OF CONTROL.
THIS CLASS IS ON THE VERGE OF A TOTAL MELT-DOWN!
BAM
QUIET!
CLASS HAS STARTED!
THAT'S THE FIRST TIME I'VE SEEN HER SO MAD.

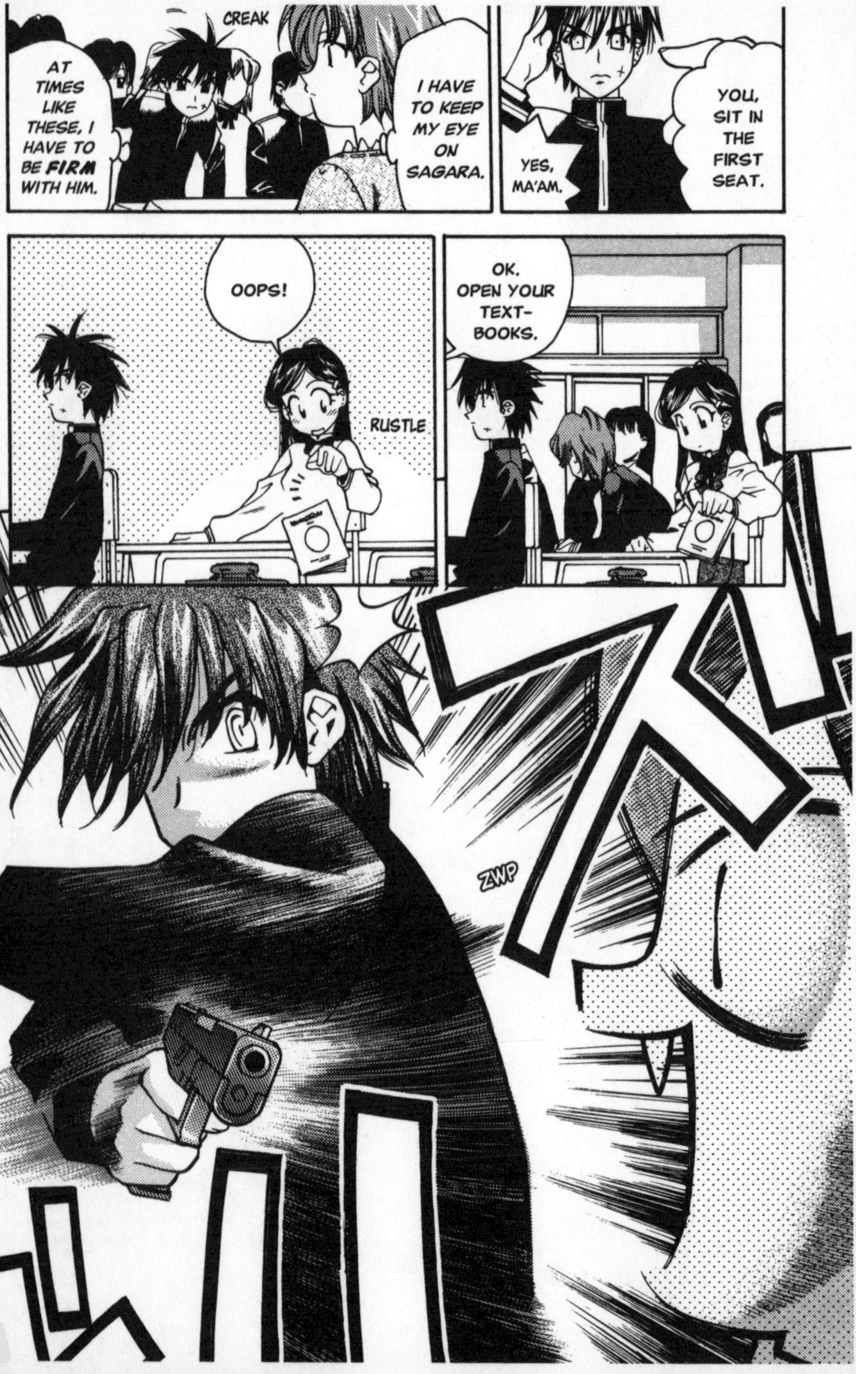
YOU, SIT IN THE FIRST SEAT.
YES, MA'AM.
I HAVE TO KEEP MY EYE ON SAGARA.
AT TIMES LIKE THESE, I HAVE TO BE **FIRM** WITH HIM.
CREAK
OK. OPEN YOUR TEXT-BOOKS.
OOPS!
RUSTLE
ZWP

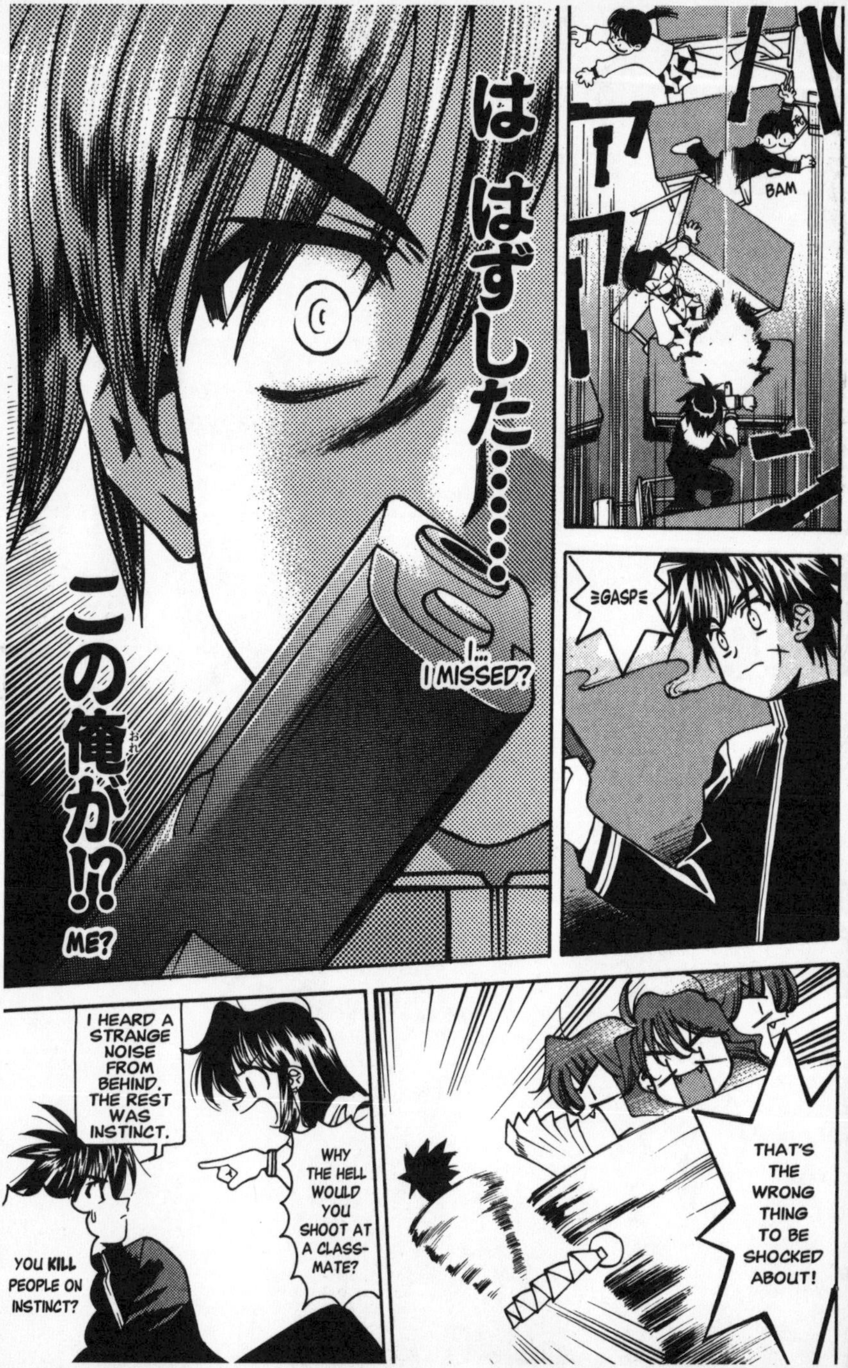
BAM
≡GASP≡
は、はずした……
I... I MISSED?
この俺が!?
ME?
THAT'S THE WRONG THING TO BE SHOCKED ABOUT!
WHY THE HELL WOULD YOU SHOOT AT A CLASSMATE?
I HEARD A STRANGE NOISE FROM BEHIND. THE REST WAS INSTINCT.
YOU KILL PEOPLE ON INSTINCT?

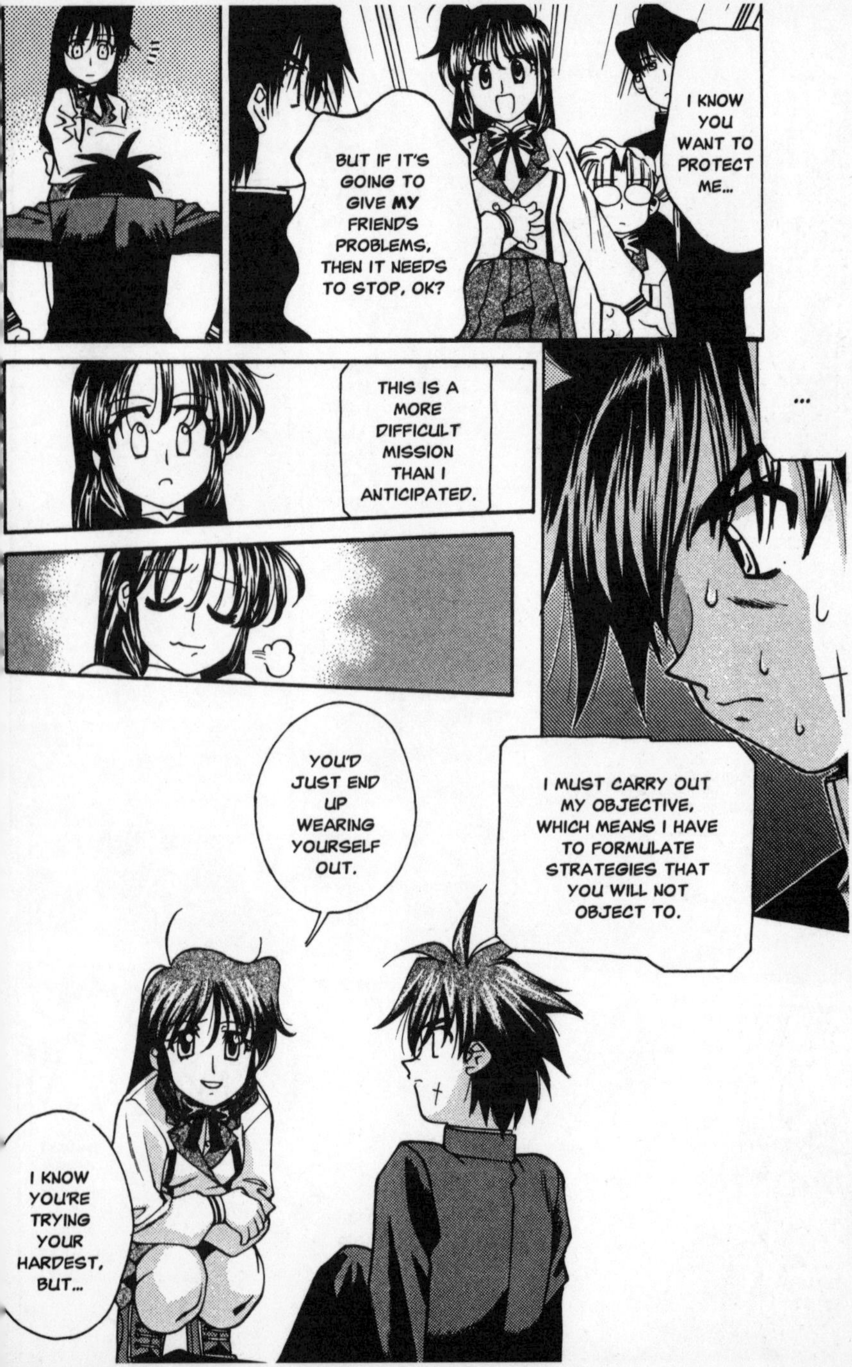
I KNOW YOU WANT TO PROTECT ME...
BUT IF IT'S GOING TO GIVE MY FRIENDS PROBLEMS, THEN IT NEEDS TO STOP, OK?
...
THIS IS A MORE DIFFICULT MISSION THAN I ANTICIPATED.
I MUST CARRY OUT MY OBJECTIVE, WHICH MEANS I HAVE TO FORMULATE STRATEGIES THAT YOU WILL NOT OBJECT TO.
YOU'D JUST END UP WEARING YOURSELF OUT.
I KNOW YOU'RE TRYING YOUR HARDEST, BUT...

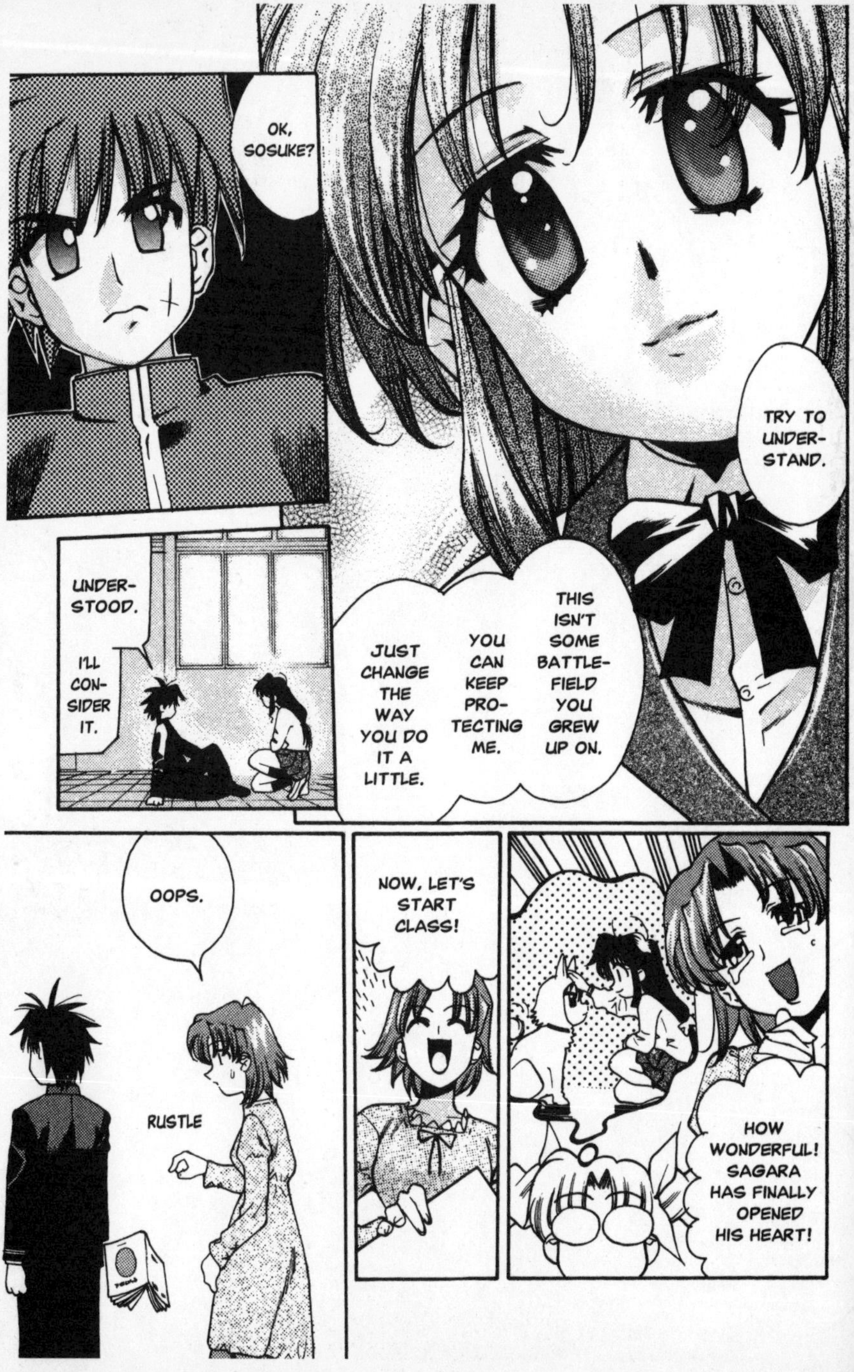
THIS ISN'T SOME BATTLEFIELD YOU GREW UP ON.
YOU CAN KEEP PROTECTING ME.
JUST CHANGE THE WAY YOU DO IT A LITTLE.
TRY TO UNDER-STAND.
OK, SOSUKE?
UNDER-STOOD.
I'LL CON-SIDER IT.
HOW WONDERFUL! SAGARA HAS FINALLY OPENED HIS HEART!
NOW, LET'S START CLASS!
OOPS.
RUSTLE

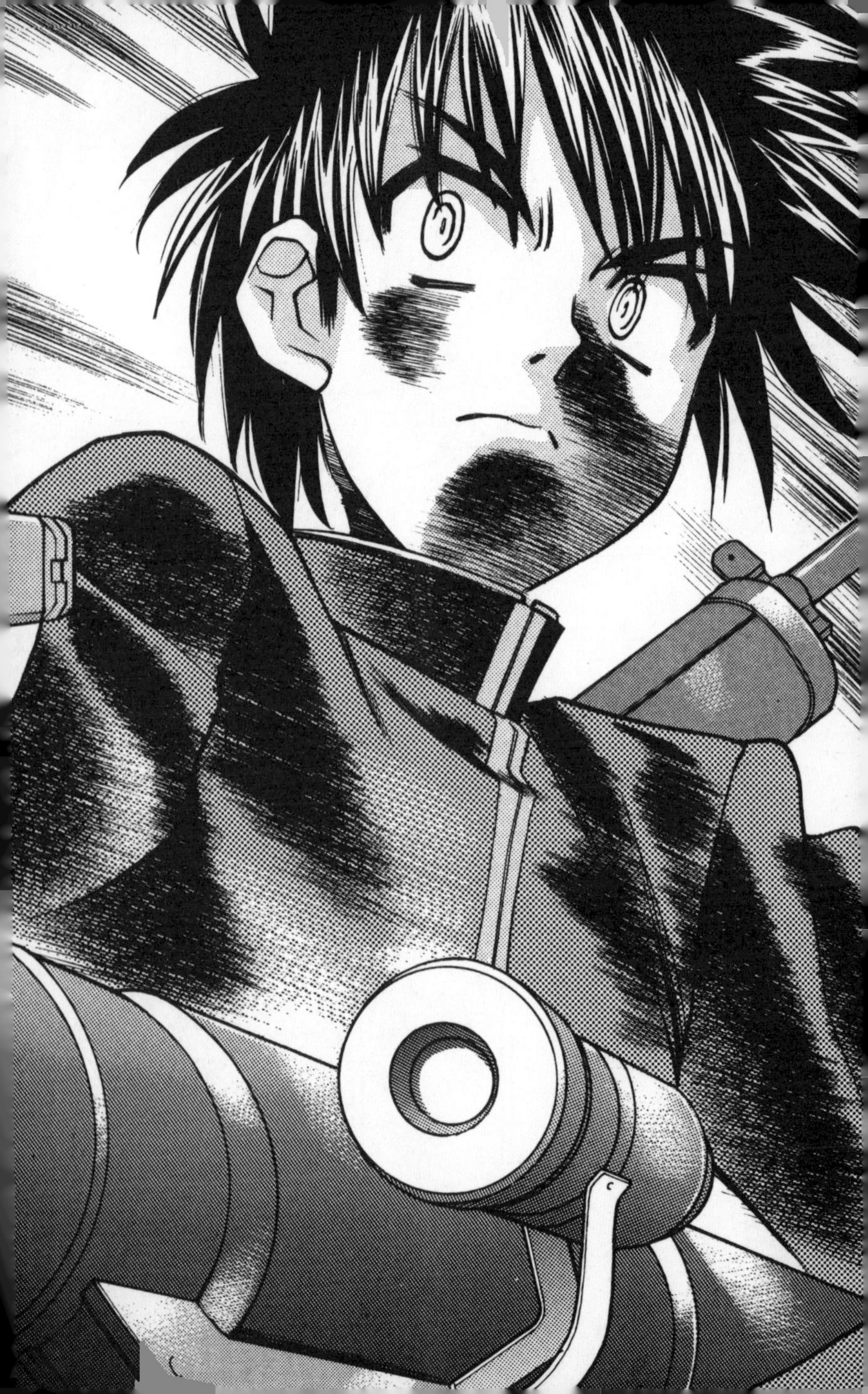

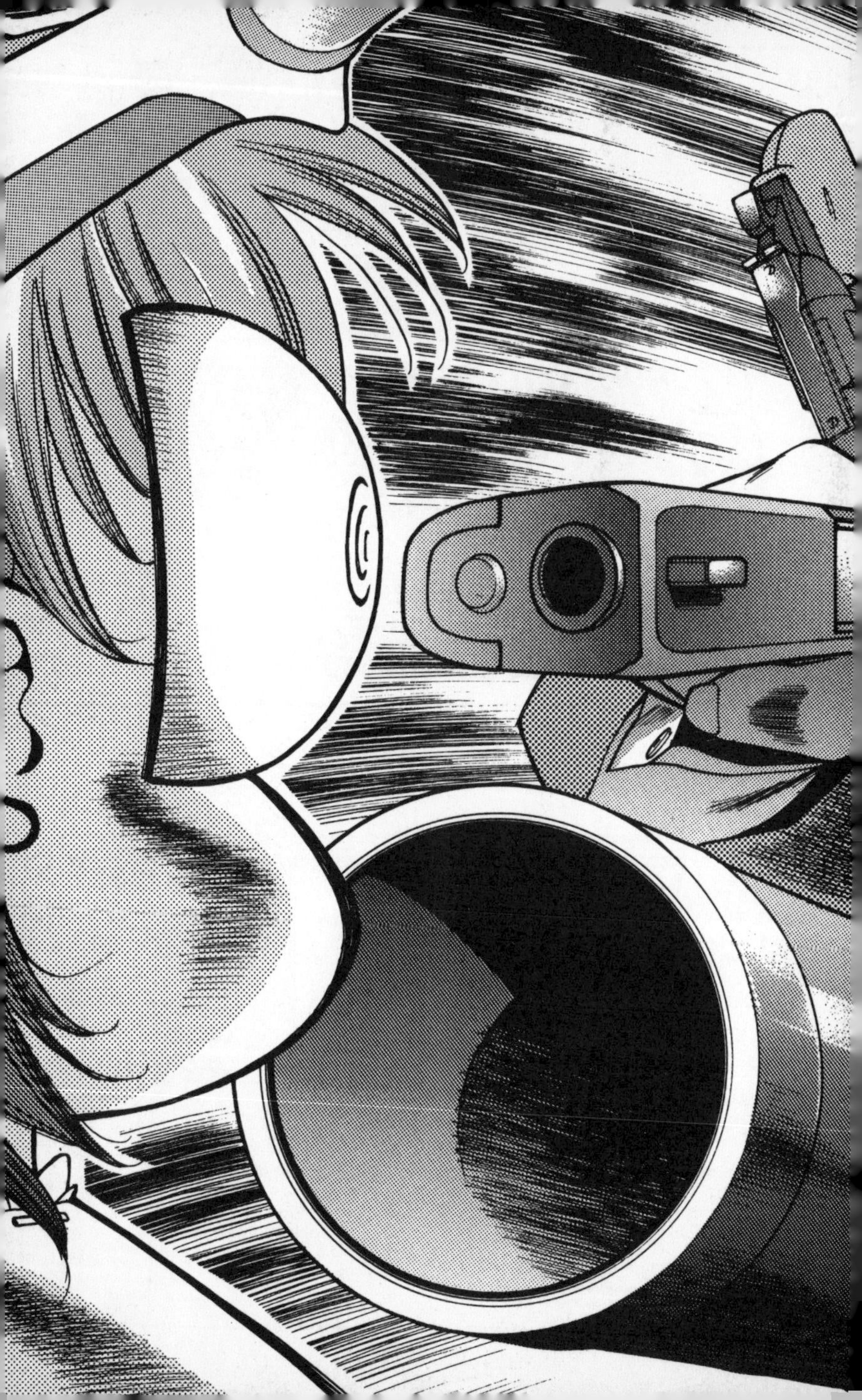

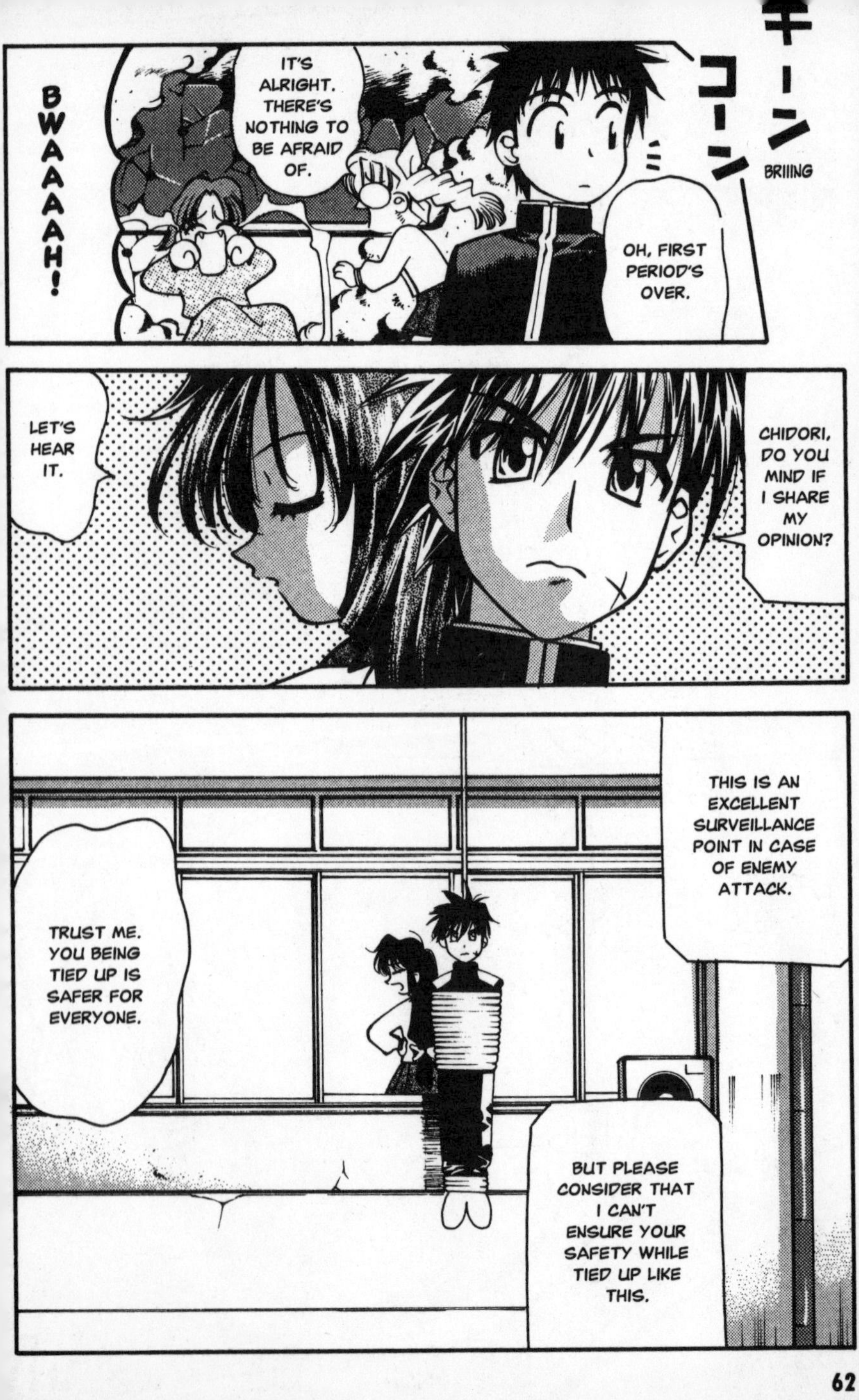
キーンコーン
BRIIING
OH, FIRST PERIOD'S OVER.
IT'S ALRIGHT. THERE'S NOTHING TO BE AFRAID OF.
BWAAAAAH!
CHIDORI, DO YOU MIND IF I SHARE MY OPINION?
LET'S HEAR IT.
THIS IS AN EXCELLENT SURVEILLANCE POINT IN CASE OF ENEMY ATTACK.
BUT PLEASE CONSIDER THAT I CAN'T ENSURE YOUR SAFETY WHILE TIED UP LIKE THIS.
TRUST ME. YOU BEING TIED UP IS SAFER FOR EVERYONE.

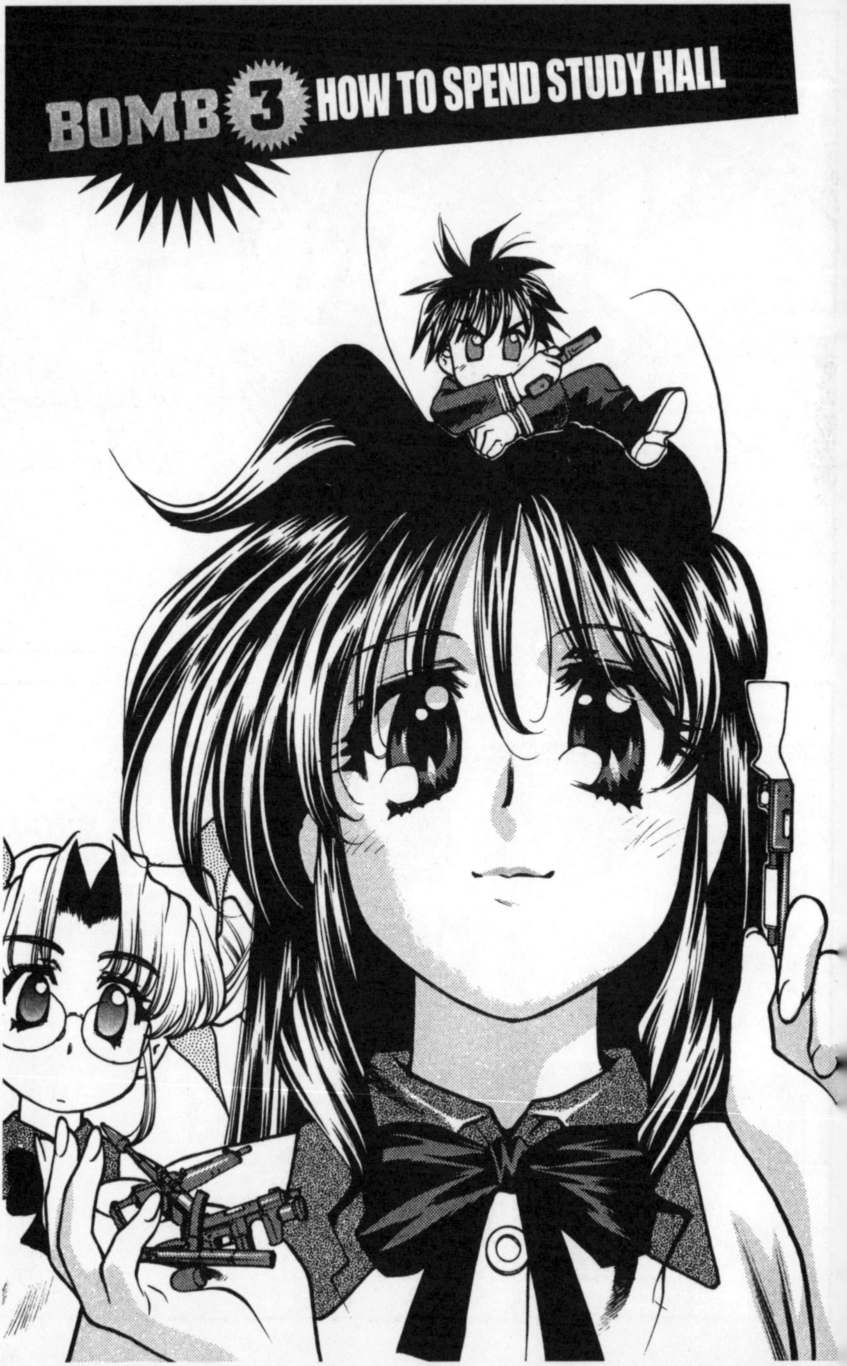
BOMB 3
HOW TO SPEND STUDY HALL

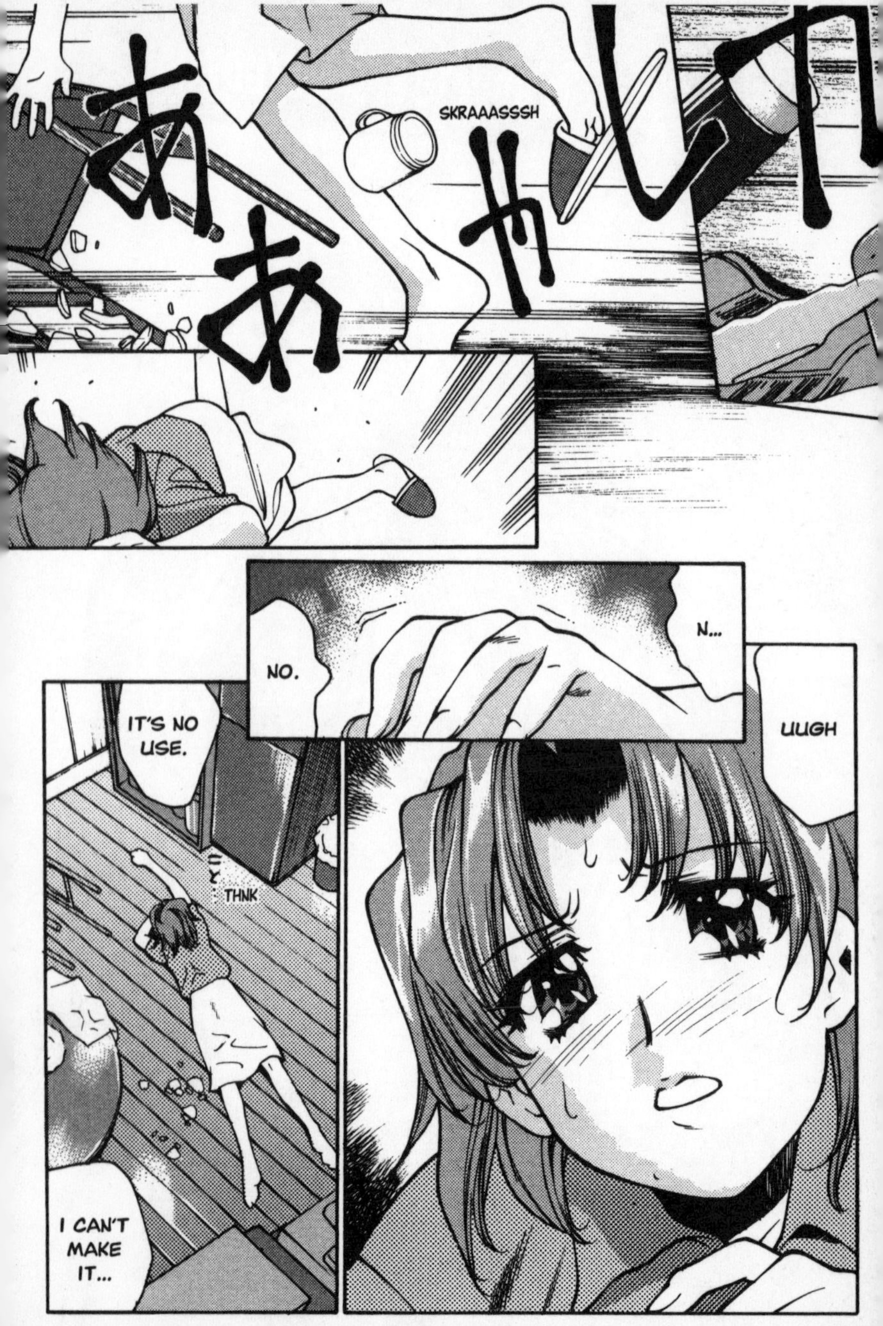
ガシャーン
SKRAAASSSH
N...
NO.
UUGH
IT'S NO USE.
THNK
I CAN'T MAKE IT...

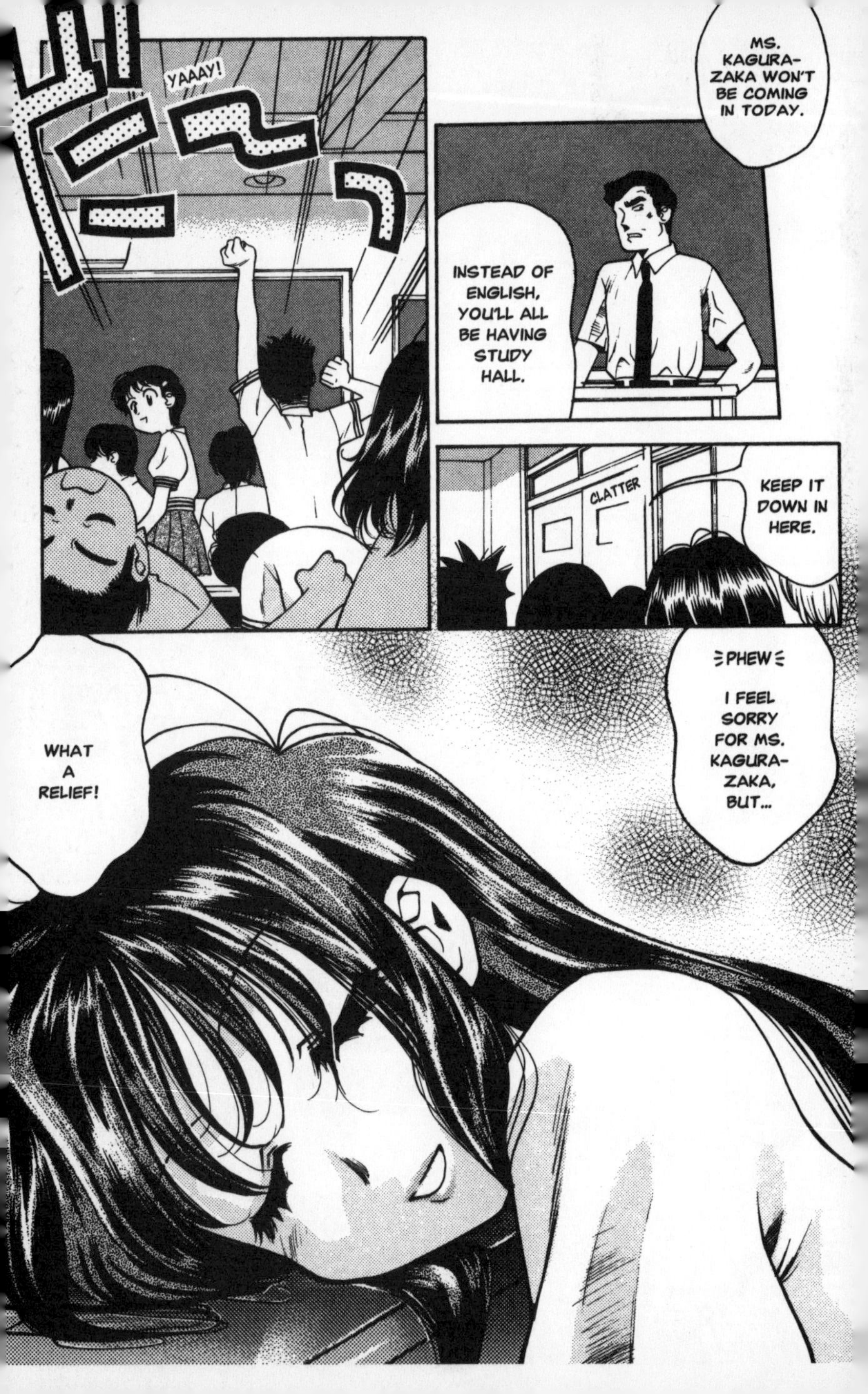
MS. KAGURA-ZAKA WON'T BE COMING IN TODAY.
INSTEAD OF ENGLISH, YOU'LL ALL BE HAVING STUDY HALL.
YAAAY!
CLATTER
KEEP IT DOWN IN HERE.
PHEW
I FEEL SORRY FOR MS. KAGURA-ZAKA, BUT...
WHAT A RELIEF!

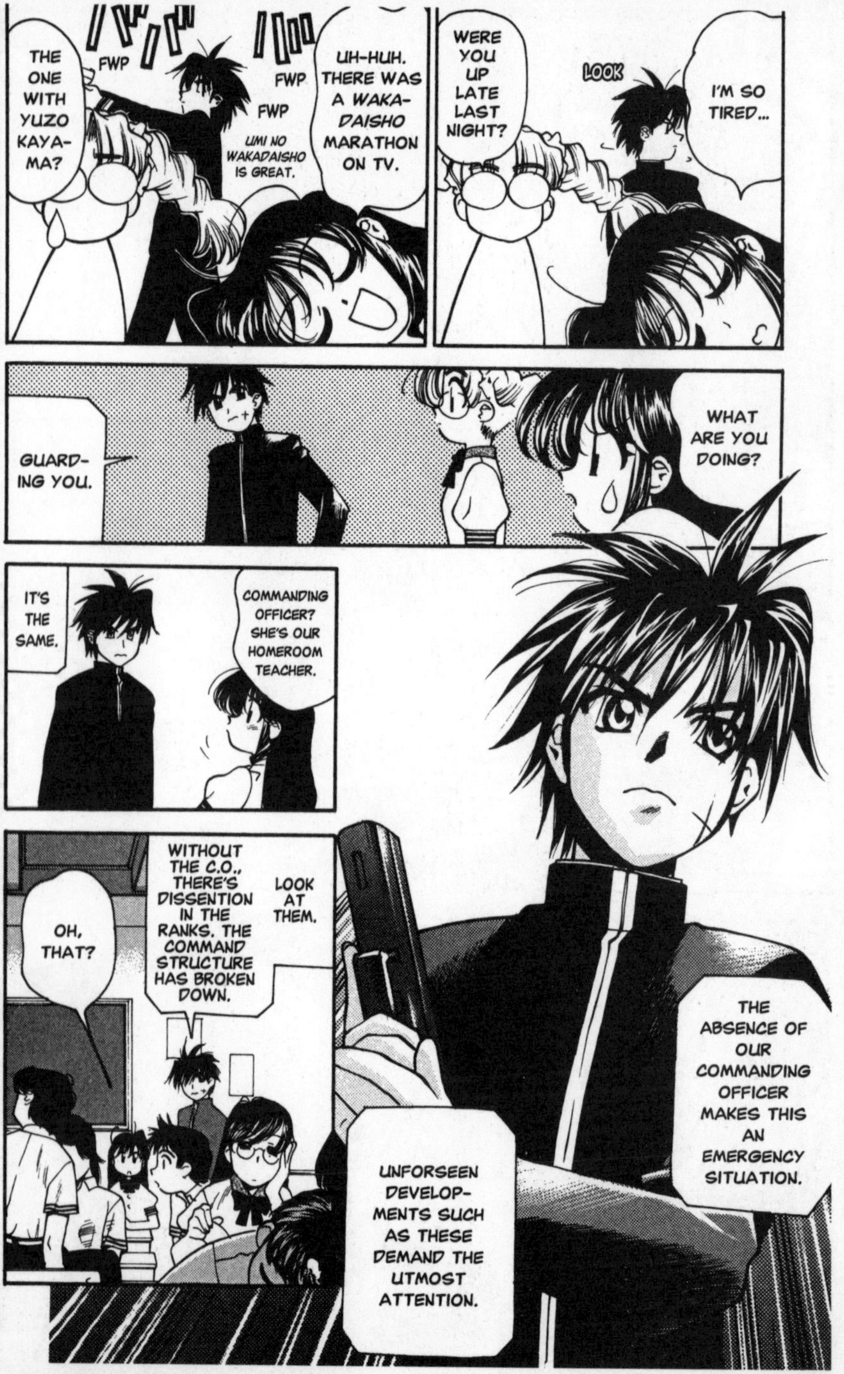
I'M SO TIRED...
LOOK
WERE YOU UP LATE LAST NIGHT?
UH-HUH. THERE WAS A WAKA-DAISHO MARATHON ON TV.
FWP
FWP
FWP
UMI NO WAKADAISHO IS GREAT.
THE ONE WITH YUZO KAYAMA?
WHAT ARE YOU DOING?
GUARDING YOU.
THE ABSENCE OF OUR COMMANDING OFFICER MAKES THIS AN EMERGENCY SITUATION.
UNFORSEEN DEVELOPMENTS SUCH AS THESE DEMAND THE UTMOST ATTENTION.
COMMANDING OFFICER? SHE'S OUR HOMEROOM TEACHER.
IT'S THE SAME.
LOOK AT THEM.
WITHOUT THE C.O., THERE'S DISSENTION IN THE RANKS. THE COMMAND STRUCTURE HAS BROKEN DOWN.
OH, THAT?

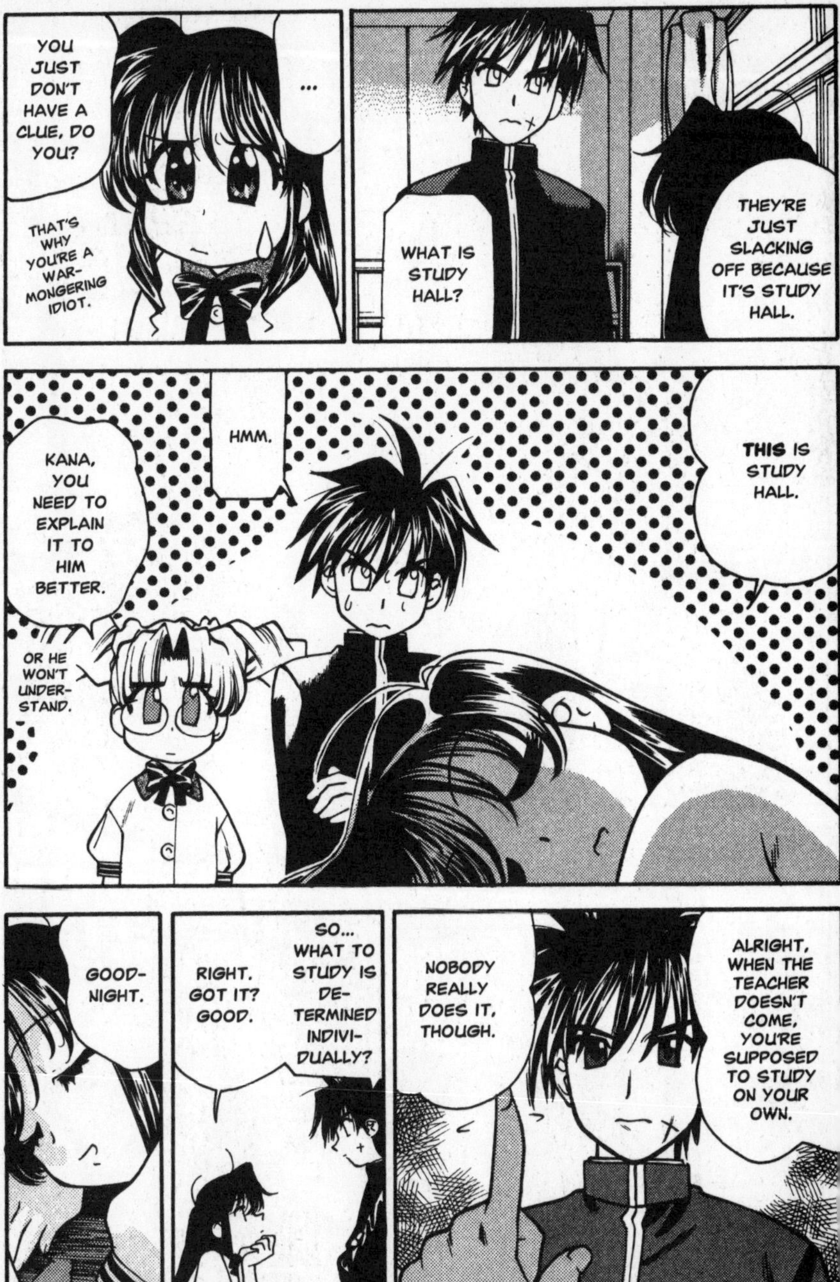
THEY'RE JUST SLACKING OFF BECAUSE IT'S STUDY HALL.
WHAT IS STUDY HALL?
...
YOU JUST DON'T HAVE A CLUE, DO YOU?
THAT'S WHY YOU'RE A WAR-MONGERING IDIOT.
THIS IS STUDY HALL.
HMM.
KANA, YOU NEED TO EXPLAIN IT TO HIM BETTER.
OR HE WON'T UNDER-STAND.
ALRIGHT, WHEN THE TEACHER DOESN'T COME, YOU'RE SUPPOSED TO STUDY ON YOUR OWN.
NOBODY REALLY DOES IT, THOUGH.
SO... WHAT TO STUDY IS DE-TERMINED INDIVI-DUALLY?
RIGHT. GOT IT? GOOD.
GOOD-NIGHT.

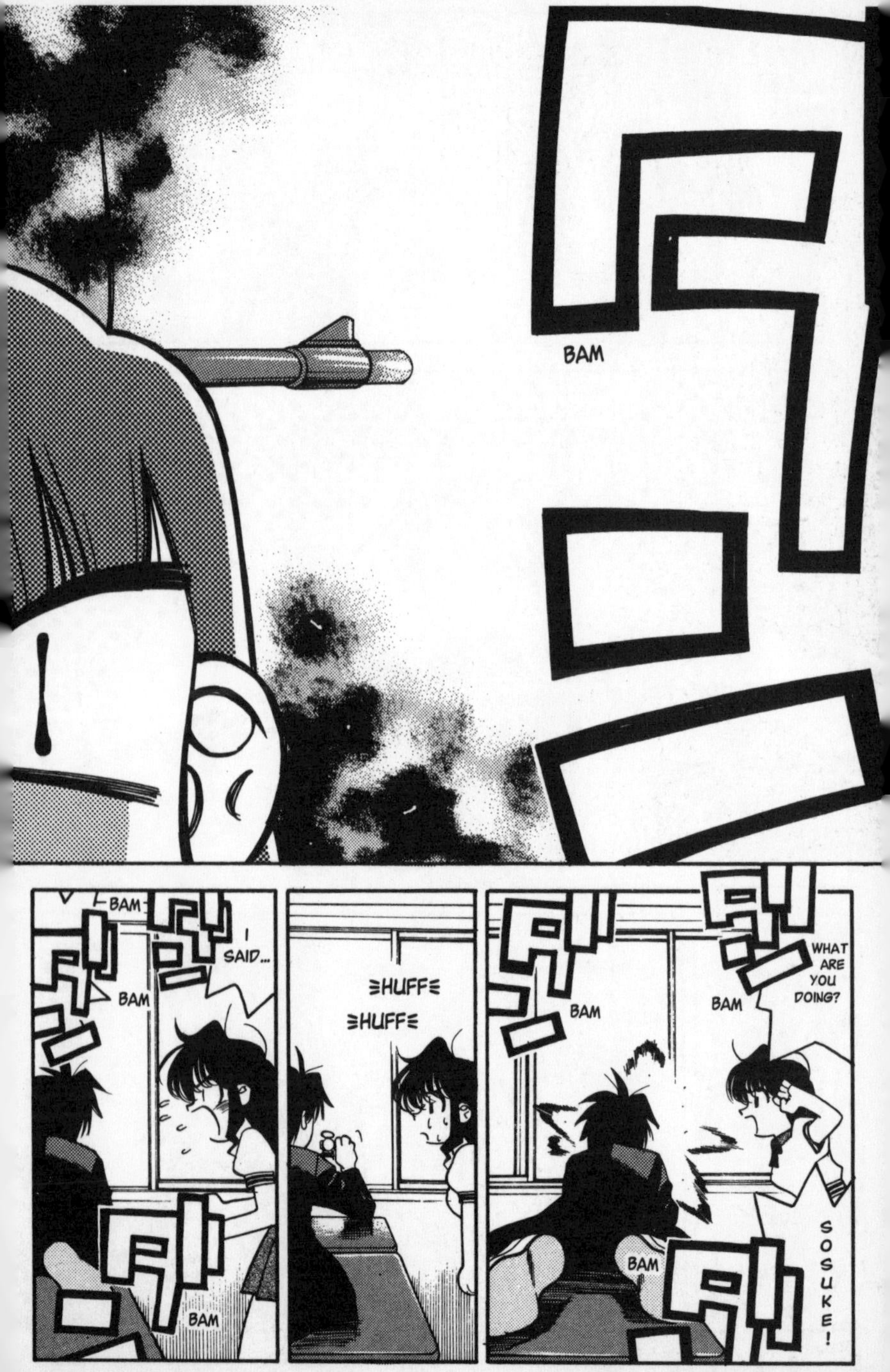
BAM
I SAID...
BAM
BAM
BAM
≡HUFF≡
≡HUFF≡
WHAT ARE YOU DOING?
BAM
BAM
BAM
SOSUKE!

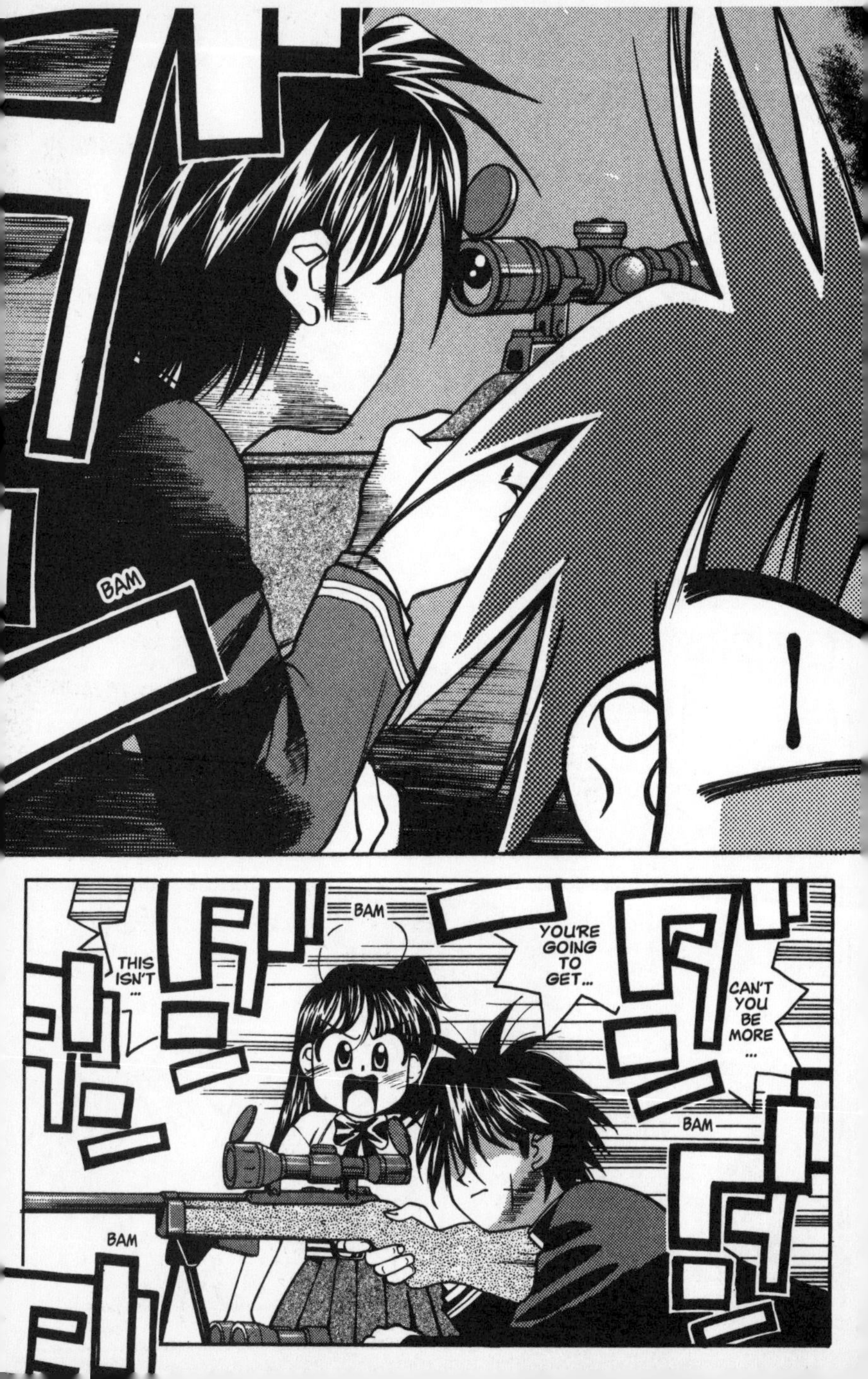
BAM
BAM
THIS ISN'T ...
YOU'RE GOING TO GET...
CAN'T YOU BE MORE ...
BAM
BAM

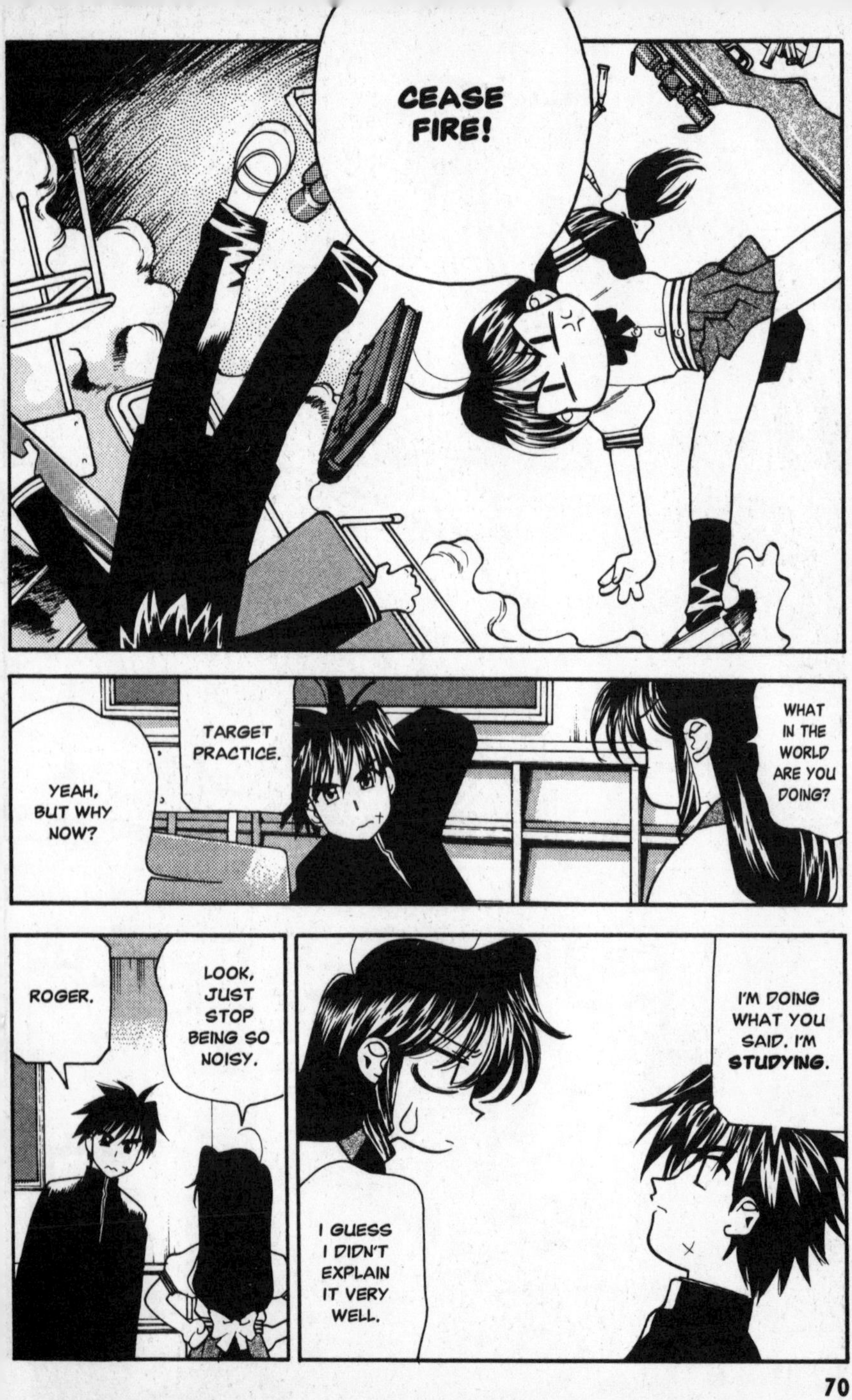
CEASE FIRE!
WHAT IN THE WORLD ARE YOU DOING?
TARGET PRACTICE.
YEAH, BUT WHY NOW?
I'M DOING WHAT YOU SAID. I'M **STUDYING**.
I GUESS I DIDN'T EXPLAIN IT VERY WELL.
LOOK, JUST STOP BEING SO NOISY.
ROGER.

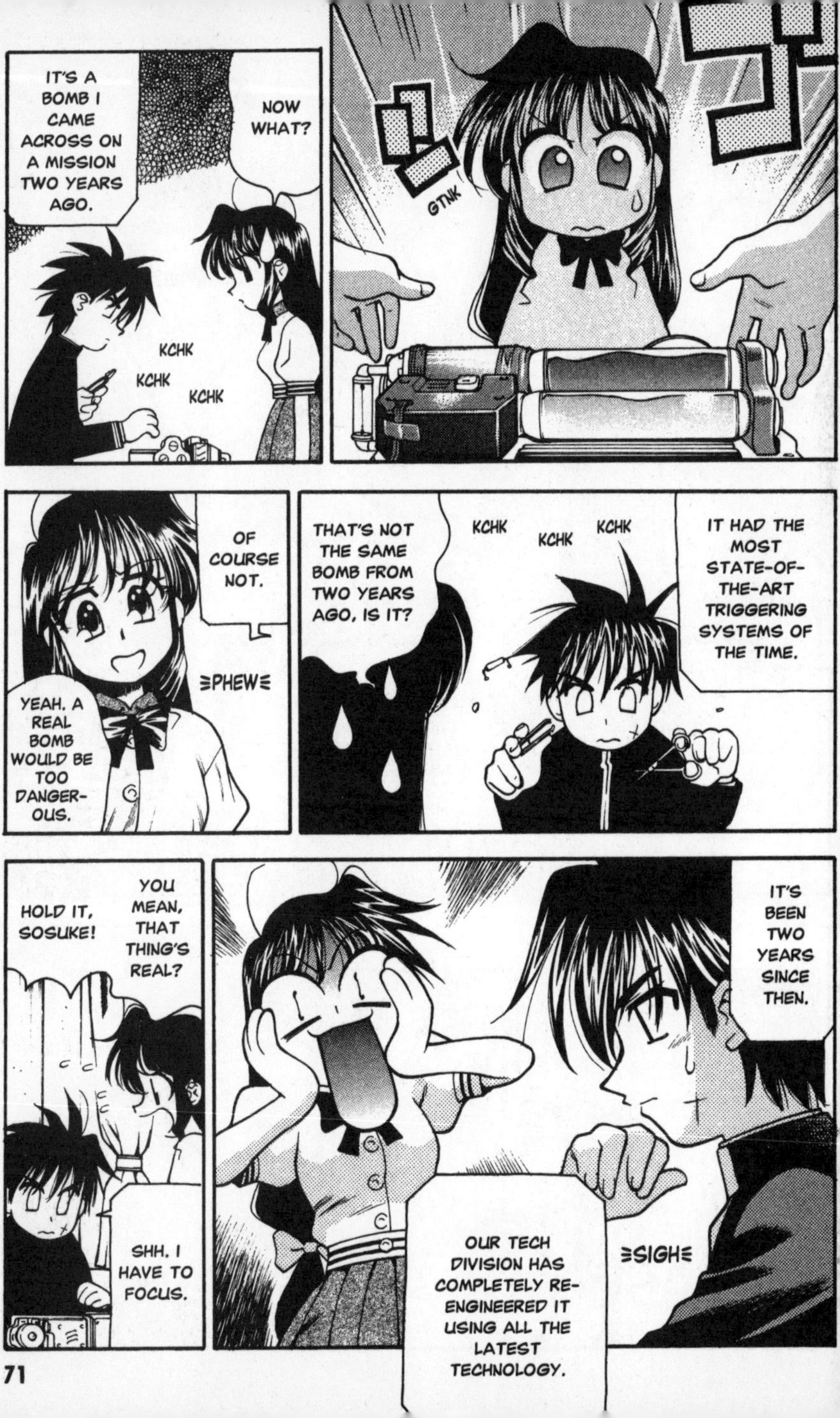
IT'S A BOMB I CAME ACROSS ON A MISSION TWO YEARS AGO.
NOW WHAT?
KCHK
KCHK
KCHK
GTNK
OF COURSE NOT.
≡PHEW≡
YEAH. A REAL BOMB WOULD BE TOO DANGER-OUS.
THAT'S NOT THE SAME BOMB FROM TWO YEARS AGO, IS IT?
KCHK
KCHK
KCHK
IT HAD THE MOST STATE-OF-THE-ART TRIGGERING SYSTEMS OF THE TIME.
HOLD IT, SOSUKE!
YOU MEAN, THAT THING'S REAL?
SHH. I HAVE TO FOCUS.
IT'S BEEN TWO YEARS SINCE THEN.
OUR TECH DIVISION HAS COMPLETELY RE-ENGINEERED IT USING ALL THE LATEST TECHNOLOGY.
≡SIGH≡

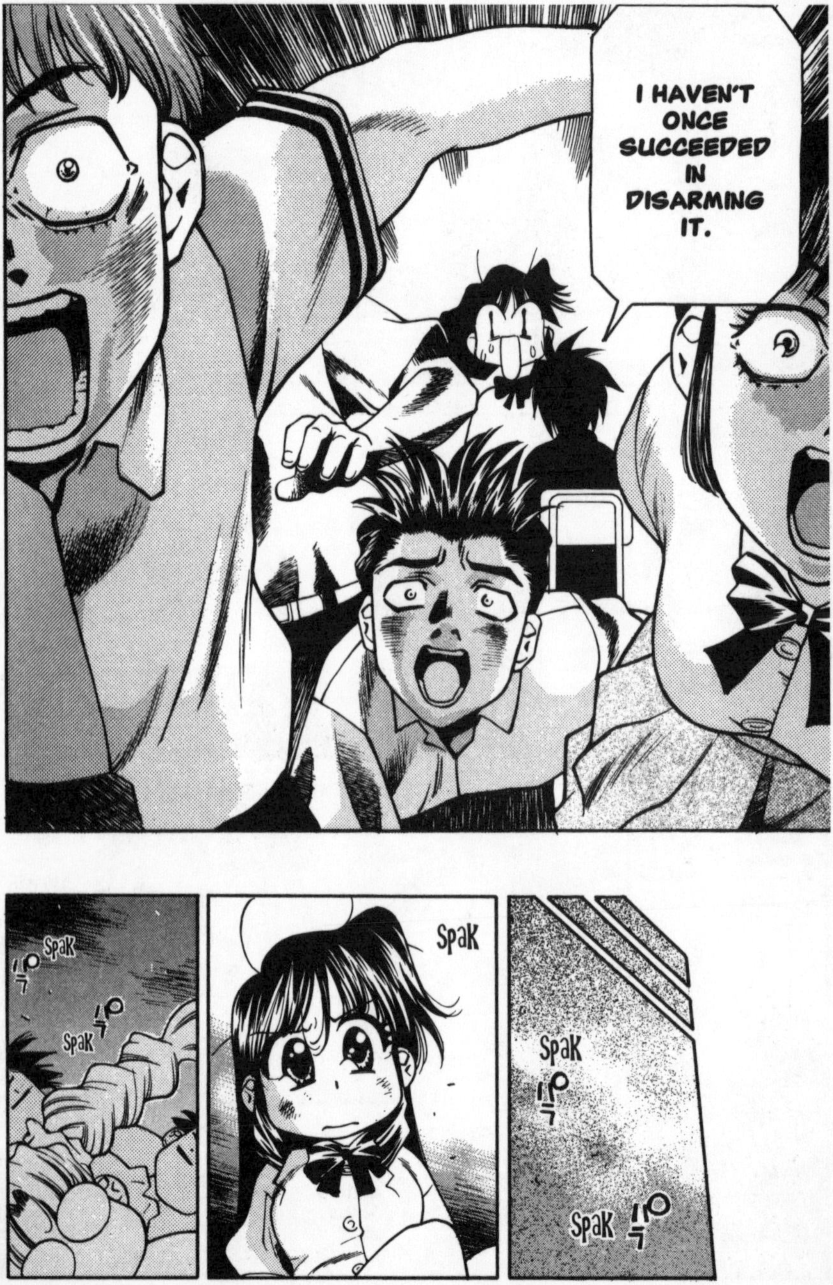
I HAVEN'T ONCE SUCCEEDED IN DISARMING IT.
Spak
Spak
Spak
Spak
Spak

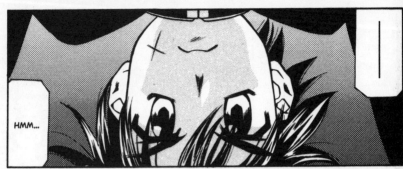

HMM...
SO THAT CODE WAS A FAKE.
IT'S A MIRACLE THERE WEREN'T ANY CASUALTIES. THAT EXPLOSIVE DIDN'T HAVE MUCH KILLING POWER.
YOU SHOULD BE **GLAD**, NOT ANGRY.
JUST SHUT UP!
HOW CAN YOU BE SO CALM?!
WHAT ARE WE GOING TO DO? WE'VE LOST OUR CLASSROOM.
HMM.

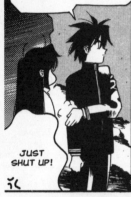

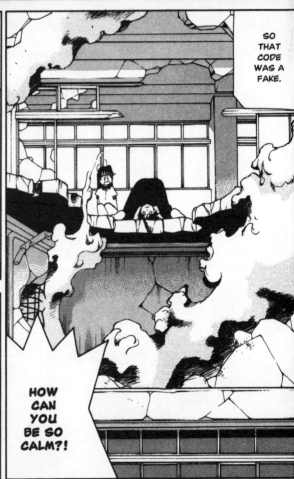

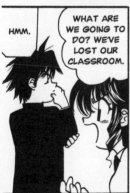

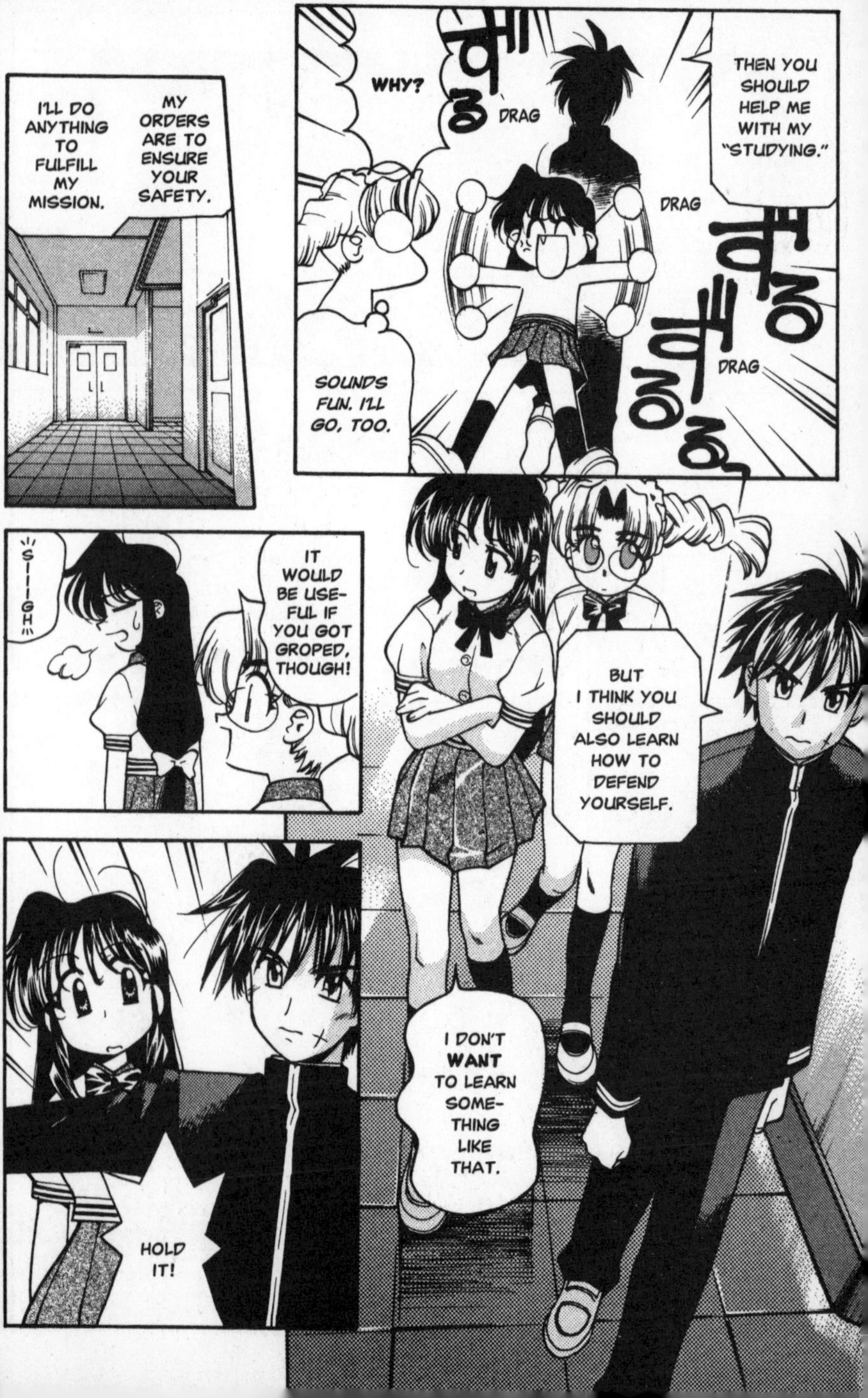
THEN YOU SHOULD HELP ME WITH MY "STUDYING."
WHY?
ずる
DRAG
DRAG
ずる
ずる
DRAG
ずる
SOUNDS FUN. I'LL GO, TOO.
MY ORDERS ARE TO ENSURE YOUR SAFETY.
I'LL DO ANYTHING TO FULFILL MY MISSION.
BUT I THINK YOU SHOULD ALSO LEARN HOW TO DEFEND YOURSELF.
I DON'T **WANT** TO LEARN SOMETHING LIKE THAT.
IT WOULD BE USEFUL IF YOU GOT GROPED, THOUGH!
SIIIGH
HOLD IT!

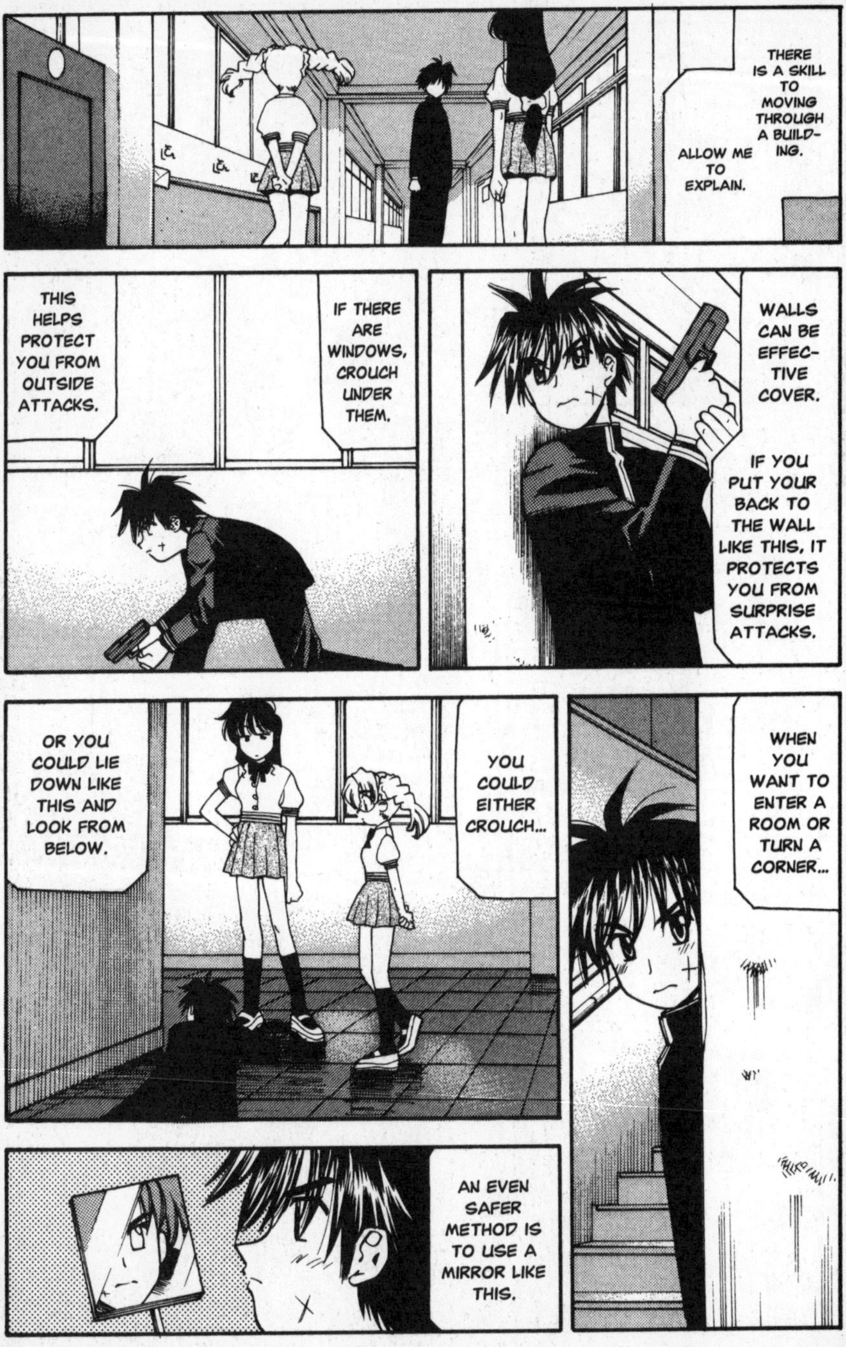
THERE IS A SKILL TO MOVING THROUGH A BUILD-ING.
ALLOW ME TO EXPLAIN.
WALLS CAN BE EFFEC-TIVE COVER.
IF YOU PUT YOUR BACK TO THE WALL LIKE THIS, IT PROTECTS YOU FROM SURPRISE ATTACKS.
IF THERE ARE WINDOWS, CROUCH UNDER THEM.
THIS HELPS PROTECT YOU FROM OUTSIDE ATTACKS.
WHEN YOU WANT TO ENTER A ROOM OR TURN A CORNER...
YOU COULD EITHER CROUCH...
OR YOU COULD LIE DOWN LIKE THIS AND LOOK FROM BELOW.
AN EVEN SAFER METHOD IS TO USE A MIRROR LIKE THIS.

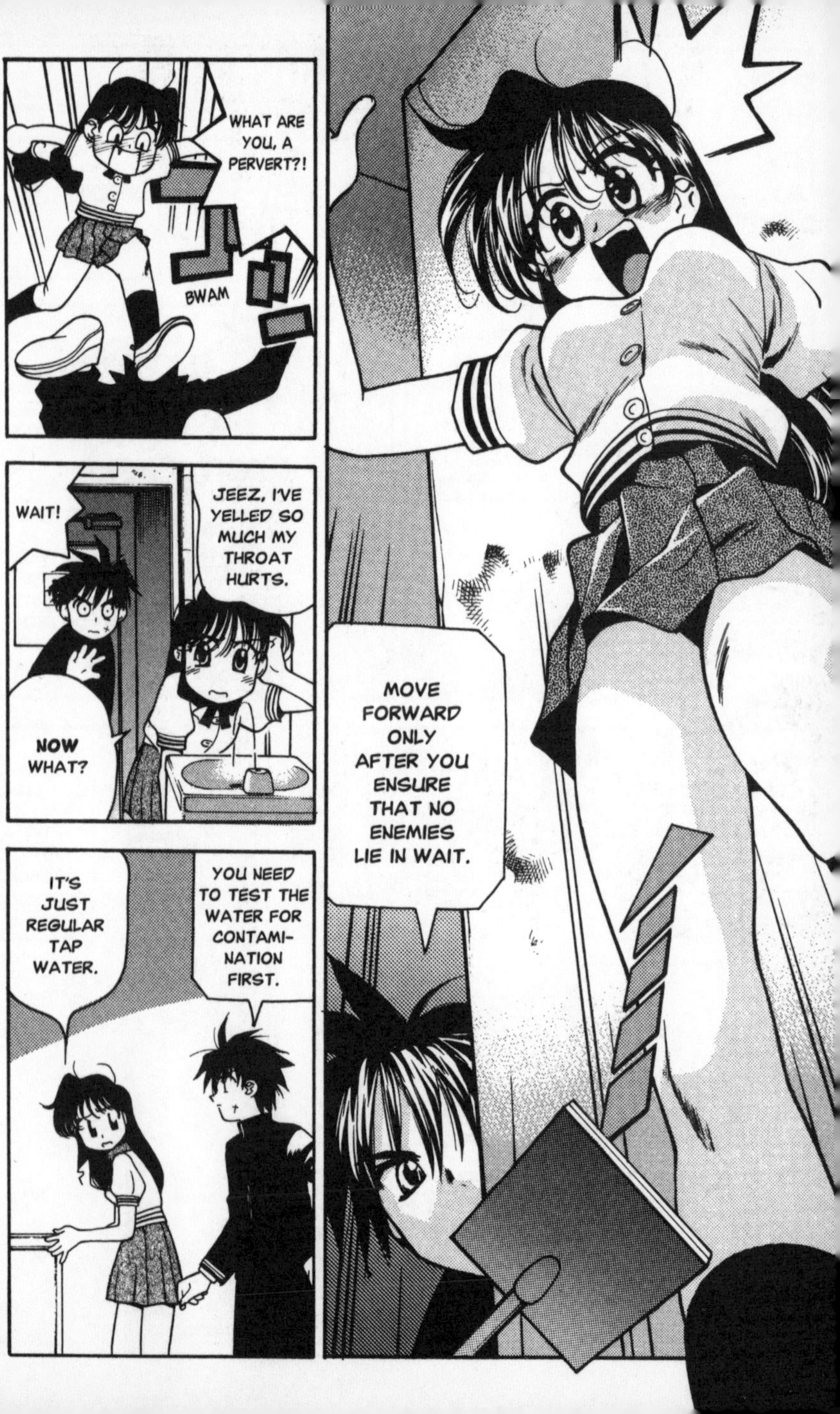
MOVE FORWARD ONLY AFTER YOU ENSURE THAT NO ENEMIES LIE IN WAIT.
WHAT ARE YOU, A PERVERT?!
BWAM
JEEZ, I'VE YELLED SO MUCH MY THROAT HURTS.
WAIT!
NOW WHAT?
YOU NEED TO TEST THE WATER FOR CONTAMI-NATION FIRST.
IT'S JUST REGULAR TAP WATER.

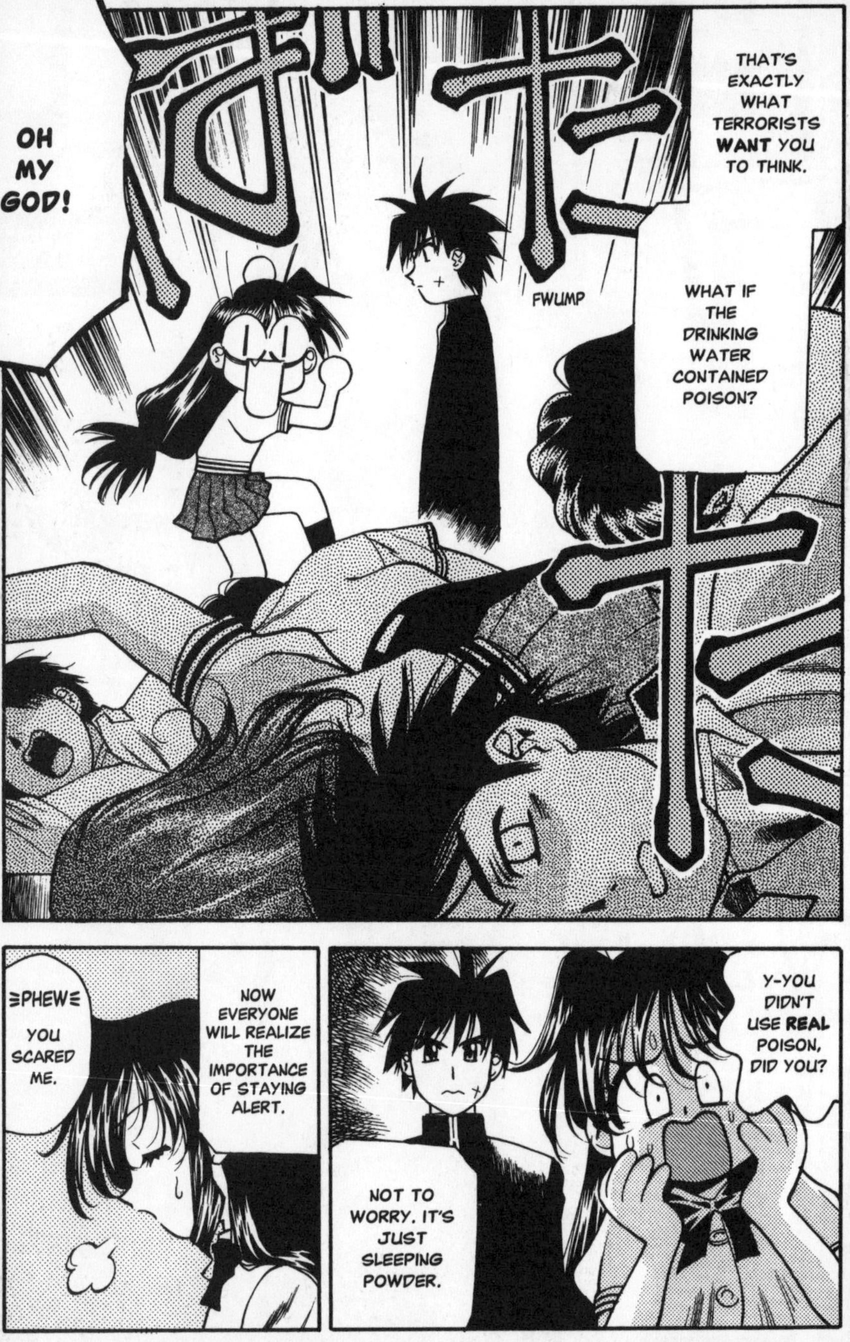
THAT'S EXACTLY WHAT TERRORISTS WANT YOU TO THINK.
OH MY GOD!
WHAT IF THE DRINKING WATER CONTAINED POISON?
FWUMP
NOW EVERYONE WILL REALIZE THE IMPORTANCE OF STAYING ALERT.
≡PHEW≡
YOU SCARED ME.
Y-YOU DIDN'T USE REAL POISON, DID YOU?
NOT TO WORRY. IT'S JUST SLEEPING POWDER.

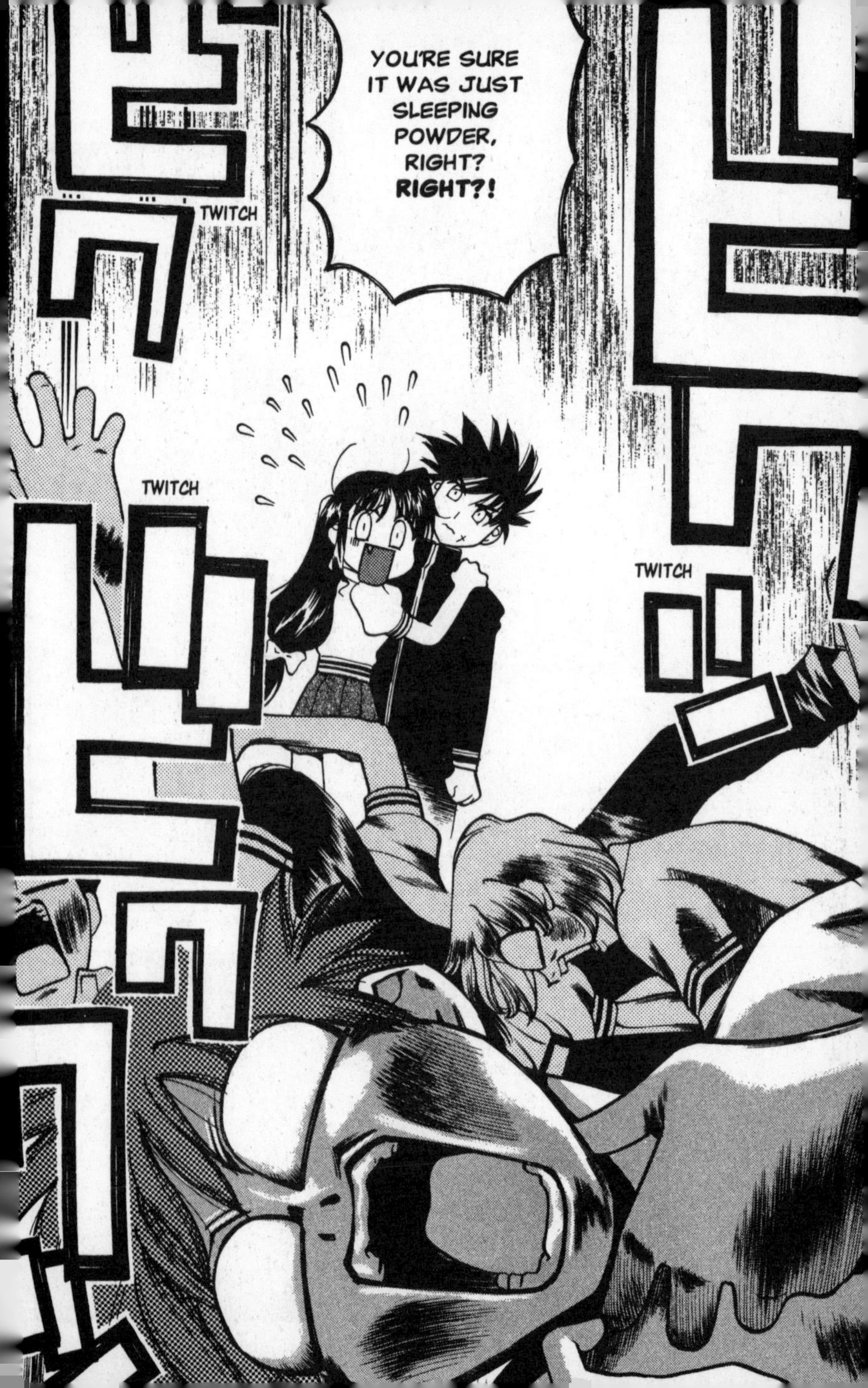
YOU'RE SURE IT WAS JUST SLEEPING POWDER, RIGHT? RIGHT?!
TWITCH
TWITCH
TWITCH

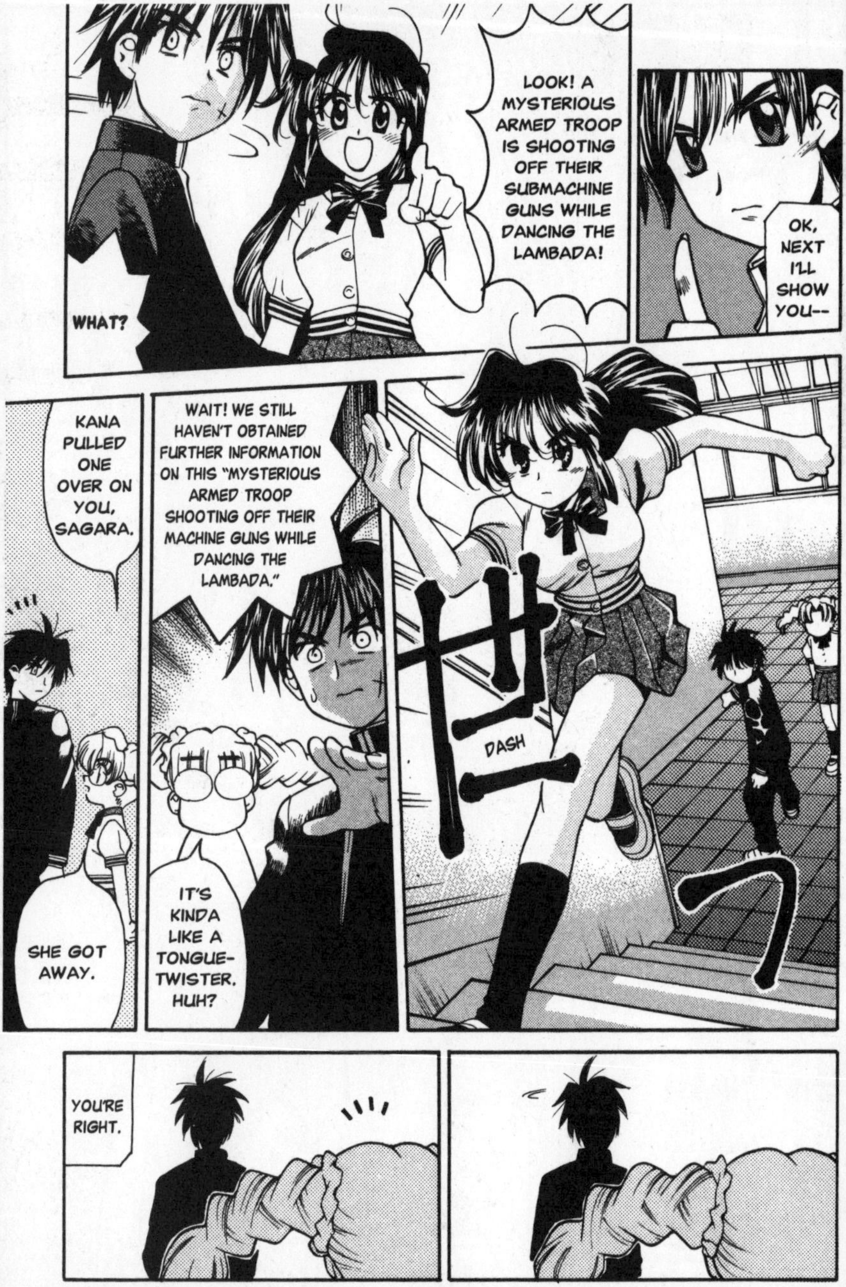
WHAT?
LOOK! A MYSTERIOUS ARMED TROOP IS SHOOTING OFF THEIR SUBMACHINE GUNS WHILE DANCING THE LAMBADA!
OK, NEXT I'LL SHOW YOU--
DASH
WAIT! WE STILL HAVEN'T OBTAINED FURTHER INFORMATION ON THIS "MYSTERIOUS ARMED TROOP SHOOTING OFF THEIR MACHINE GUNS WHILE DANCING THE LAMBADA."
IT'S KINDA LIKE A TONGUE-TWISTER. HUH?
KANA PULLED ONE OVER ON YOU, SAGARA.
SHE GOT AWAY.
YOU'RE RIGHT.

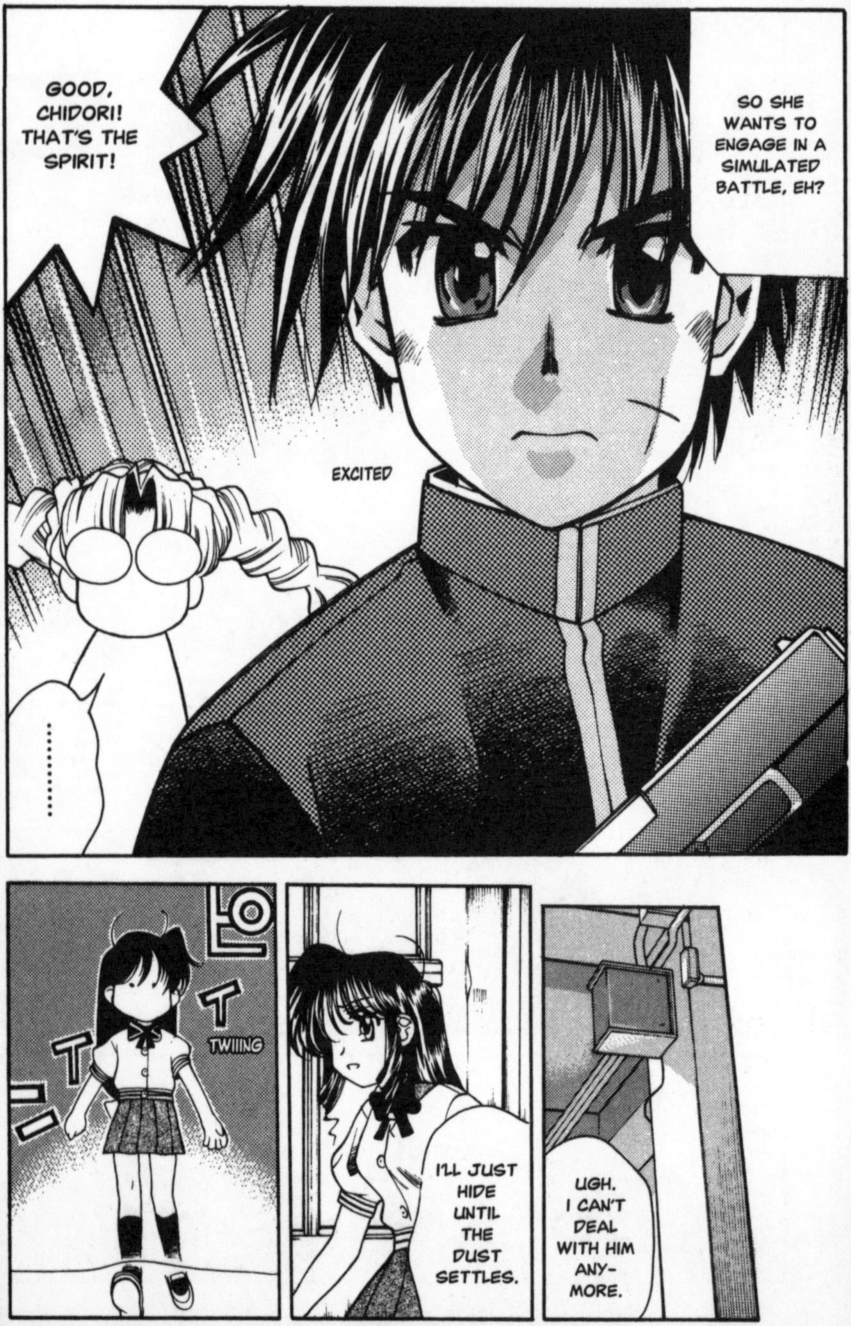
SO SHE WANTS TO ENGAGE IN A SIMULATED BATTLE, EH?
GOOD, CHIDORI! THAT'S THE SPIRIT!
EXCITED
....
UGH. I CAN'T DEAL WITH HIM ANY-MORE.
I'LL JUST HIDE UNTIL THE DUST SETTLES.
TWIIING

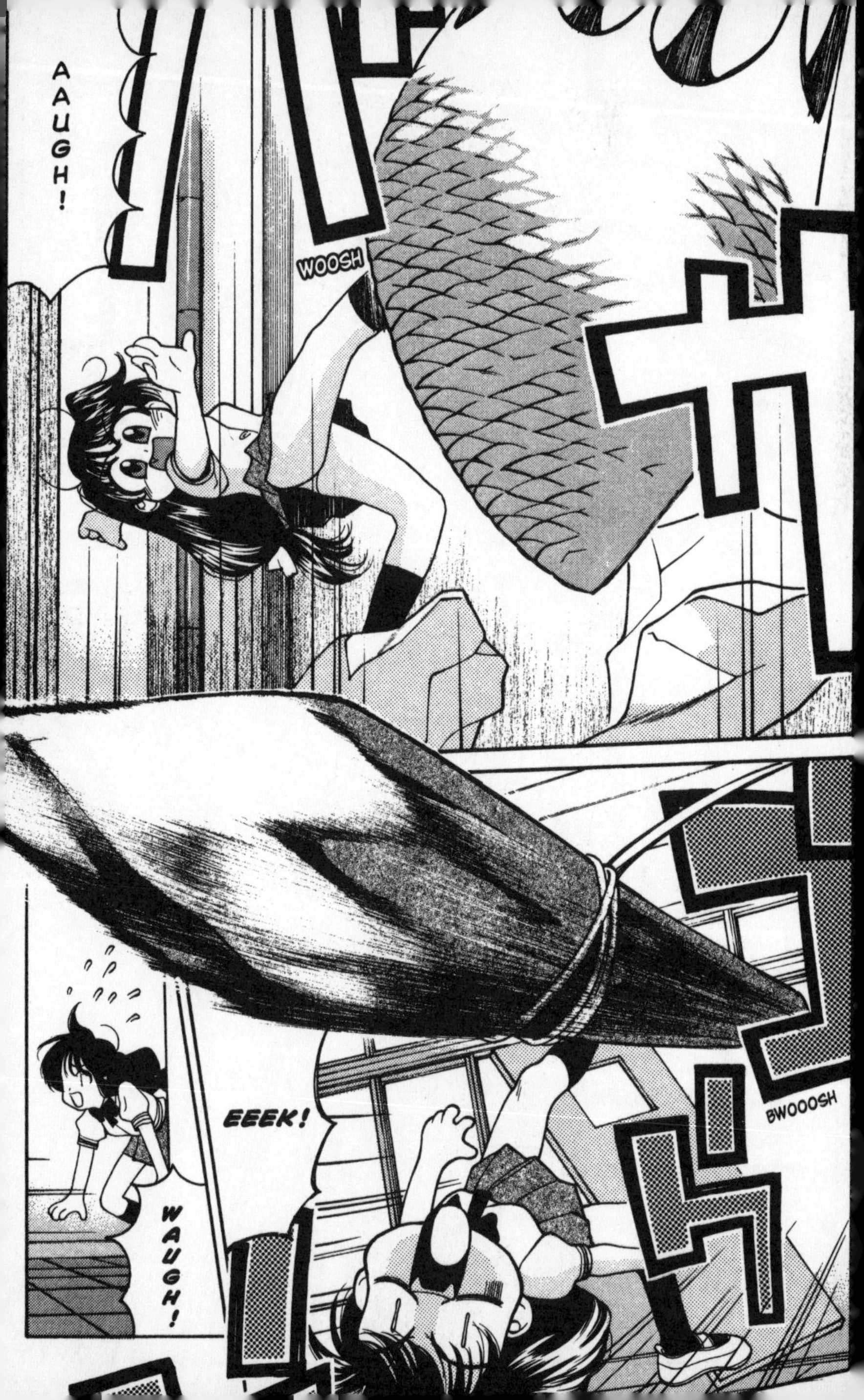
WOOSH
AAUGH!
BWOOOSH
EEEK!
WAUGH!

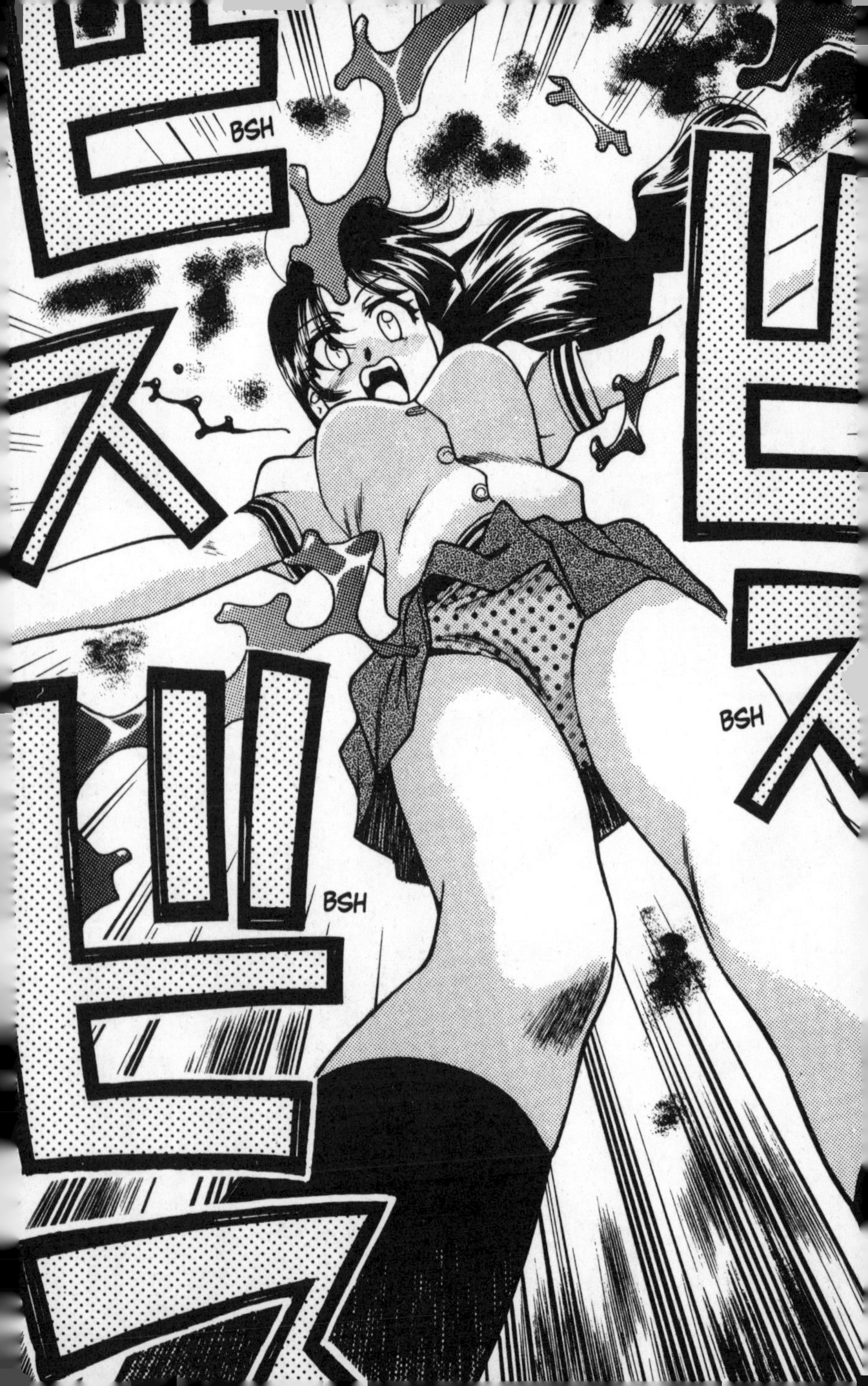
BSH
BSH
BSH

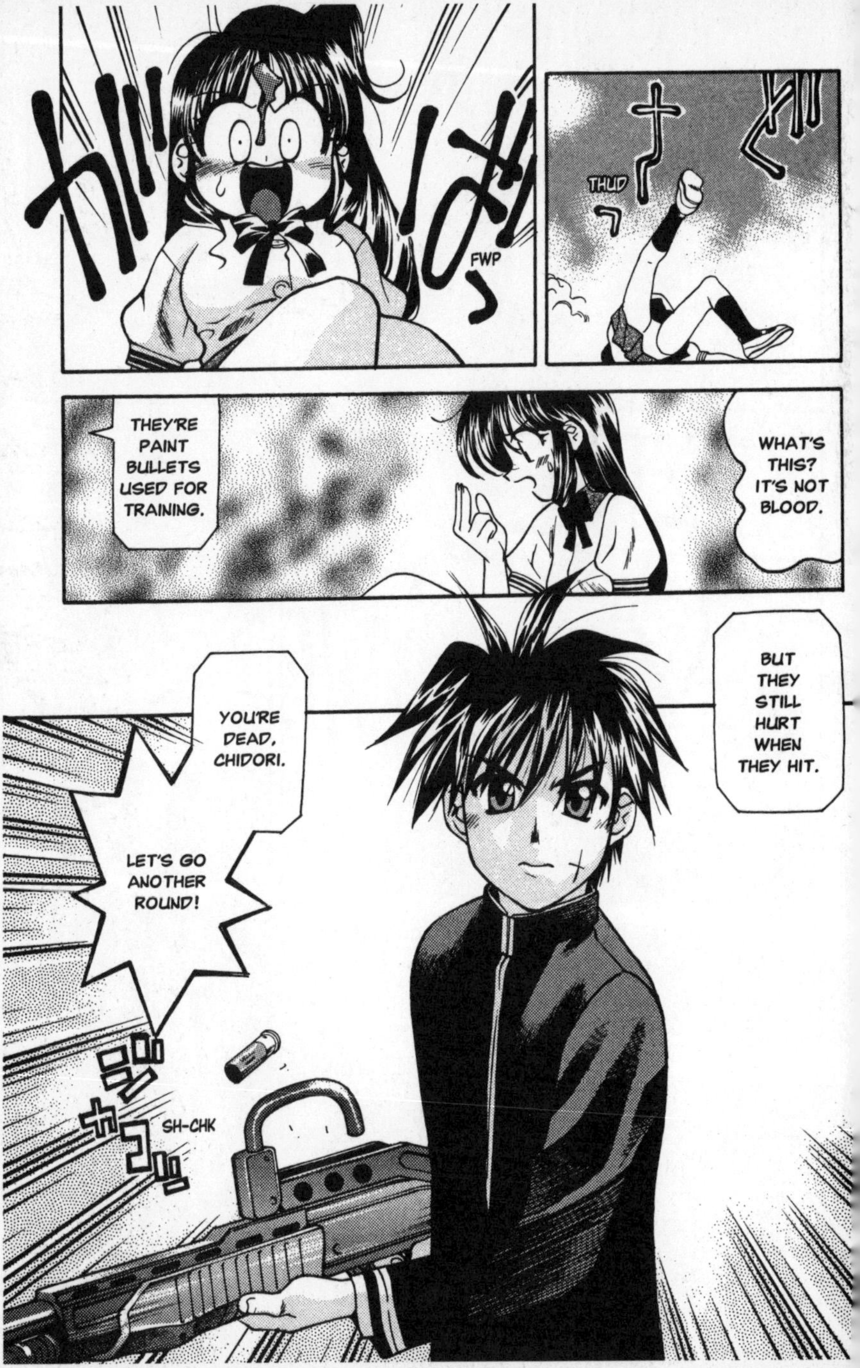
THUD
FWP
WHAT'S THIS? IT'S NOT BLOOD.
THEY'RE PAINT BULLETS USED FOR TRAINING.
BUT THEY STILL HURT WHEN THEY HIT.
YOU'RE DEAD, CHIDORI.
LET'S GO ANOTHER ROUND!
SH-CHK

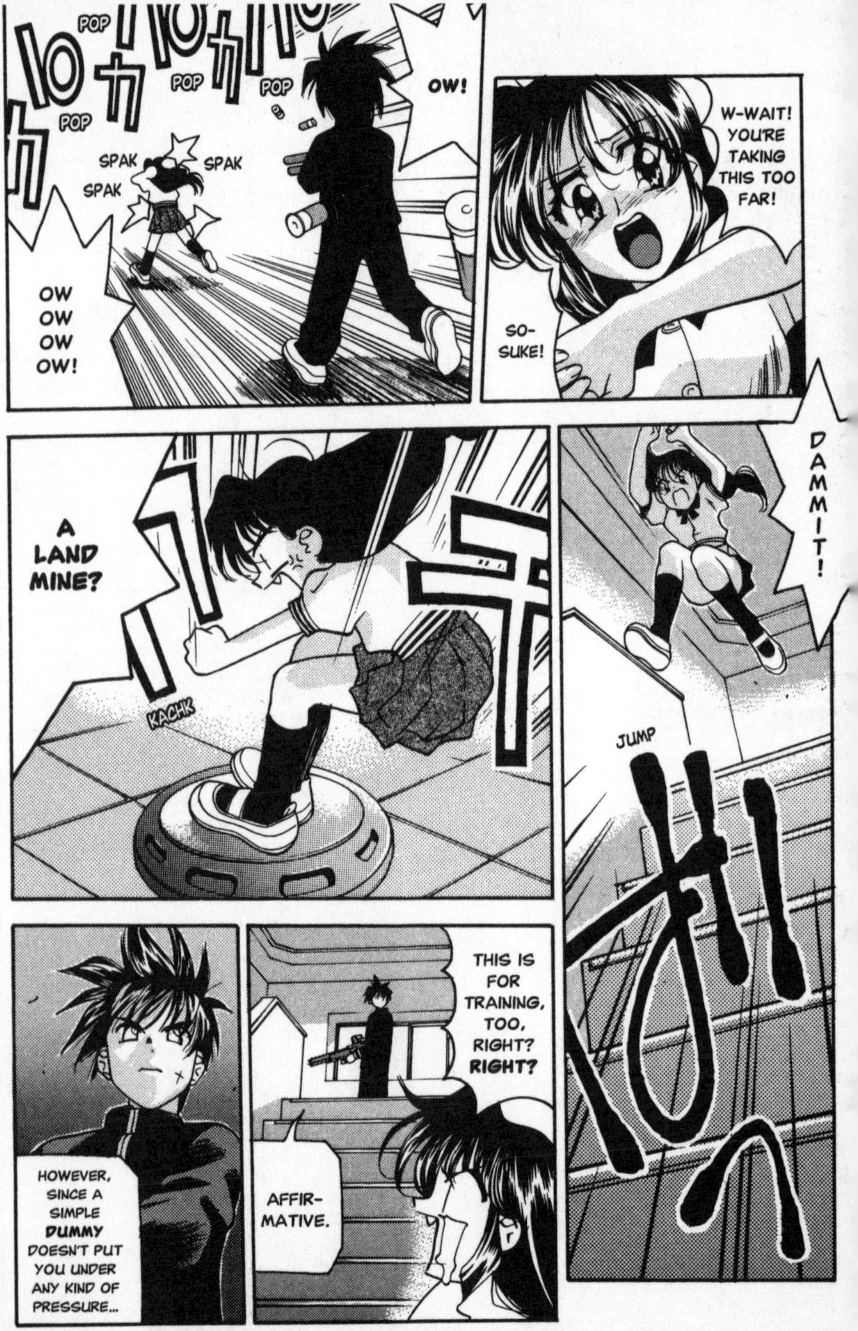
W-WAIT! YOU'RE TAKING THIS TOO FAR!
SO-SUKE!
POP
POP
POP
POP
OW!
SPAK
SPAK
SPAK
OW OW OW OW!
DAMMIT!
JUMP
A LAND MINE?
KACHK
THIS IS FOR TRAINING, TOO, RIGHT? RIGHT?
AFFIRMATIVE.
HOWEVER, SINCE A SIMPLE DUMMY DOESN'T PUT YOU UNDER ANY KIND OF PRESSURE...

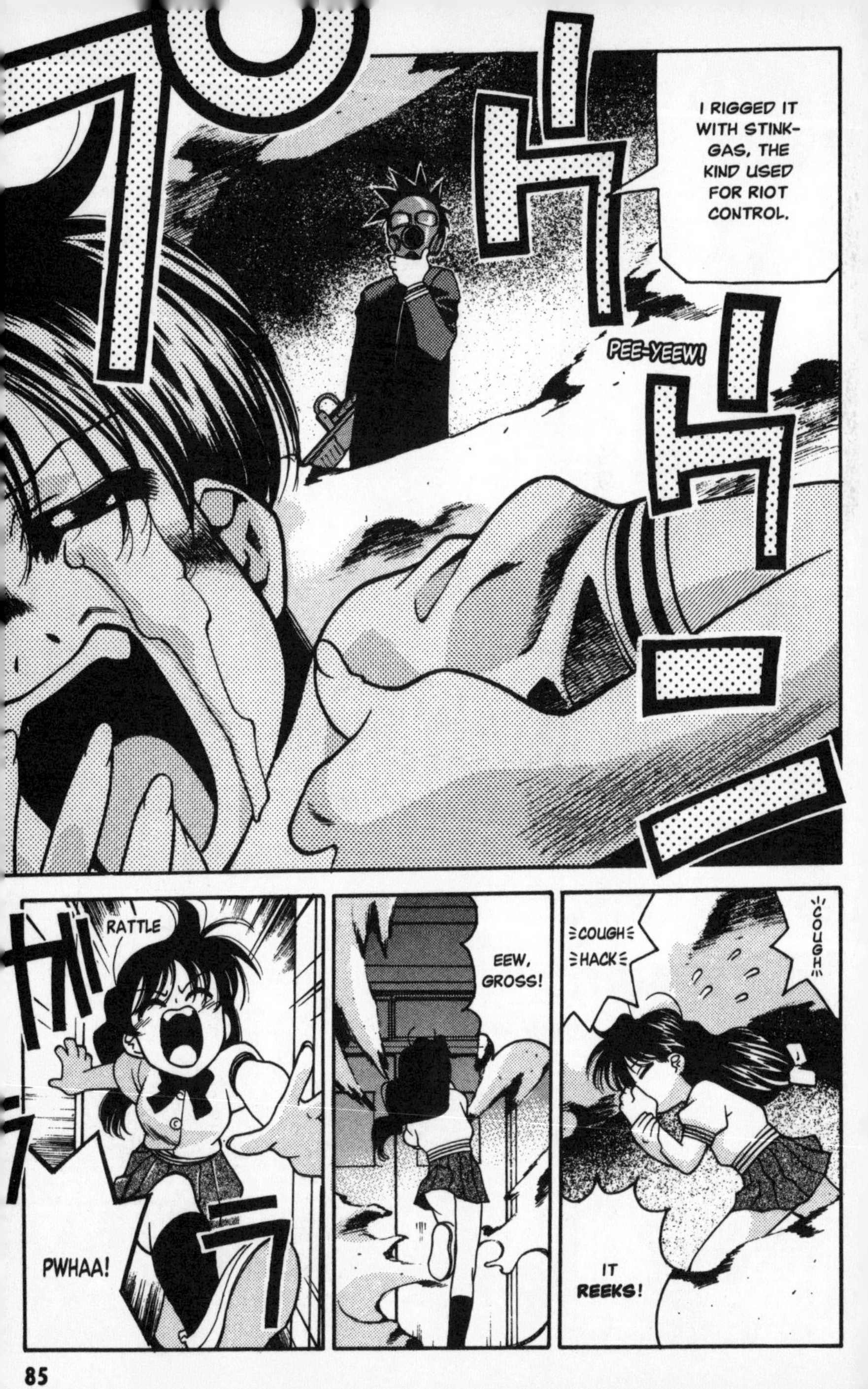
I RIGGED IT WITH STINK-GAS, THE KIND USED FOR RIOT CONTROL.
PEE-YEEW!
COUGH
COUGH
HACK
IT REEKS!
EEW, GROSS!
RATTLE
PWHAA!

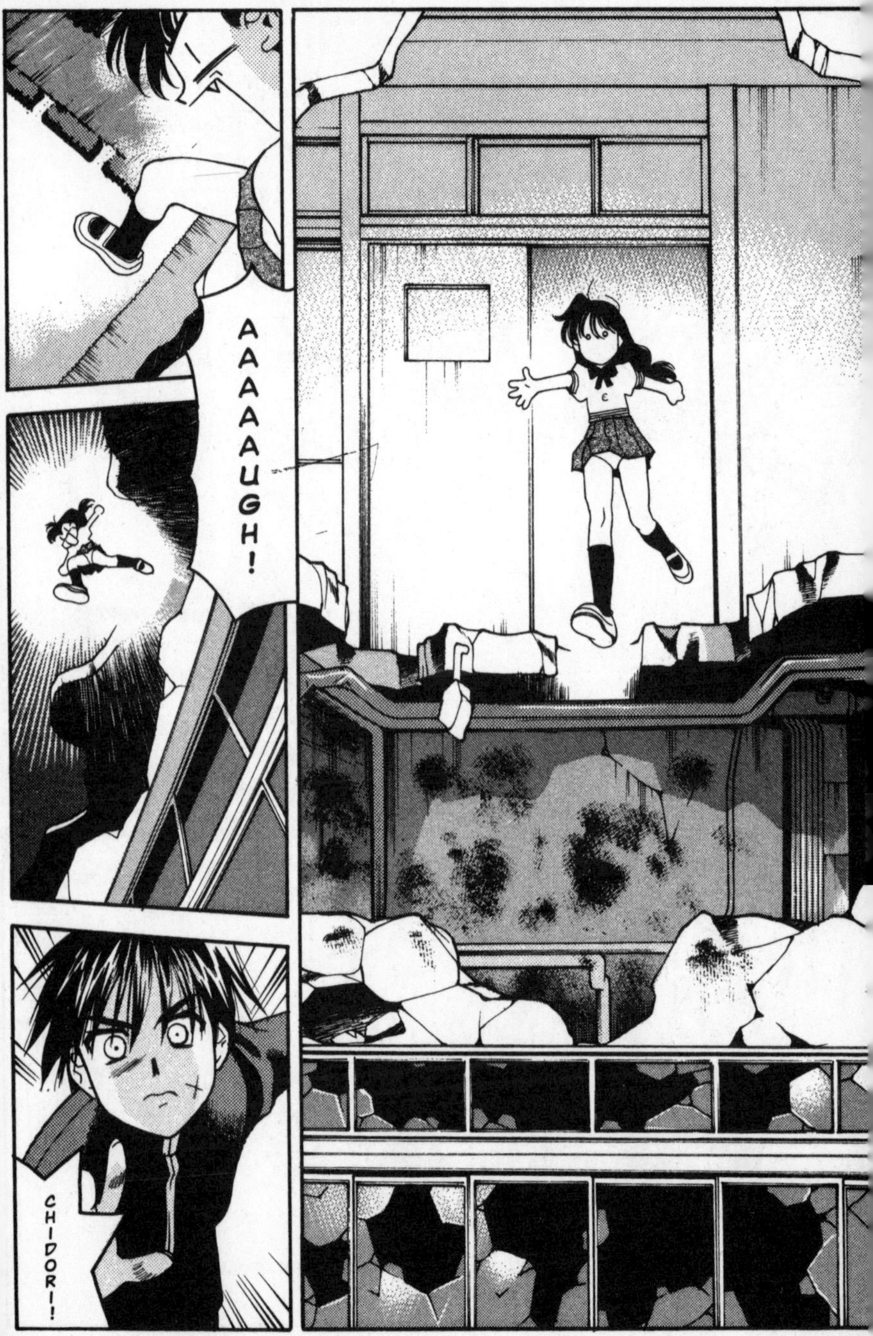
AAAAAAUGH!
CHIDORI!

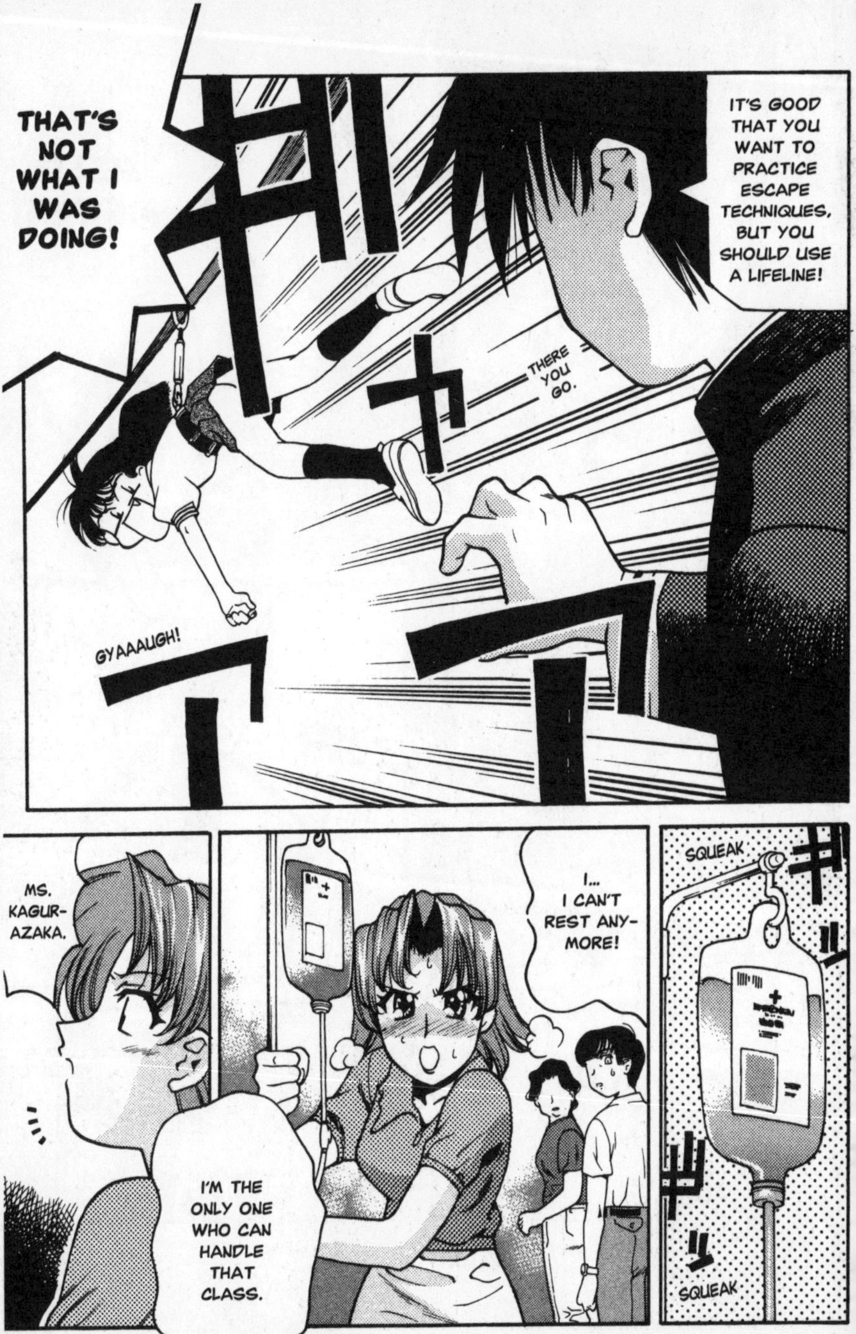
IT'S GOOD THAT YOU WANT TO PRACTICE ESCAPE TECHNIQUES, BUT YOU SHOULD USE A LIFELINE!
THERE YOU GO.
THAT'S NOT WHAT I WAS DOING!
GYAAAUGH!
SQUEAK
SQUEAK
I... I CAN'T REST ANY-MORE!
I'M THE ONLY ONE WHO CAN HANDLE THAT CLASS.
MS. KAGUR-AZAKA.

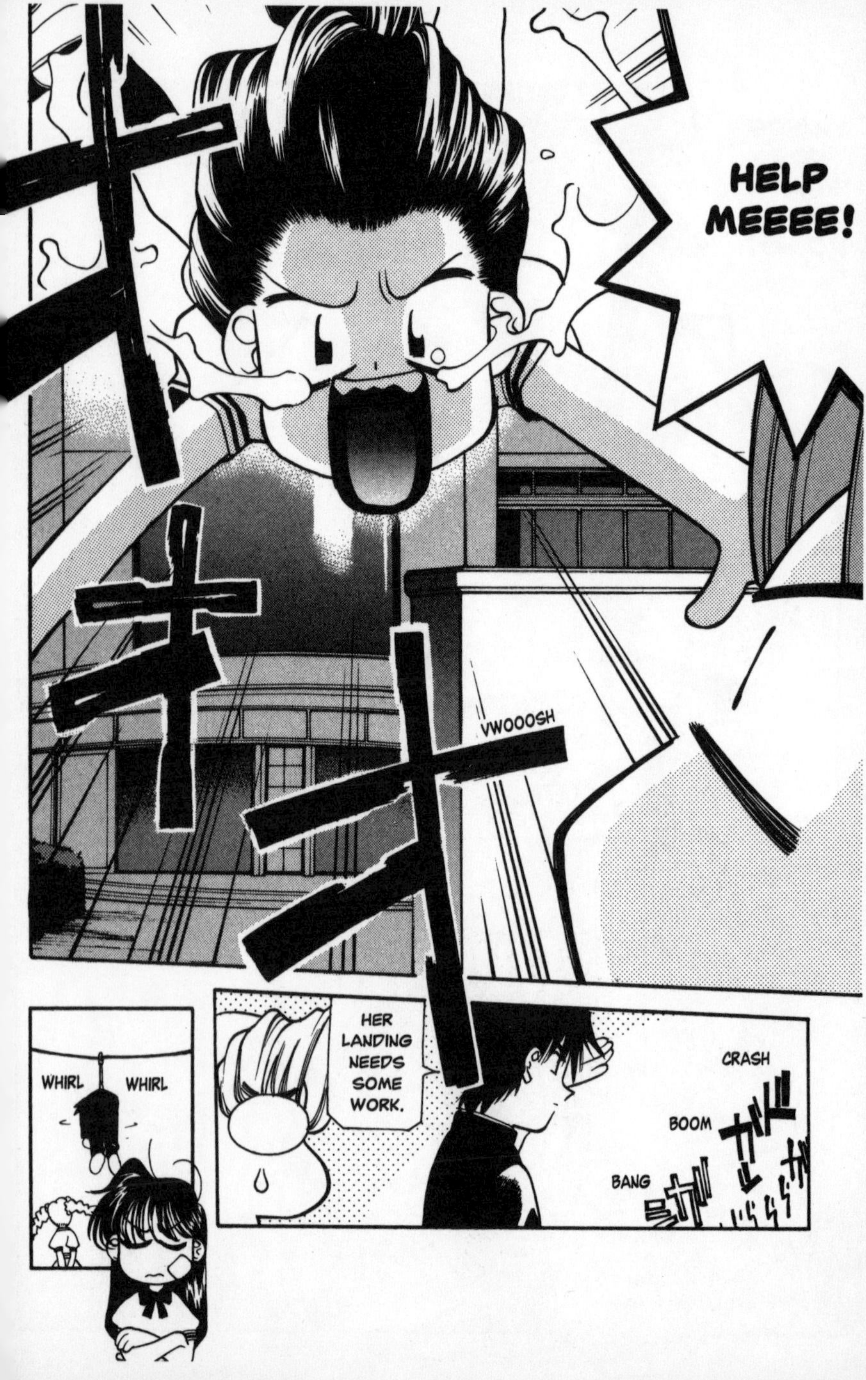
HELP MEEEE!
VWOOOSH
CRASH
BOOM
BANG
HER LANDING NEEDS SOME WORK.
WHIRL
WHIRL

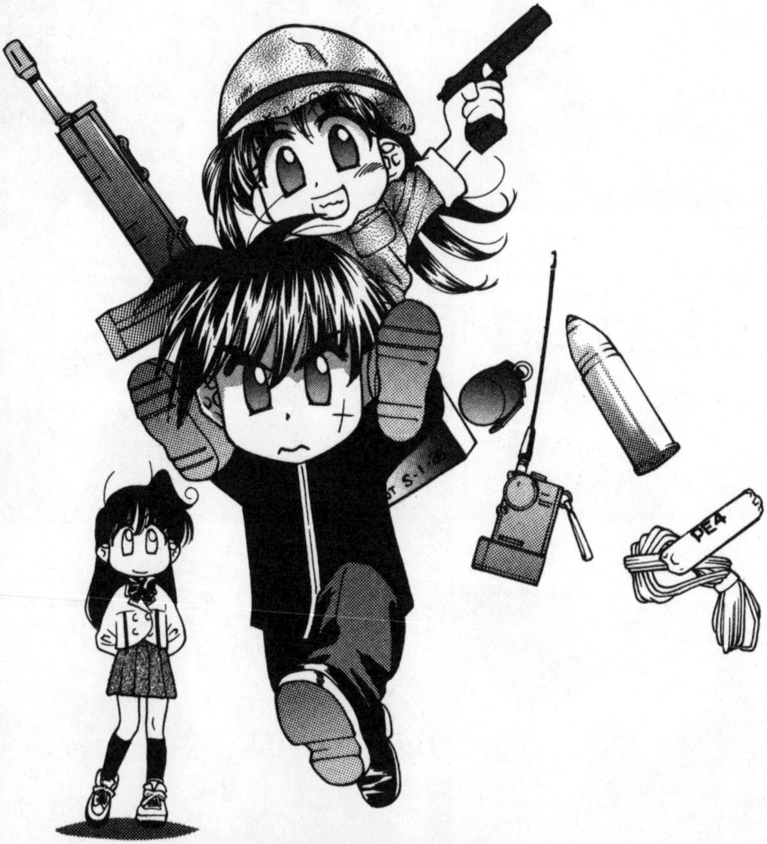
PE4

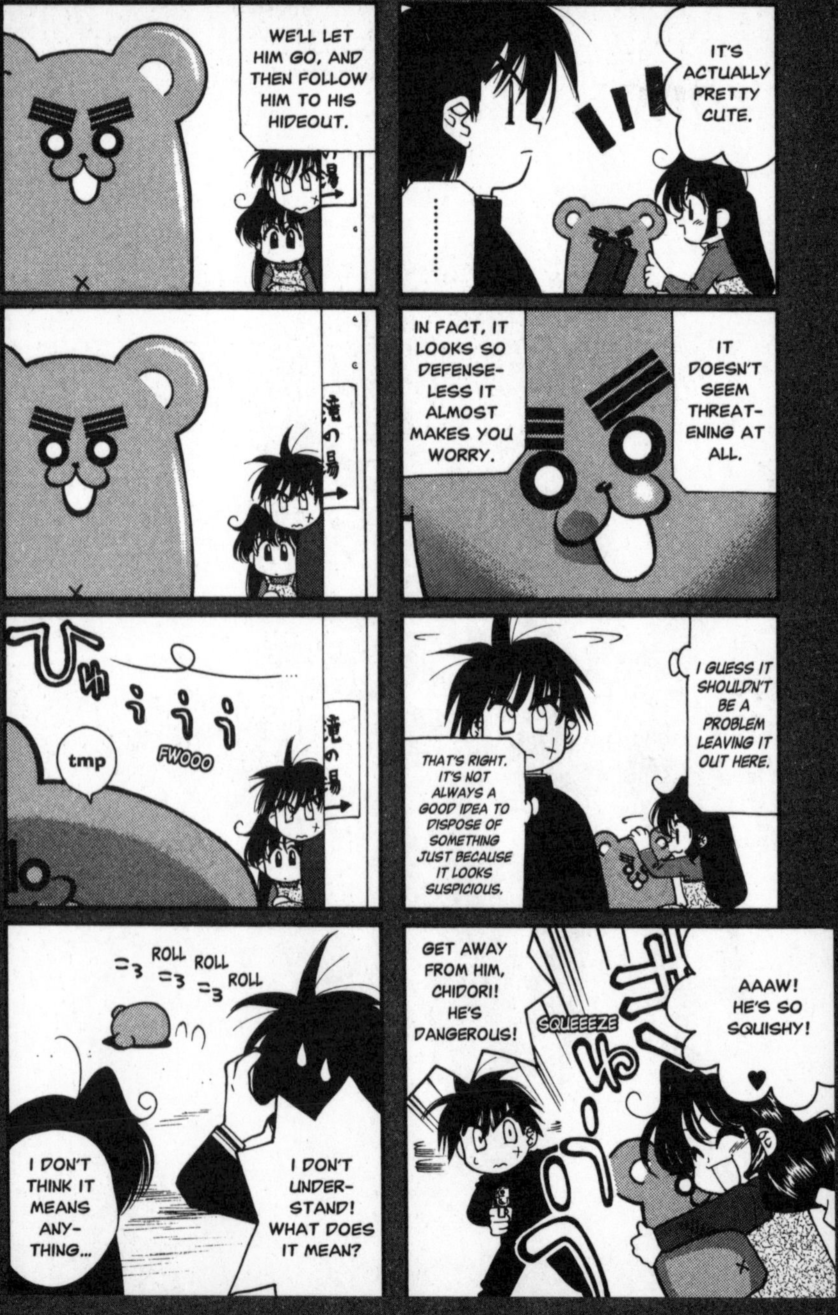
IT'S ACTUALLY PRETTY CUTE.
IT DOESN'T SEEM THREAT-ENING AT ALL.
IN FACT, IT LOOKS SO DEFENSE-LESS IT ALMOST MAKES YOU WORRY.
I GUESS IT SHOULDN'T BE A PROBLEM LEAVING IT OUT HERE.
THAT'S RIGHT. IT'S NOT ALWAYS A GOOD IDEA TO DISPOSE OF SOMETHING JUST BECAUSE IT LOOKS SUSPICIOUS.
AAAW! HE'S SO SQUISHY!
SQUEEEZE
GET AWAY FROM HIM, CHIDORI! HE'S DANGEROUS!
WE'LL LET HIM GO, AND THEN FOLLOW HIM TO HIS HIDEOUT.
滝の湯
tmp
FWOOO
ROLL
ROLL
ROLL
I DON'T UNDER-STAND! WHAT DOES IT MEAN?
I DON'T THINK IT MEANS ANY-THING...

BOMB 4 TOGETHER WITH SOSUKE

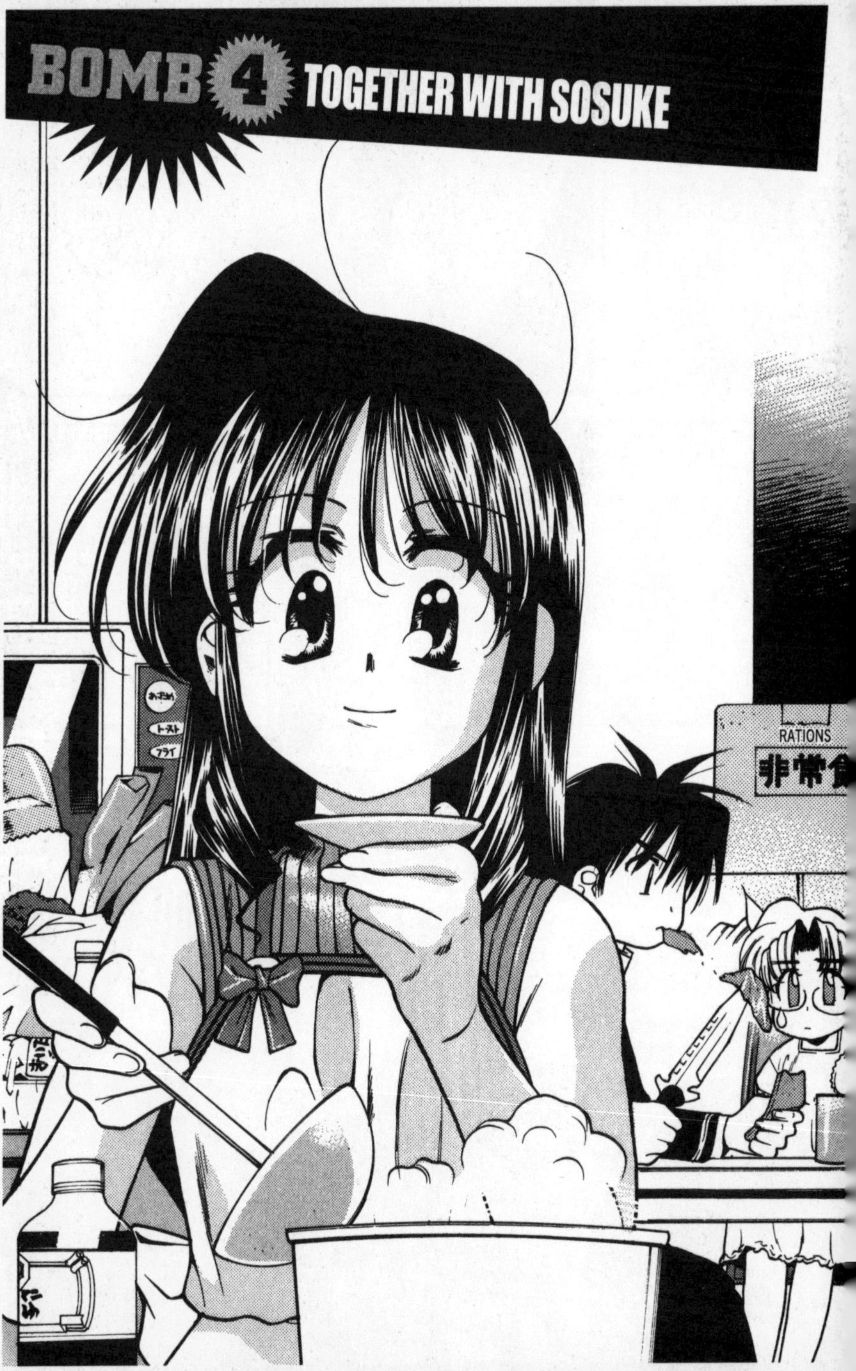

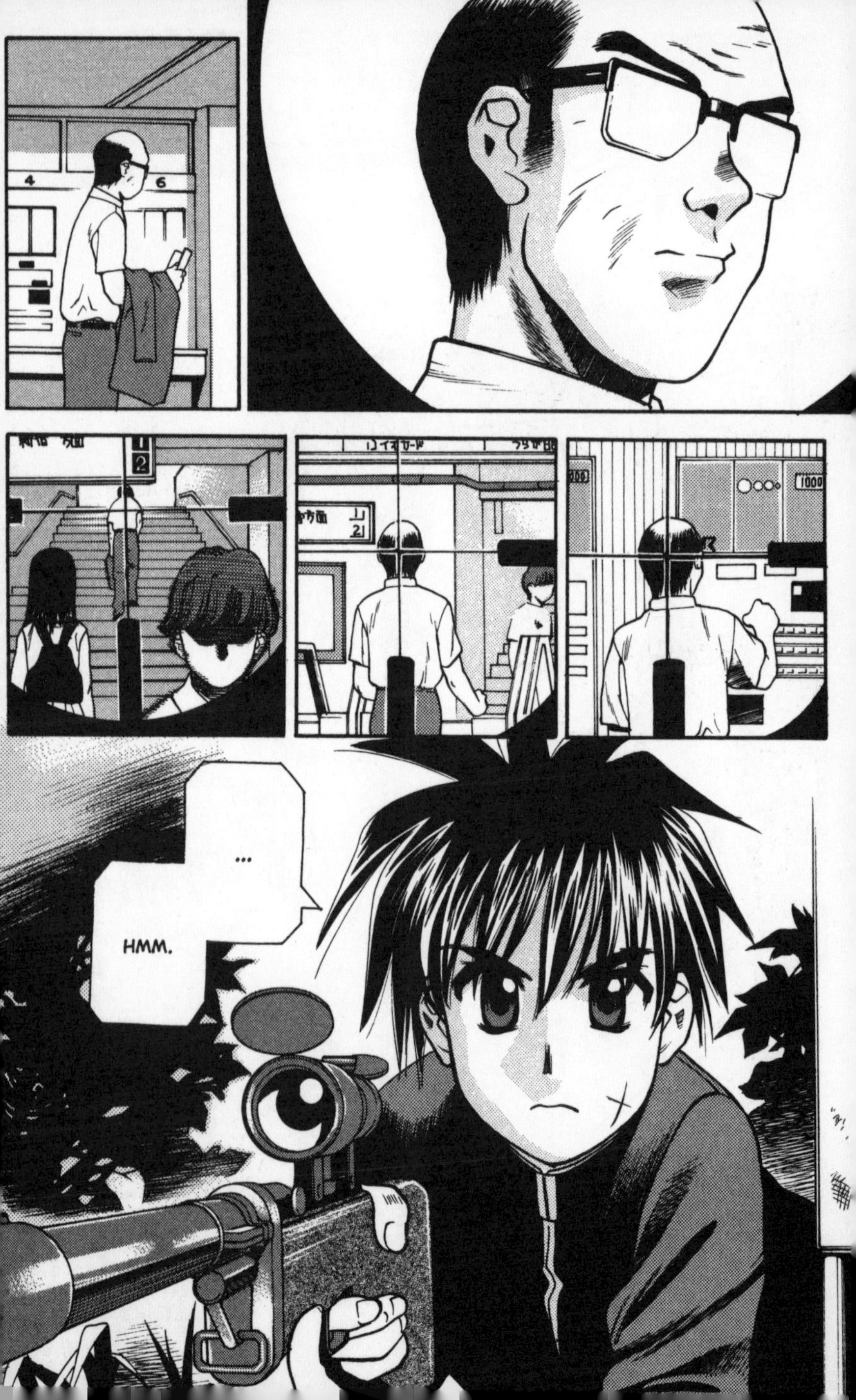
...
HMM.

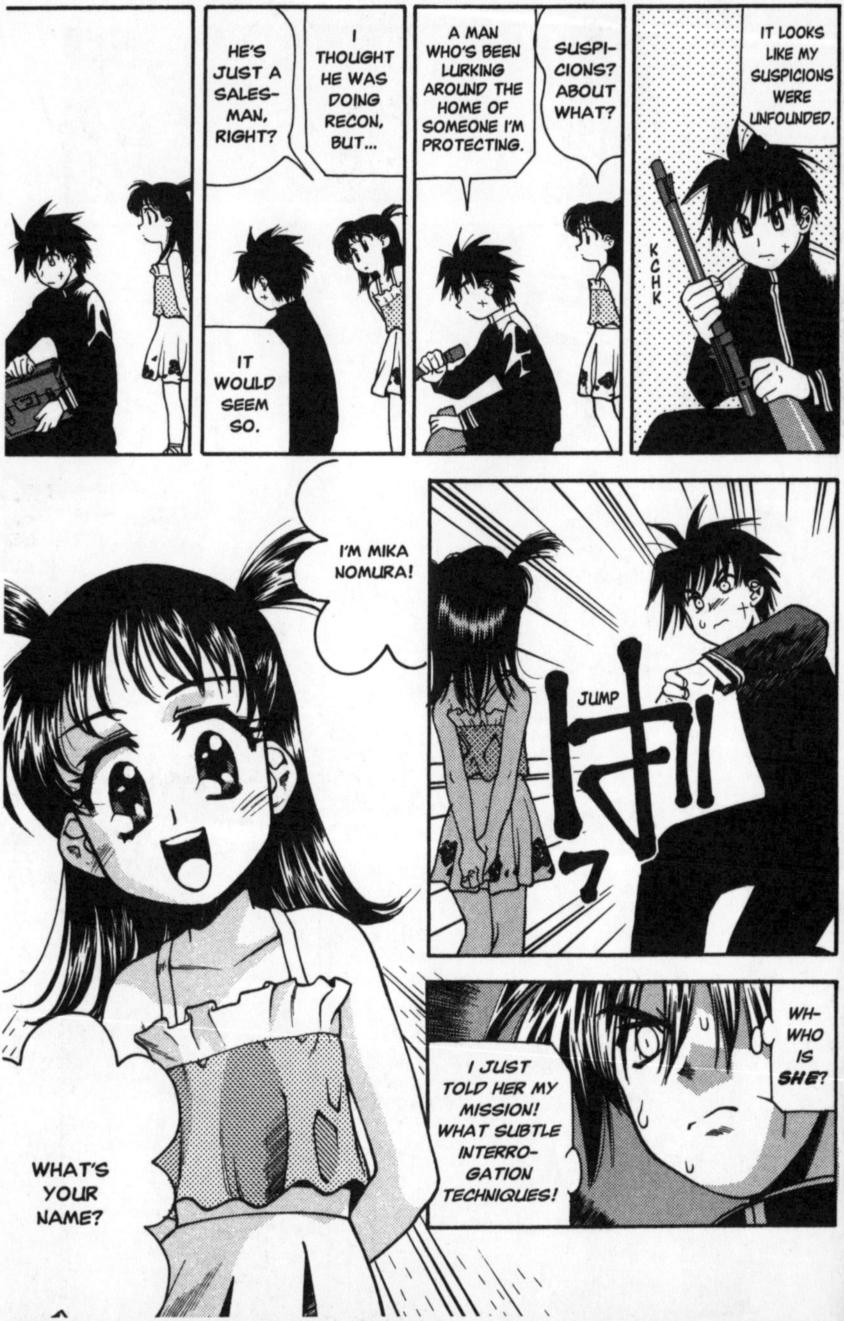
IT LOOKS LIKE MY SUSPICIONS WERE UNFOUNDED.
KCHK
SUSPICIONS? ABOUT WHAT?
A MAN WHO'S BEEN LURKING AROUND THE HOME OF SOMEONE I'M PROTECTING.
I THOUGHT HE WAS DOING RECON, BUT...
HE'S JUST A SALESMAN, RIGHT?
IT WOULD SEEM SO.
JUMP
WH-WHO IS SHE?
I JUST TOLD HER MY MISSION! WHAT SUBTLE INTERROGATION TECHNIQUES!
I'M MIKA NOMURA!
WHAT'S YOUR NAME?

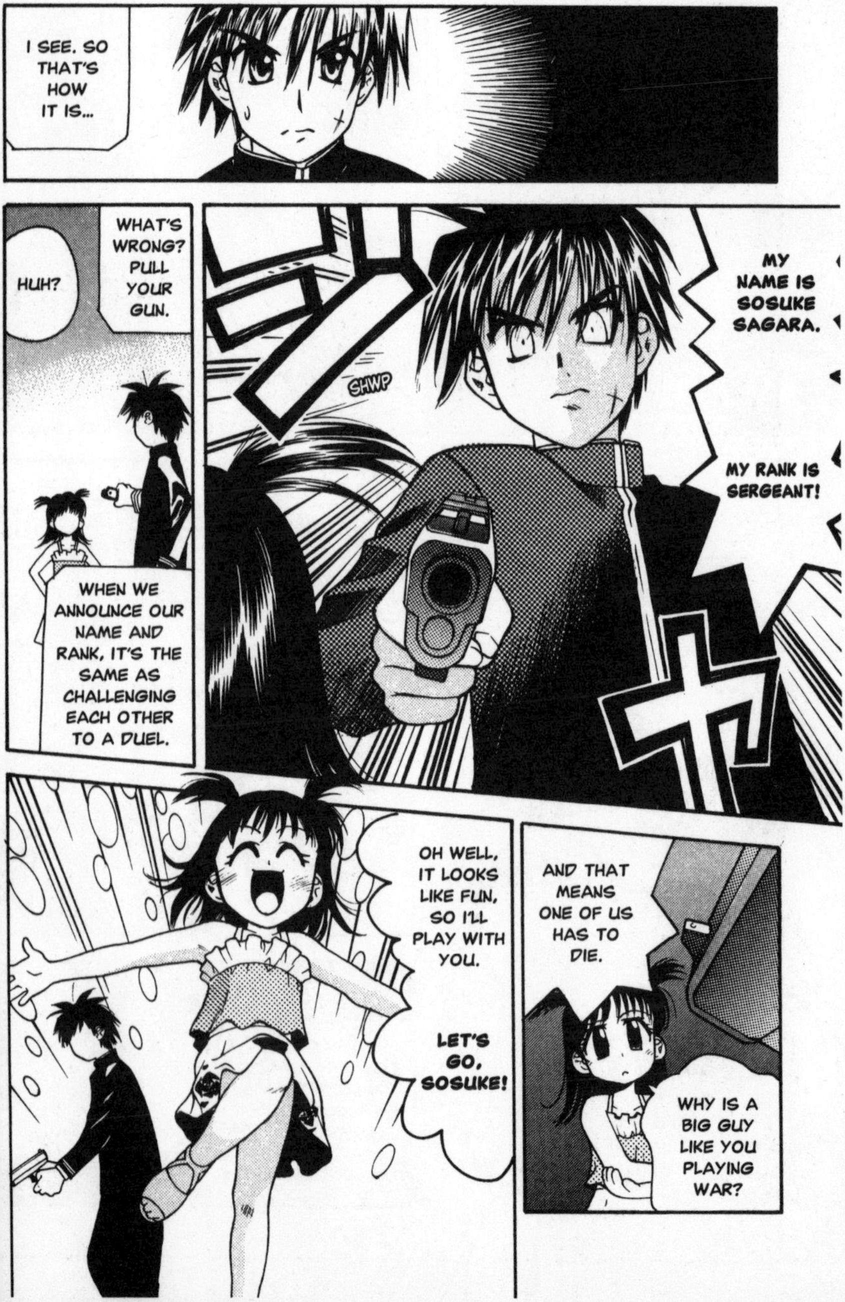
I SEE. SO THAT'S HOW IT IS...
MY NAME IS SOSUKE SAGARA.
MY RANK IS SERGEANT!
SHWP
WHAT'S WRONG? PULL YOUR GUN.
HUH?
WHEN WE ANNOUNCE OUR NAME AND RANK, IT'S THE SAME AS CHALLENGING EACH OTHER TO A DUEL.
AND THAT MEANS ONE OF US HAS TO DIE.
WHY IS A BIG GUY LIKE YOU PLAYING WAR?
OH WELL, IT LOOKS LIKE FUN, SO I'LL PLAY WITH YOU.
LET'S GO, SOSUKE!

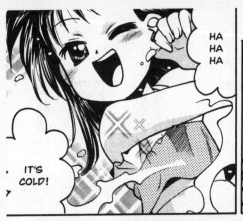

SPLASH
HA HA HA
IT'S COLD!
WHAT IS SHE TRYING TO DO?
WHAT IS SHE AFTER?
SHE SEEMS INNOCENT ENOUGH...AND DEFENSELESS, TOO.
MAYBE SHE REALLY **IS** JUST A REGULAR GIRL.
NO. SHE'S EXACTLY THE KIND OF CHILD THAT TER-RORISTS LIKE TO USE AS PAWNS.
SHE MUST HAVE BEEN THROUGH THE SAME KIND OF HELLISH TRAINING AS ME.
JUMP
SO-SUKE!

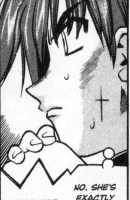

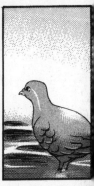

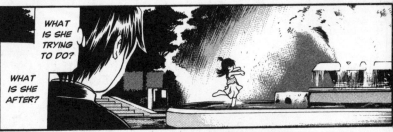

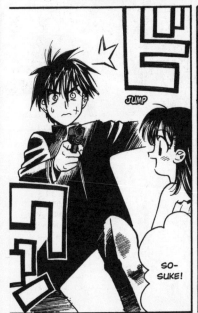

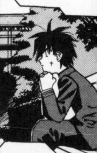

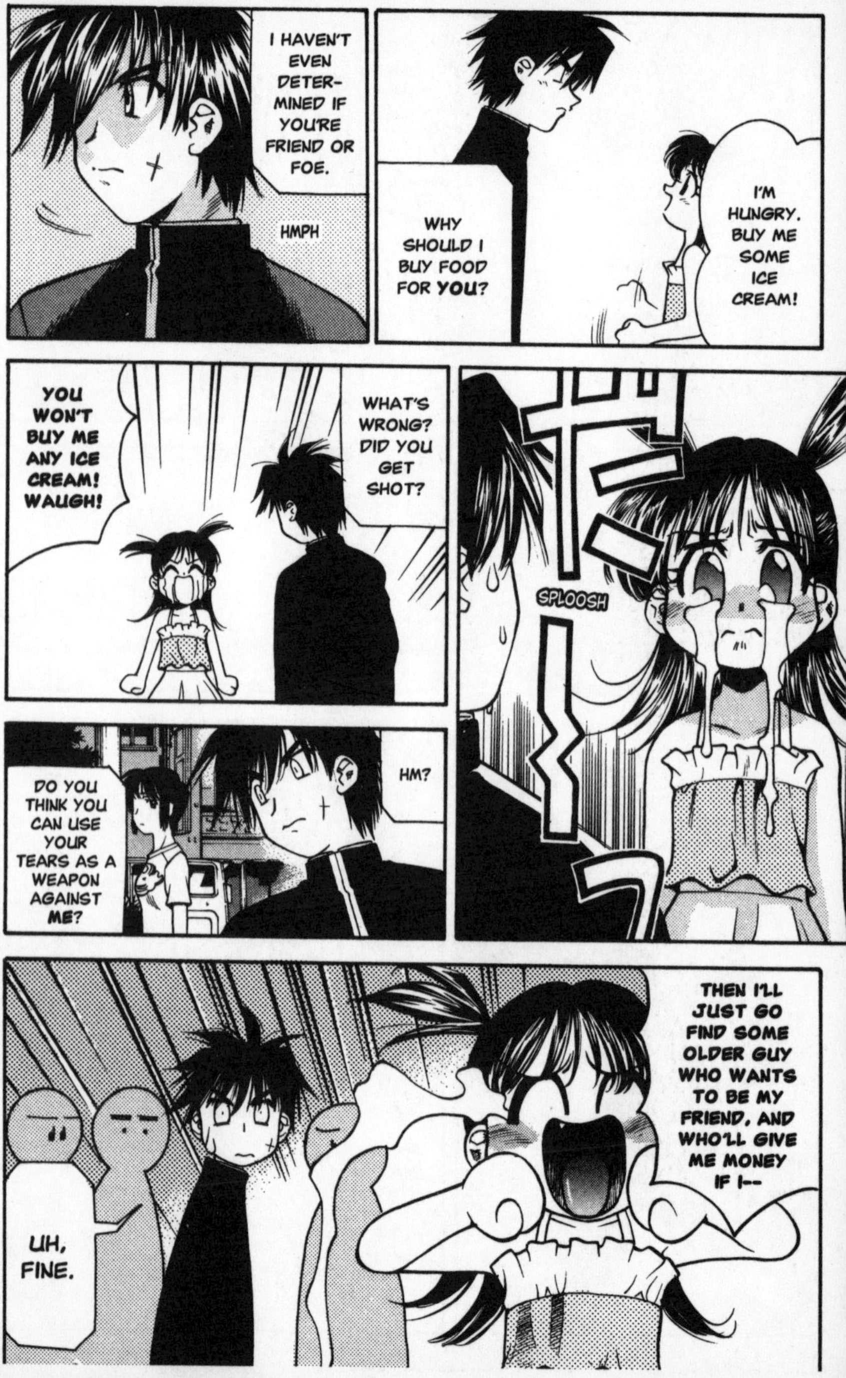
I'M HUNGRY. BUY ME SOME ICE CREAM!
WHY SHOULD I BUY FOOD FOR YOU?
I HAVEN'T EVEN DETER-MINED IF YOU'RE FRIEND OR FOE.
HMPH
SPLOOSH
WHAT'S WRONG? DID YOU GET SHOT?
YOU WON'T BUY ME ANY ICE CREAM! WAUGH!
HM?
DO YOU THINK YOU CAN USE YOUR TEARS AS A WEAPON AGAINST ME?
THEN I'LL JUST GO FIND SOME OLDER GUY WHO WANTS TO BE MY FRIEND, AND WHO'LL GIVE ME MONEY IF I--
UH, FINE.

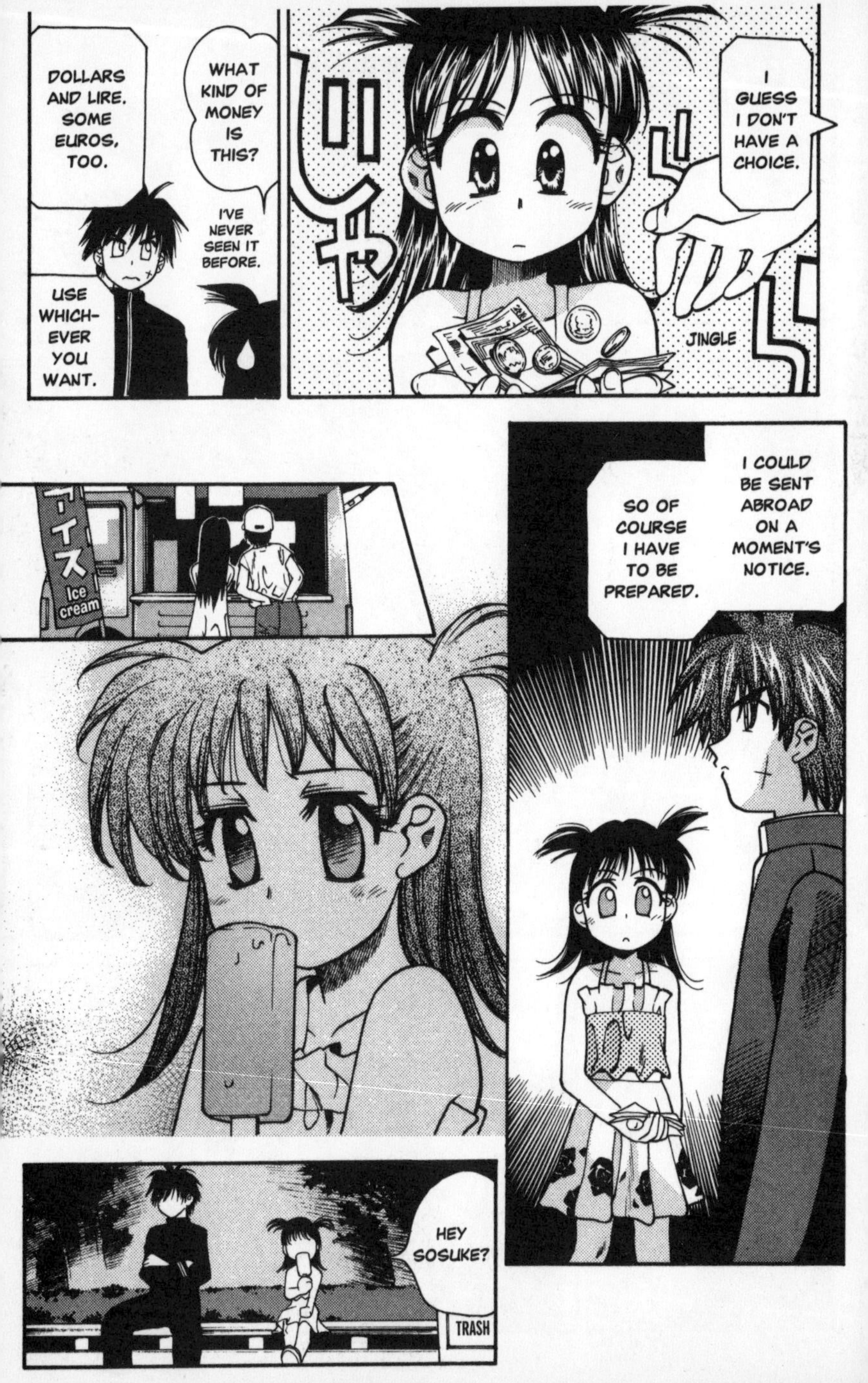
I GUESS I DON'T HAVE A CHOICE.
JINGLE
WHAT KIND OF MONEY IS THIS?
I'VE NEVER SEEN IT BEFORE.
DOLLARS AND LIRE. SOME EUROS, TOO.
USE WHICH-EVER YOU WANT.
I COULD BE SENT ABROAD ON A MOMENT'S NOTICE.
SO OF COURSE I HAVE TO BE PREPARED.
Ice cream
HEY SOSUKE?
TRASH

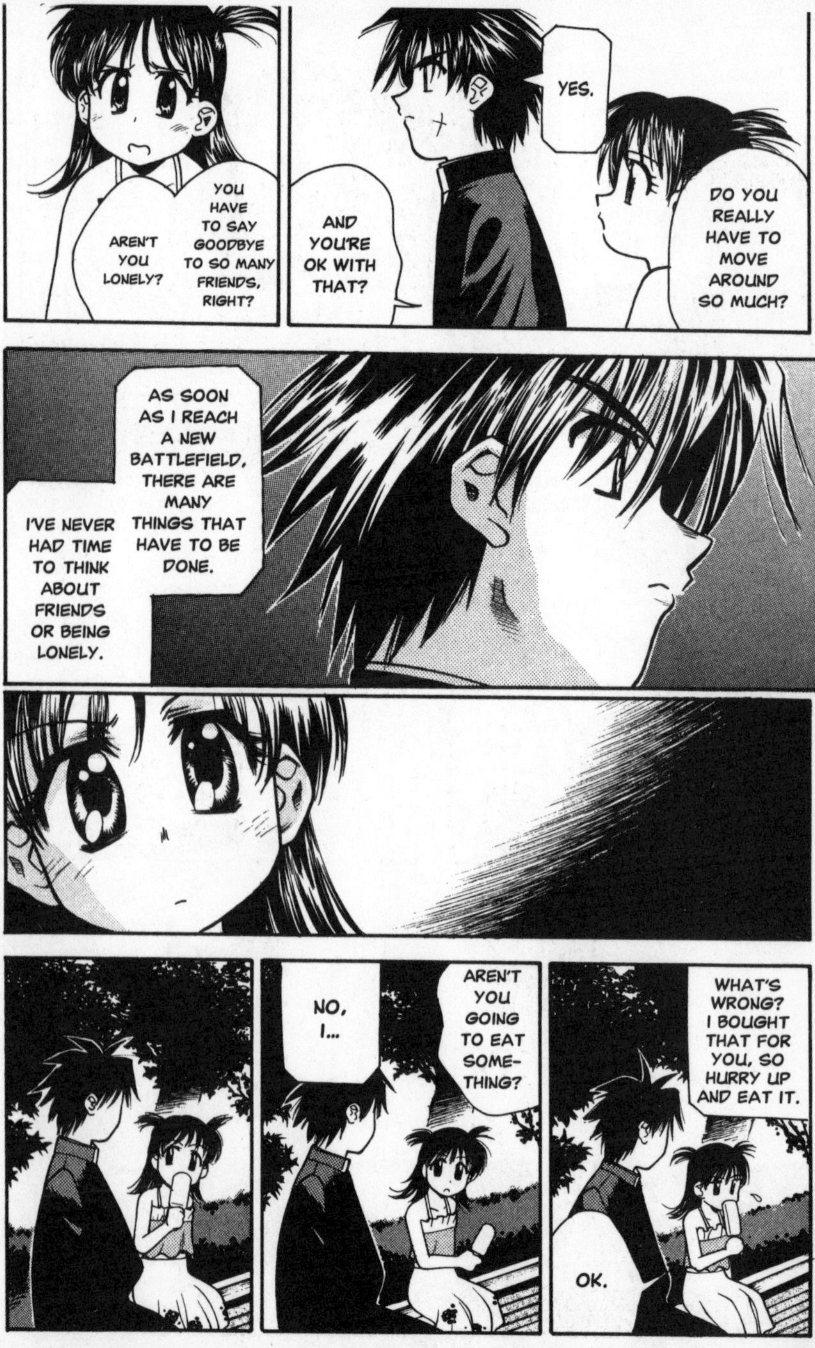
DO YOU REALLY HAVE TO MOVE AROUND SO MUCH?
YES.
AND YOU'RE OK WITH THAT?
YOU HAVE TO SAY GOODBYE TO SO MANY FRIENDS, RIGHT?
AREN'T YOU LONELY?
AS SOON AS I REACH A NEW BATTLEFIELD, THERE ARE MANY THINGS THAT HAVE TO BE DONE.
I'VE NEVER HAD TIME TO THINK ABOUT FRIENDS OR BEING LONELY.
WHAT'S WRONG? I BOUGHT THAT FOR YOU, SO HURRY UP AND EAT IT.
OK.
AREN'T YOU GOING TO EAT SOMETHING?
NO, I...

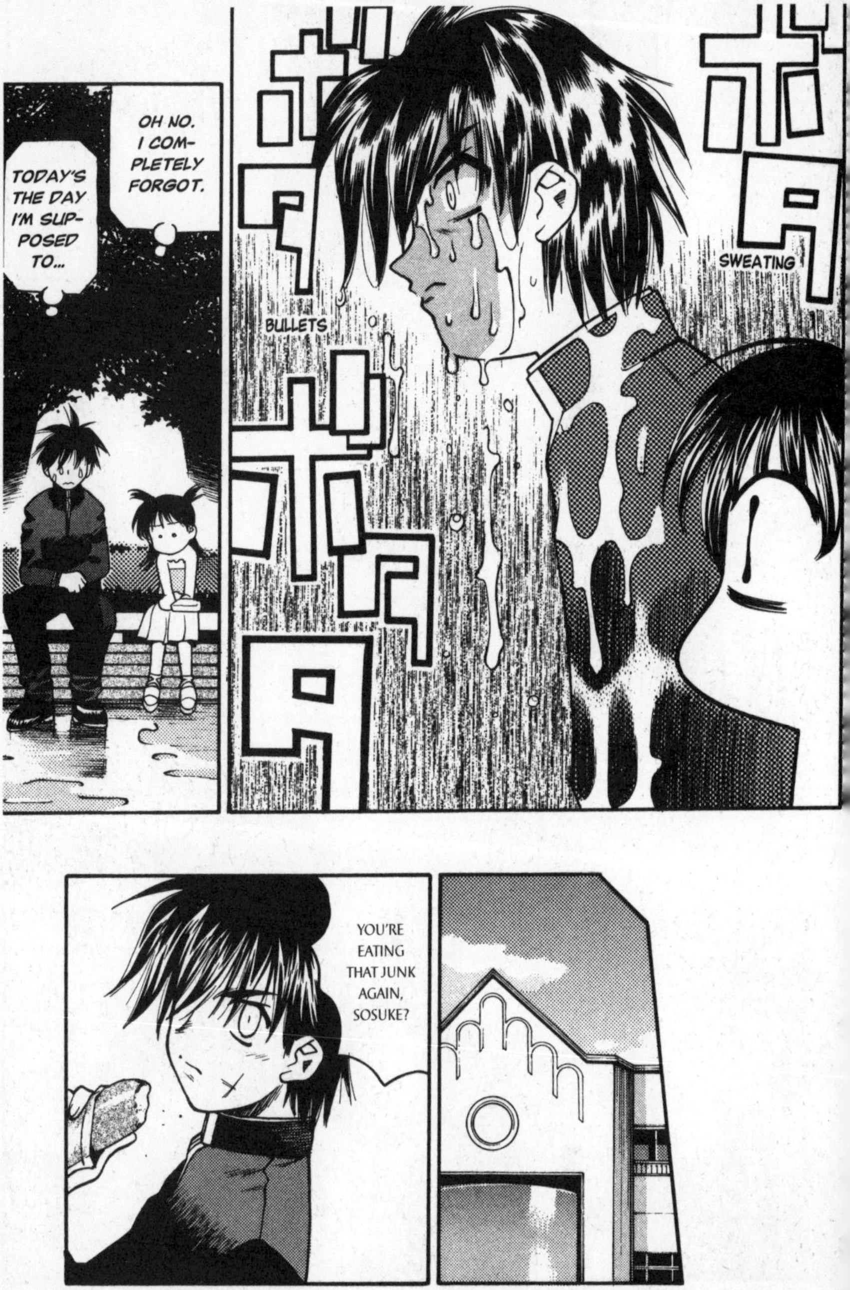
SWEATING
BULLETS
OH NO. I COMPLETELY FORGOT.
TODAY'S THE DAY I'M SUPPOSED TO...
YOU'RE EATING THAT JUNK AGAIN, SOSUKE?

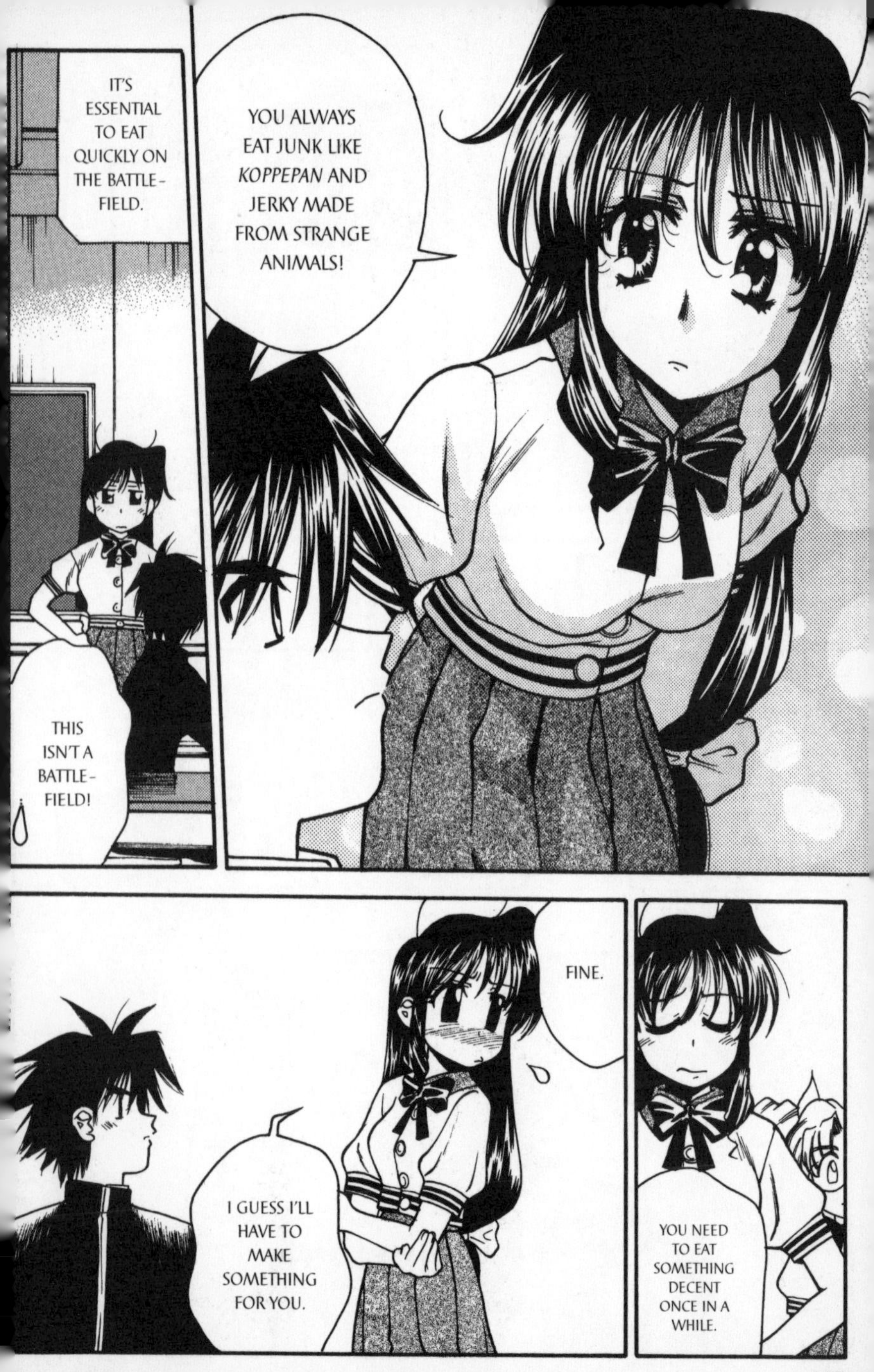
YOU ALWAYS EAT JUNK LIKE *KOPPEPAN* AND JERKY MADE FROM STRANGE ANIMALS!
IT'S ESSENTIAL TO EAT QUICKLY ON THE BATTLE-FIELD.
THIS ISN'T A BATTLE-FIELD!
YOU NEED TO EAT SOMETHING DECENT ONCE IN A WHILE.
FINE.
I GUESS I'LL HAVE TO MAKE SOMETHING FOR YOU.

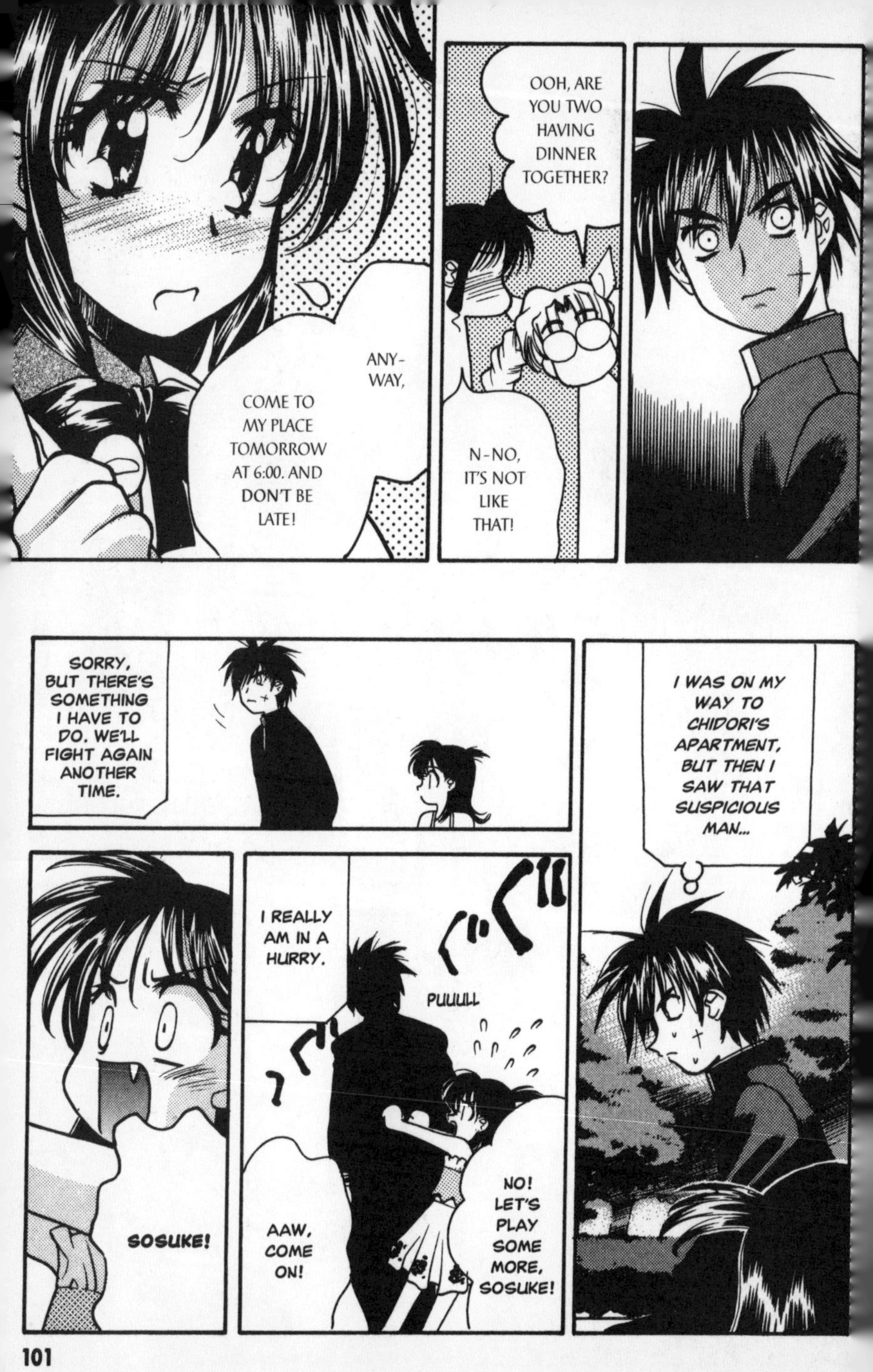
OOH, ARE YOU TWO HAVING DINNER TOGETHER?
N-NO, IT'S NOT LIKE THAT!
ANY-WAY,
COME TO MY PLACE TOMORROW AT 6:00. AND DON'T BE LATE!
I WAS ON MY WAY TO CHIDORI'S APARTMENT, BUT THEN I SAW THAT SUSPICIOUS MAN...
SORRY, BUT THERE'S SOMETHING I HAVE TO DO. WE'LL FIGHT AGAIN ANOTHER TIME.
NO! LET'S PLAY SOME MORE, SOSUKE!
PUUULL
I REALLY AM IN A HURRY.
AAW, COME ON!
SOSUKE!

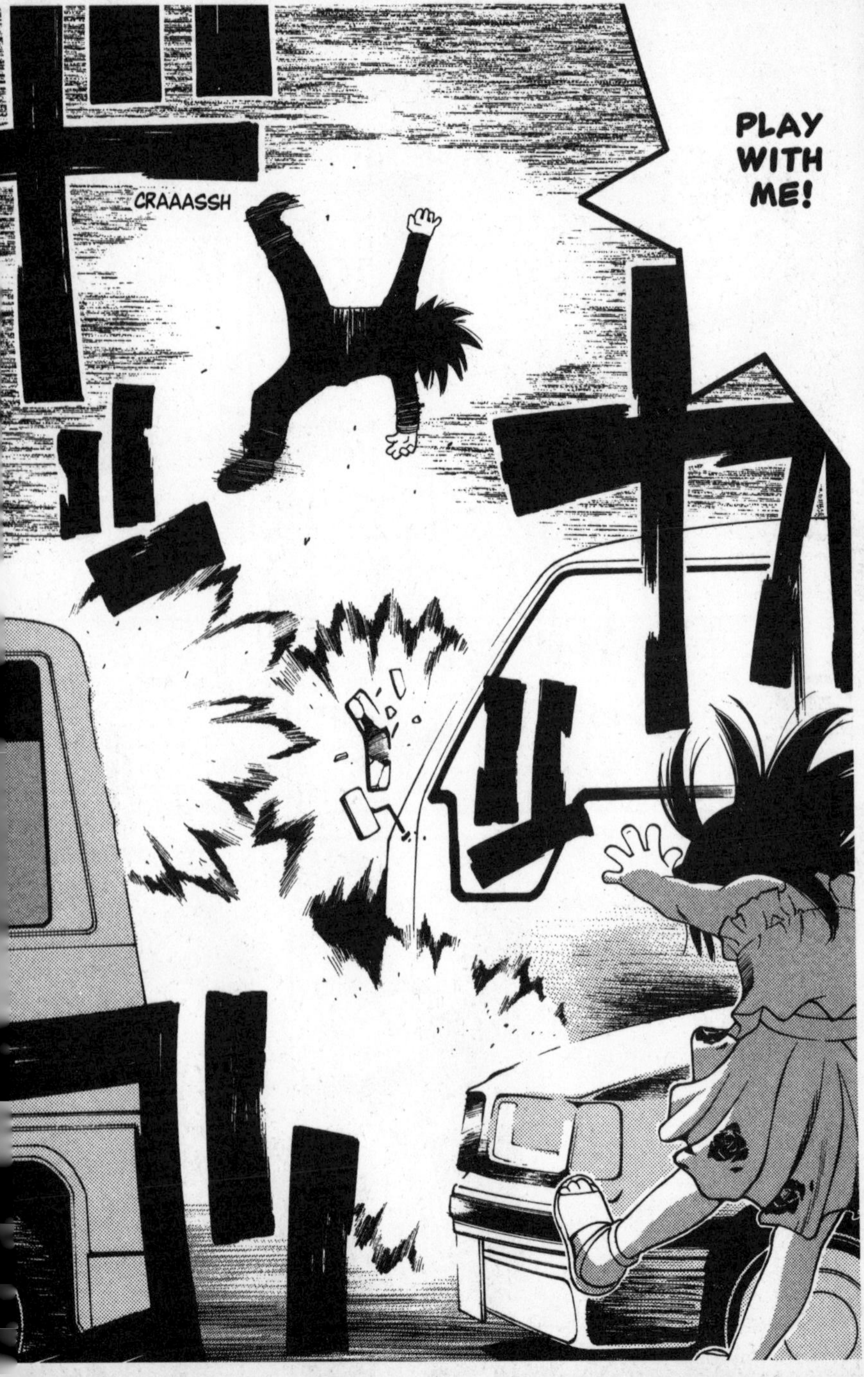
CRAAASSH
PLAY WITH ME!

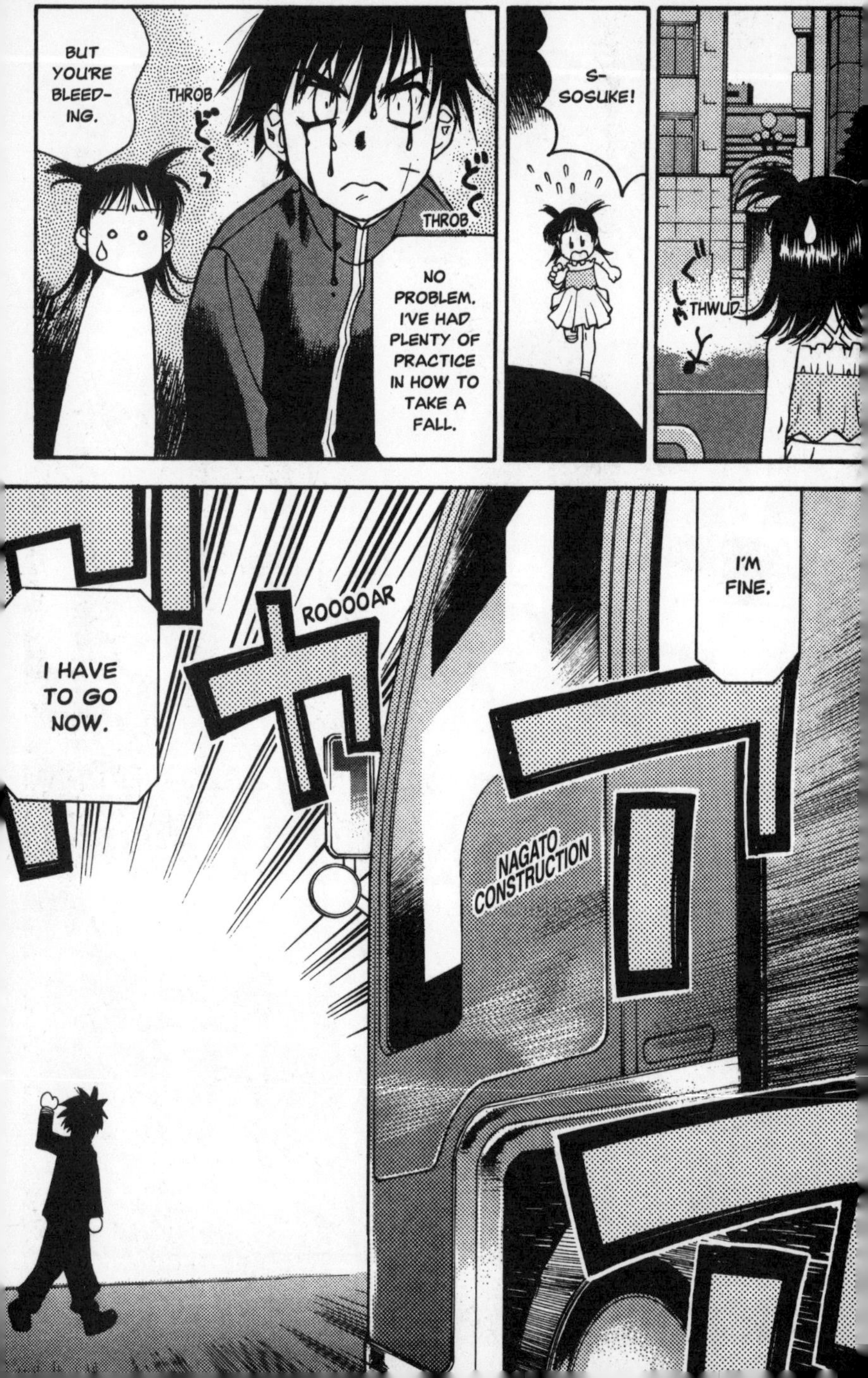
THWUD
S-SOSUKE!
THROB
THROB
BUT YOU'RE BLEEDING.
NO PROBLEM. I'VE HAD PLENTY OF PRACTICE IN HOW TO TAKE A FALL.
I'M FINE.
ROOOOAR
NAGATO CONSTRUCTION
I HAVE TO GO NOW.

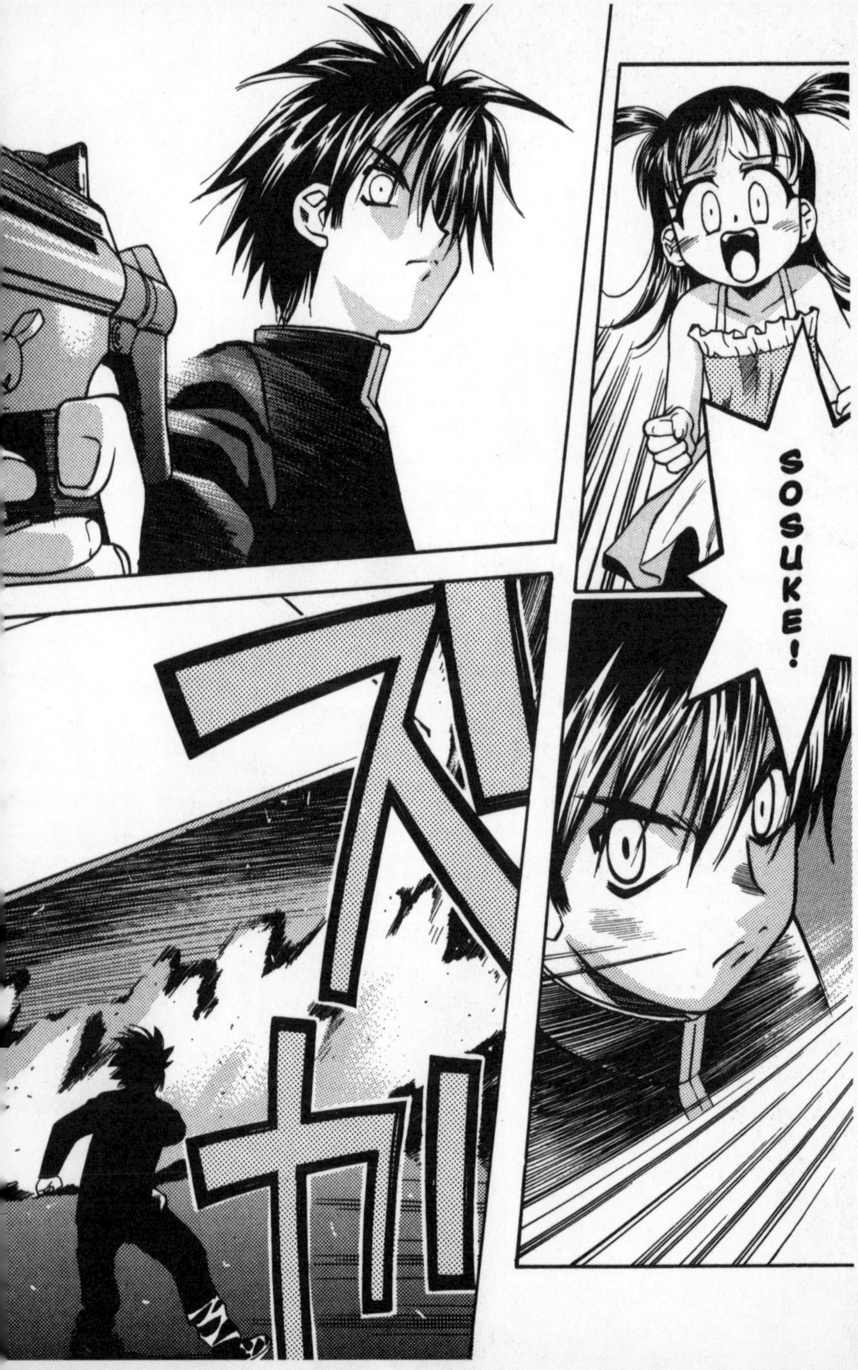
SOSUKE!

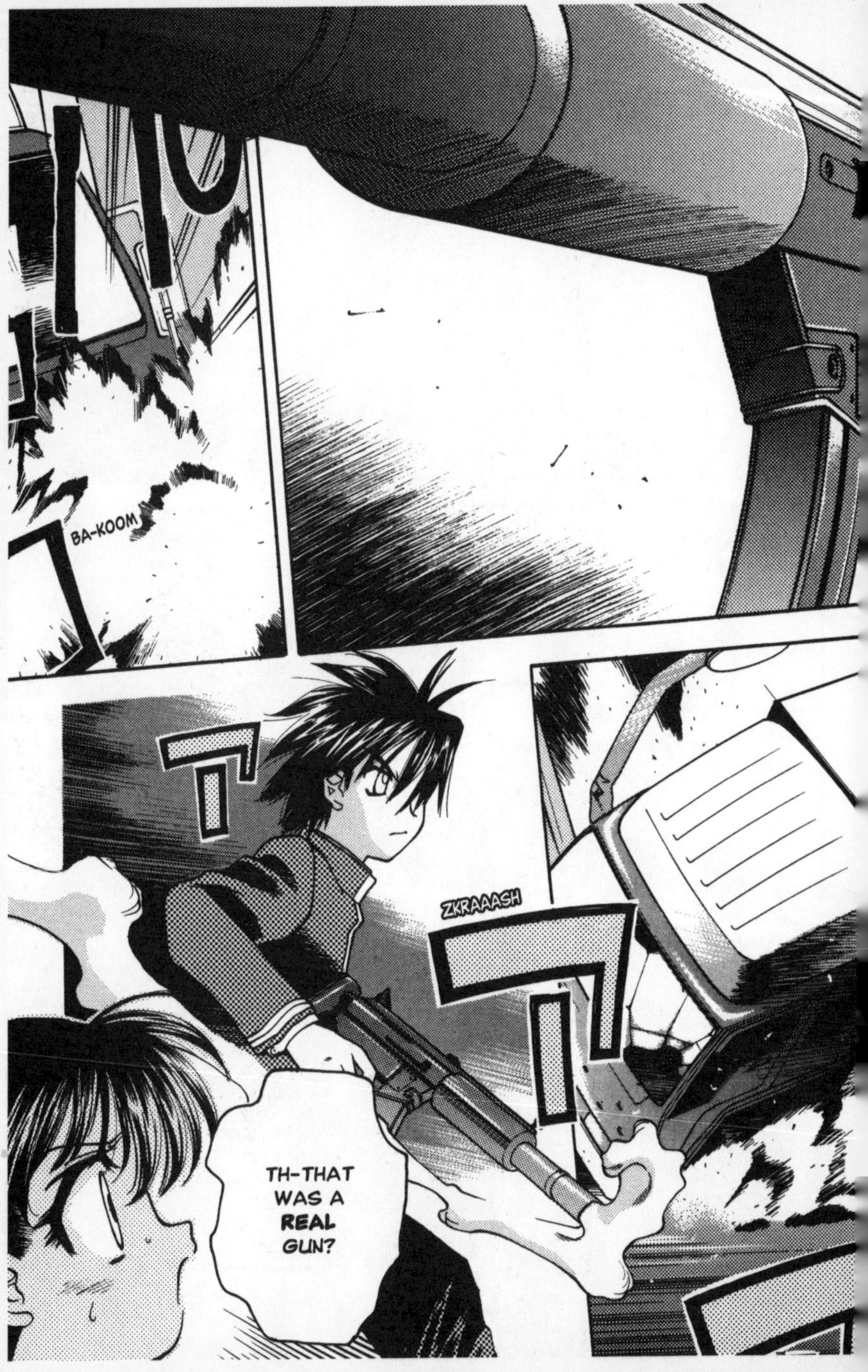
BA-KOOM
ZKRAAASH
TH-THAT WAS A REAL GUN?

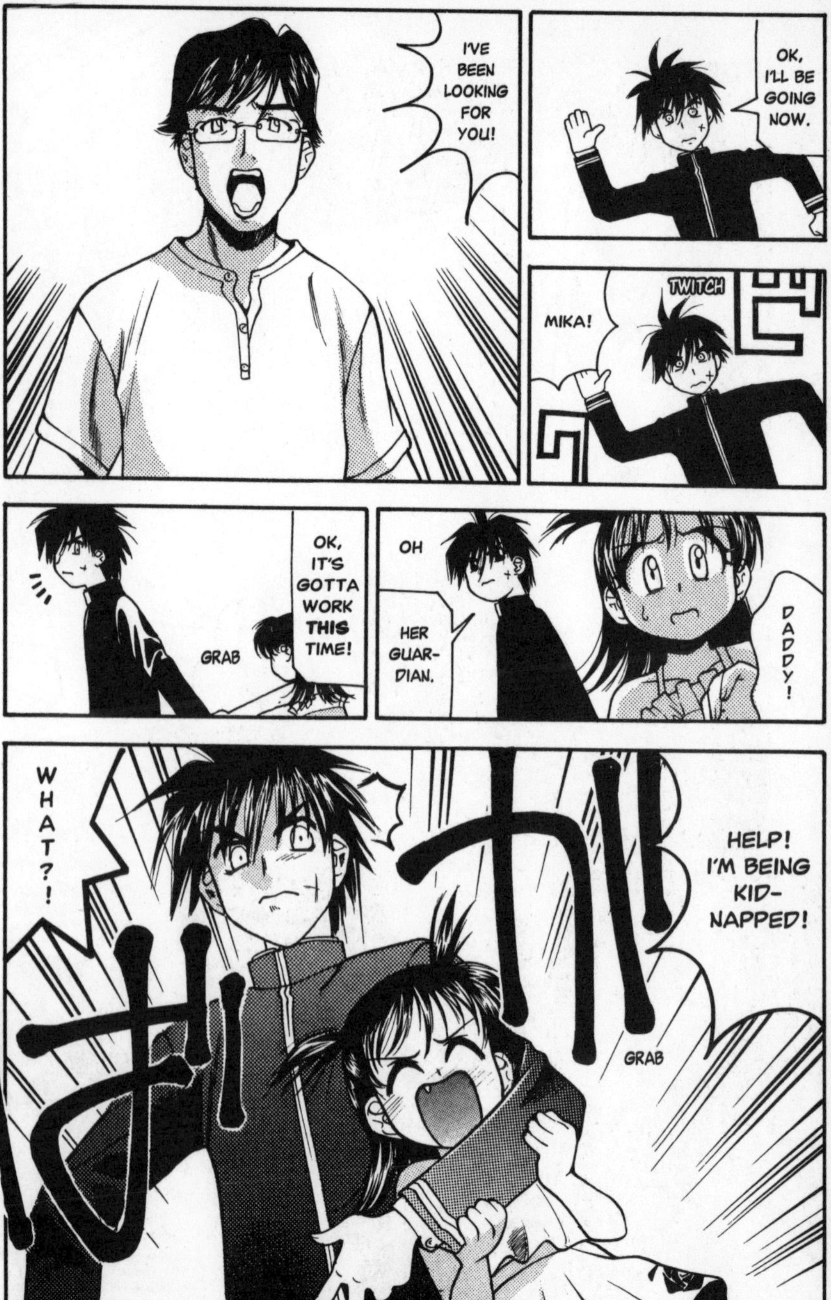
OK, I'LL BE GOING NOW.
TWITCH
MIKA!
I'VE BEEN LOOKING FOR YOU!
DADDY!
OH
HER GUARDIAN.
OK, IT'S GOTTA WORK **THIS** TIME!
GRAB
HELP! I'M BEING KID-NAPPED!
GRAB
WHAT?!

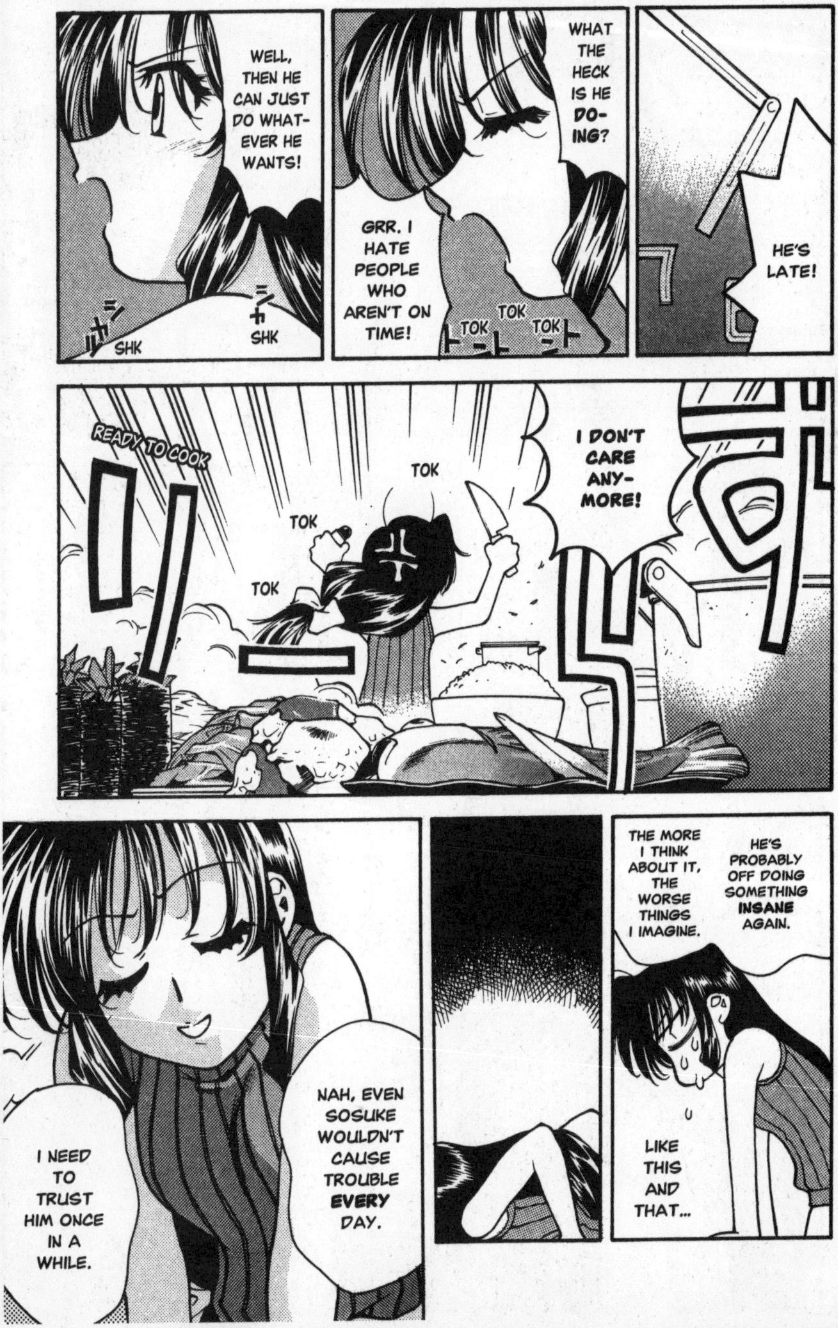

HE'S LATE!
WHAT THE HECK IS HE DOING?
GRR. I HATE PEOPLE WHO AREN'T ON TIME!
TOK TOK TOK
WELL, THEN HE CAN JUST DO WHATEVER HE WANTS!
SHK SHK
I DON'T CARE ANYMORE!
TOK TOK TOK
READY TO COOK
HE'S PROBABLY OFF DOING SOMETHING **INSANE** AGAIN.
THE MORE I THINK ABOUT IT, THE WORSE THINGS I IMAGINE.
LIKE THIS AND THAT...
NAH, EVEN SOSUKE WOULDN'T CAUSE TROUBLE **EVERY** DAY.
I NEED TO TRUST HIM ONCE IN A WHILE.

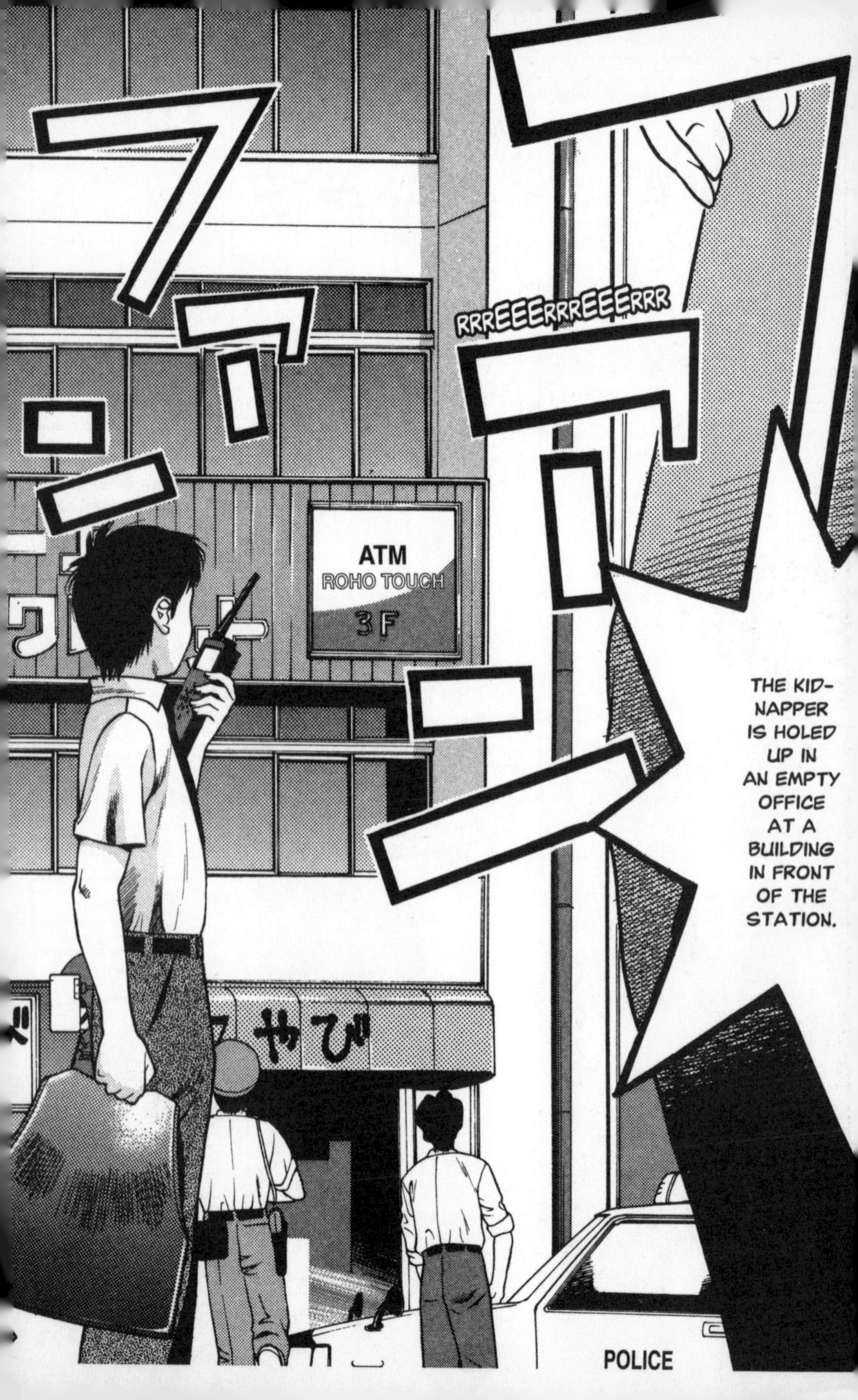
RRREEERRREEERRR
ATM
ROHO TOUCH
3 F
THE KID-
NAPPER
IS HOLED
UP IN
AN EMPTY
OFFICE
AT A
BUILDING
IN FRONT
OF THE
STATION.
POLICE

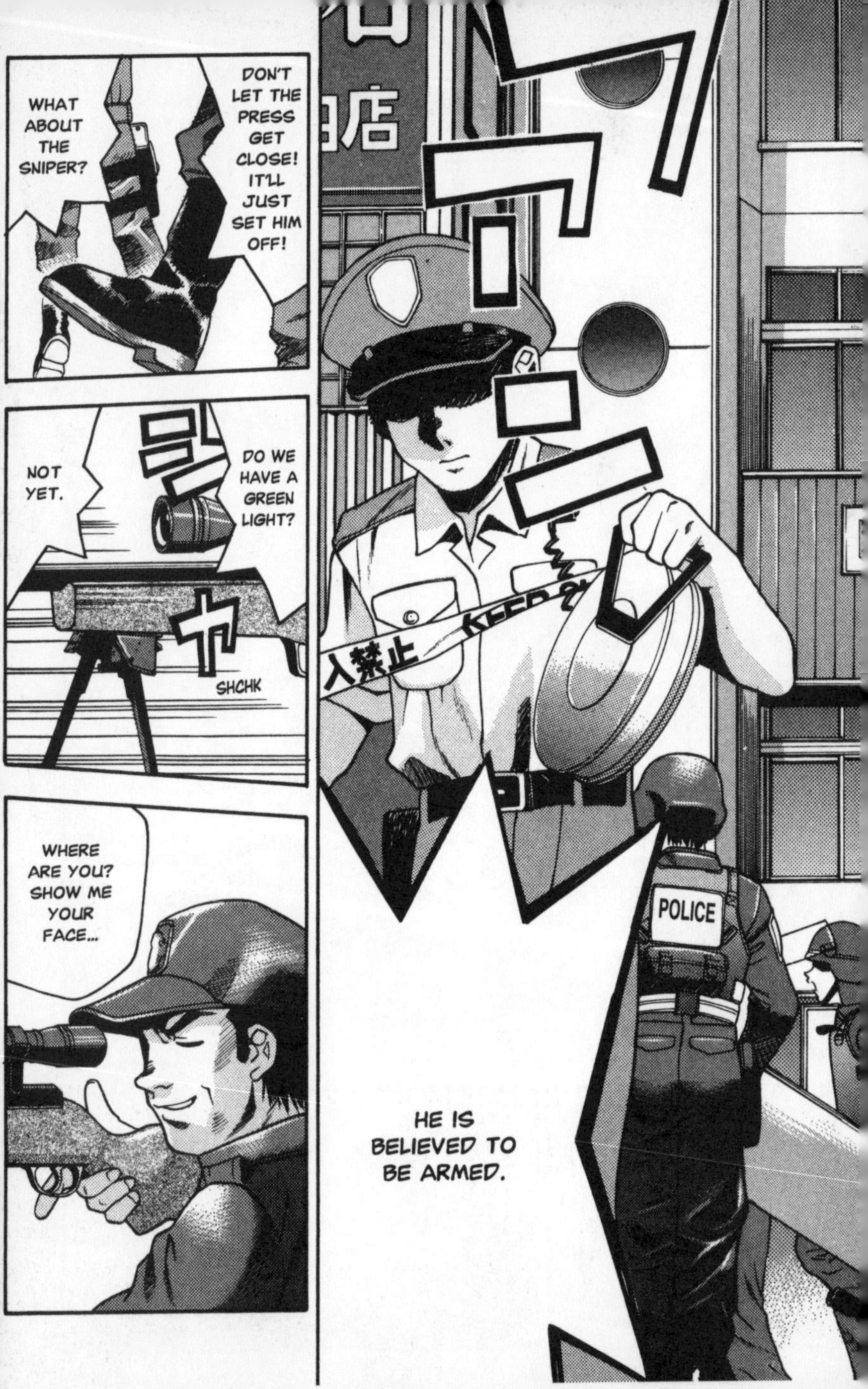

入禁止
POLICE
HE IS BELIEVED TO BE ARMED.
DON'T LET THE PRESS GET CLOSE! IT'LL JUST SET HIM OFF!
WHAT ABOUT THE SNIPER?
DO WE HAVE A GREEN LIGHT?
NOT YET.
SHCHK
WHERE ARE YOU? SHOW ME YOUR FACE...

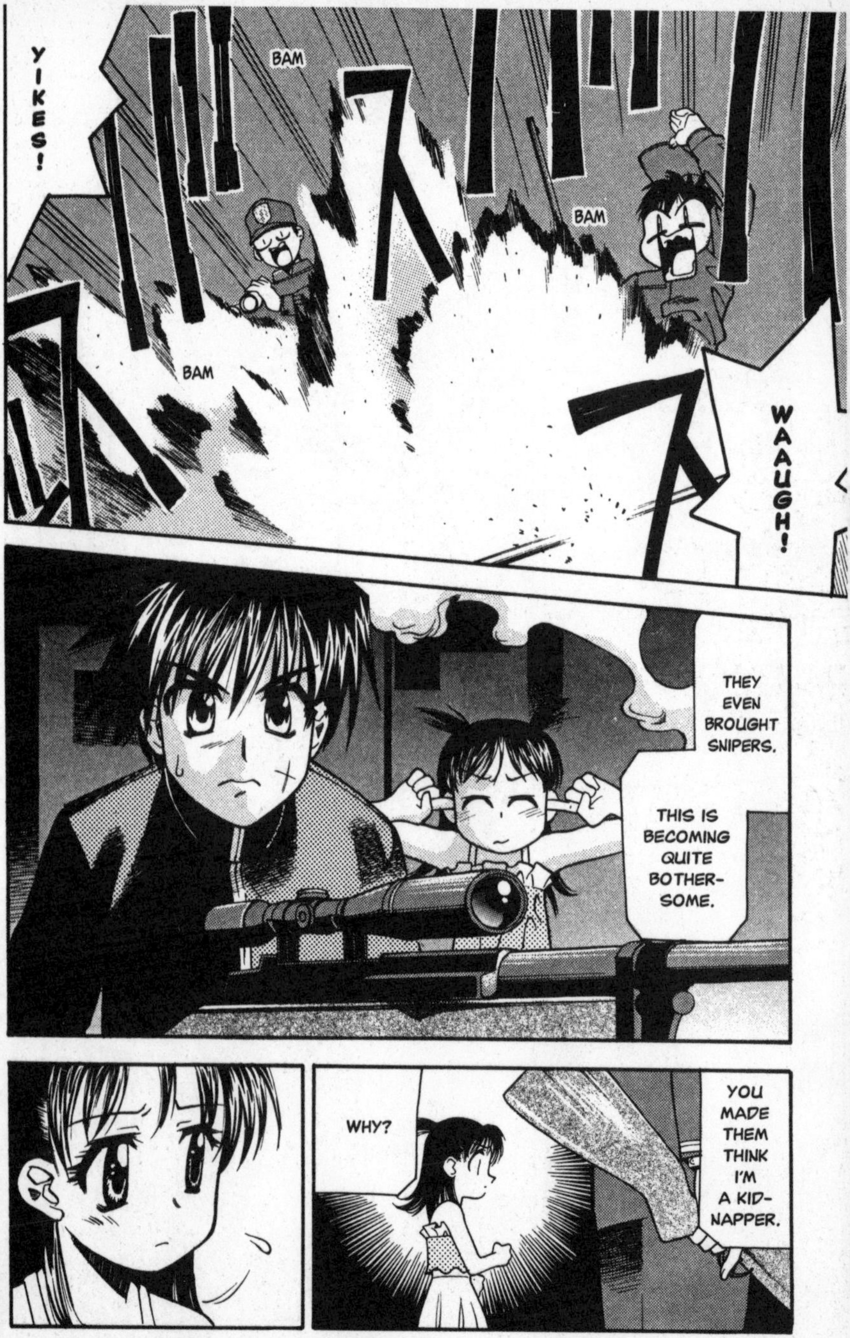
WAAUGH!
BAM
BAM
BAM
YIKES!
THEY EVEN BROUGHT SNIPERS.
THIS IS BECOMING QUITE BOTHER-SOME.
YOU MADE THEM THINK I'M A KID-NAPPER.
WHY?

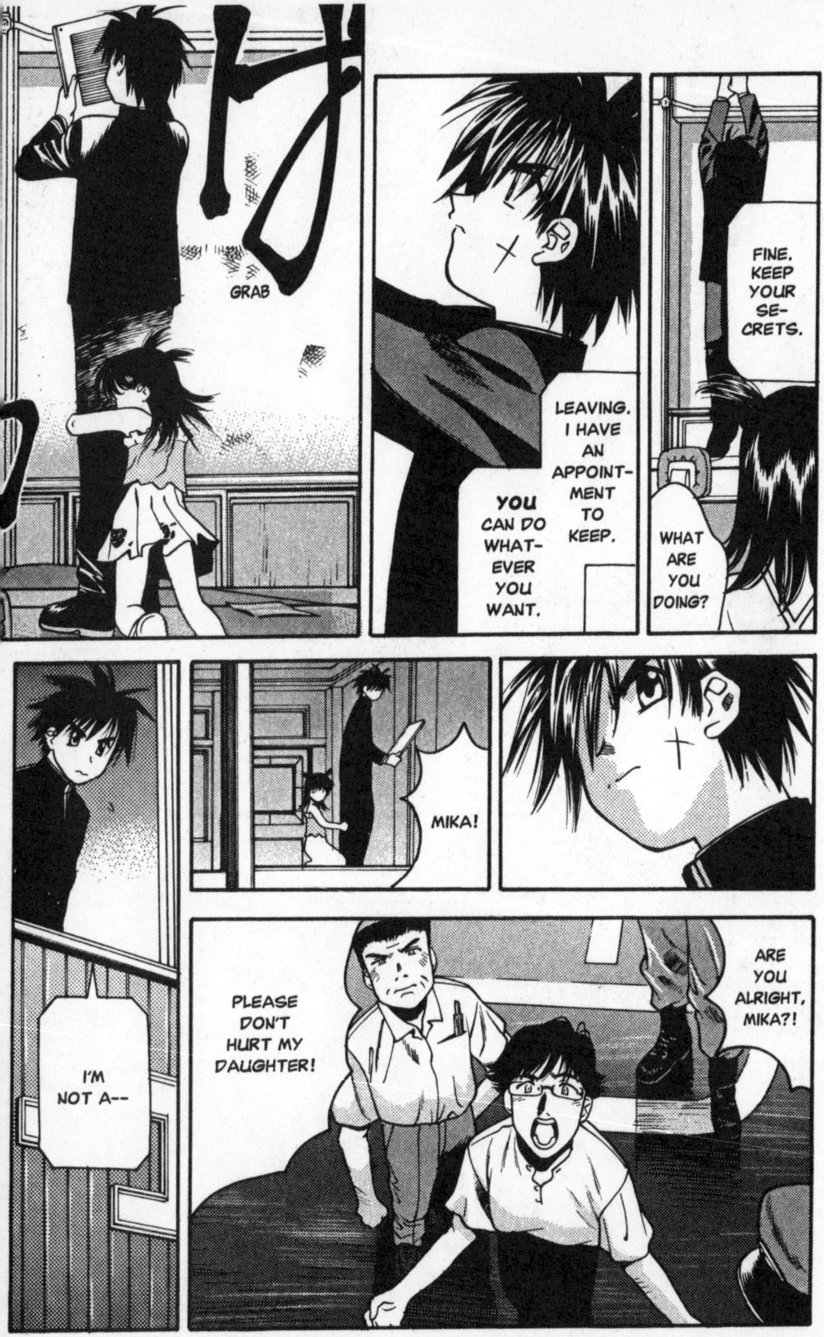
FINE. KEEP YOUR SE-CRETS.
WHAT ARE YOU DOING?
LEAVING. I HAVE AN APPOINTMENT TO KEEP.
YOU CAN DO WHATEVER YOU WANT.
GRAB
MIKA!
ARE YOU ALRIGHT, MIKA?!
PLEASE DON'T HURT MY DAUGHTER!
I'M NOT A--

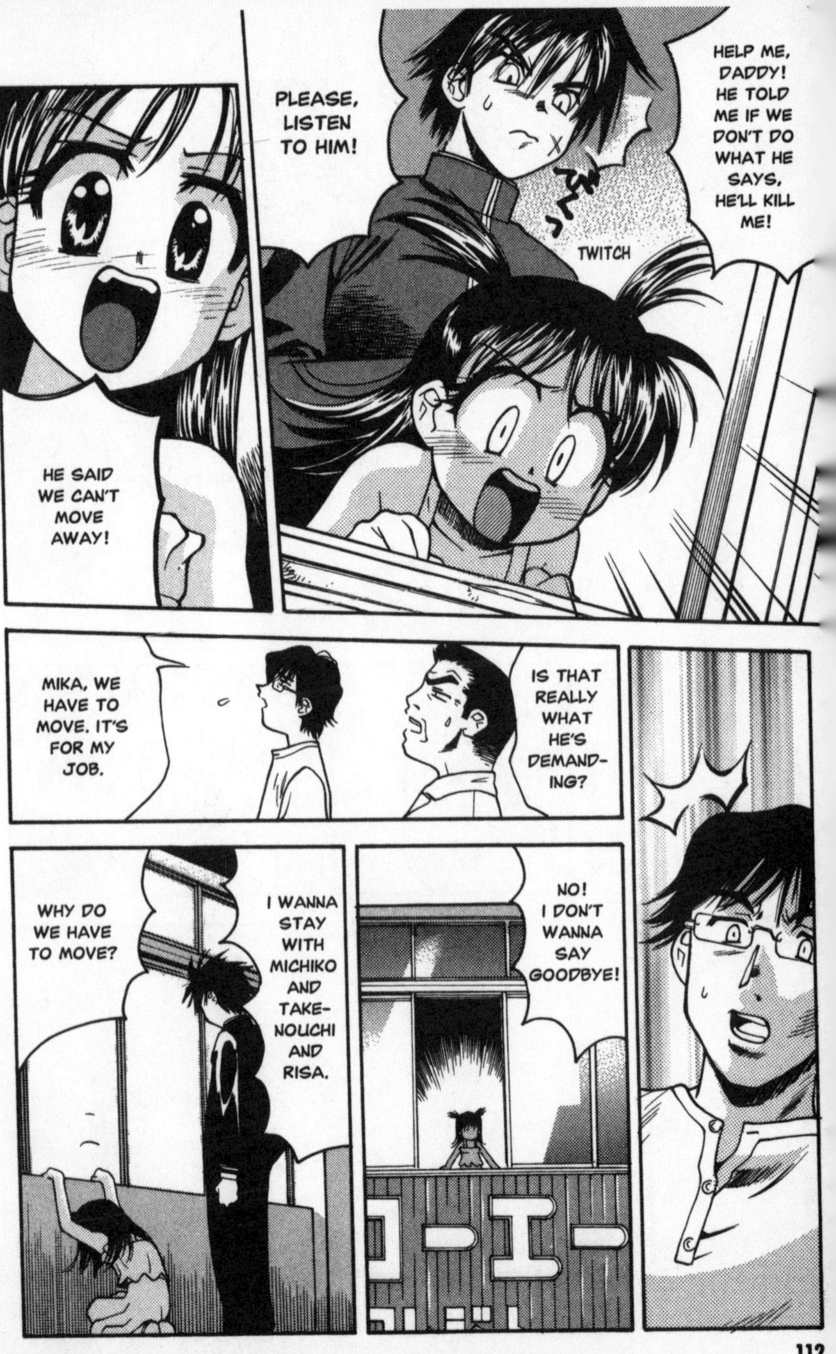
HELP ME, DADDY! HE TOLD ME IF WE DON'T DO WHAT HE SAYS, HE'LL KILL ME!
TWITCH
PLEASE, LISTEN TO HIM!
HE SAID WE CAN'T MOVE AWAY!
IS THAT REALLY WHAT HE'S DEMAND-ING?
MIKA, WE HAVE TO MOVE. IT'S FOR MY JOB.
NO! I DON'T WANNA SAY GOODBYE!
I WANNA STAY WITH MICHIKO AND TAKE-NOUCHI AND RISA.
WHY DO WE HAVE TO MOVE?

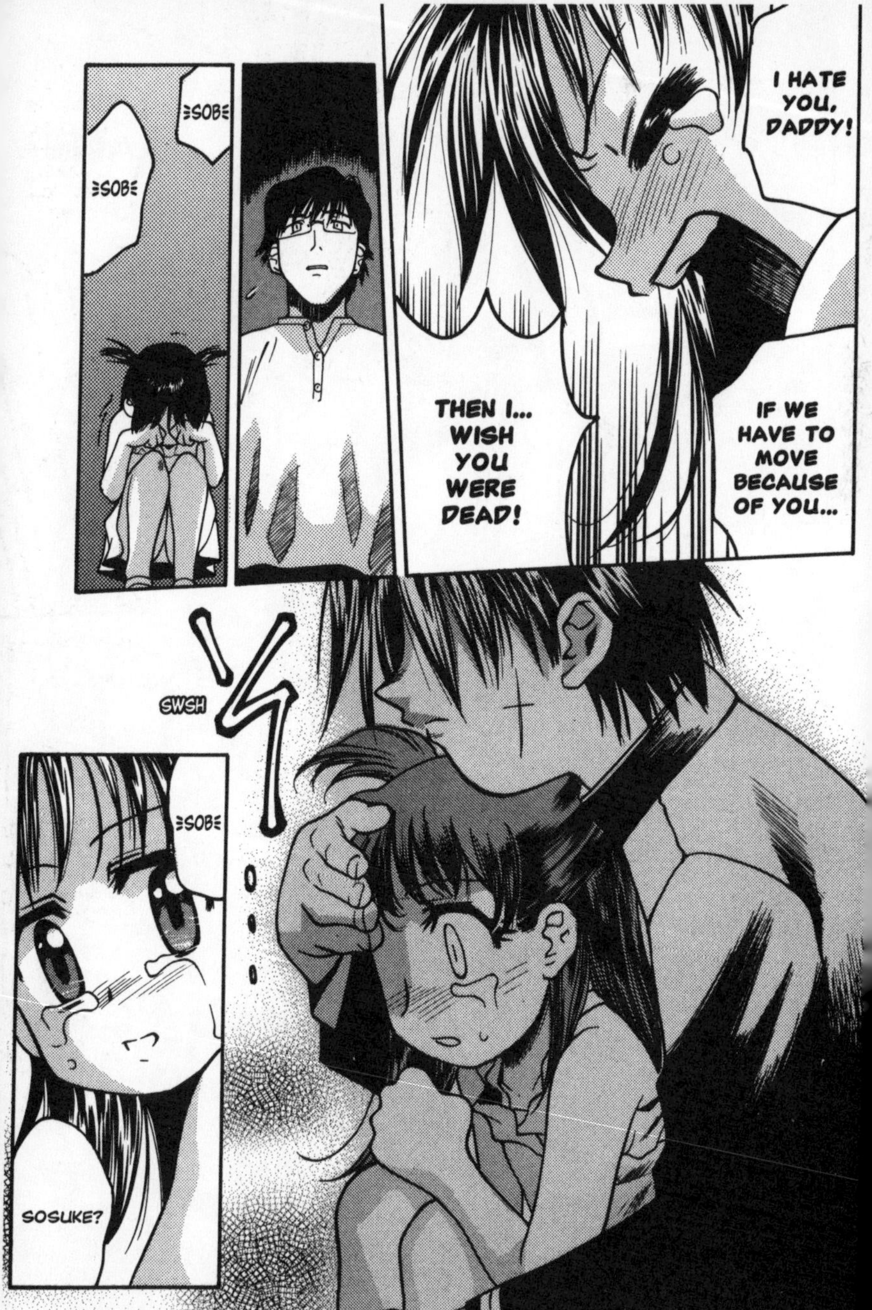

I HATE YOU, DADDY!
IF WE HAVE TO MOVE BECAUSE OF YOU...
THEN I... WISH YOU WERE DEAD!
SOB
SOB
SWSH
...
SOB
SOSUKE?

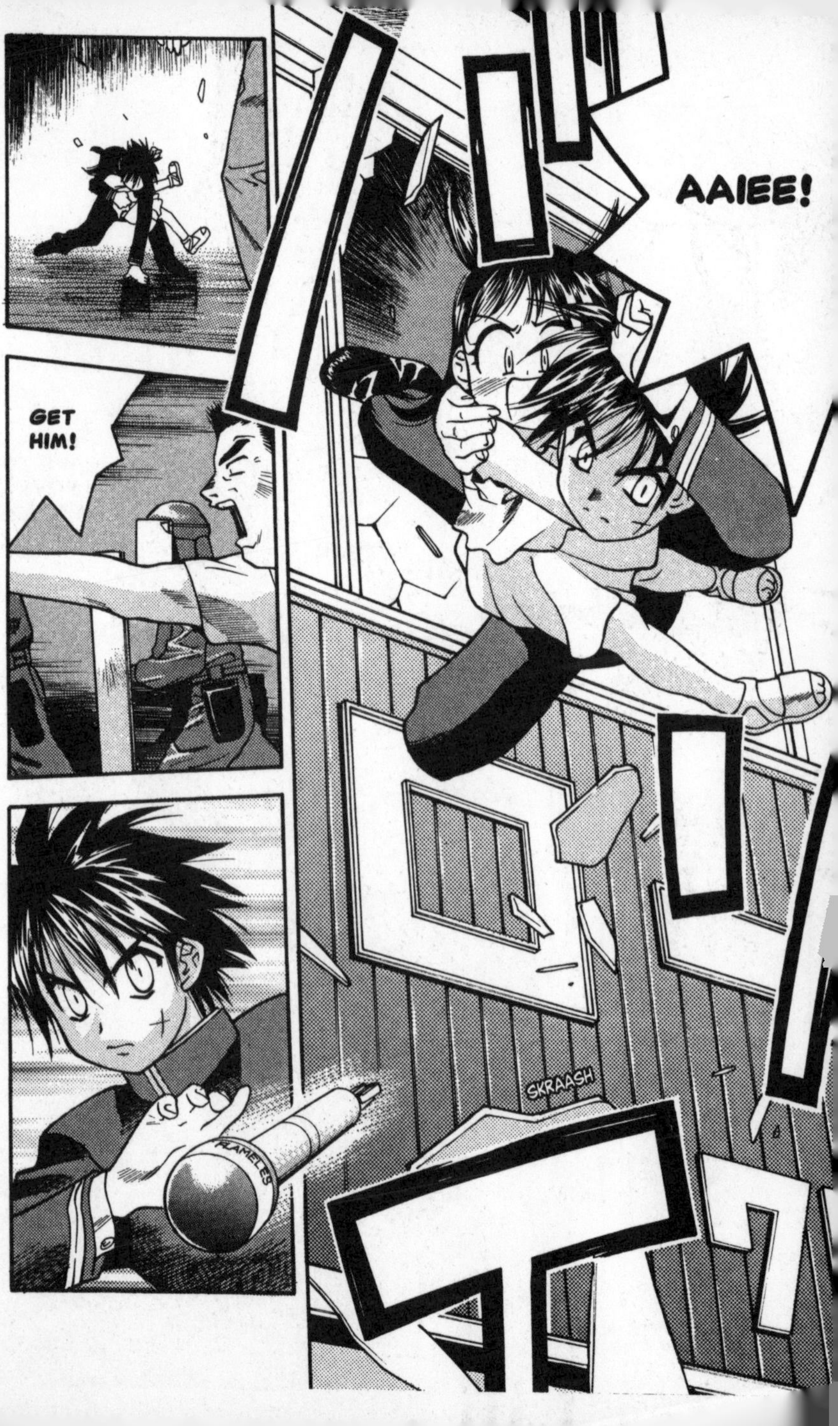
AAIEE!
SKRAASH
GET HIM!

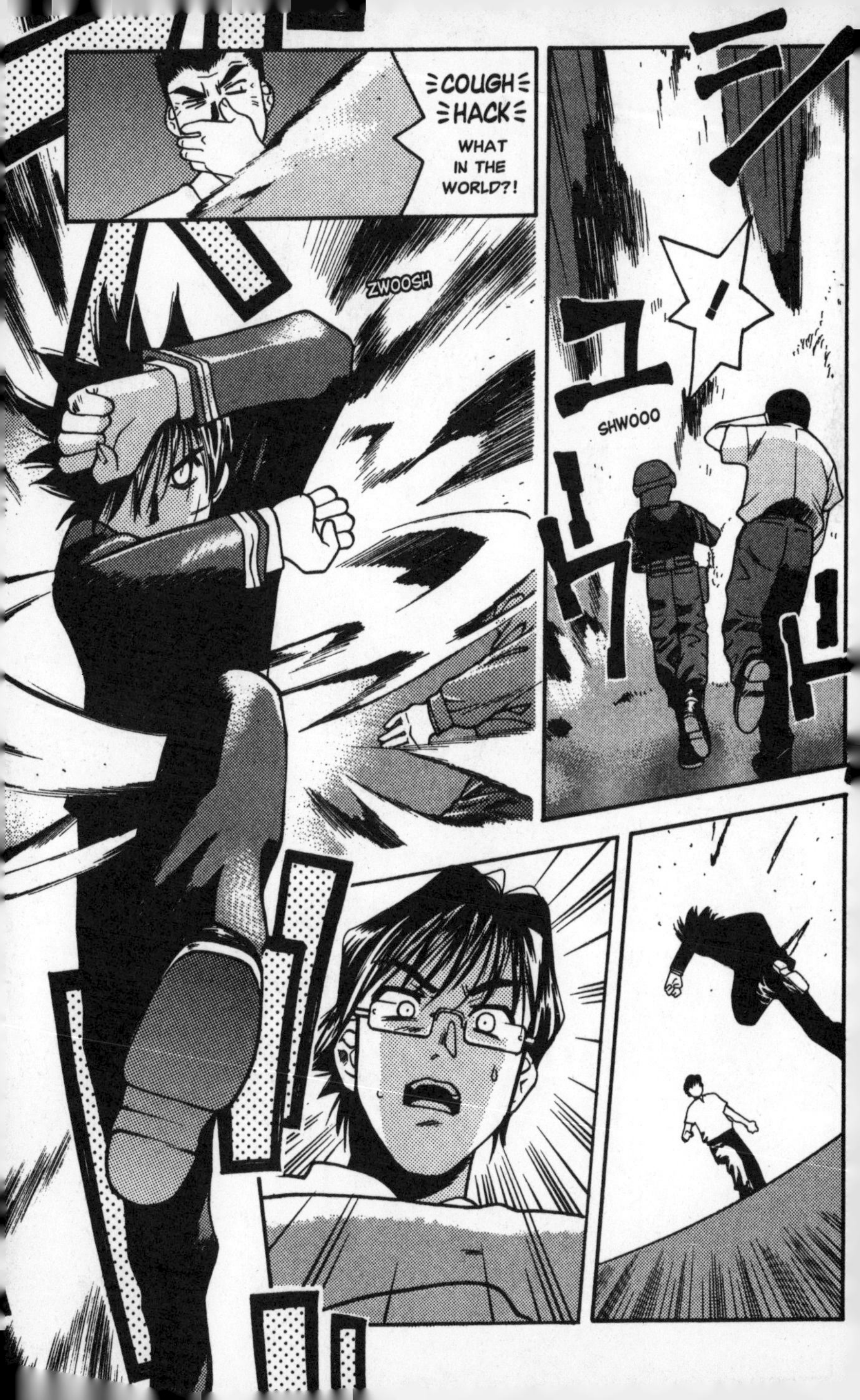
COUGH
HACK
WHAT IN THE WORLD?!
SHWOOO
ZWOOSH

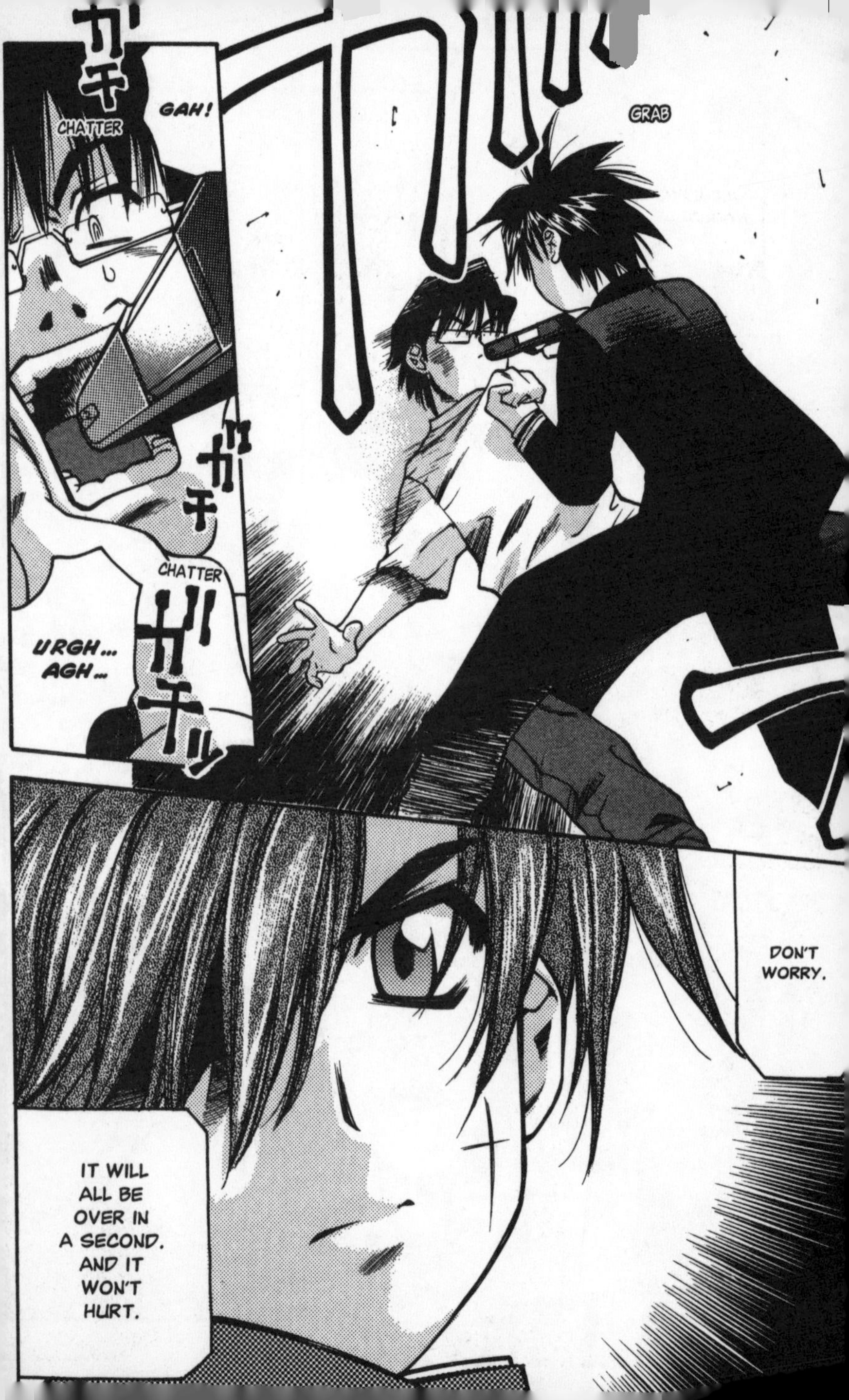
GRAB
ガチ
GAH!
CHATTER
ガチ
CHATTER
ガチガチッ
URGH... AGH...
DON'T WORRY.
IT WILL ALL BE OVER IN A SECOND. AND IT WON'T HURT.

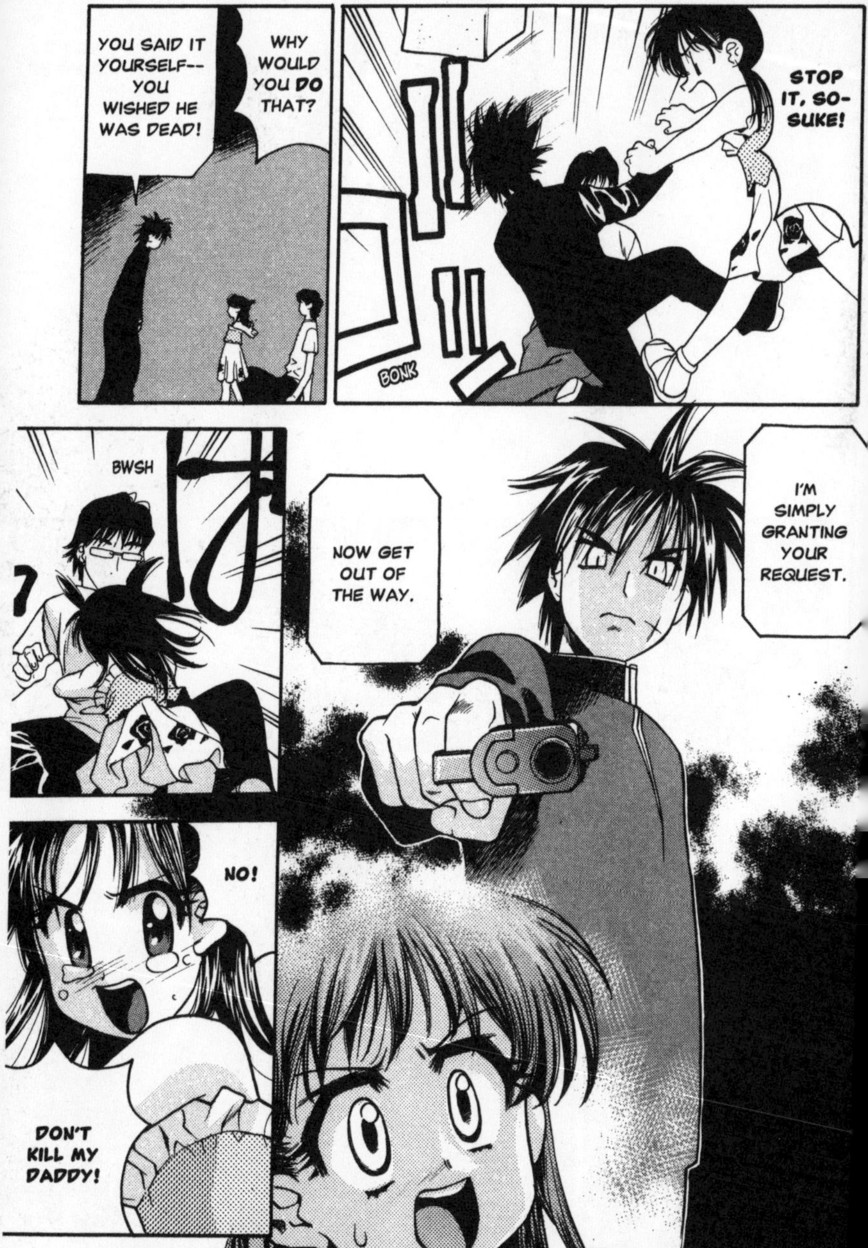
STOP IT, SO-SUKE!
BONK
WHY WOULD YOU DO THAT?
YOU SAID IT YOURSELF-- YOU WISHED HE WAS DEAD!
I'M SIMPLY GRANTING YOUR REQUEST.
NOW GET OUT OF THE WAY.
BWSH
NO!
DON'T KILL MY DADDY!

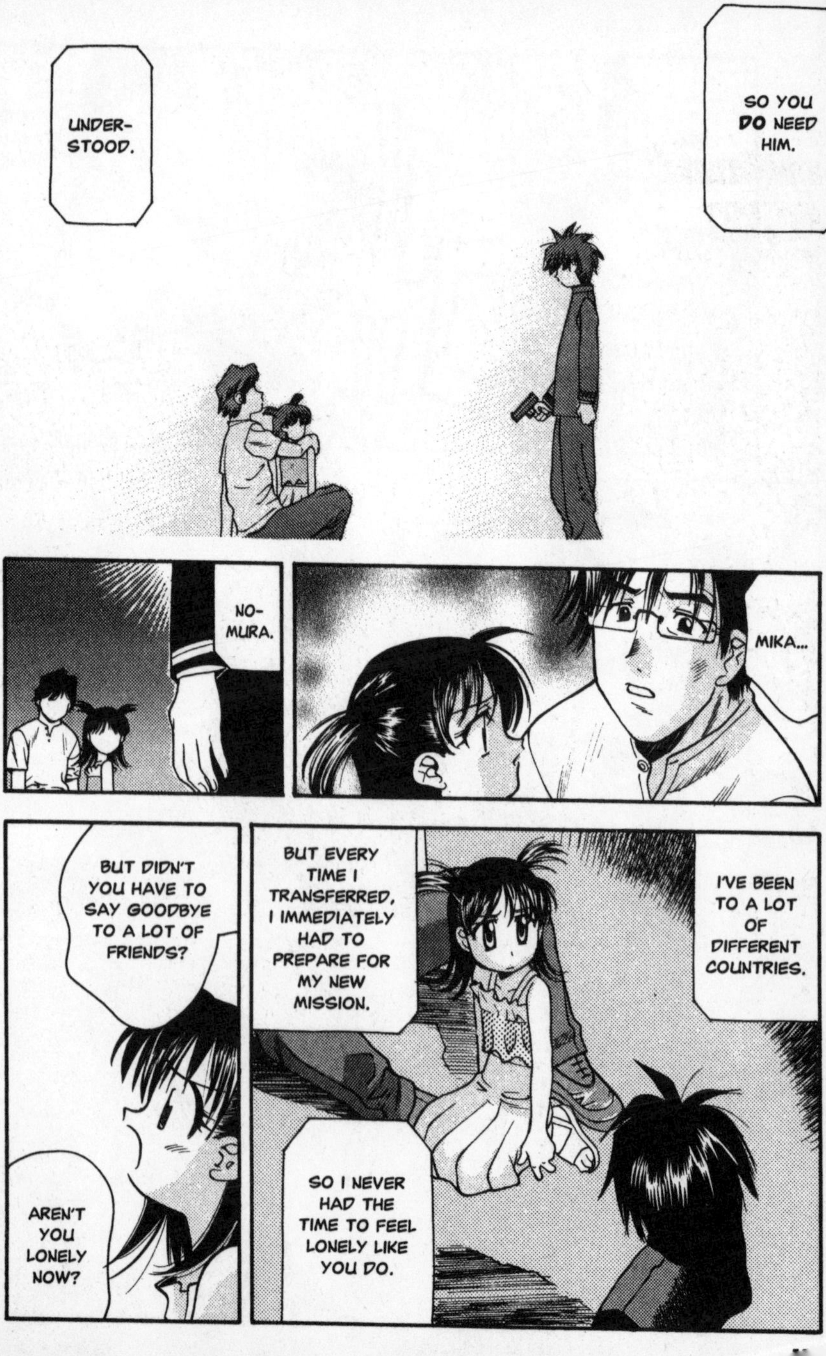
SO YOU DO NEED HIM.
UNDER-STOOD.
MIKA...
NO-MURA.
I'VE BEEN TO A LOT OF DIFFERENT COUNTRIES.
BUT EVERY TIME I TRANSFERRED, I IMMEDIATELY HAD TO PREPARE FOR MY NEW MISSION.
SO I NEVER HAD THE TIME TO FEEL LONELY LIKE YOU DO.
BUT DIDN'T YOU HAVE TO SAY GOODBYE TO A LOT OF FRIENDS?
AREN'T YOU LONELY NOW?

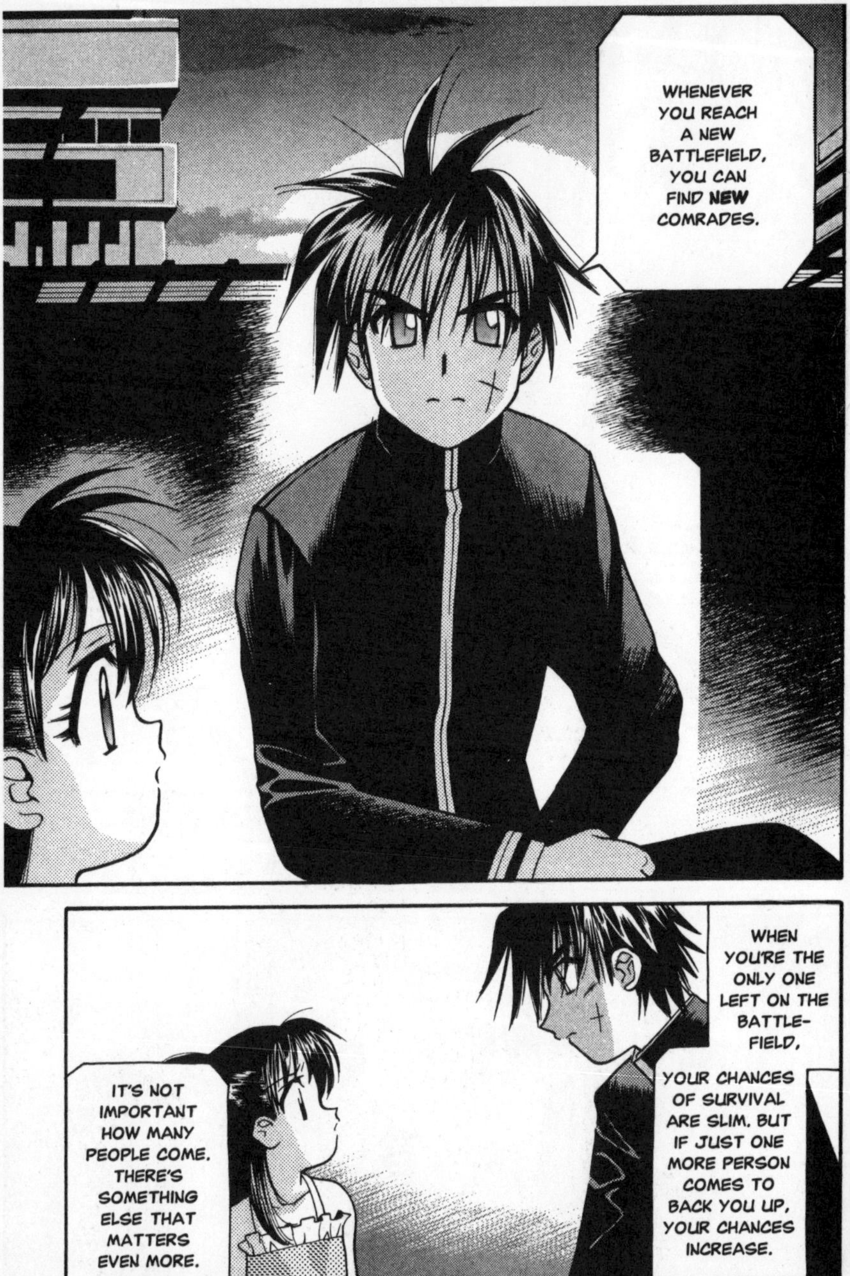
WHENEVER YOU REACH A NEW BATTLEFIELD, YOU CAN FIND **NEW** COMRADES.
WHEN YOU'RE THE ONLY ONE LEFT ON THE BATTLE-FIELD,
YOUR CHANCES OF SURVIVAL ARE SLIM. BUT IF JUST ONE MORE PERSON COMES TO BACK YOU UP, YOUR CHANCES INCREASE.
IT'S NOT IMPORTANT HOW MANY PEOPLE COME. THERE'S SOMETHING ELSE THAT MATTERS EVEN MORE.

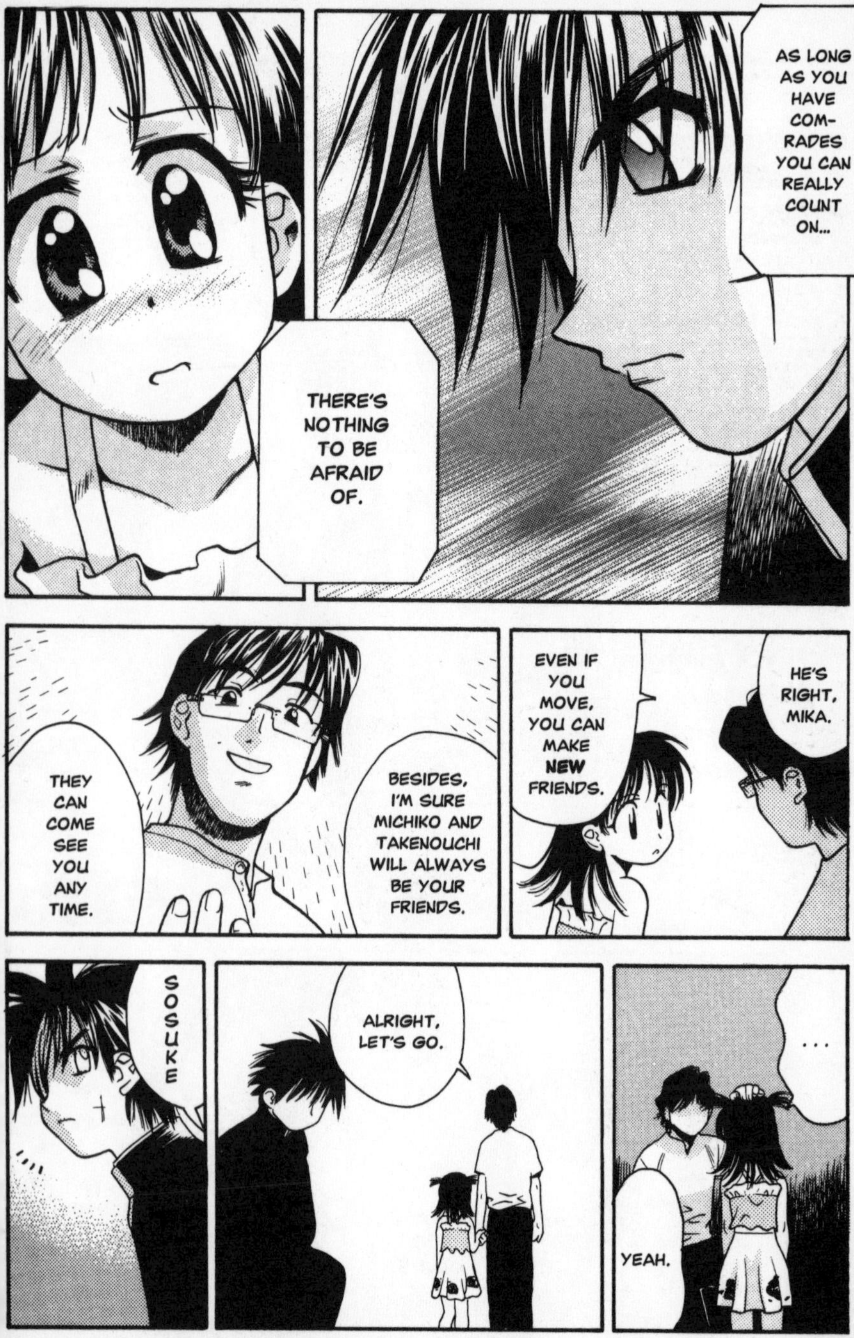
AS LONG AS YOU HAVE COM-RADES YOU CAN REALLY COUNT ON...
THERE'S NOTHING TO BE AFRAID OF.
HE'S RIGHT, MIKA.
EVEN IF YOU MOVE, YOU CAN MAKE NEW FRIENDS.
BESIDES, I'M SURE MICHIKO AND TAKENOUCHI WILL ALWAYS BE YOUR FRIENDS.
THEY CAN COME SEE YOU ANY TIME.
...
YEAH.
ALRIGHT, LET'S GO.
SOSUKE

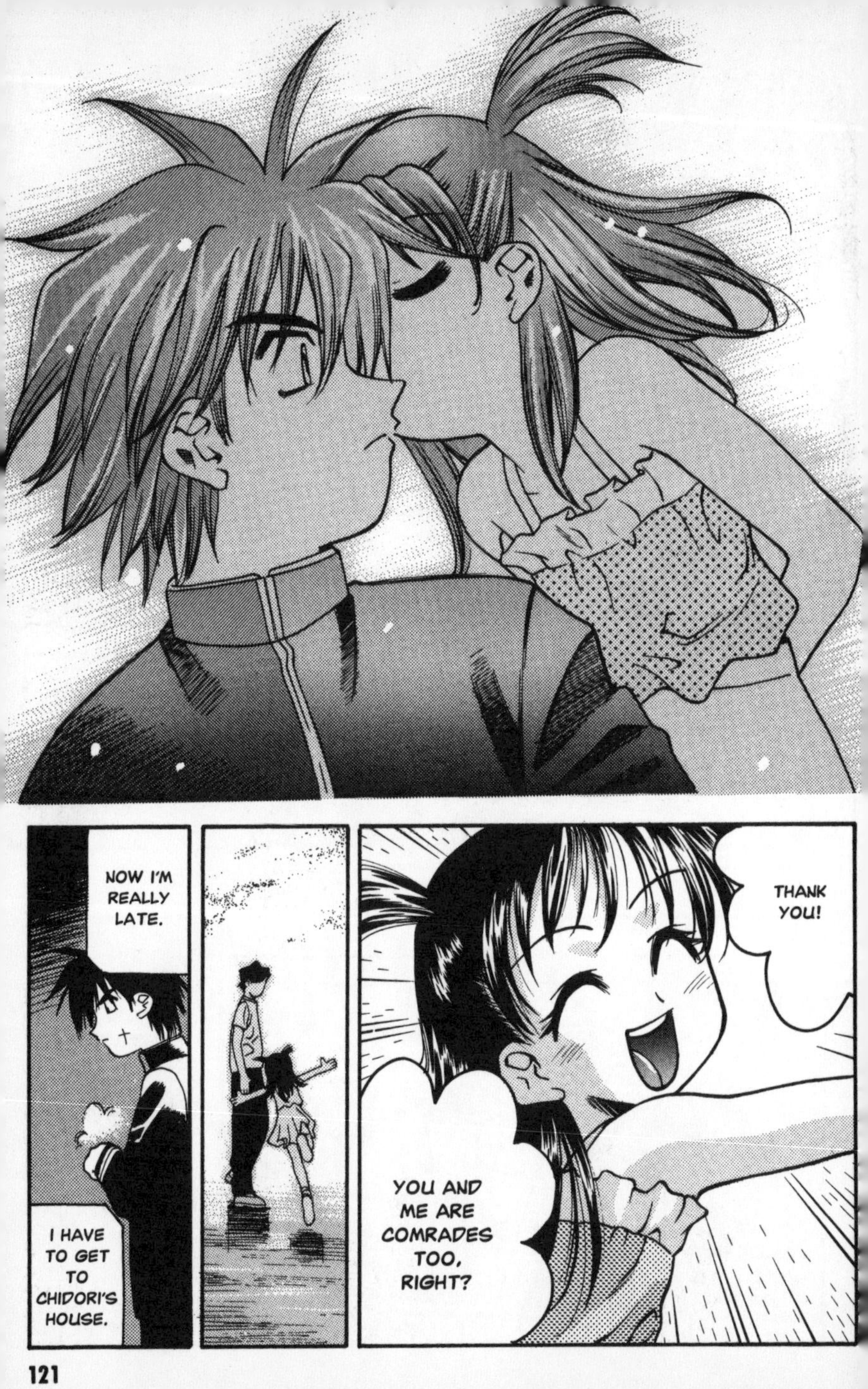
THANK YOU!
YOU AND ME ARE COMRADES TOO, RIGHT?
NOW I'M REALLY LATE.
I HAVE TO GET TO CHIDORI'S HOUSE.

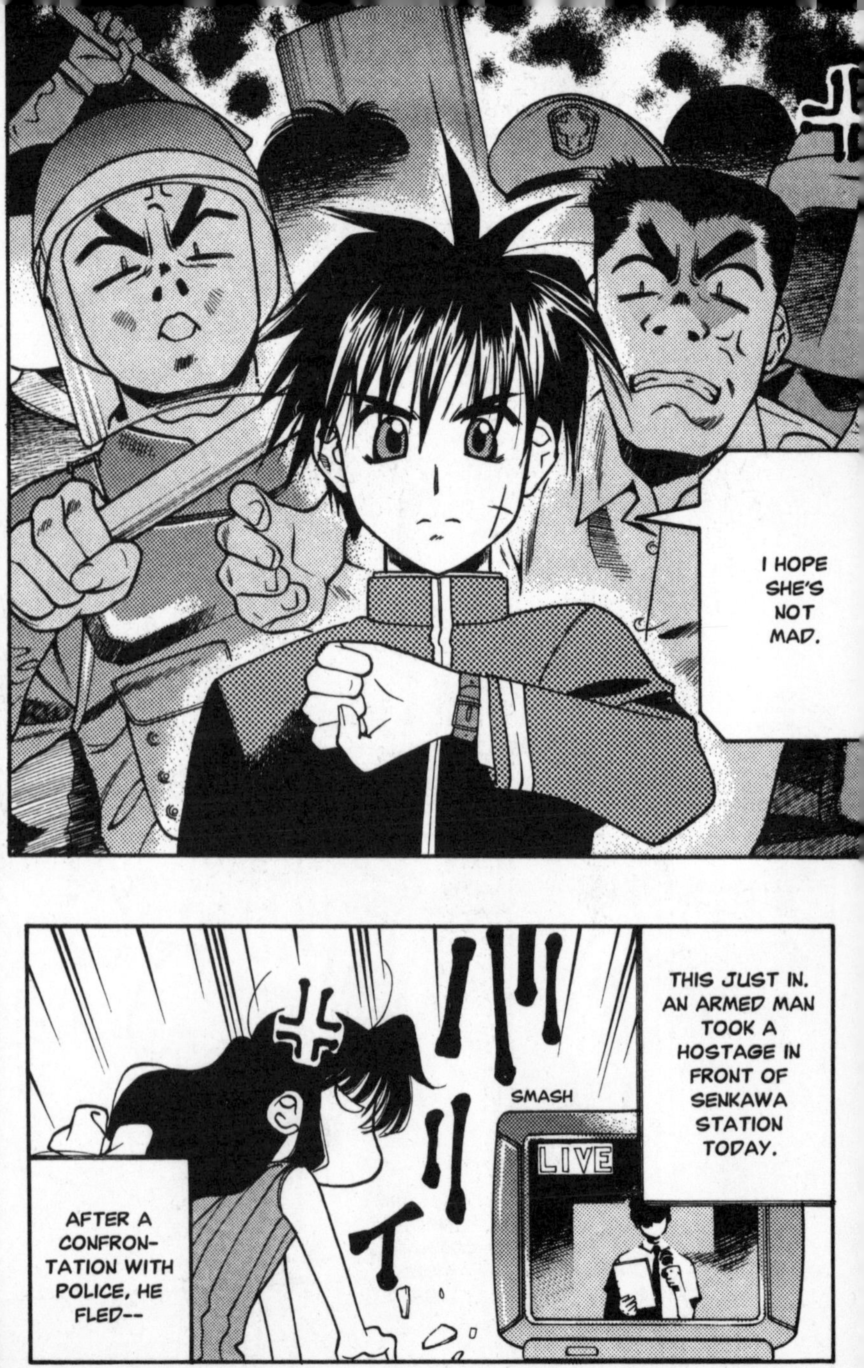
I HOPE SHE'S NOT MAD.
THIS JUST IN. AN ARMED MAN TOOK A HOSTAGE IN FRONT OF SENKAWA STATION TODAY.
LIVE
SMASH
AFTER A CONFRON-TATION WITH POLICE, HE FLED--

BOMB 5 THE LURE OF THE POOL

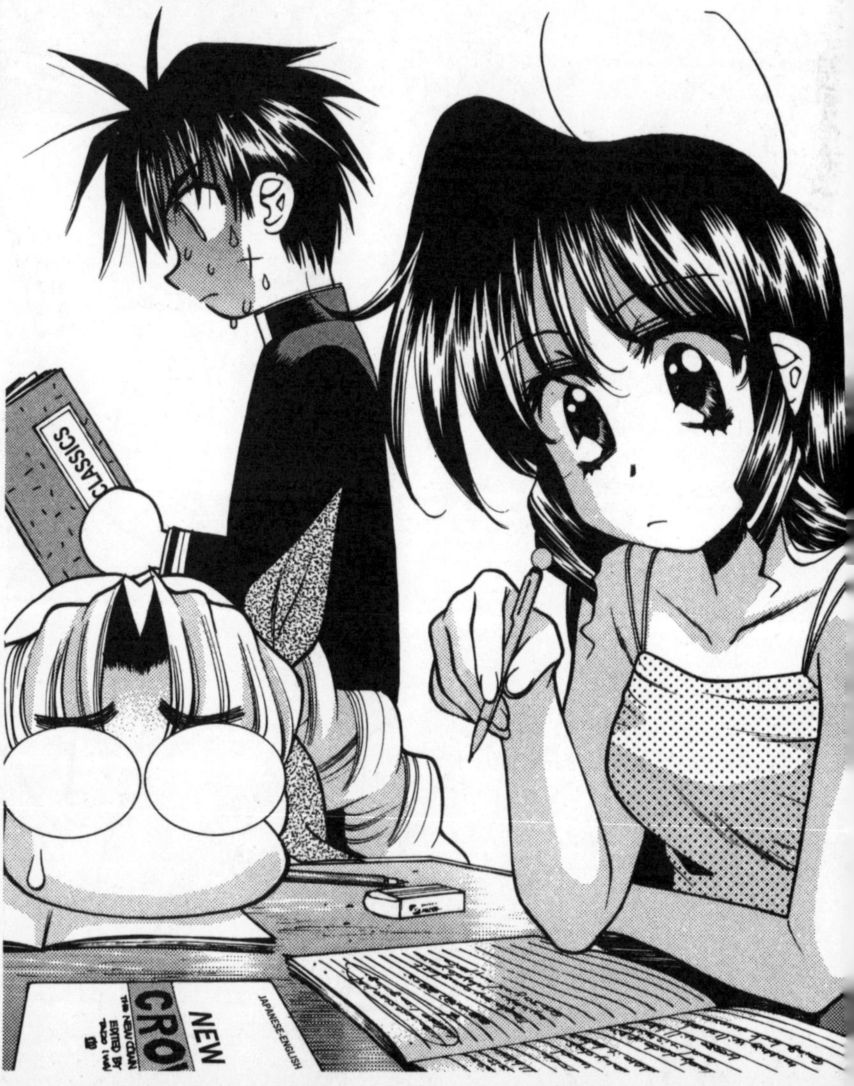

CLASSICS
NEW
CRO
JAPANESE-ENGLISH

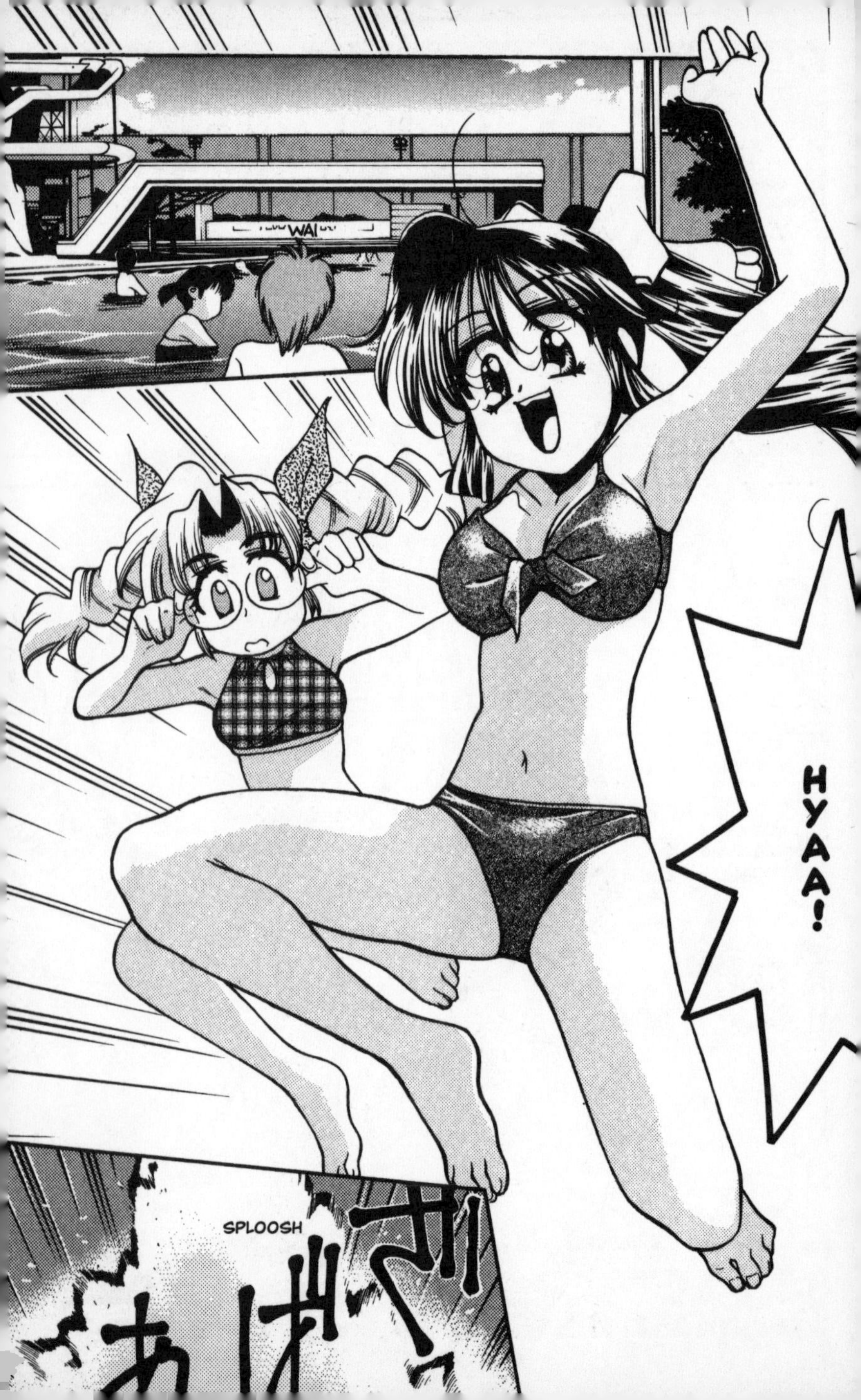
WAI
HYAA!
SPLOOSH

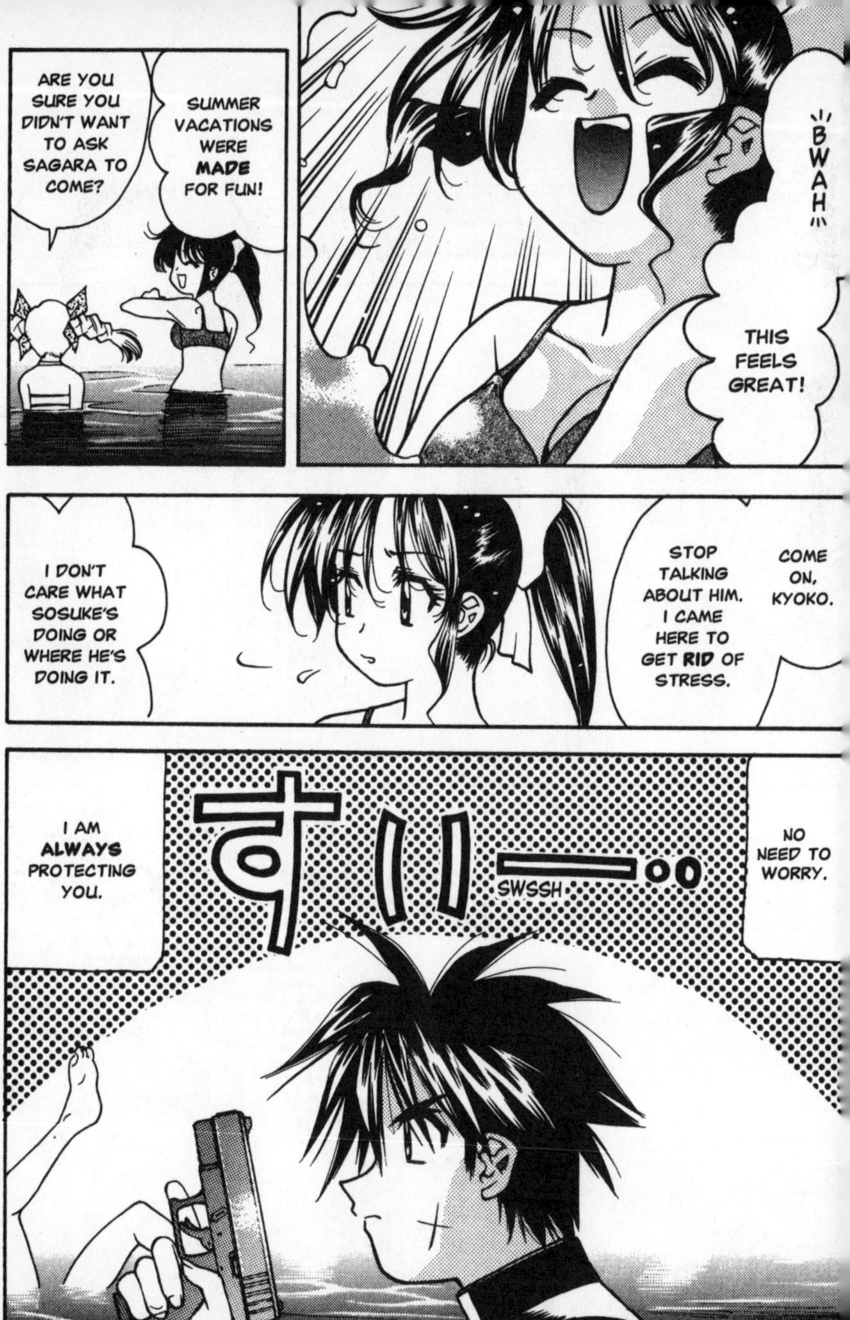
BWAH
THIS FEELS GREAT!
SUMMER VACATIONS WERE MADE FOR FUN!
ARE YOU SURE YOU DIDN'T WANT TO ASK SAGARA TO COME?
COME ON, KYOKO.
STOP TALKING ABOUT HIM. I CAME HERE TO GET RID OF STRESS.
I DON'T CARE WHAT SOSUKE'S DOING OR WHERE HE'S DOING IT.
NO NEED TO WORRY.
すいーっ
SWSSH
I AM ALWAYS PROTECTING YOU.

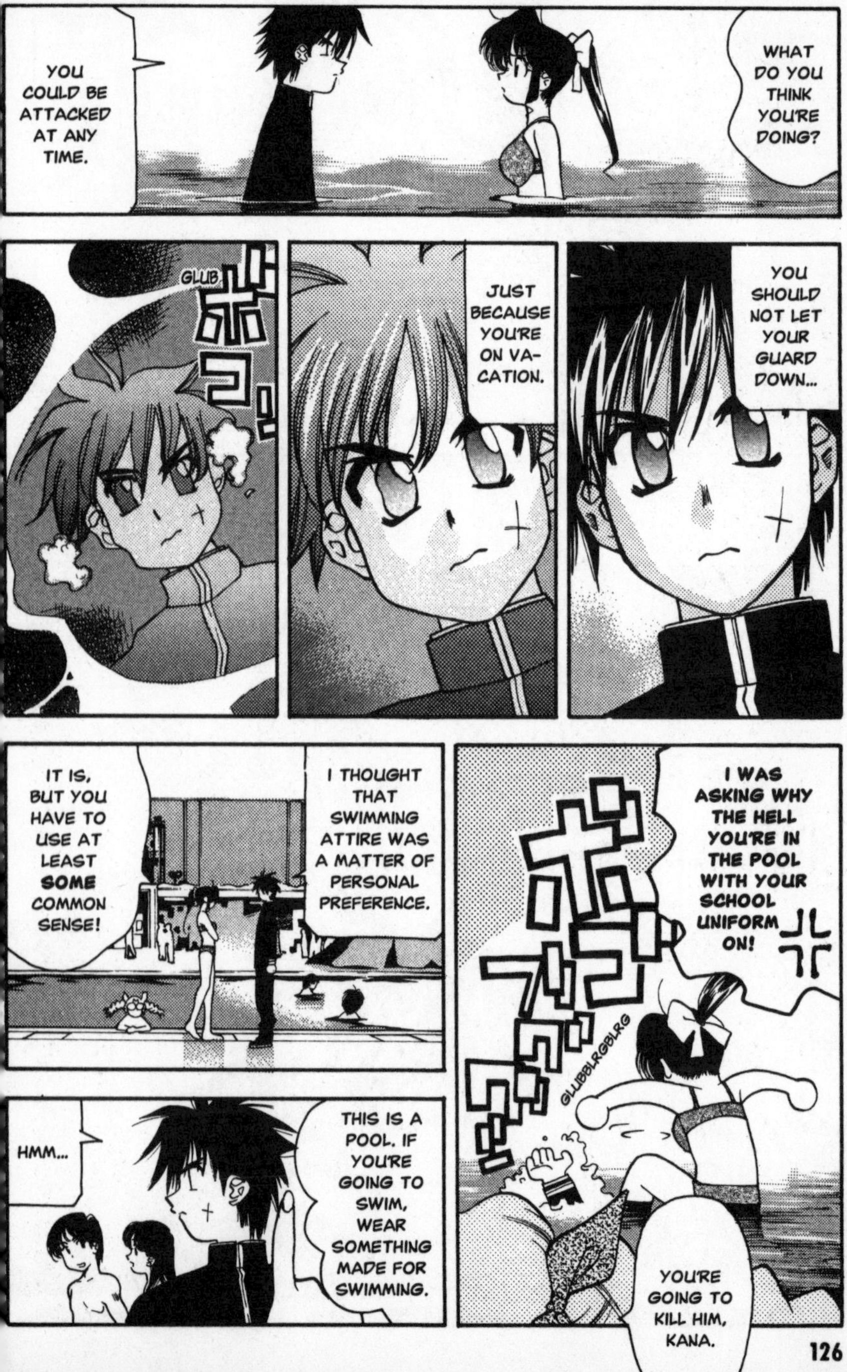
WHAT DO YOU THINK YOU'RE DOING?
YOU COULD BE ATTACKED AT ANY TIME.
YOU SHOULD NOT LET YOUR GUARD DOWN...
JUST BECAUSE YOU'RE ON VACATION.
GLUB
I WAS ASKING WHY THE HELL YOU'RE IN THE POOL WITH YOUR SCHOOL UNIFORM ON!
GLUBBLRGBLRG
YOU'RE GOING TO KILL HIM, KANA.
I THOUGHT THAT SWIMMING ATTIRE WAS A MATTER OF PERSONAL PREFERENCE.
IT IS, BUT YOU HAVE TO USE AT LEAST SOME COMMON SENSE!
THIS IS A POOL. IF YOU'RE GOING TO SWIM, WEAR SOMETHING MADE FOR SWIMMING.
HMM...

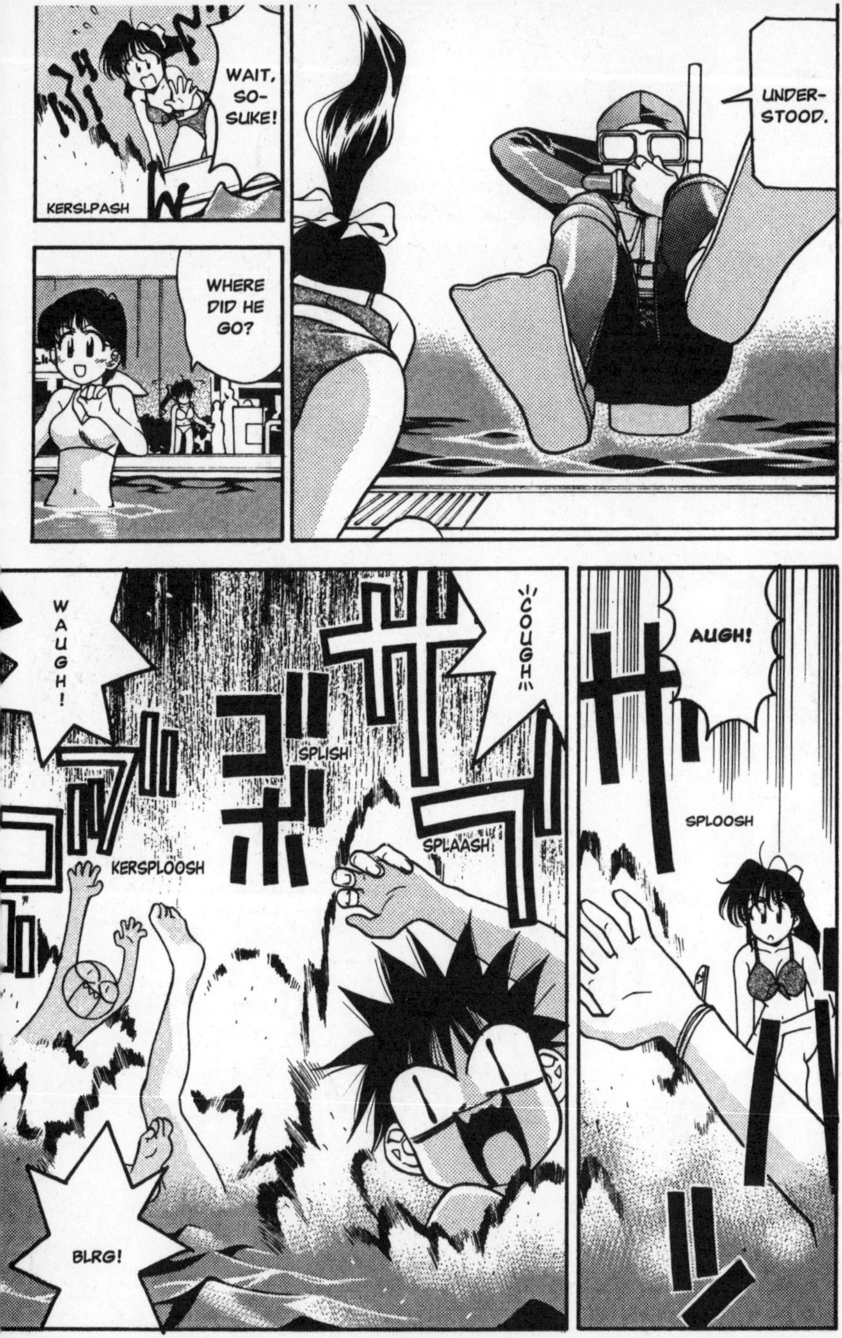
UNDER-STOOD.
WAIT, SO-SUKE!
KERSLPASH
WHERE DID HE GO?
AUGH!
SPLOOSH
COUGH
SPLAASH
SPLISH
WAUGH!
KERSPLOOSH
BLRG!

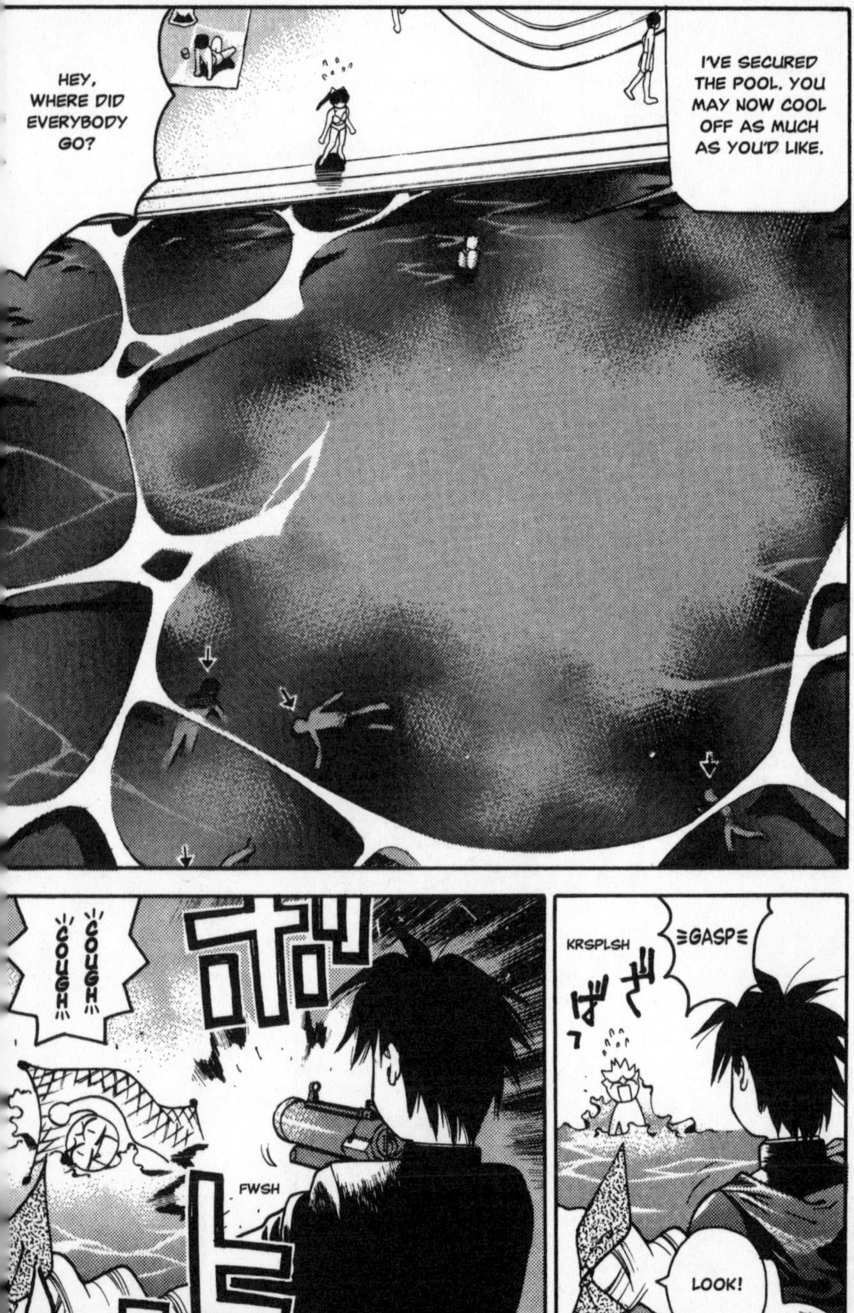
I'VE SECURED THE POOL. YOU MAY NOW COOL OFF AS MUCH AS YOU'D LIKE.
HEY, WHERE DID EVERYBODY GO?
≡GASP≡
KRSPLSH
LOOK!
COUGH COUGH
FWSH

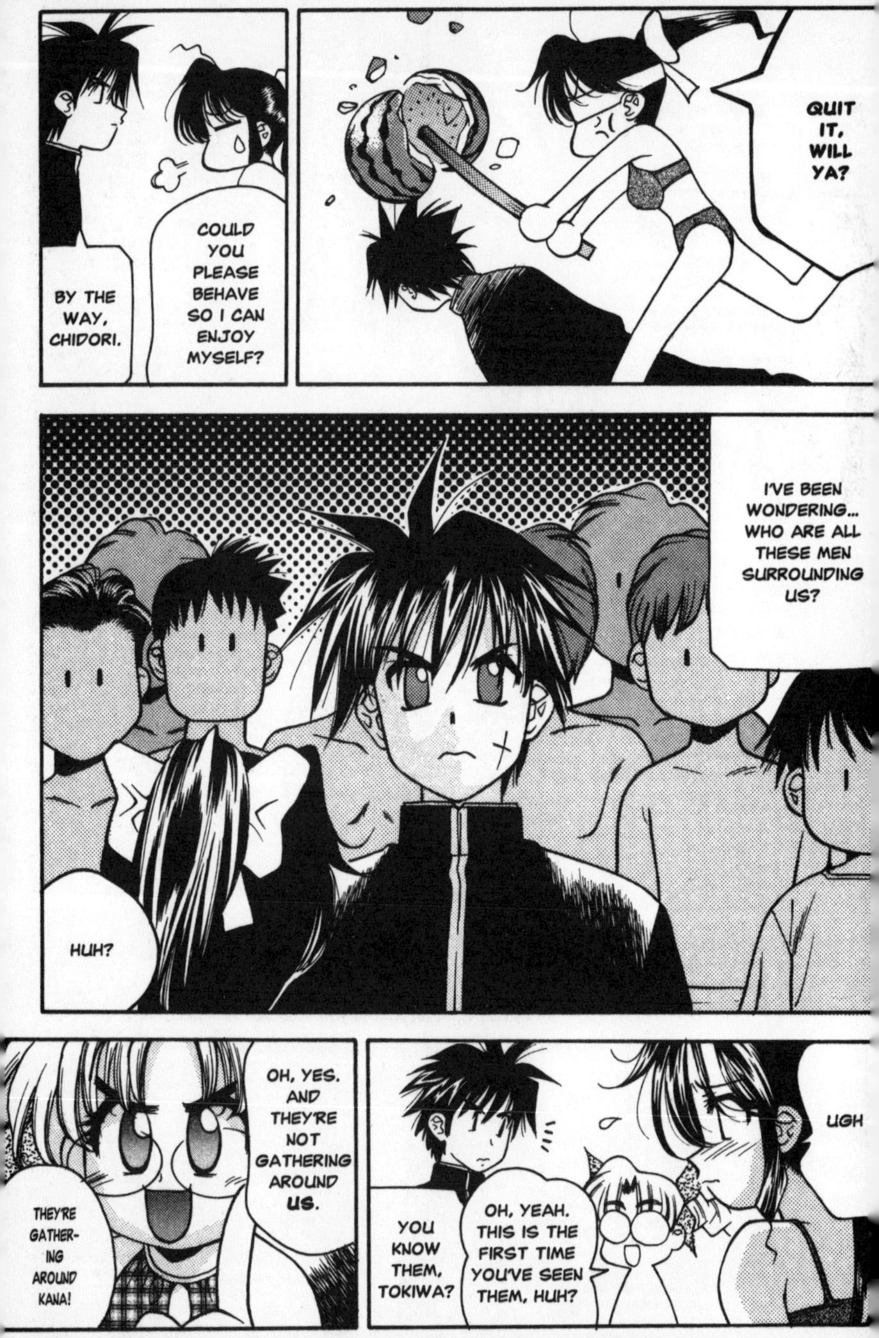

QUIT IT, WILL YA?
COULD YOU PLEASE BEHAVE SO I CAN ENJOY MYSELF?
BY THE WAY, CHIDORI.
I'VE BEEN WONDERING... WHO ARE ALL THESE MEN SURROUNDING US?
HUH?
UGH
OH, YEAH. THIS IS THE FIRST TIME YOU'VE SEEN THEM, HUH?
YOU KNOW THEM, TOKIWA?
OH, YES. AND THEY'RE NOT GATHERING AROUND US.
THEY'RE GATHERING AROUND KANA!

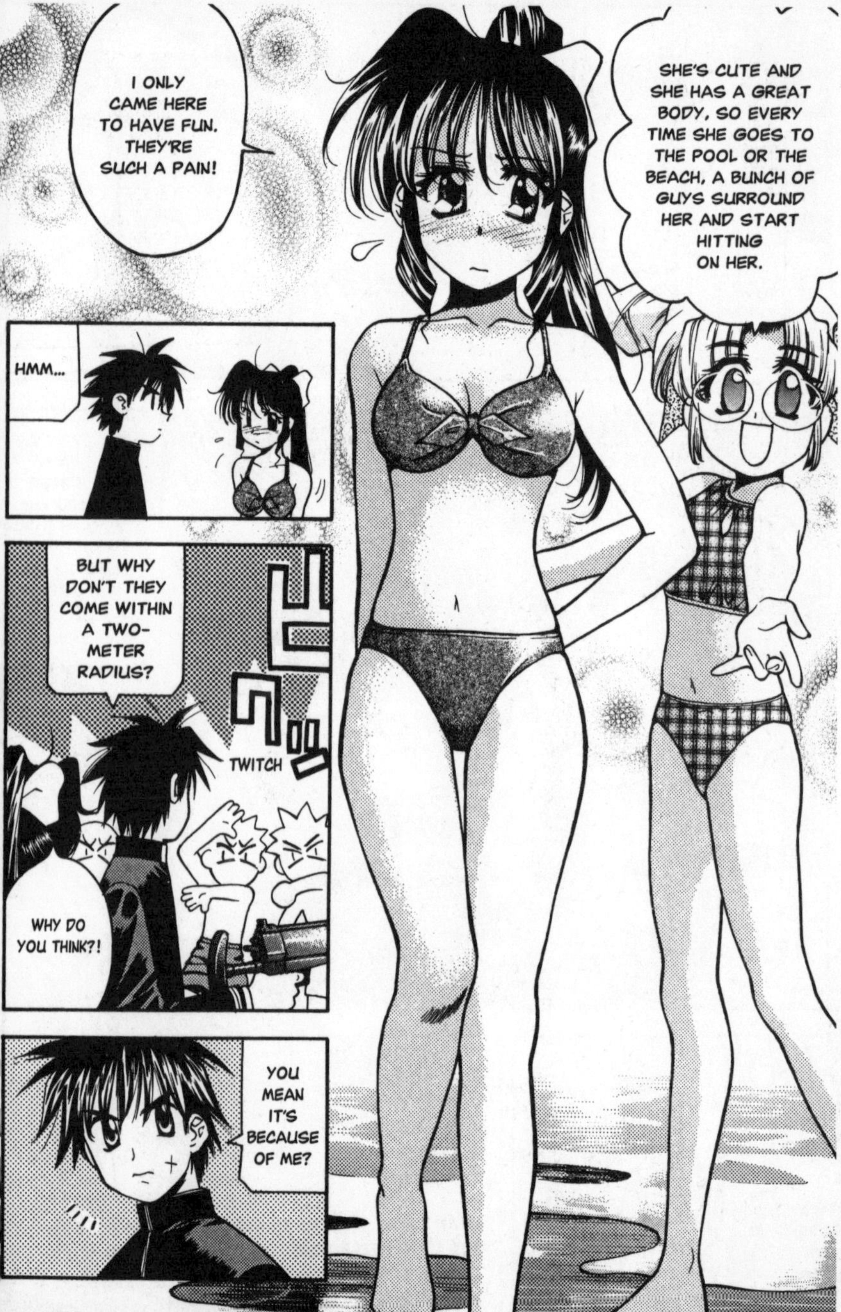
SHE'S CUTE AND SHE HAS A GREAT BODY, SO EVERY TIME SHE GOES TO THE POOL OR THE BEACH, A BUNCH OF GUYS SURROUND HER AND START HITTING ON HER.
I ONLY CAME HERE TO HAVE FUN. THEY'RE SUCH A PAIN!
HMM...
BUT WHY DON'T THEY COME WITHIN A TWO-METER RADIUS?
TWITCH
WHY DO YOU THINK?!
YOU MEAN IT'S BECAUSE OF ME?

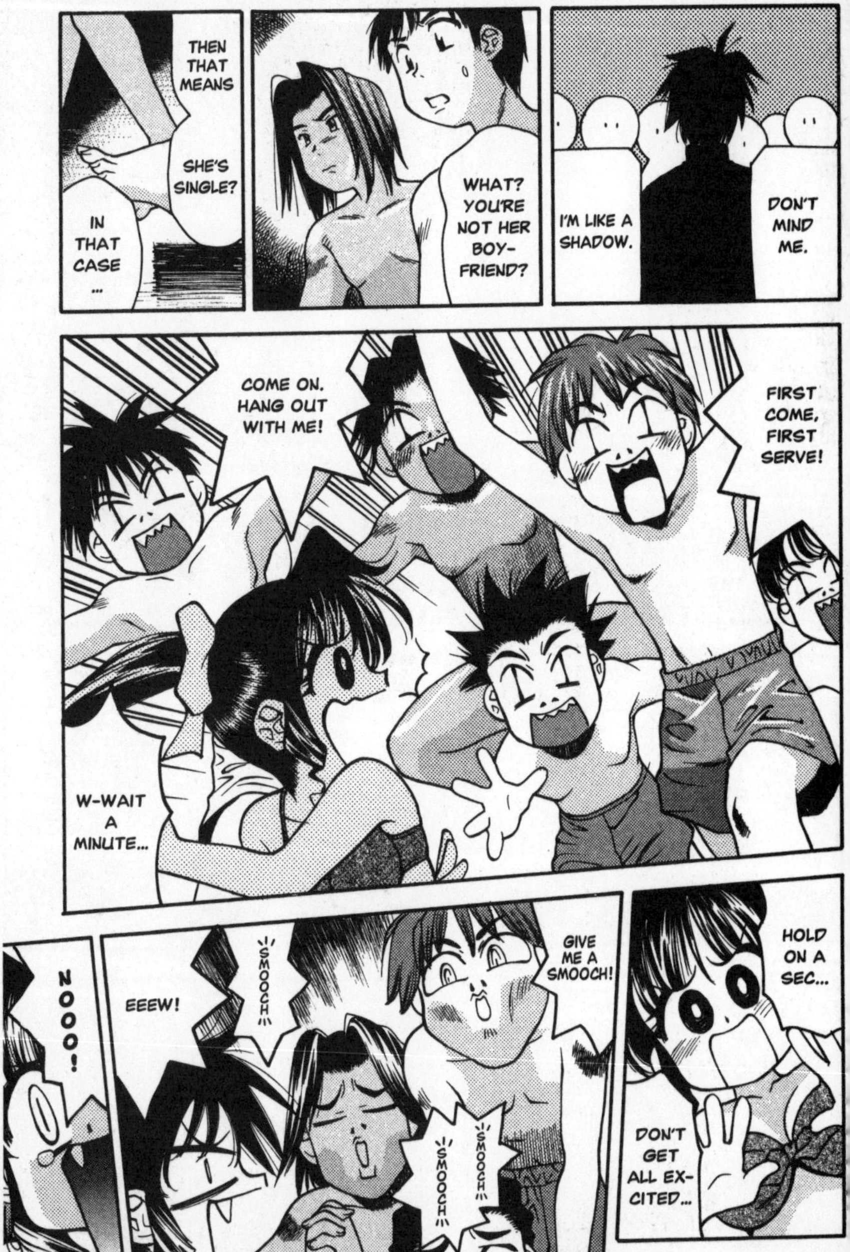
DON'T MIND ME.
I'M LIKE A SHADOW.
WHAT? YOU'RE NOT HER BOY-FRIEND?
THEN THAT MEANS
SHE'S SINGLE?
IN THAT CASE ...
FIRST COME, FIRST SERVE!
COME ON. HANG OUT WITH ME!
W-WAIT A MINUTE...
HOLD ON A SEC...
DON'T GET ALL EX-CITED...
GIVE ME A SMOOCH!
SMOOCH
SMOOCH
SMOOCH
EEEW!
SMOOCH
NOOOO!

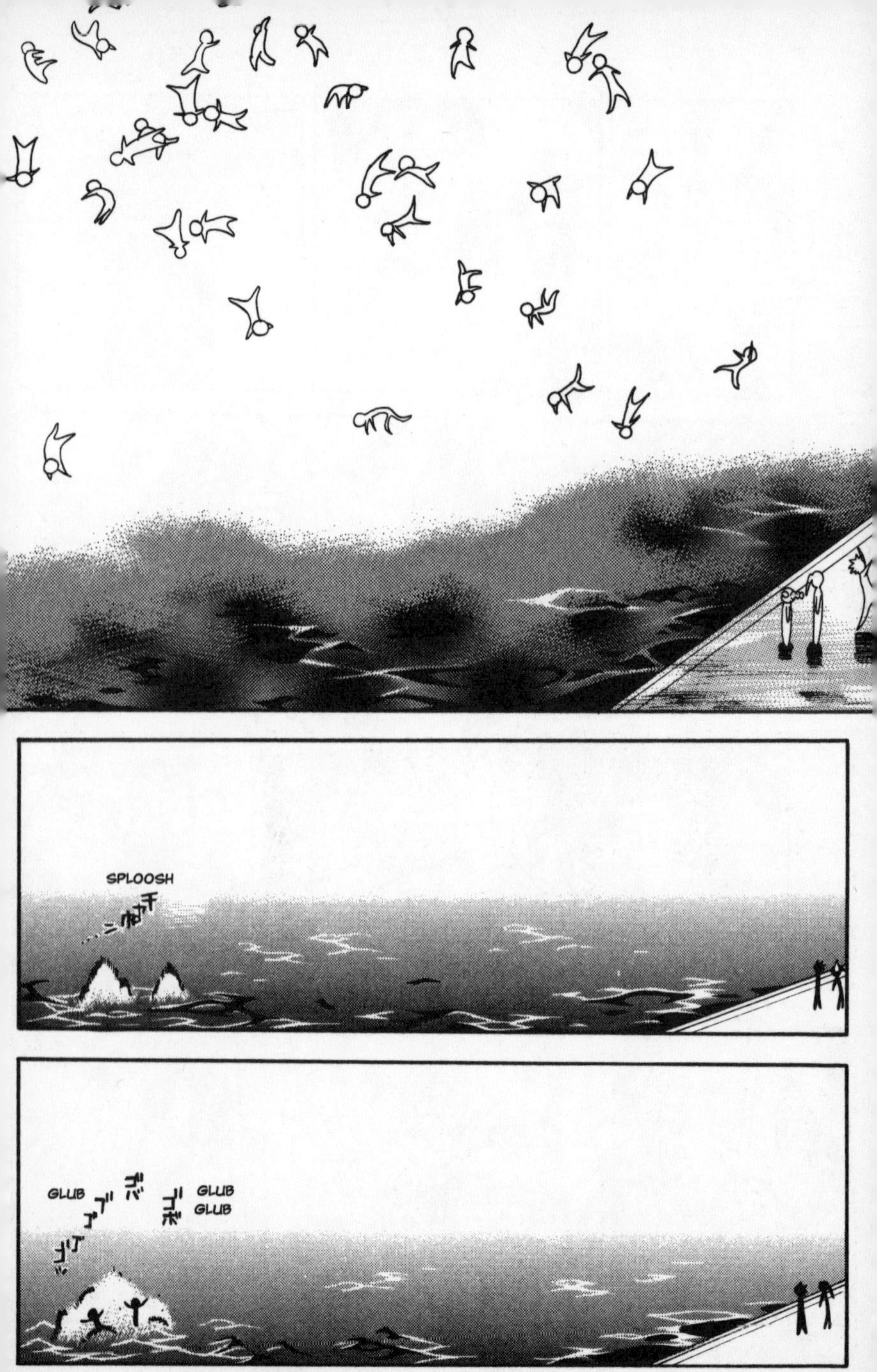
SPLOOSH
GLUB
GLUB
GLUB

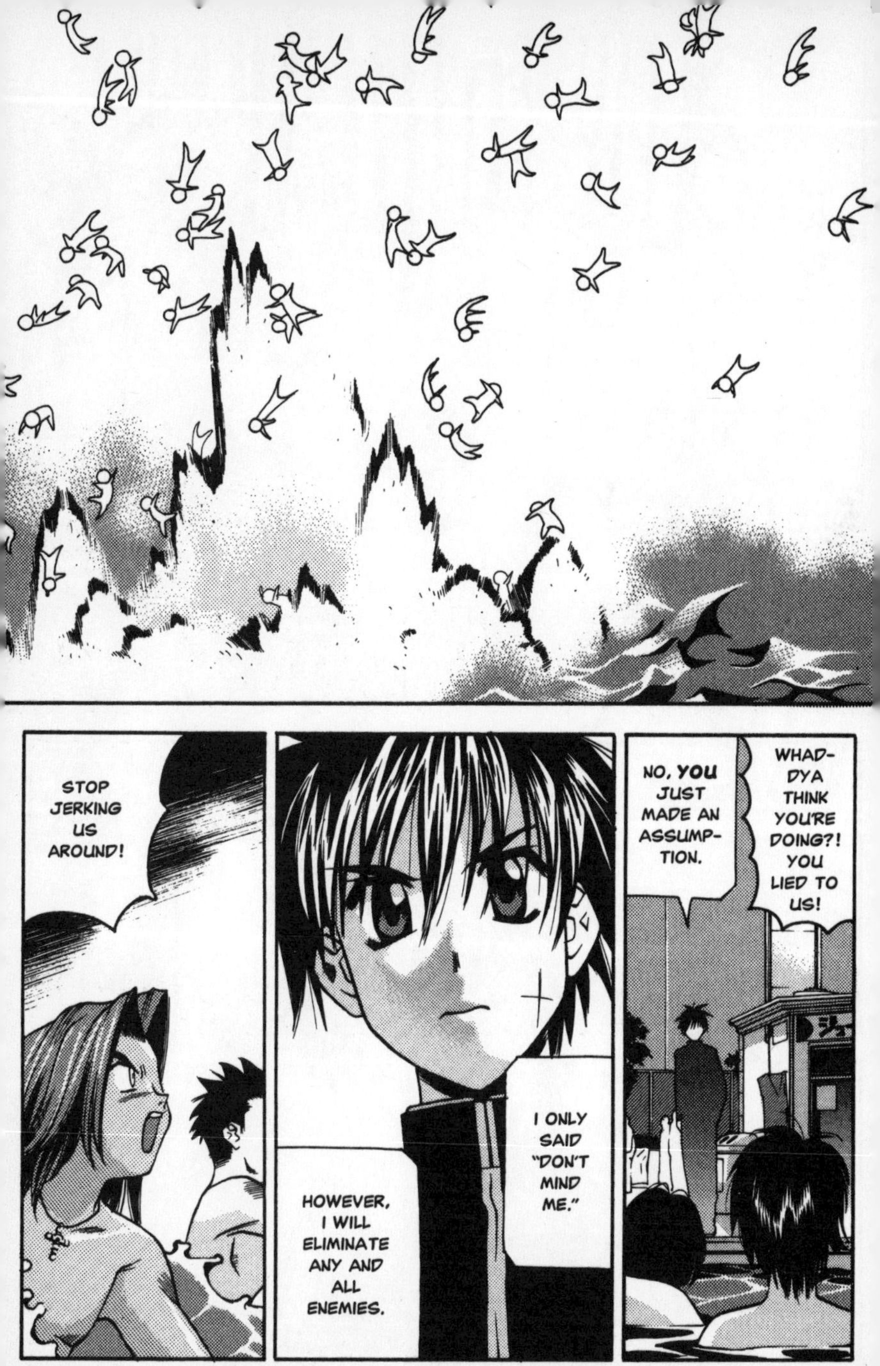
WHAD-DYA THINK YOU'RE DOING?! YOU LIED TO US!
NO, YOU JUST MADE AN ASSUMP-TION.
I ONLY SAID "DON'T MIND ME."
HOWEVER, I WILL ELIMINATE ANY AND ALL ENEMIES.
STOP JERKING US AROUND!

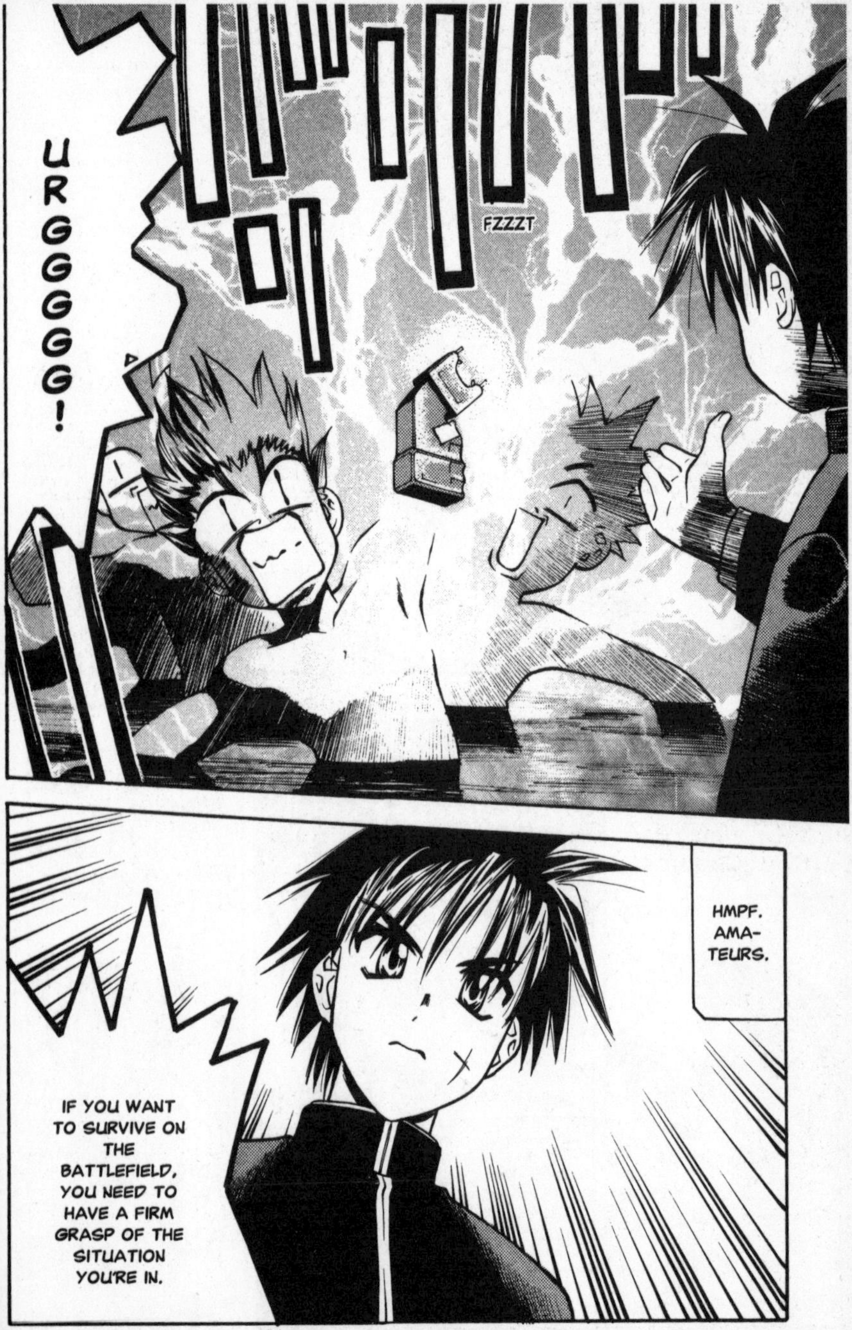
URGGGGGG!
FZZZT
HMPF. AMA-TEURS.
IF YOU WANT TO SURVIVE ON THE BATTLEFIELD, YOU NEED TO HAVE A FIRM GRASP OF THE SITUATION YOU'RE IN.

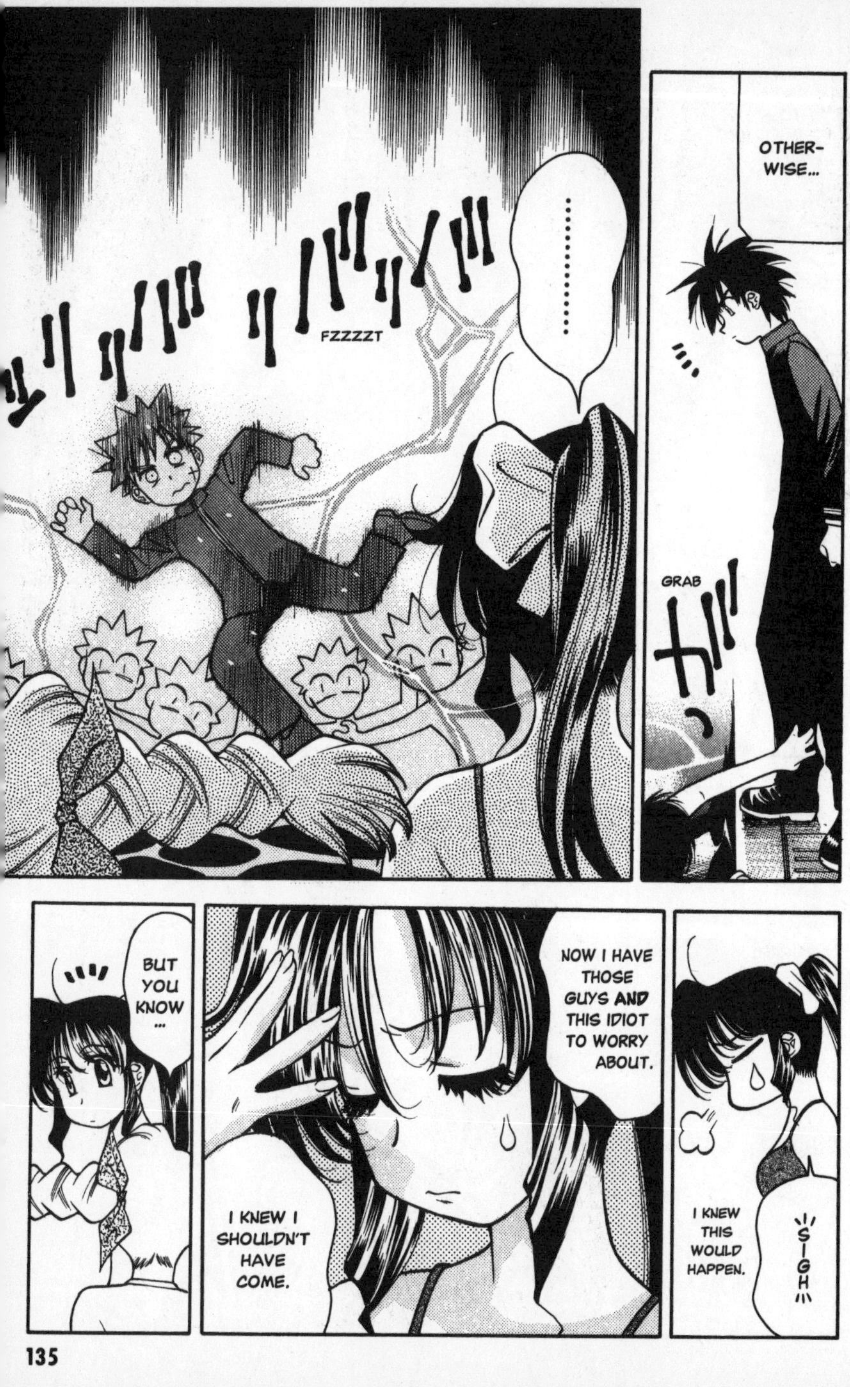
OTHER-WISE...
GRAB
FZZZZT
......
I KNEW THIS WOULD HAPPEN.
SIGH
NOW I HAVE THOSE GUYS AND THIS IDIOT TO WORRY ABOUT.
I KNEW I SHOULDN'T HAVE COME.
BUT YOU KNOW ...

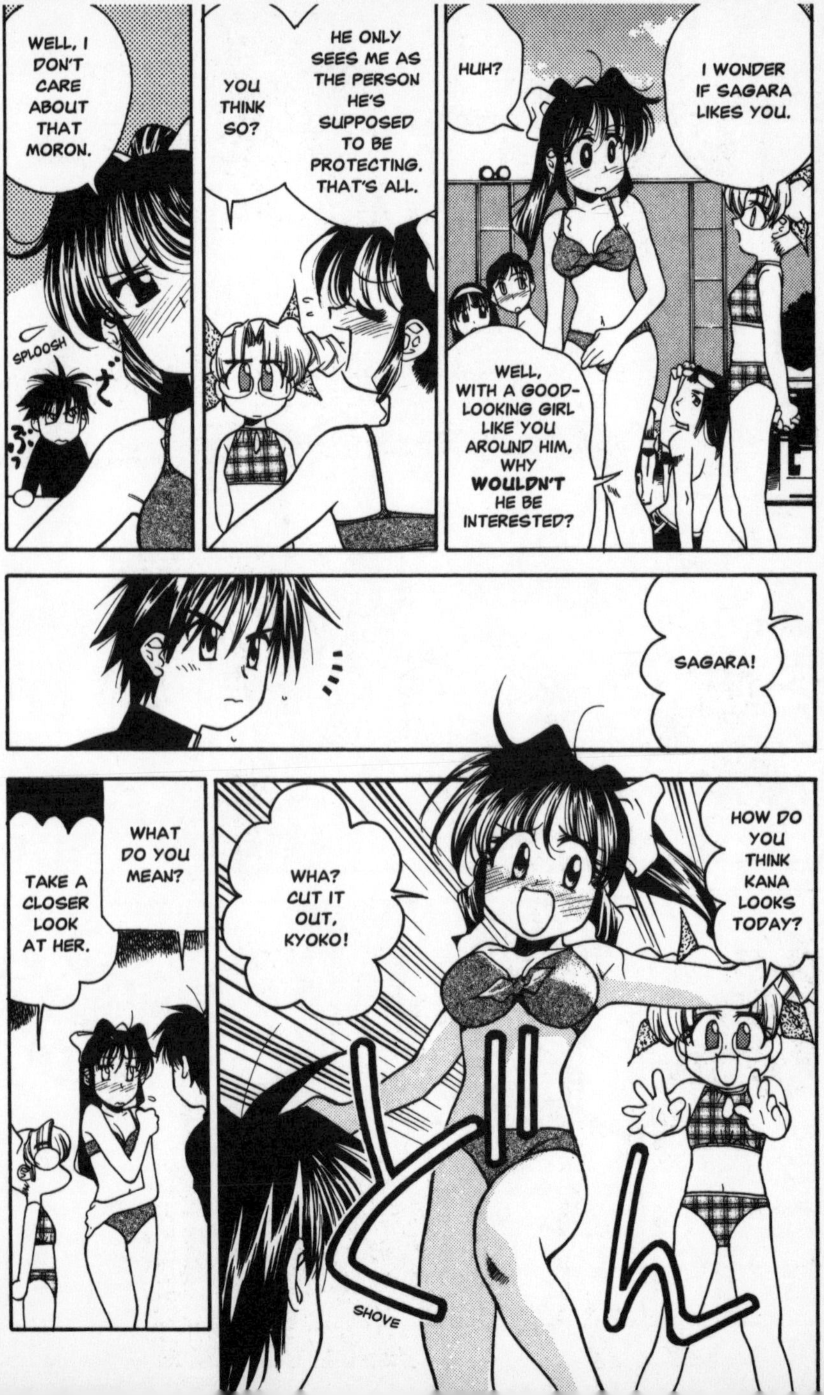
I WONDER IF SAGARA LIKES YOU.
HUH?
WELL, WITH A GOOD-LOOKING GIRL LIKE YOU AROUND HIM, WHY **WOULDN'T** HE BE INTERESTED?
HE ONLY SEES ME AS THE PERSON HE'S SUPPOSED TO BE PROTECTING. THAT'S ALL.
YOU THINK SO?
WELL, I DON'T CARE ABOUT THAT MORON.
SPLOOSH
SAGARA!
HOW DO YOU THINK KANA LOOKS TODAY?
WHA? CUT IT OUT, KYOKO!
SHOVE
WHAT DO YOU MEAN?
TAKE A CLOSER LOOK AT HER.

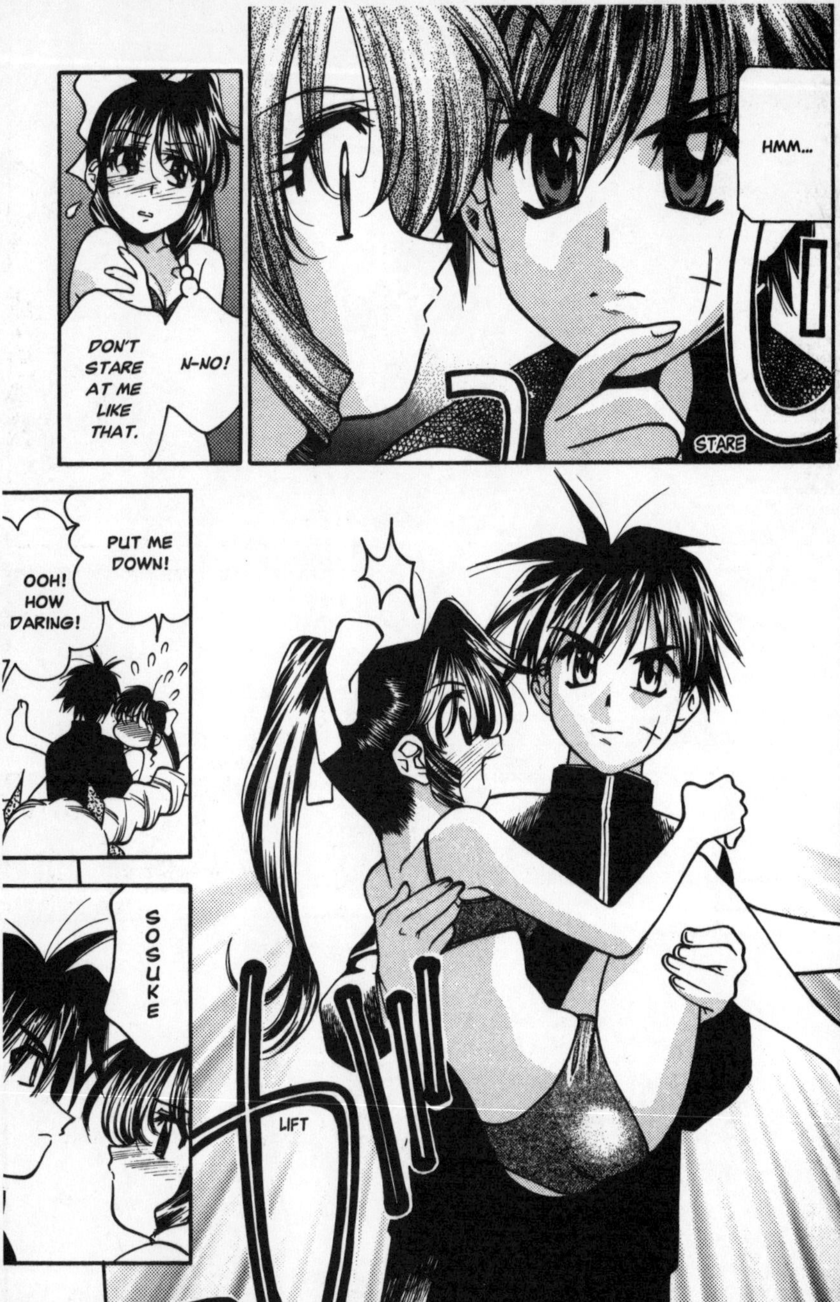
HMM...
STARE
N-NO!
DON'T STARE AT ME LIKE THAT.
LIFT
PUT ME DOWN!
OOH! HOW DARING!
SOSUKE

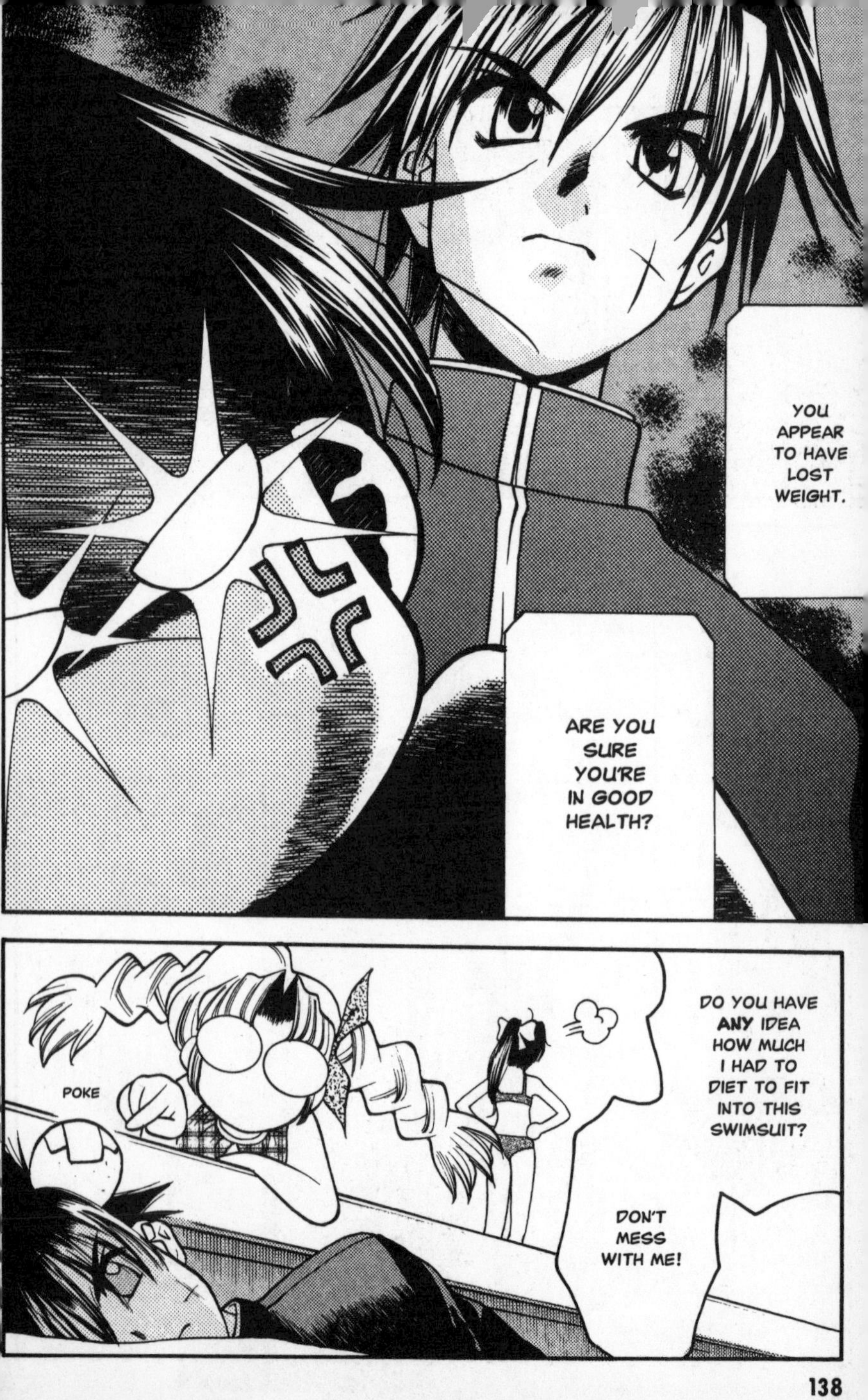
YOU APPEAR TO HAVE LOST WEIGHT.
ARE YOU SURE YOU'RE IN GOOD HEALTH?
DO YOU HAVE ANY IDEA HOW MUCH I HAD TO DIET TO FIT INTO THIS SWIMSUIT?
DON'T MESS WITH ME!
POKE

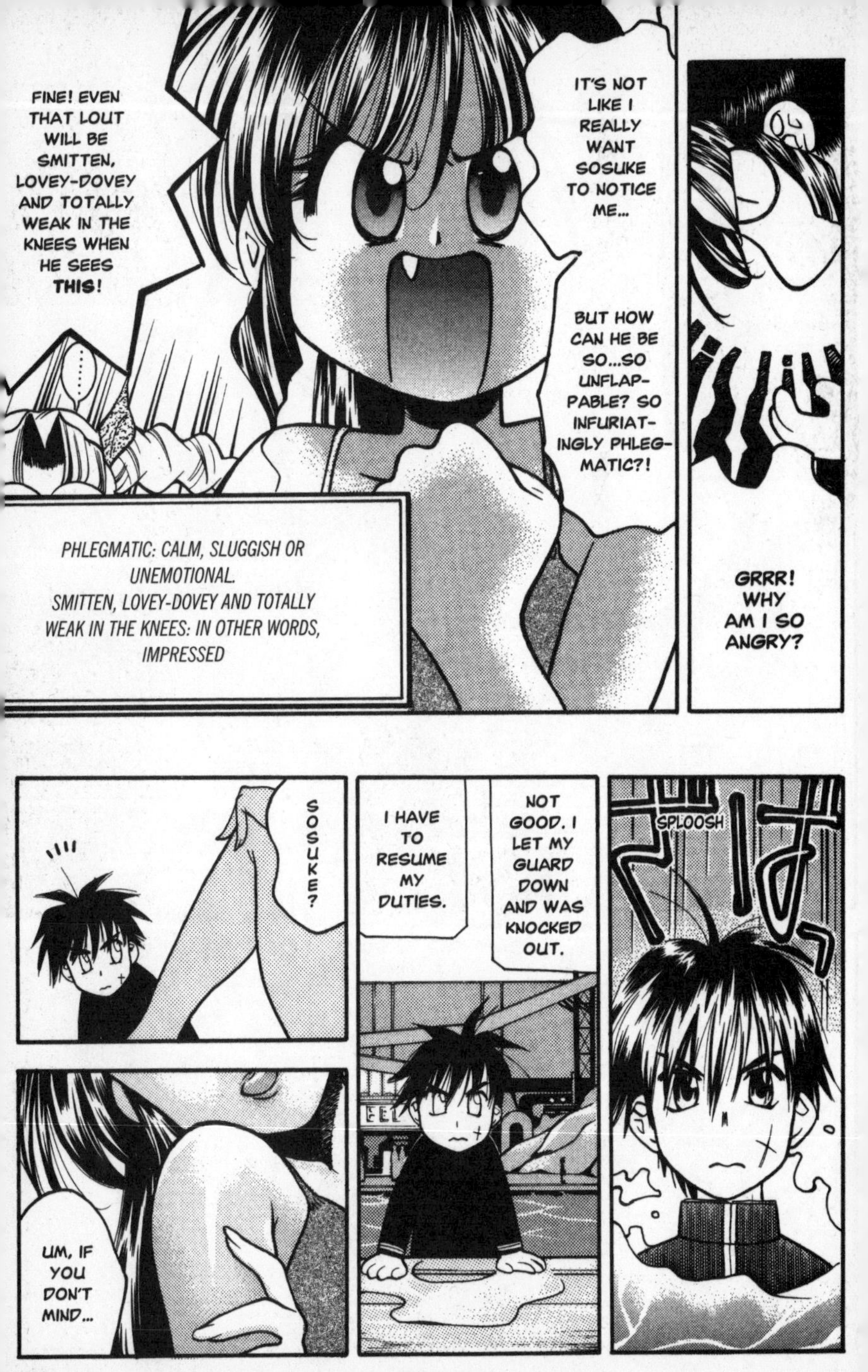

IT'S NOT LIKE I REALLY WANT SOSUKE TO NOTICE ME...
BUT HOW CAN HE BE SO...SO UNFLAP-PABLE? SO INFURIAT-INGLY PHLEG-MATIC?!
FINE! EVEN THAT LOUT WILL BE SMITTEN, LOVEY-DOVEY AND TOTALLY WEAK IN THE KNEES WHEN HE SEES **THIS**!
PHLEGMATIC: CALM, SLUGGISH OR UNEMOTIONAL.
SMITTEN, LOVEY-DOVEY AND TOTALLY WEAK IN THE KNEES: IN OTHER WORDS, IMPRESSED
GRRR! WHY AM I SO ANGRY?
SPLOOSH
NOT GOOD. I LET MY GUARD DOWN AND WAS KNOCKED OUT.
I HAVE TO RESUME MY DUTIES.
SOSUKE?
UM, IF YOU DON'T MIND...

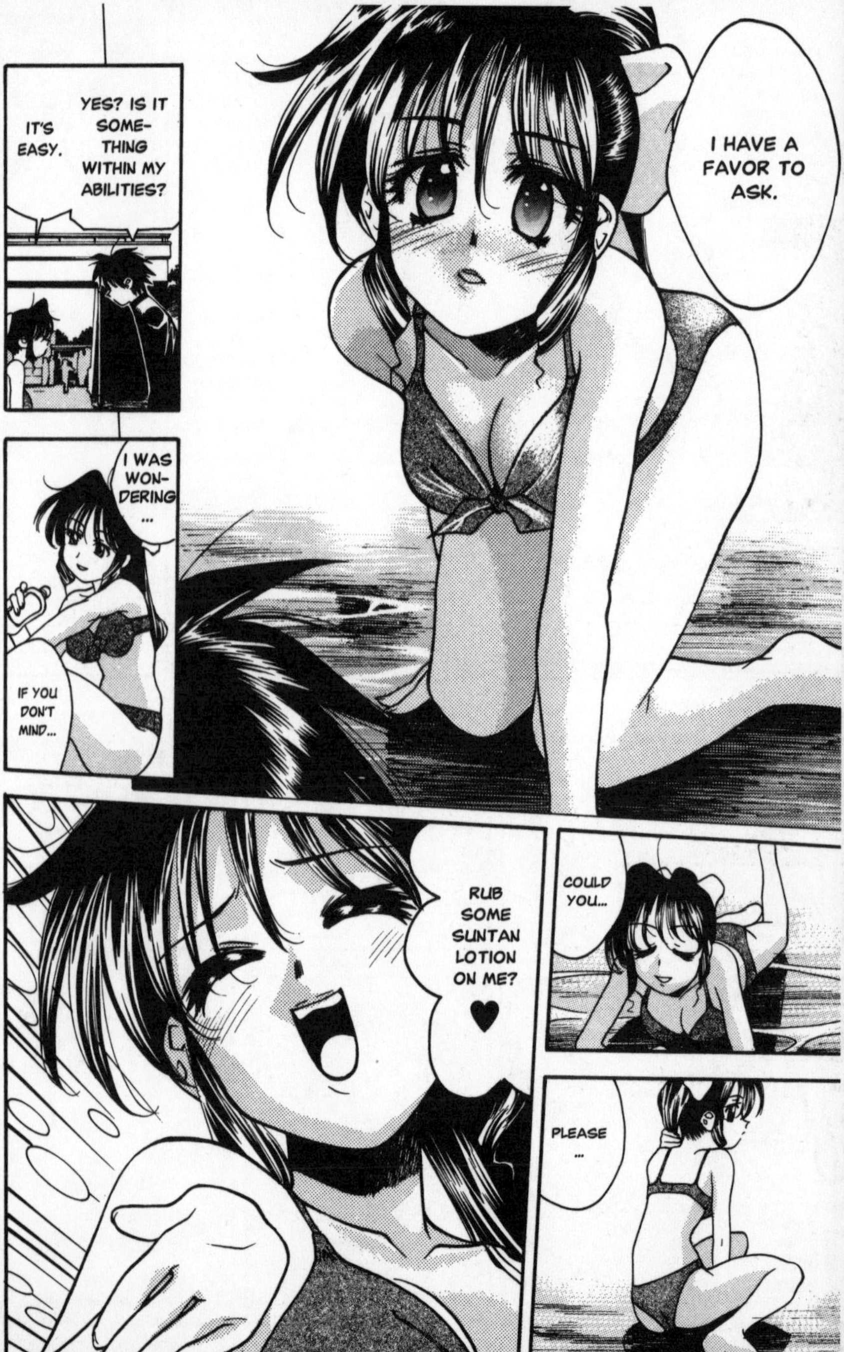
I HAVE A FAVOR TO ASK.
YES? IS IT SOME-THING WITHIN MY ABILITIES?
IT'S EASY.
I WAS WON-DERING ...
IF YOU DON'T MIND...
COULD YOU...
RUB SOME SUNTAN LOTION ON ME? ♥
PLEASE ...

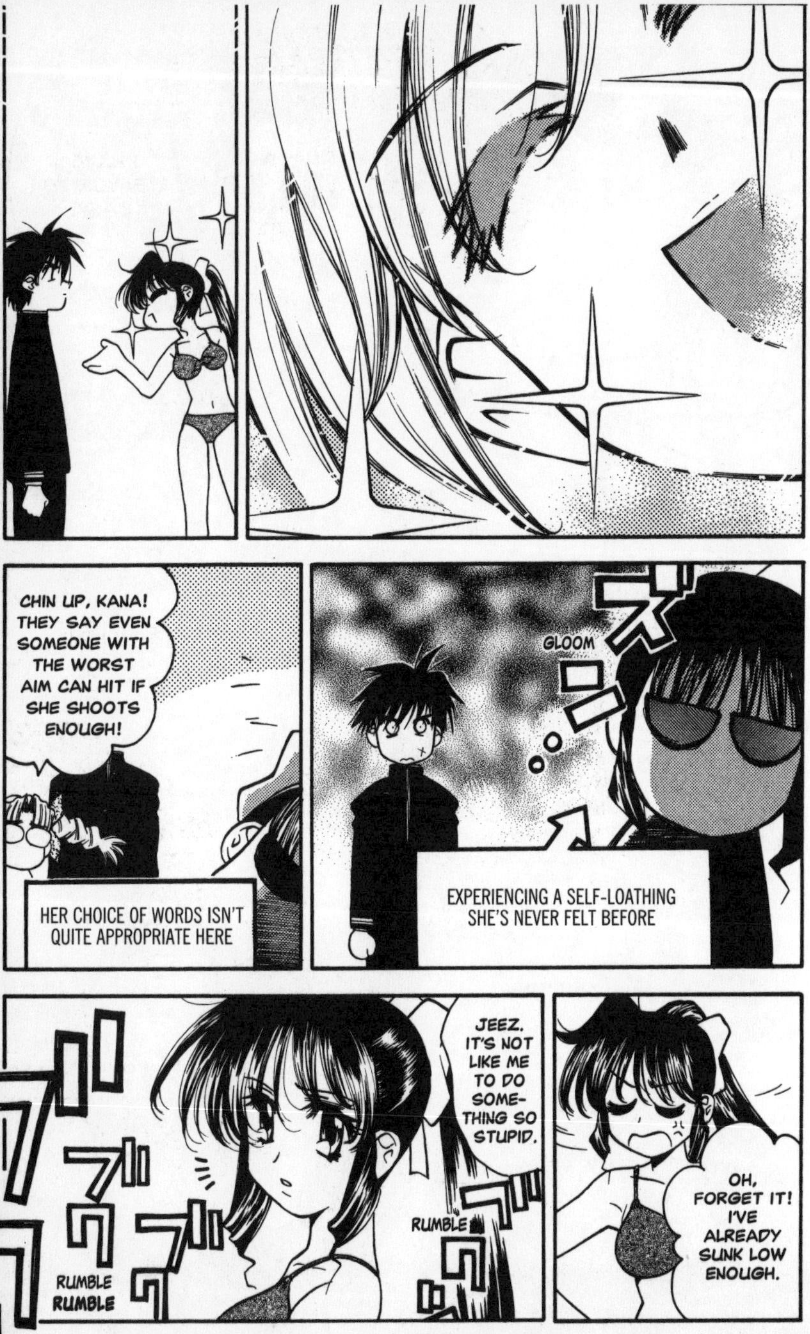
GLOOM
EXPERIENCING A SELF-LOATHING SHE'S NEVER FELT BEFORE
CHIN UP, KANA! THEY SAY EVEN SOMEONE WITH THE WORST AIM CAN HIT IF SHE SHOOTS ENOUGH!
HER CHOICE OF WORDS ISN'T QUITE APPROPRIATE HERE
OH, FORGET IT! I'VE ALREADY SUNK LOW ENOUGH.
JEEZ. IT'S NOT LIKE ME TO DO SOME-THING SO STUPID.
RUMBLE
RUMBLE RUMBLE

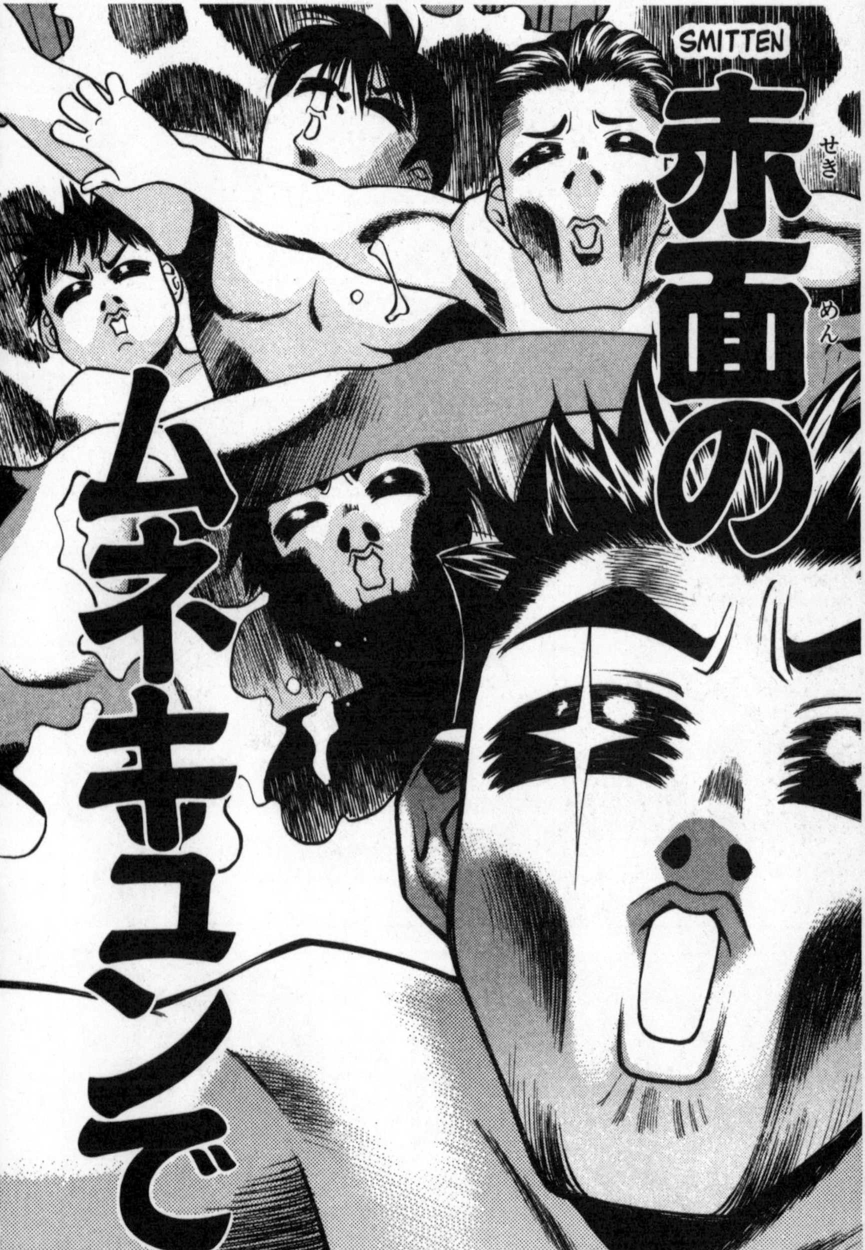
SMITTEN
赤面(せきめん)の
ムネキュンで
LOVEY-DOVEY

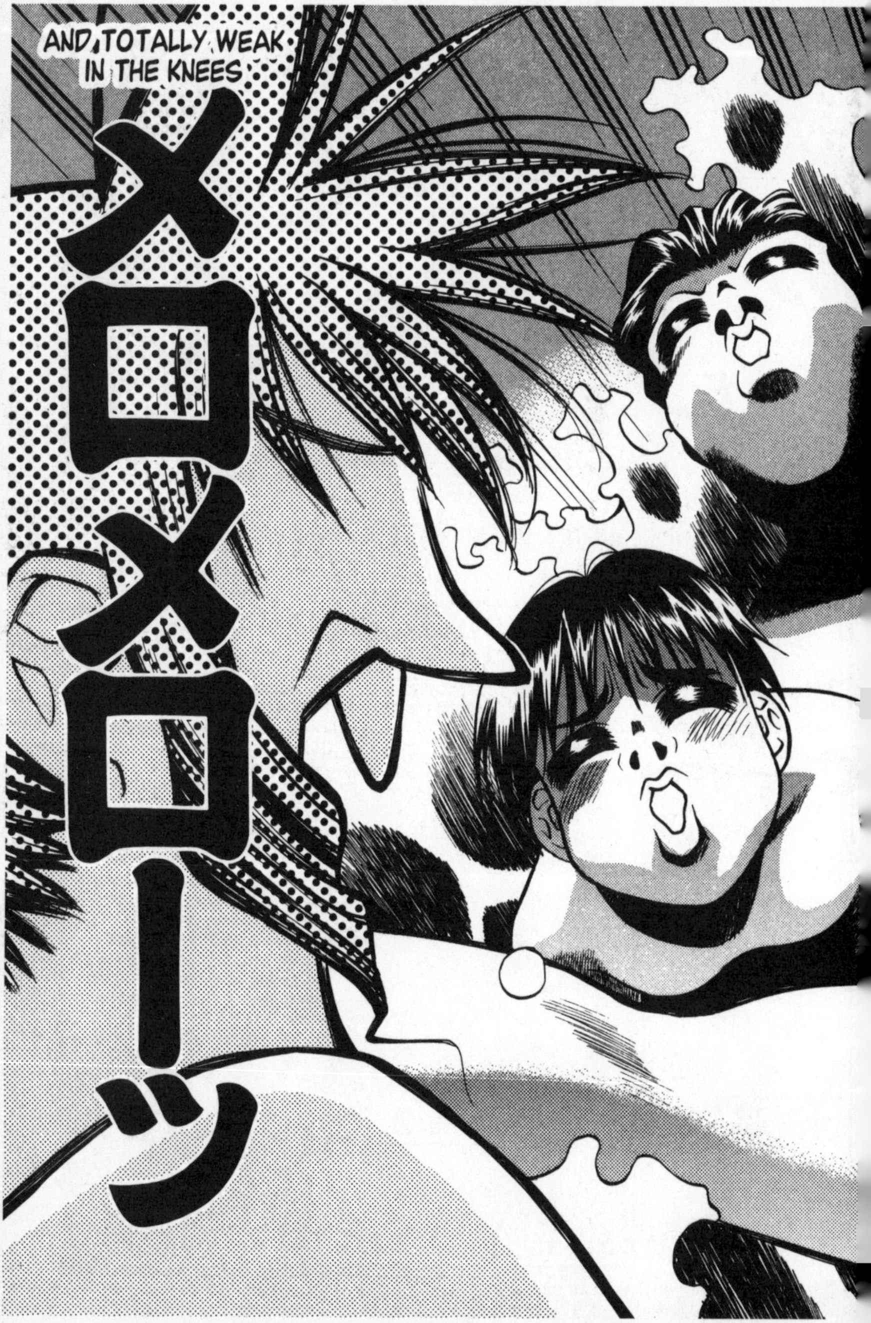
AND TOTALLY WEAK IN THE KNEES
メロメローッ

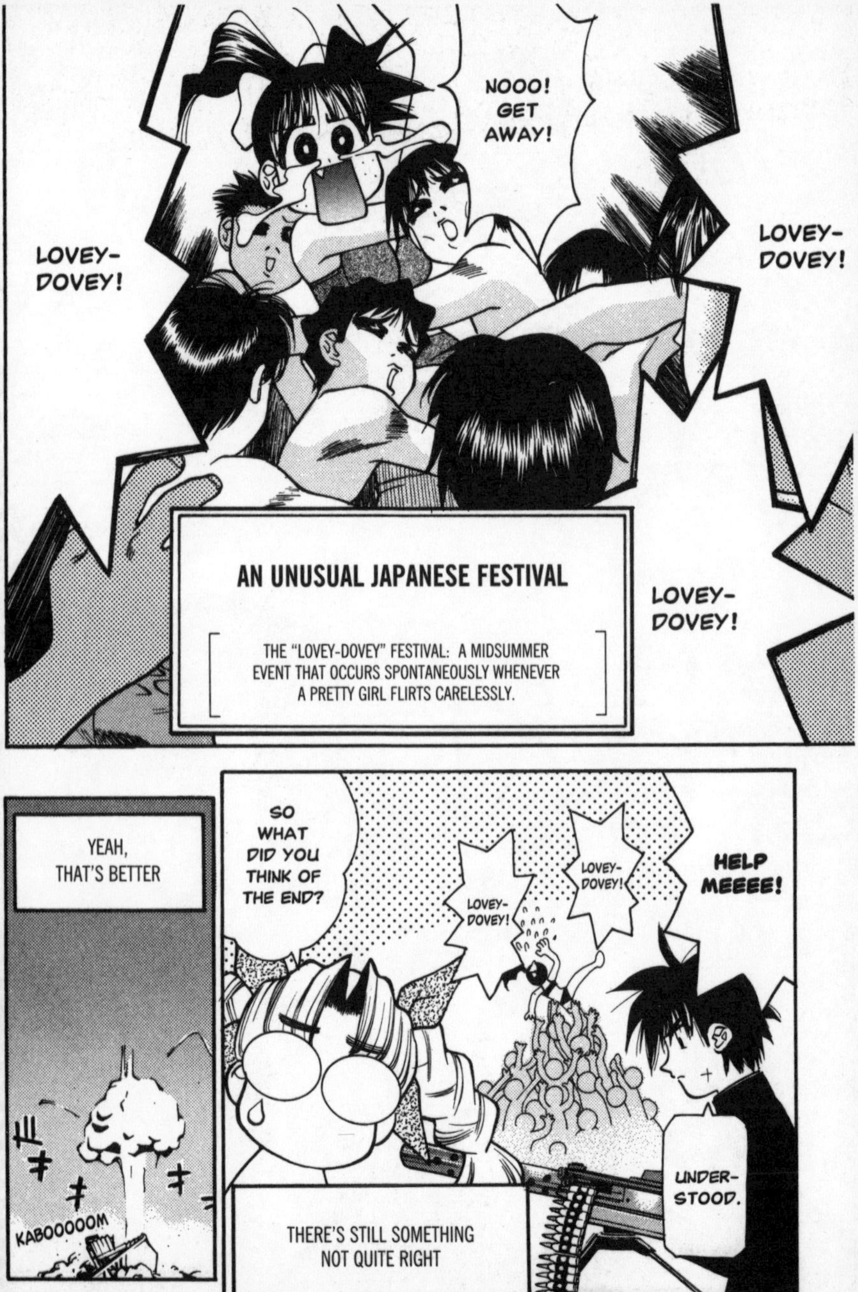
NOOO! GET AWAY!
LOVEY-DOVEY!
LOVEY-DOVEY!
AN UNUSUAL JAPANESE FESTIVAL
THE "LOVEY-DOVEY" FESTIVAL: A MIDSUMMER EVENT THAT OCCURS SPONTANEOUSLY WHENEVER A PRETTY GIRL FLIRTS CARELESSLY.
LOVEY-DOVEY!
HELP MEEEE!
LOVEY-DOVEY!
LOVEY-DOVEY!
SO WHAT DID YOU THINK OF THE END?
UNDERSTOOD.
THERE'S STILL SOMETHING NOT QUITE RIGHT
YEAH, THAT'S BETTER
KABOOOOOM

BOMB 6 WAR NUT AND FESTIVAL NUT?

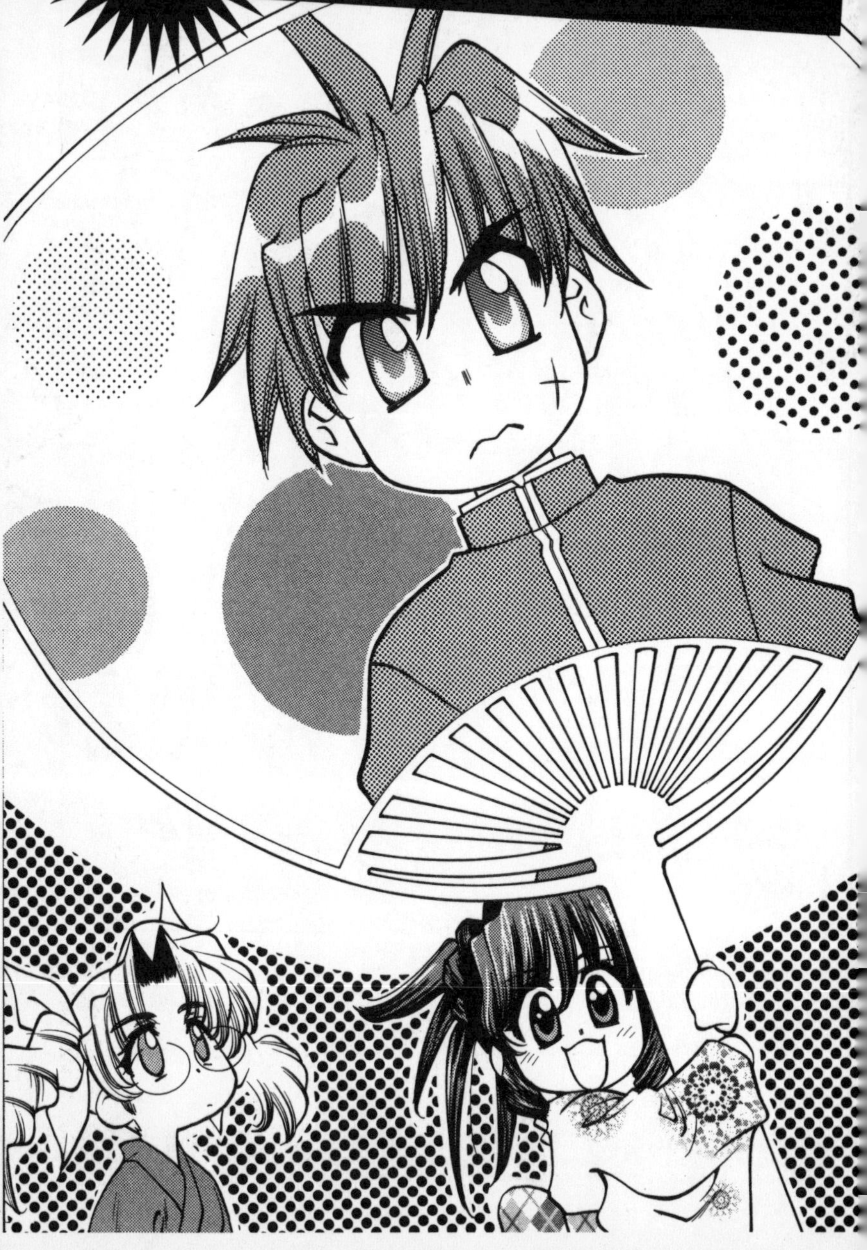

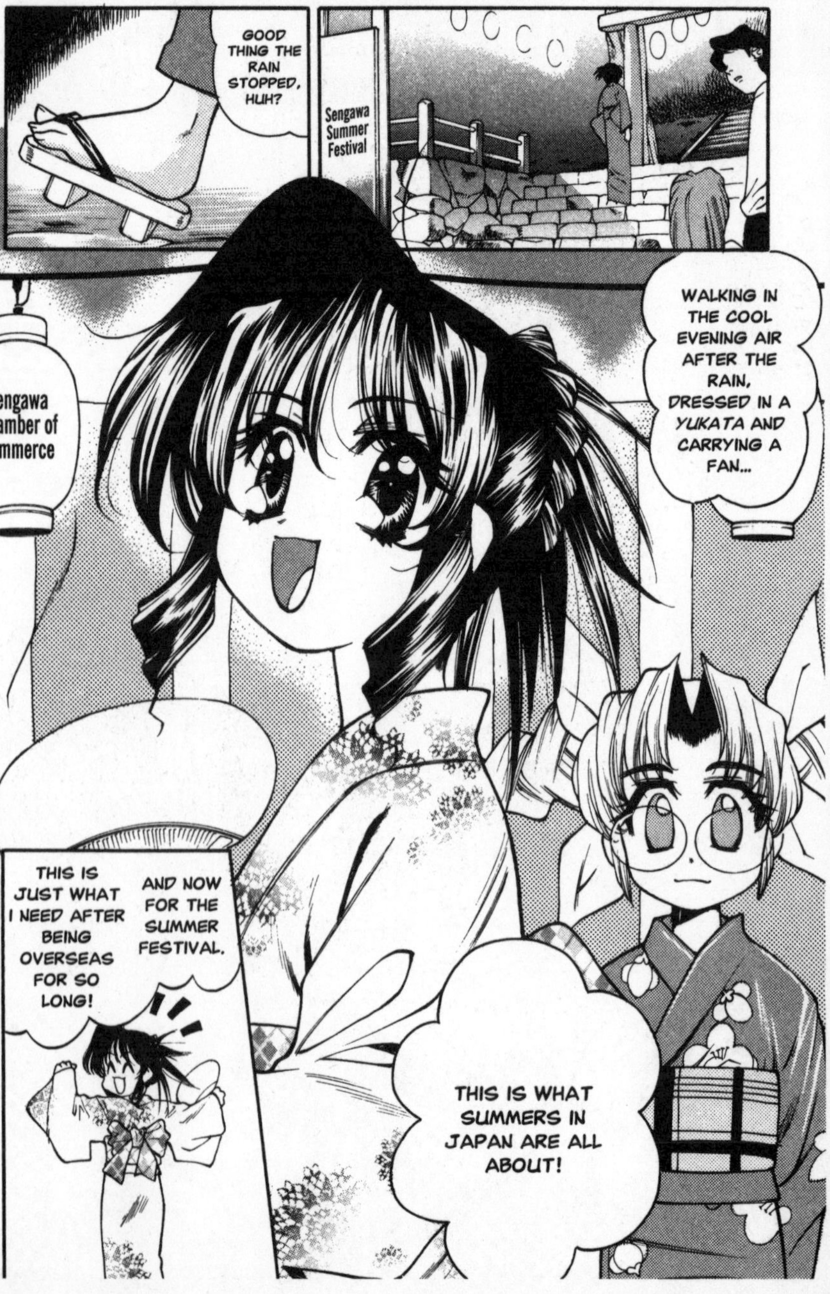

Sengawa Summer Festival
GOOD THING THE RAIN STOPPED, HUH?
WALKING IN THE COOL EVENING AIR AFTER THE RAIN, DRESSED IN A YUKATA AND CARRYING A FAN...
Sengawa Chamber of Commerce
AND NOW FOR THE SUMMER FESTIVAL.
THIS IS JUST WHAT I NEED AFTER BEING OVERSEAS FOR SO LONG!
THIS IS WHAT SUMMERS IN JAPAN ARE ALL ABOUT!

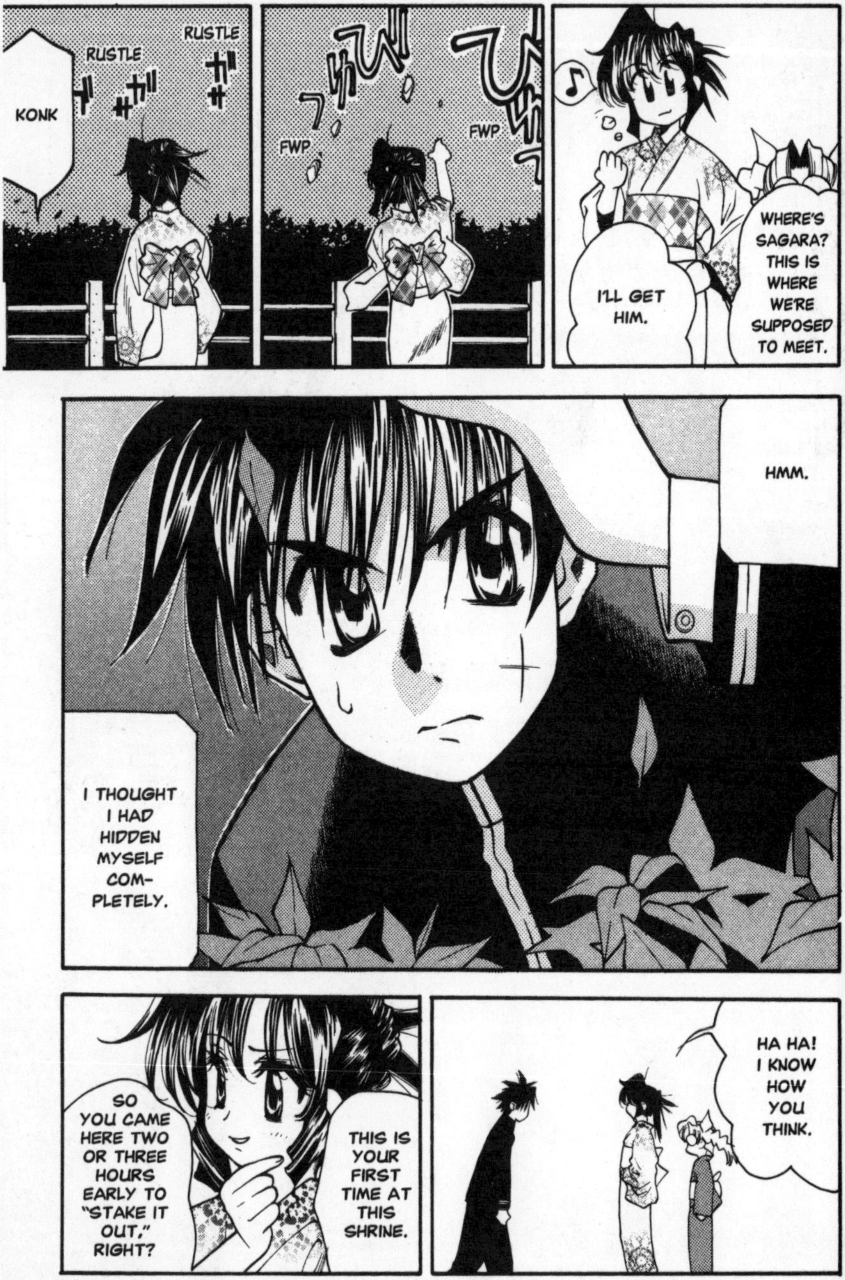
WHERE'S SAGARA? THIS IS WHERE WE'RE SUPPOSED TO MEET.
I'LL GET HIM.
FWP
FWP
RUSTLE
RUSTLE
KONK
HMM.
I THOUGHT I HAD HIDDEN MYSELF COM-PLETELY.
HA HA! I KNOW HOW YOU THINK.
THIS IS YOUR FIRST TIME AT THIS SHRINE.
SO YOU CAME HERE TWO OR THREE HOURS EARLY TO "STAKE IT OUT," RIGHT?

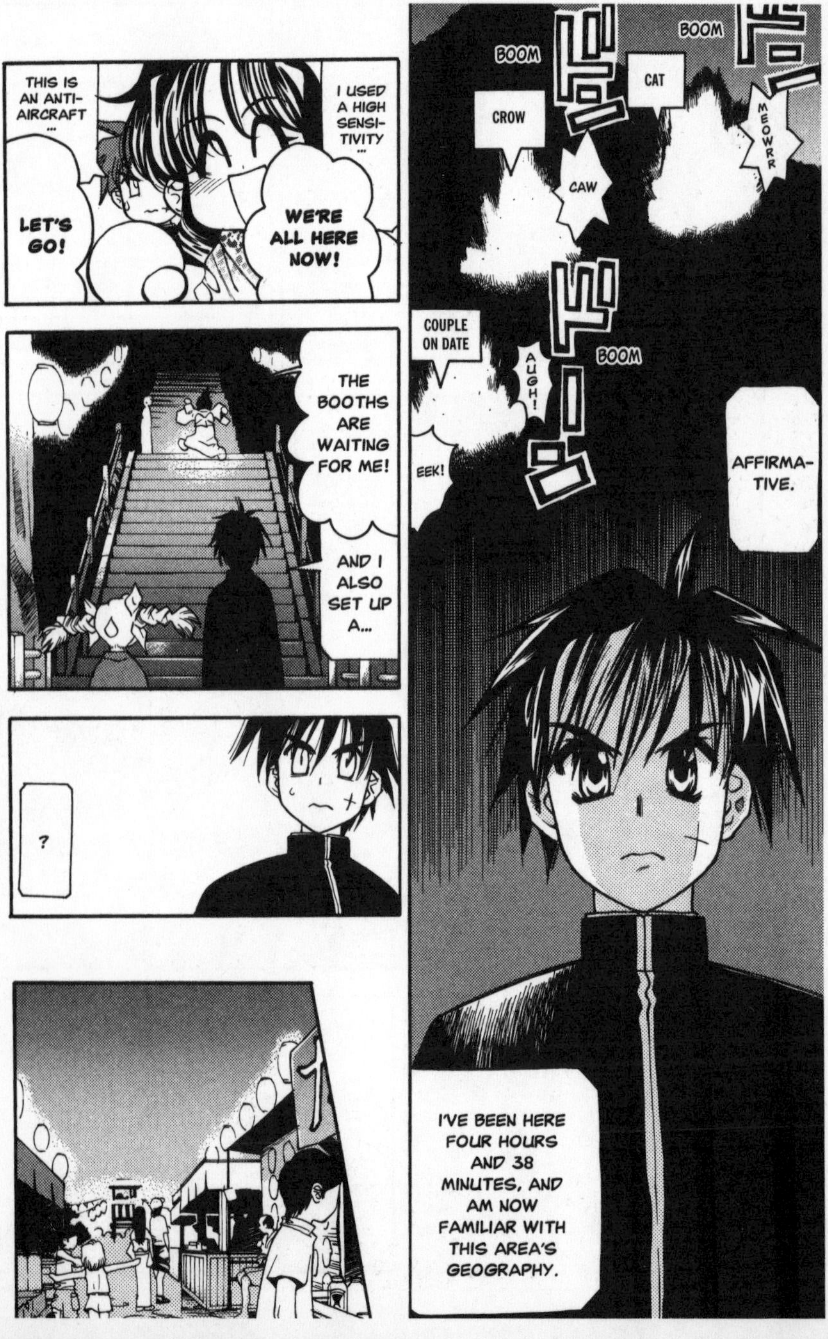
BOOM
MEOWRR
CAT
CAW
BOOM
CROW
BOOM
COUPLE ON DATE
AUGH!
EEK!
AFFIRMATIVE.
I'VE BEEN HERE FOUR HOURS AND 38 MINUTES, AND AM NOW FAMILIAR WITH THIS AREA'S GEOGRAPHY.
I USED A HIGH SENSITIVITY...
WE'RE ALL HERE NOW!
THIS IS AN ANTI-AIRCRAFT...
LET'S GO!
THE BOOTHS ARE WAITING FOR ME!
AND I ALSO SET UP A...
?

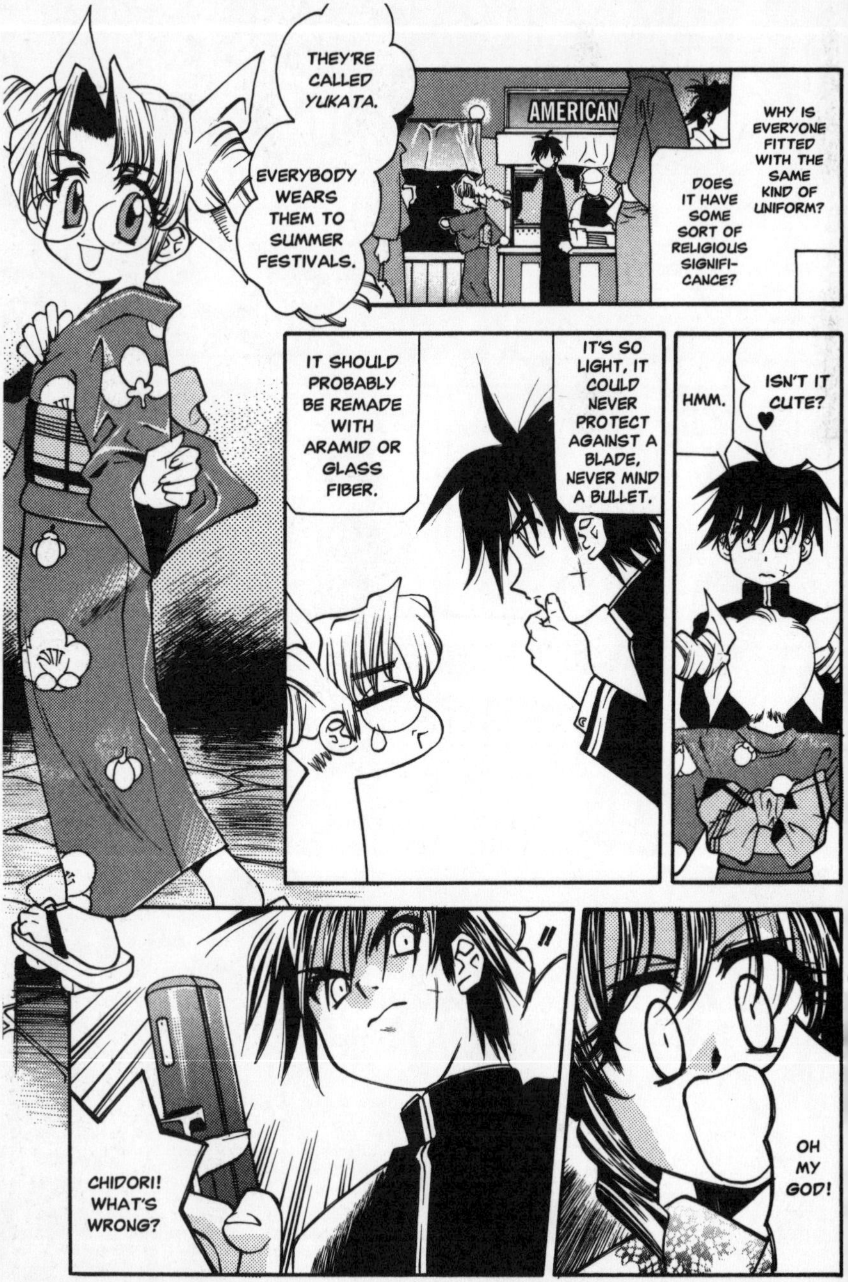
AMERICAN
WHY IS EVERYONE FITTED WITH THE SAME KIND OF UNIFORM?
DOES IT HAVE SOME SORT OF RELIGIOUS SIGNIFI-CANCE?
THEY'RE CALLED YUKATA.
EVERYBODY WEARS THEM TO SUMMER FESTIVALS.
ISN'T IT CUTE?
HMM.
IT'S SO LIGHT, IT COULD NEVER PROTECT AGAINST A BLADE, NEVER MIND A BULLET.
IT SHOULD PROBABLY BE REMADE WITH ARAMID OR GLASS FIBER.
OH MY GOD!
CHIDORI! WHAT'S WRONG?

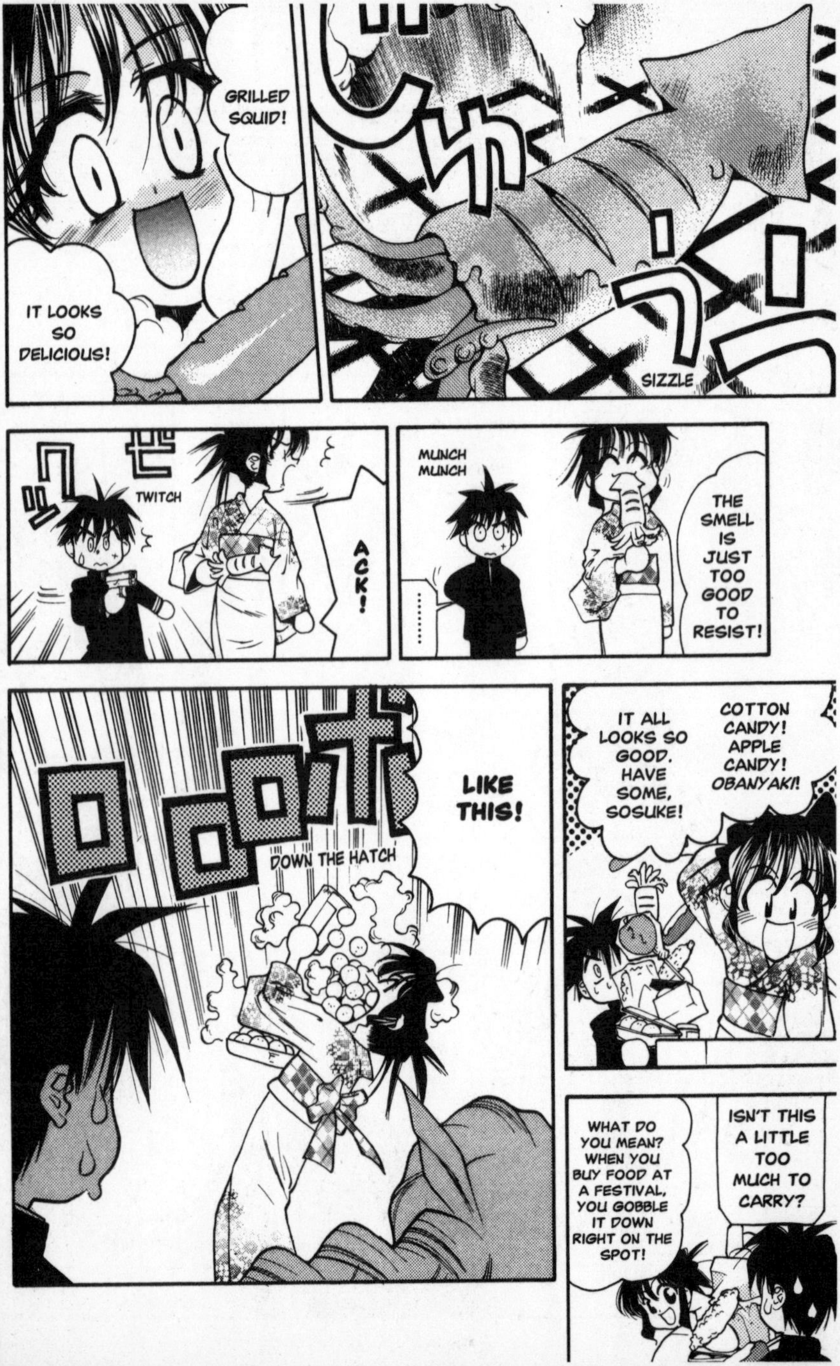
SIZZLE
GRILLED SQUID!
IT LOOKS SO DELICIOUS!
MUNCH MUNCH
THE SMELL IS JUST TOO GOOD TO RESIST!
......
TWITCH
ACK!
COTTON CANDY! APPLE CANDY! OBANYAKI!
IT ALL LOOKS SO GOOD. HAVE SOME, SOSUKE!
ISN'T THIS A LITTLE TOO MUCH TO CARRY?
WHAT DO YOU MEAN? WHEN YOU BUY FOOD AT A FESTIVAL, YOU GOBBLE IT DOWN RIGHT ON THE SPOT!
LIKE THIS!
DOWN THE HATCH

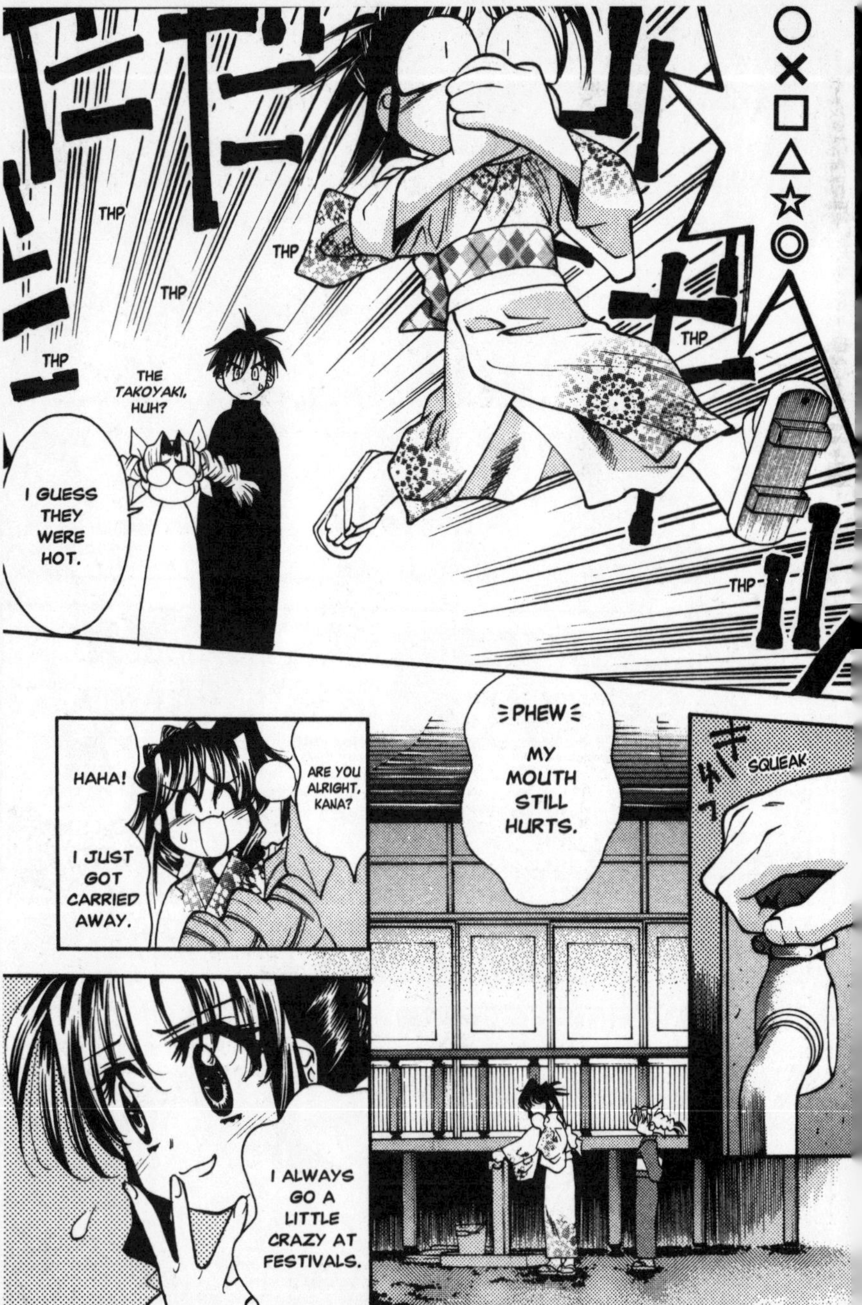
○×□△☆◎
THP
THP
THP
THP
THP
THP
THE TAKOYAKI, HUH?
I GUESS THEY WERE HOT.
PHEW
MY MOUTH STILL HURTS.
SQUEAK
ARE YOU ALRIGHT, KANA?
HAHA!
I JUST GOT CARRIED AWAY.
I ALWAYS GO A LITTLE CRAZY AT FESTIVALS.

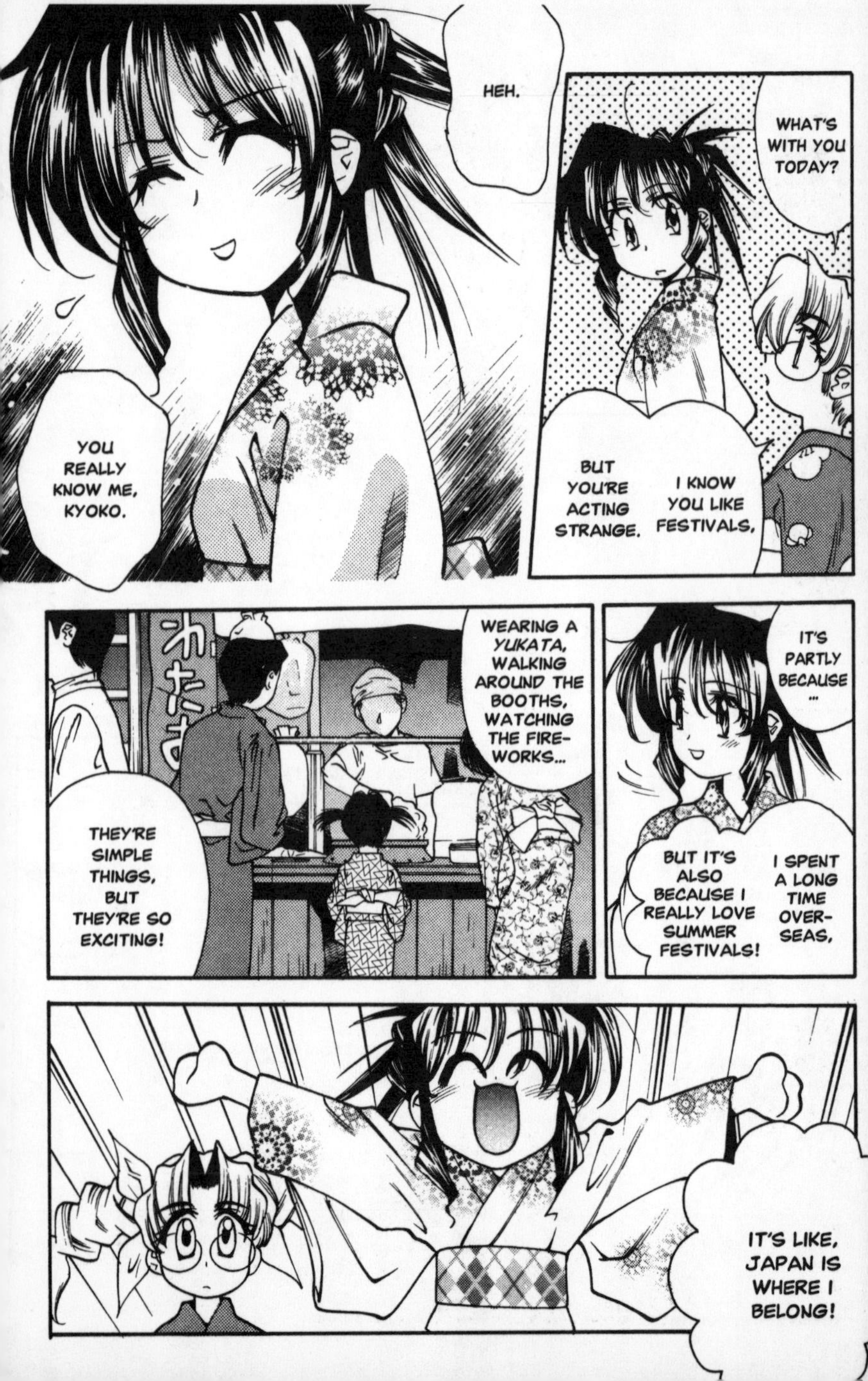

WHAT'S WITH YOU TODAY?
I KNOW YOU LIKE FESTIVALS,
BUT YOU'RE ACTING STRANGE.
HEH.
YOU REALLY KNOW ME, KYOKO.
IT'S PARTLY BECAUSE ...
I SPENT A LONG TIME OVER-SEAS,
BUT IT'S ALSO BECAUSE I REALLY LOVE SUMMER FESTIVALS!
WEARING A *YUKATA*, WALKING AROUND THE BOOTHS, WATCHING THE FIRE-WORKS...
THEY'RE SIMPLE THINGS, BUT THEY'RE SO EXCITING!
IT'S LIKE, JAPAN IS WHERE I BELONG!

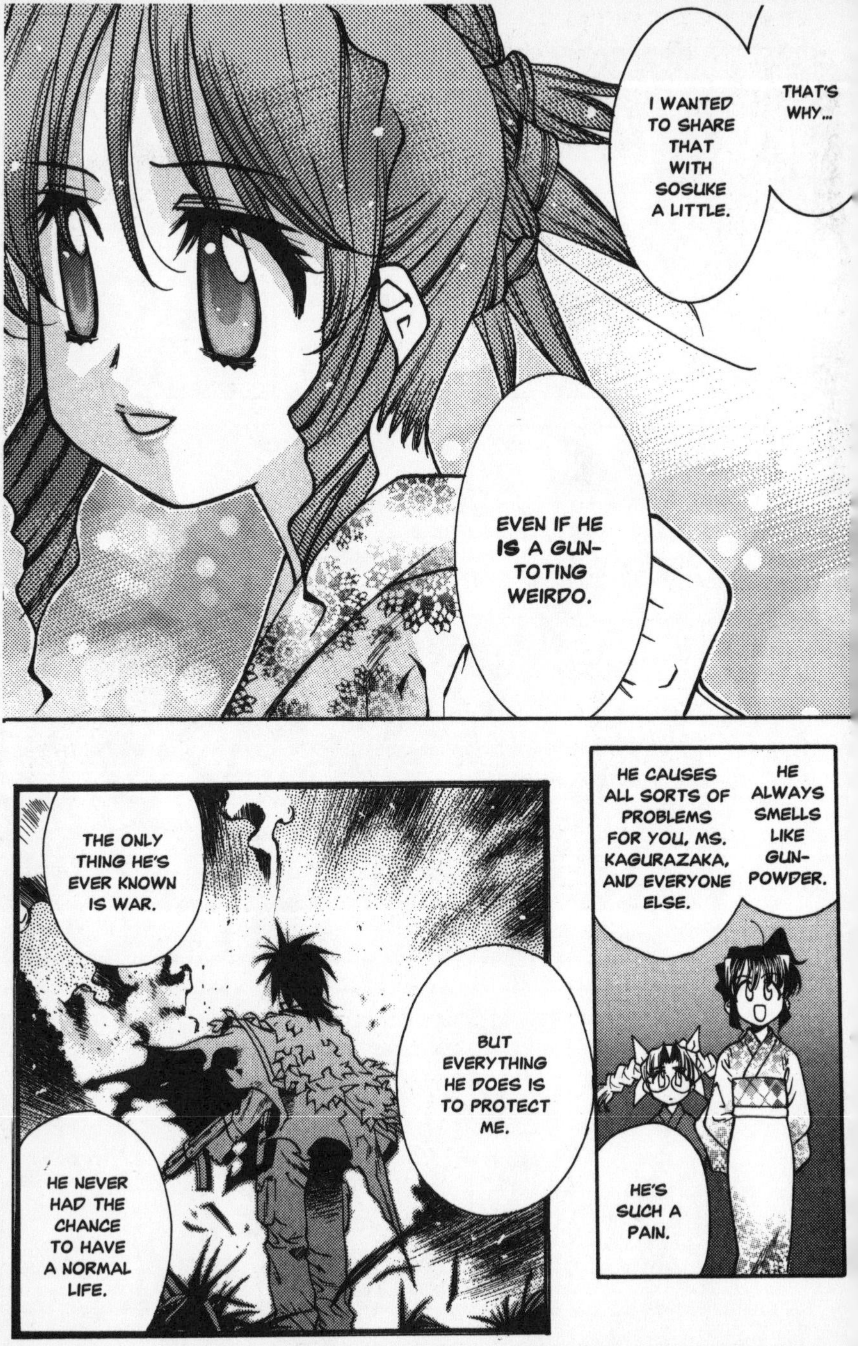
THAT'S WHY...
I WANTED TO SHARE THAT WITH SOSUKE A LITTLE.
EVEN IF HE IS A GUN-TOTING WEIRDO.
HE ALWAYS SMELLS LIKE GUN-POWDER.
HE CAUSES ALL SORTS OF PROBLEMS FOR YOU, MS. KAGURAZAKA, AND EVERYONE ELSE.
HE'S SUCH A PAIN.
THE ONLY THING HE'S EVER KNOWN IS WAR.
HE NEVER HAD THE CHANCE TO HAVE A NORMAL LIFE.
BUT EVERYTHING HE DOES IS TO PROTECT ME.

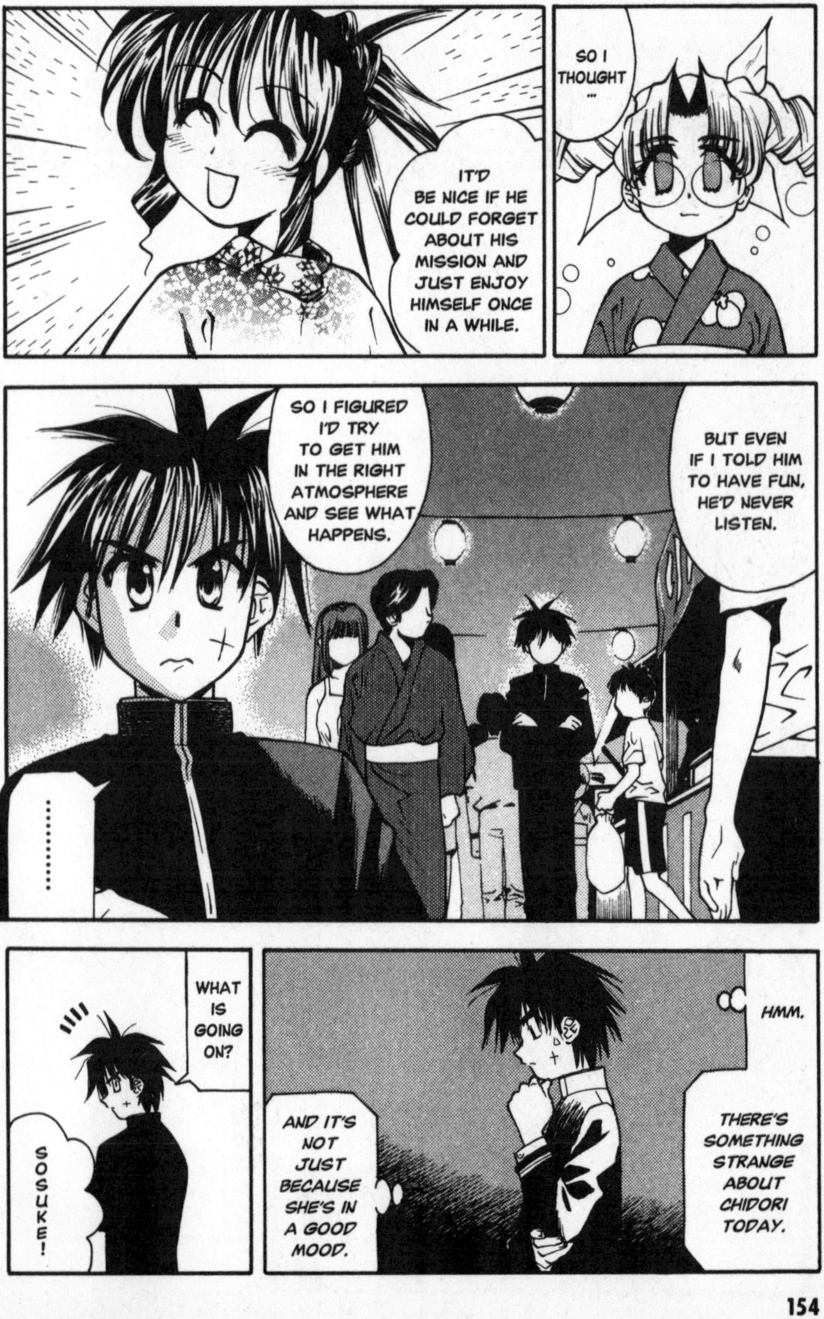

SO I THOUGHT ...
IT'D BE NICE IF HE COULD FORGET ABOUT HIS MISSION AND JUST ENJOY HIMSELF ONCE IN A WHILE.
BUT EVEN IF I TOLD HIM TO HAVE FUN, HE'D NEVER LISTEN.
SO I FIGURED I'D TRY TO GET HIM IN THE RIGHT ATMOSPHERE AND SEE WHAT HAPPENS.
....
HMM.
THERE'S SOMETHING STRANGE ABOUT CHIDORI TODAY.
AND IT'S NOT JUST BECAUSE SHE'S IN A GOOD MOOD.
SOSUKE!
WHAT IS GOING ON?

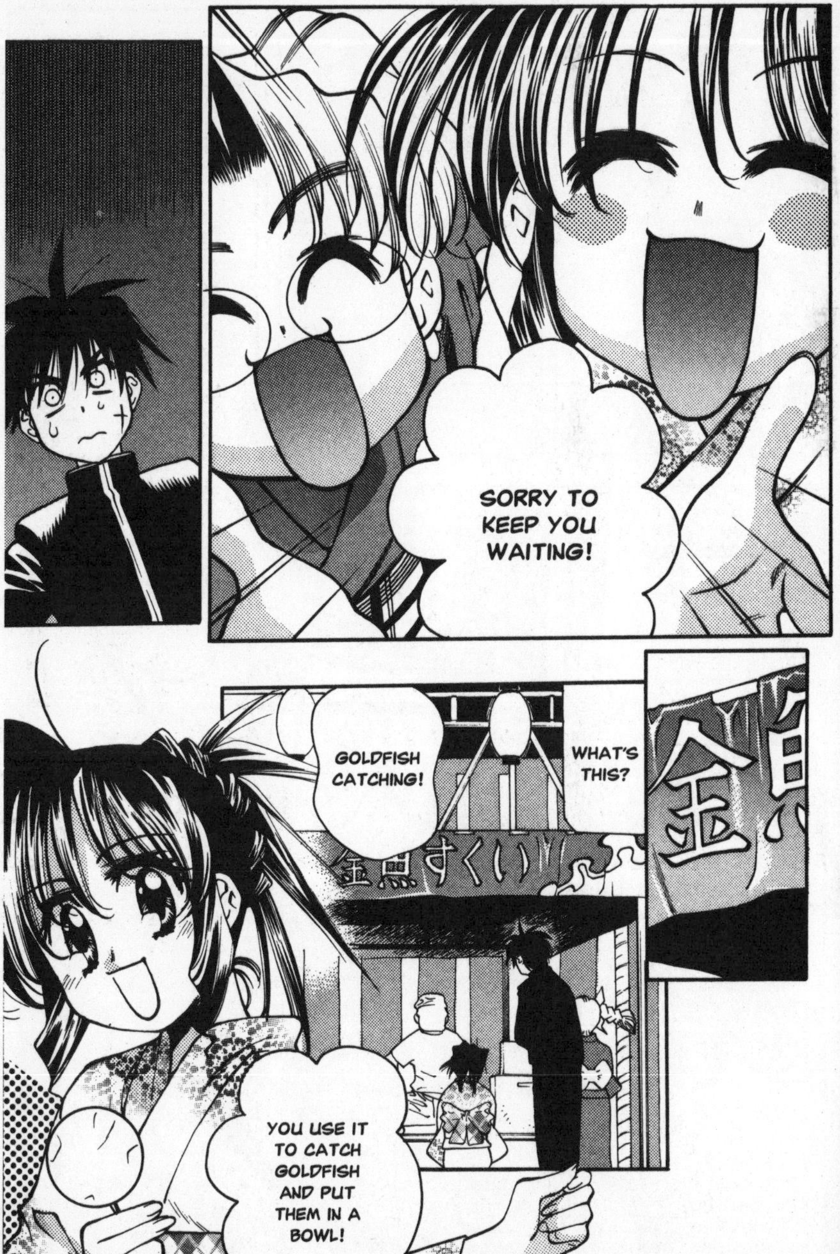
SORRY TO KEEP YOU WAITING!
WHAT'S THIS?
GOLDFISH CATCHING!
金魚すくい
YOU USE IT TO CATCH GOLDFISH AND PUT THEM IN A BOWL!

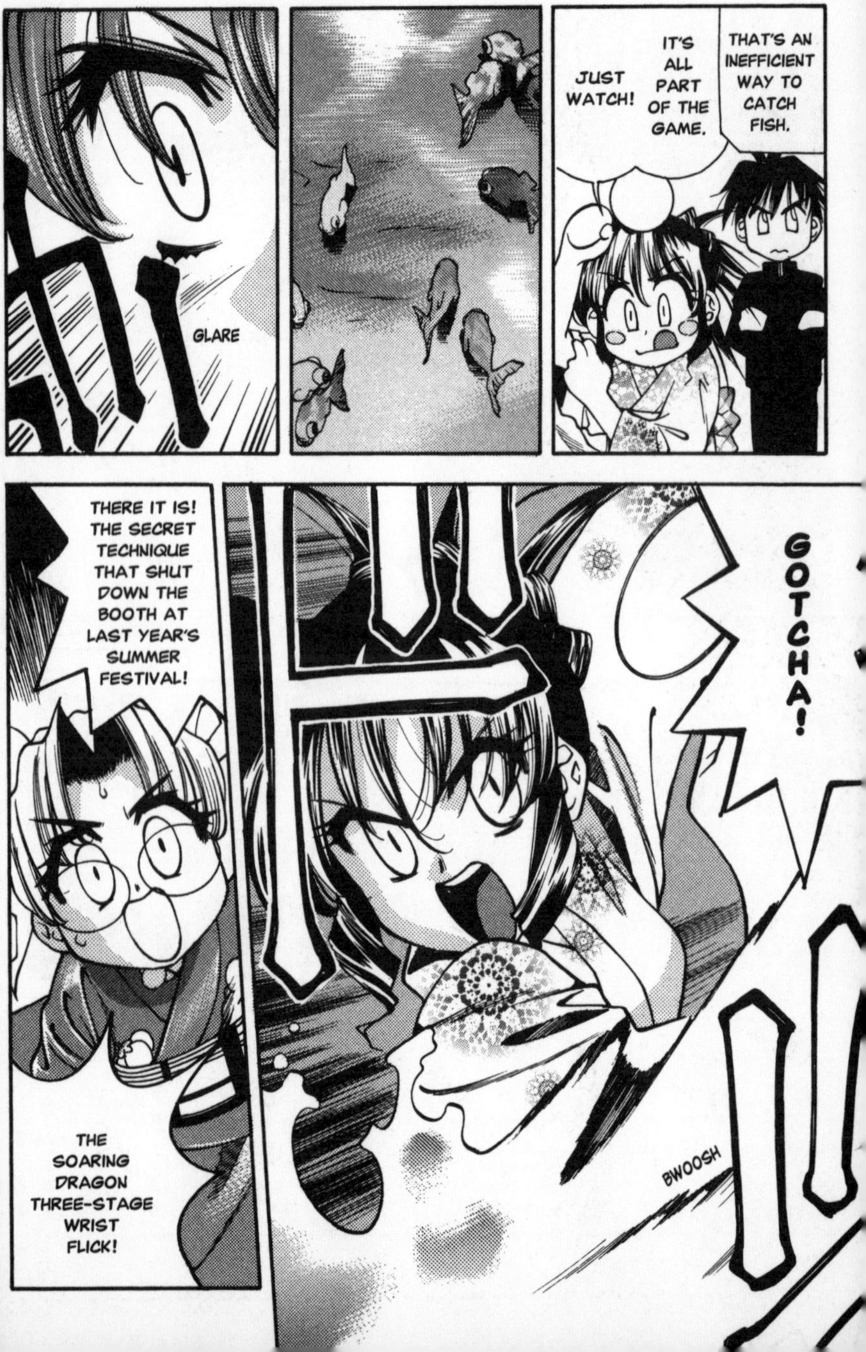
THAT'S AN INEFFICIENT WAY TO CATCH FISH.
IT'S ALL PART OF THE GAME.
JUST WATCH!
GLARE
GOTCHA!
BWOOSH
THERE IT IS! THE SECRET TECHNIQUE THAT SHUT DOWN THE BOOTH AT LAST YEAR'S SUMMER FESTIVAL!
THE SOARING DRAGON THREE-STAGE WRIST FLICK!

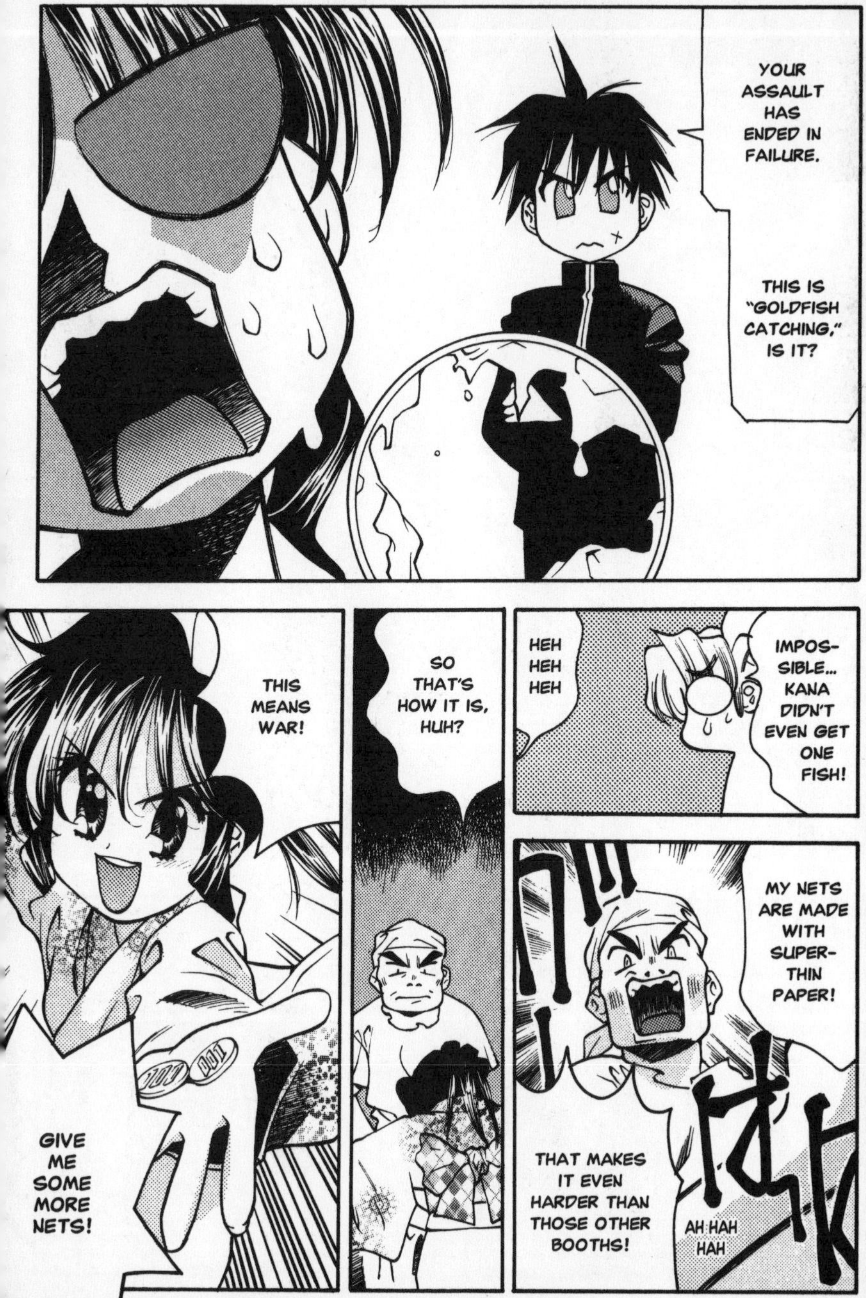
YOUR ASSAULT HAS ENDED IN FAILURE.
THIS IS "GOLDFISH CATCHING," IS IT?
IMPOSSIBLE... KANA DIDN'T EVEN GET ONE FISH!
HEH HEH HEH
MY NETS ARE MADE WITH SUPER-THIN PAPER!
THAT MAKES IT EVEN HARDER THAN THOSE OTHER BOOTHS!
AH HAH HAH
SO THAT'S HOW IT IS, HUH?
THIS MEANS WAR!
GIVE ME SOME MORE NETS!

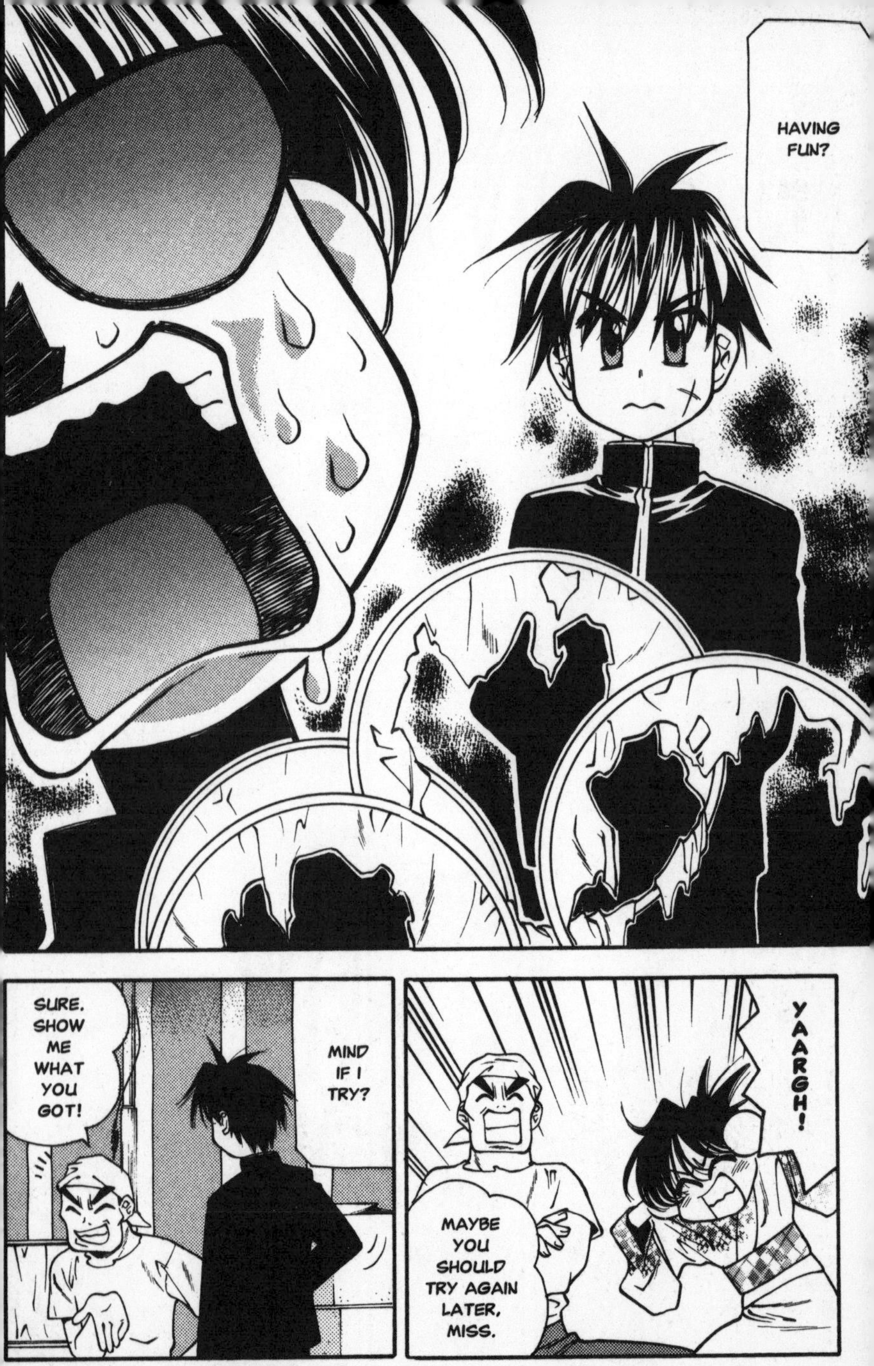
HAVING FUN?
YAAARGH!
MAYBE YOU SHOULD TRY AGAIN LATER, MISS.
MIND IF I TRY?
SURE. SHOW ME WHAT YOU GOT!

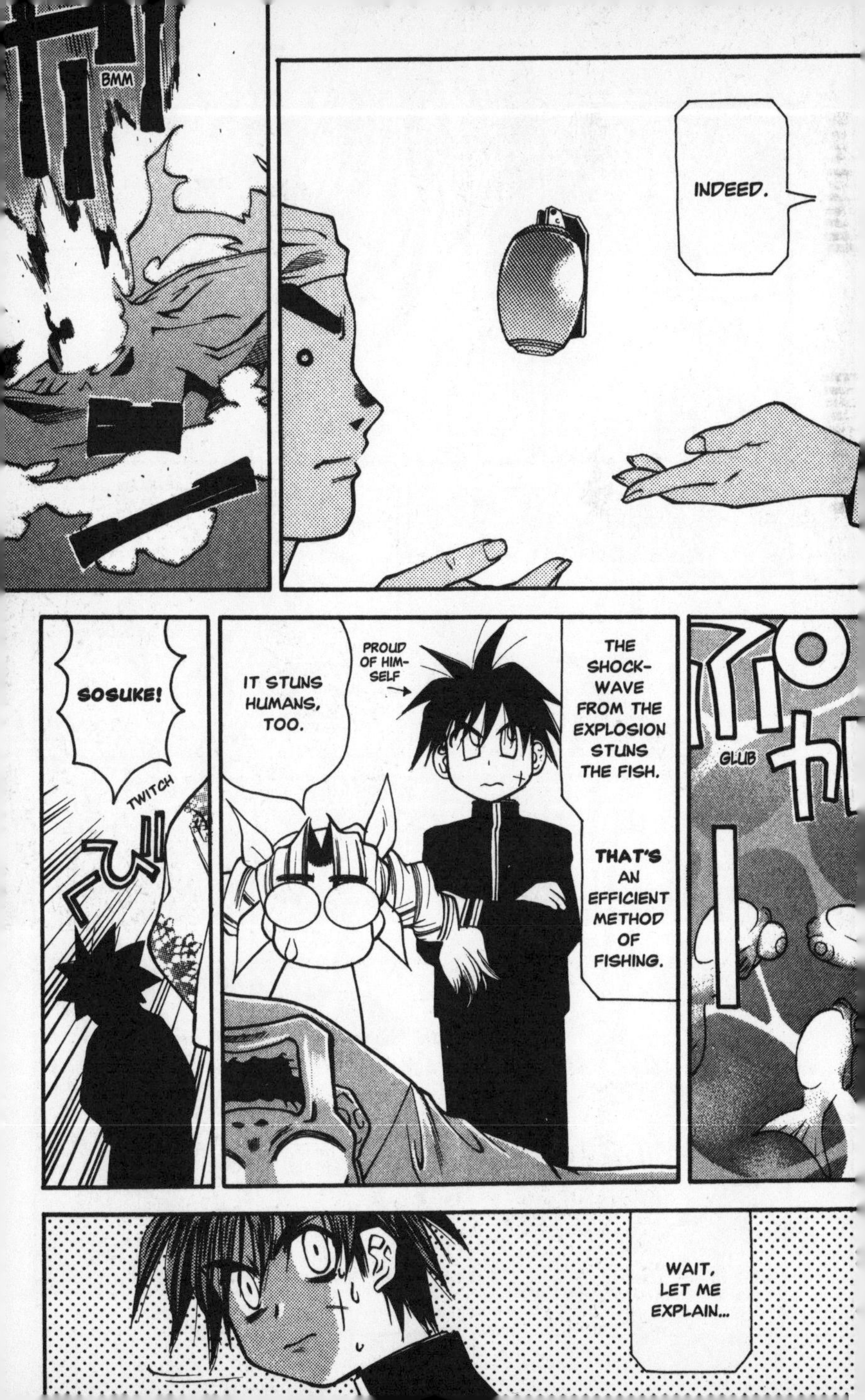
INDEED.
BMM
GLUB
THE SHOCK-WAVE FROM THE EXPLOSION STUNS THE FISH.
THAT'S AN EFFICIENT METHOD OF FISHING.
PROUD OF HIM-SELF
IT STUNS HUMANS, TOO.
SOSUKE!
TWITCH
WAIT, LET ME EXPLAIN...

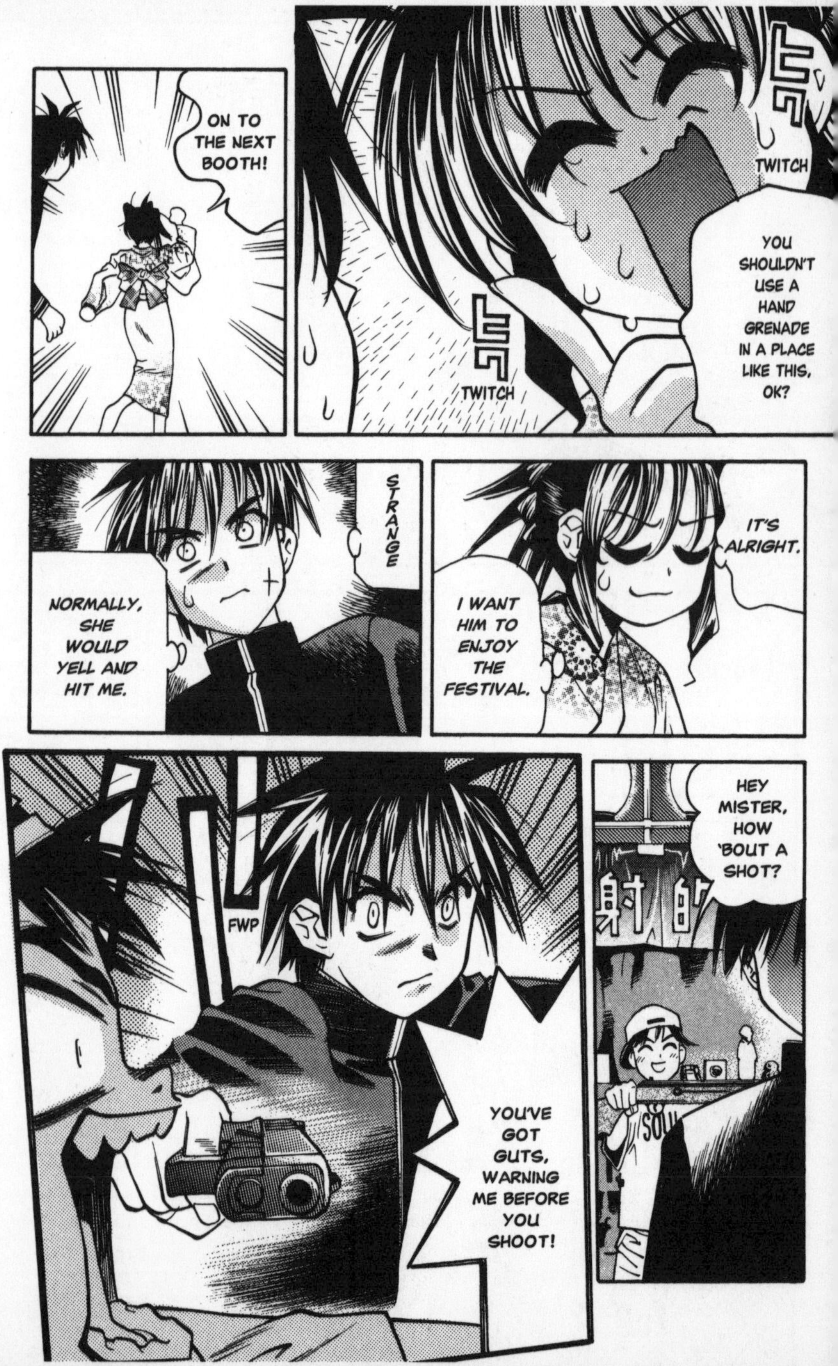
TWITCH
YOU SHOULDN'T USE A HAND GRENADE IN A PLACE LIKE THIS, OK?
TWITCH
ON TO THE NEXT BOOTH!
IT'S ALRIGHT.
I WANT HIM TO ENJOY THE FESTIVAL.
STRANGE
NORMALLY, SHE WOULD YELL AND HIT ME.
HEY MISTER, HOW 'BOUT A SHOT?
FWP
YOU'VE GOT GUTS, WARNING ME BEFORE YOU SHOOT!

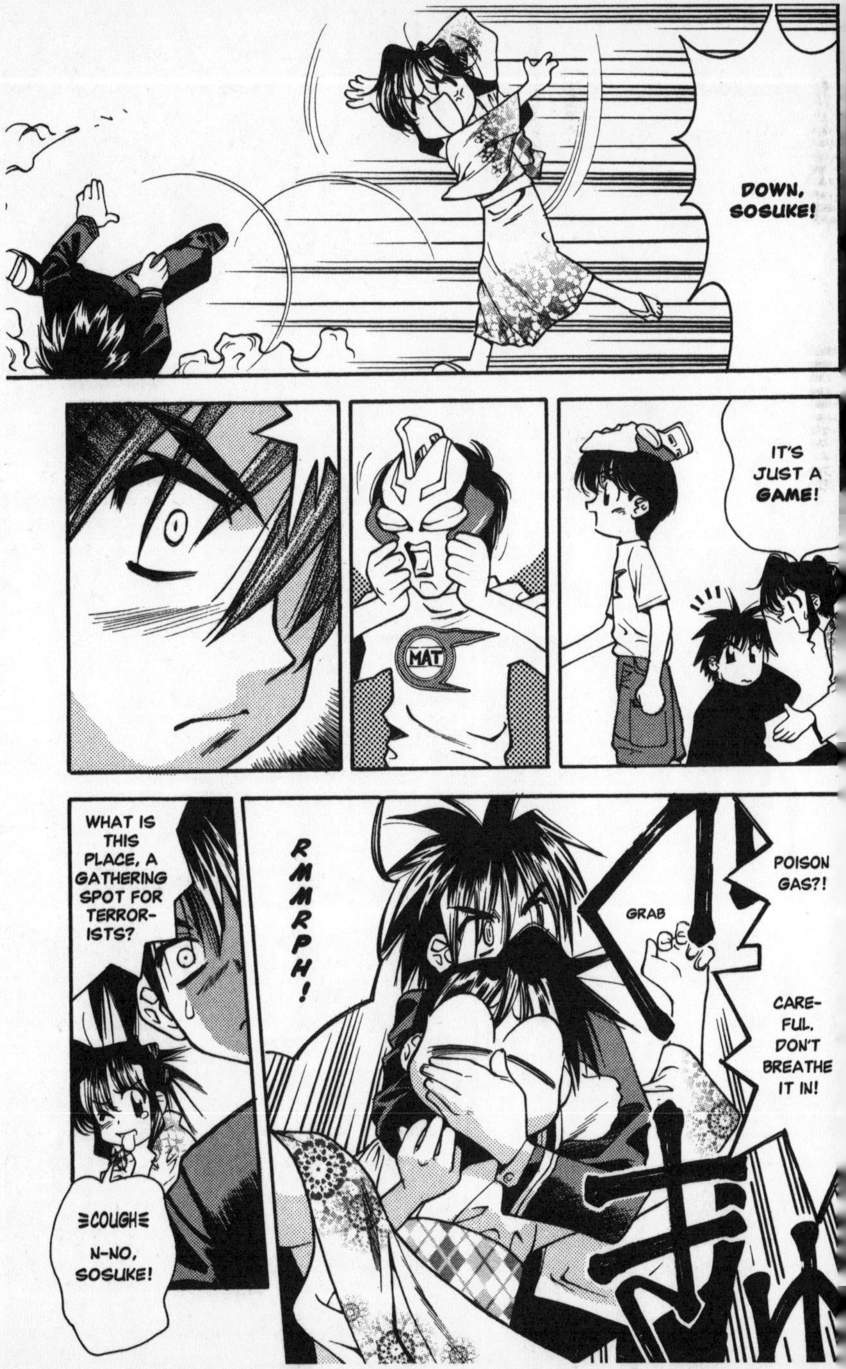
DOWN, SOSUKE!
IT'S JUST A GAME!
POISON GAS?!
GRAB
CARE-FUL. DON'T BREATHE IT IN!
RMMRPH!
WHAT IS THIS PLACE, A GATHERING SPOT FOR TERROR-ISTS?
COUGH
N-NO, SOSUKE!

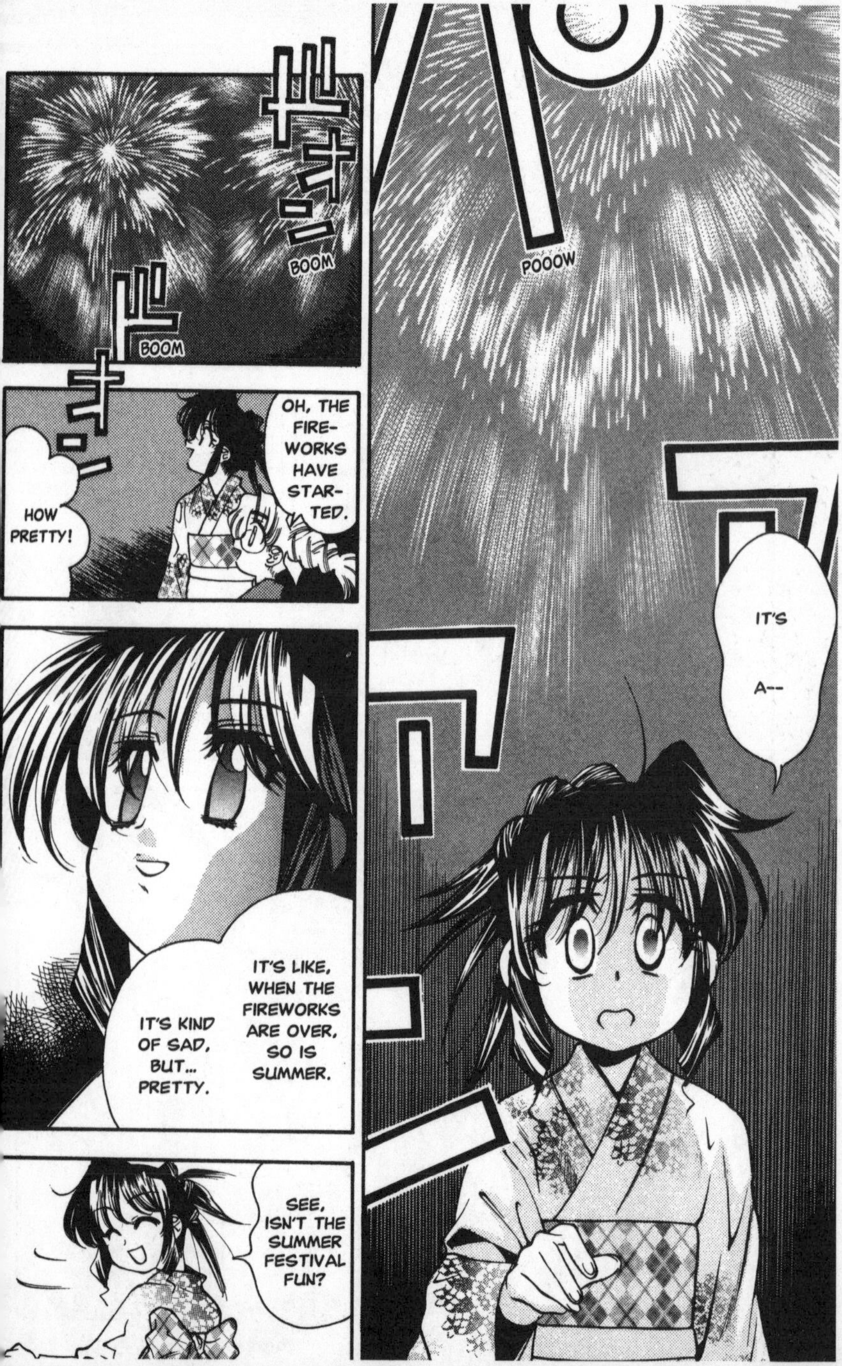
POOOW
IT'S A--
BOOM
BOOM
OH, THE FIRE-WORKS HAVE STAR-TED.
HOW PRETTY!
IT'S LIKE, WHEN THE FIREWORKS ARE OVER, SO IS SUMMER.
IT'S KIND OF SAD, BUT... PRETTY.
SEE, ISN'T THE SUMMER FESTIVAL FUN?

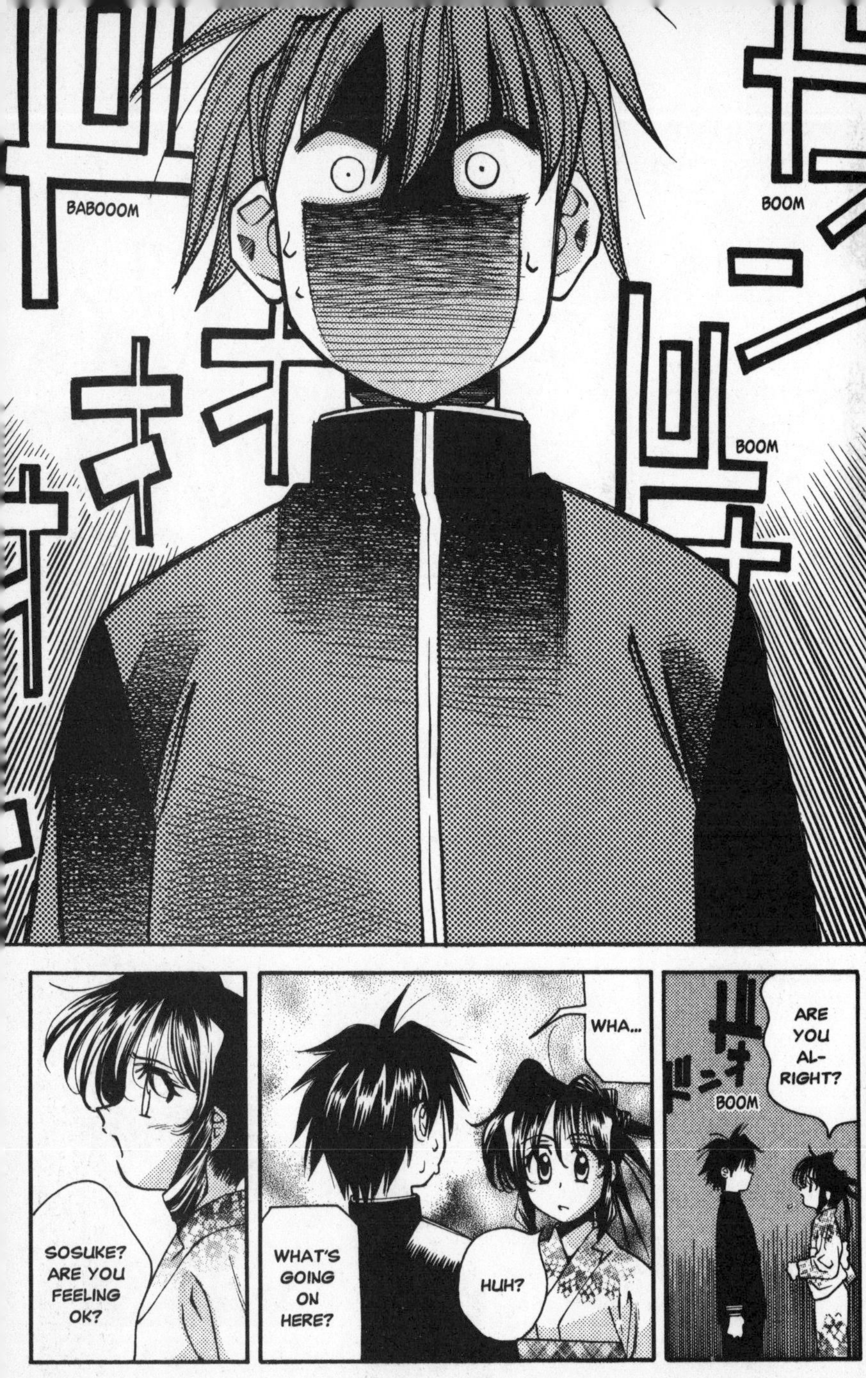
BOOM
BOOM
BABOOOM
BOOM
ARE YOU AL- RIGHT?
WHA...
HUH?
WHAT'S GOING ON HERE?
SOSUKE? ARE YOU FEELING OK?

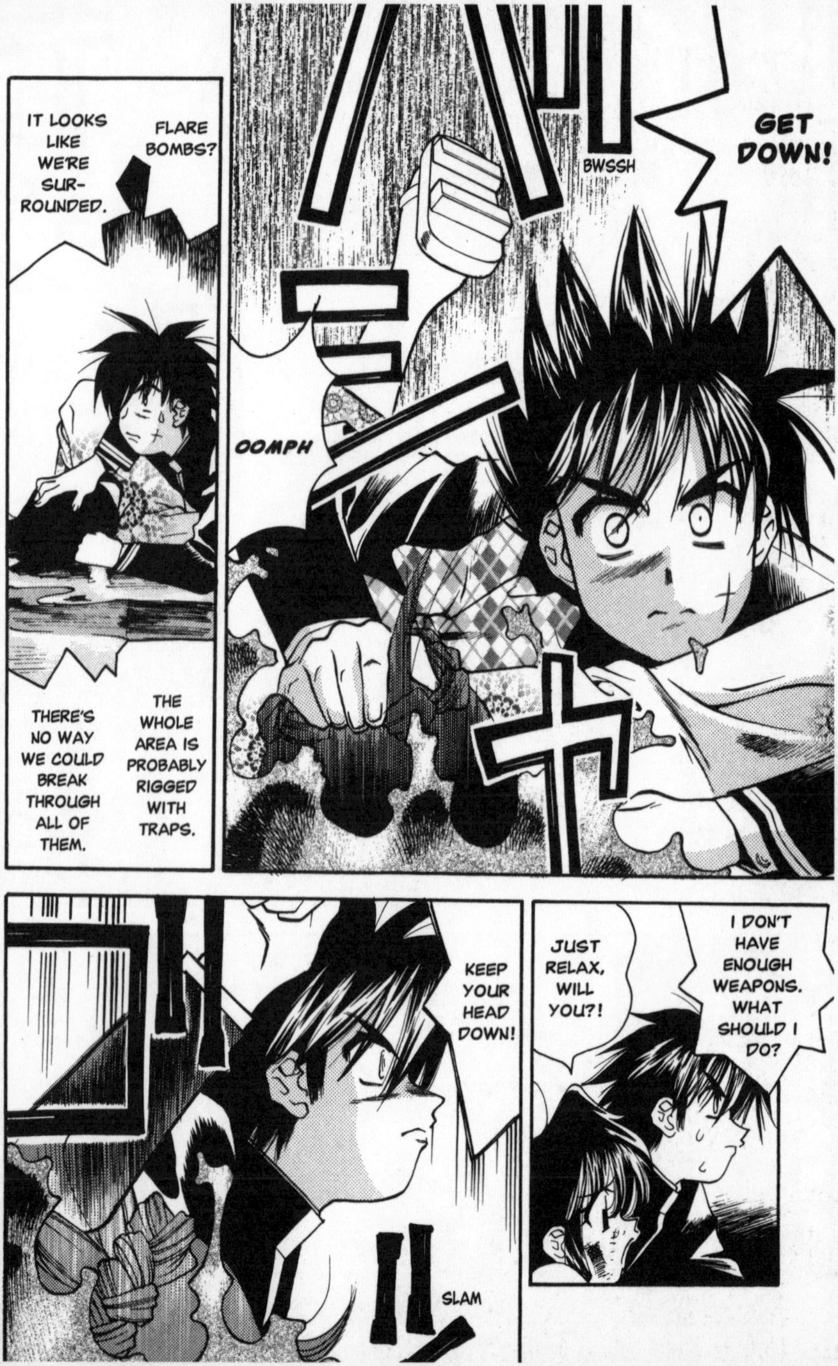
GET DOWN!
BWSSH
OOMPH
FLARE BOMBS?
IT LOOKS LIKE WE'RE SUR-ROUNDED.
THE WHOLE AREA IS PROBABLY RIGGED WITH TRAPS.
THERE'S NO WAY WE COULD BREAK THROUGH ALL OF THEM.
I DON'T HAVE ENOUGH WEAPONS. WHAT SHOULD I DO?
JUST RELAX, WILL YOU?!
KEEP YOUR HEAD DOWN!
SLAM

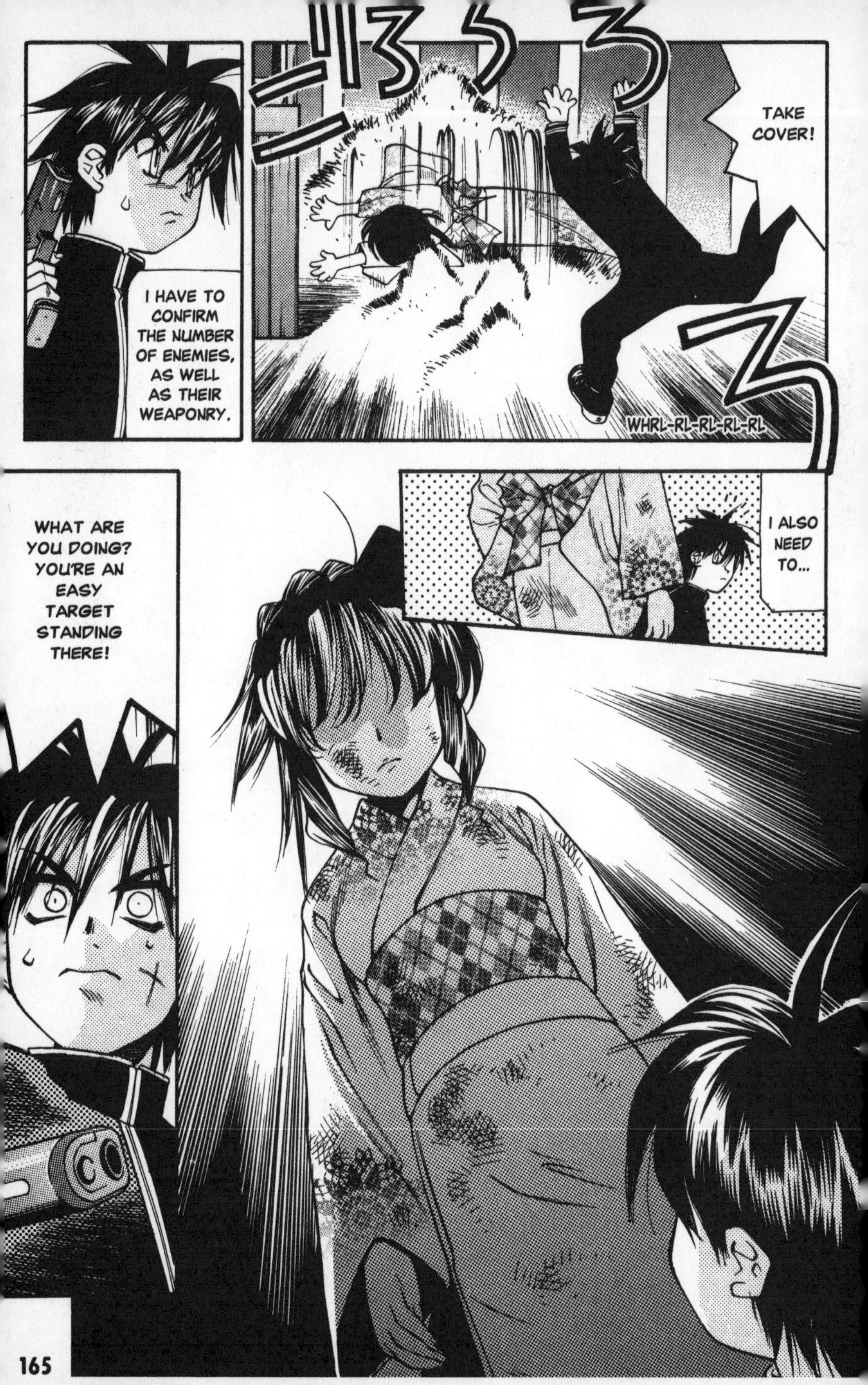
TAKE COVER!
WHRL-RL-RL-RL-RL
I HAVE TO CONFIRM THE NUMBER OF ENEMIES, AS WELL AS THEIR WEAPONRY.
I ALSO NEED TO...
WHAT ARE YOU DOING? YOU'RE AN EASY TARGET STANDING THERE!

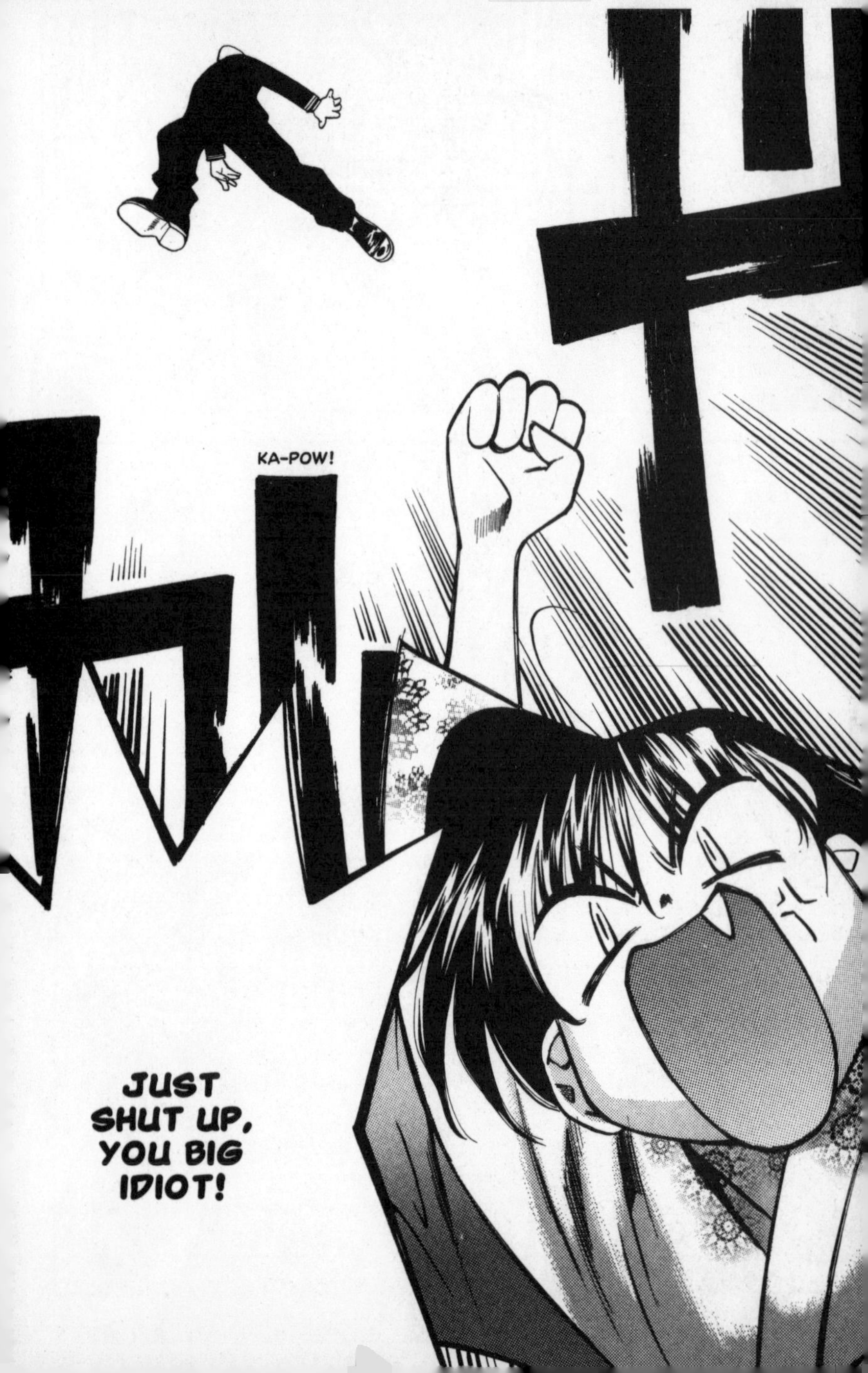
KA-POW!
JUST SHUT UP, YOU BIG IDIOT!

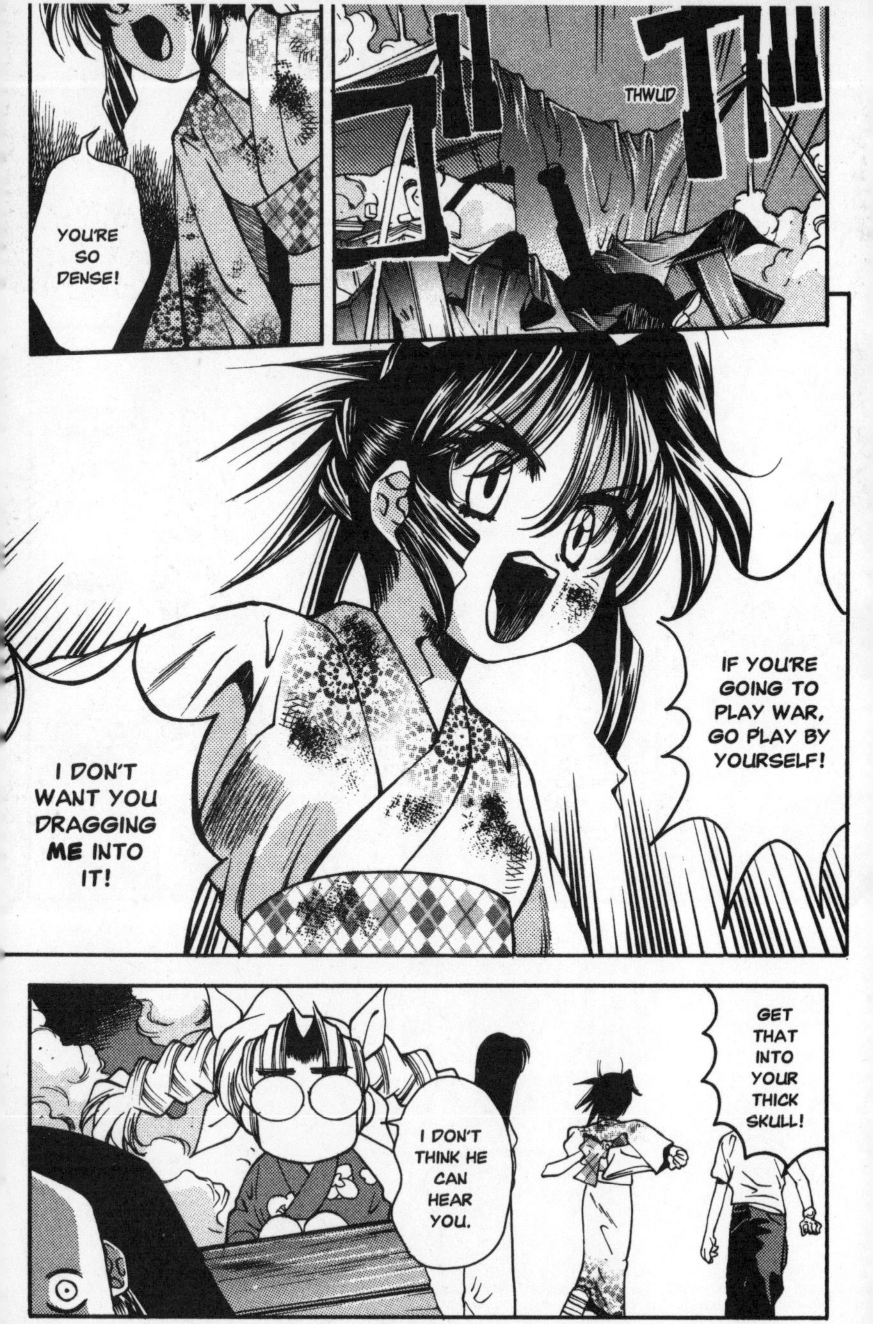
YOU'RE SO DENSE!
THWUD
IF YOU'RE GOING TO PLAY WAR, GO PLAY BY YOURSELF!
I DON'T WANT YOU DRAGGING ME INTO IT!
GET THAT INTO YOUR THICK SKULL!
I DON'T THINK HE CAN HEAR YOU.

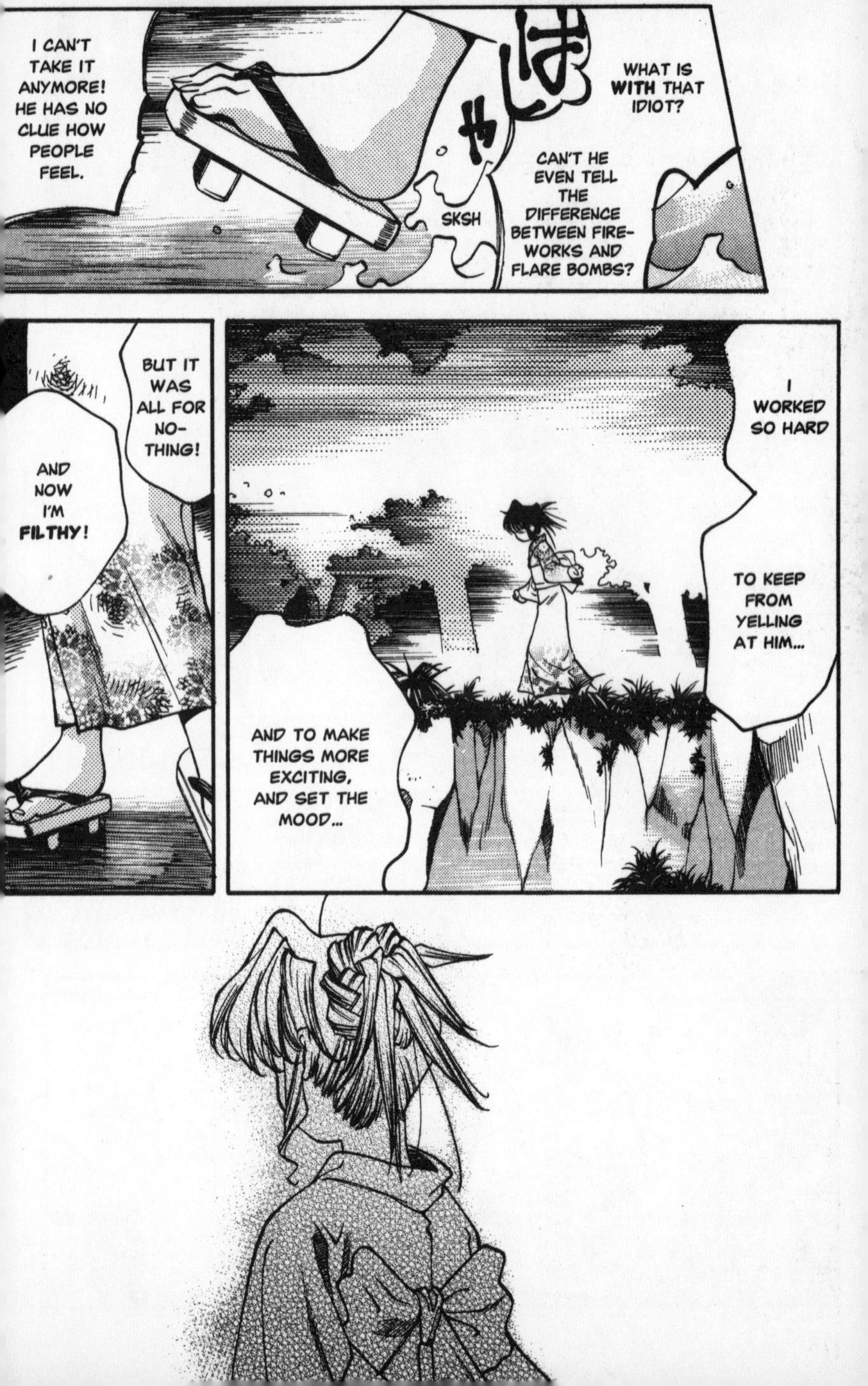
WHAT IS WITH THAT IDIOT?
CAN'T HE EVEN TELL THE DIFFERENCE BETWEEN FIRE-WORKS AND FLARE BOMBS?
ばしゃ
SKSH
I CAN'T TAKE IT ANYMORE! HE HAS NO CLUE HOW PEOPLE FEEL.
I WORKED SO HARD
TO KEEP FROM YELLING AT HIM...
AND TO MAKE THINGS MORE EXCITING, AND SET THE MOOD...
BUT IT WAS ALL FOR NO-THING!
AND NOW I'M FILTHY!

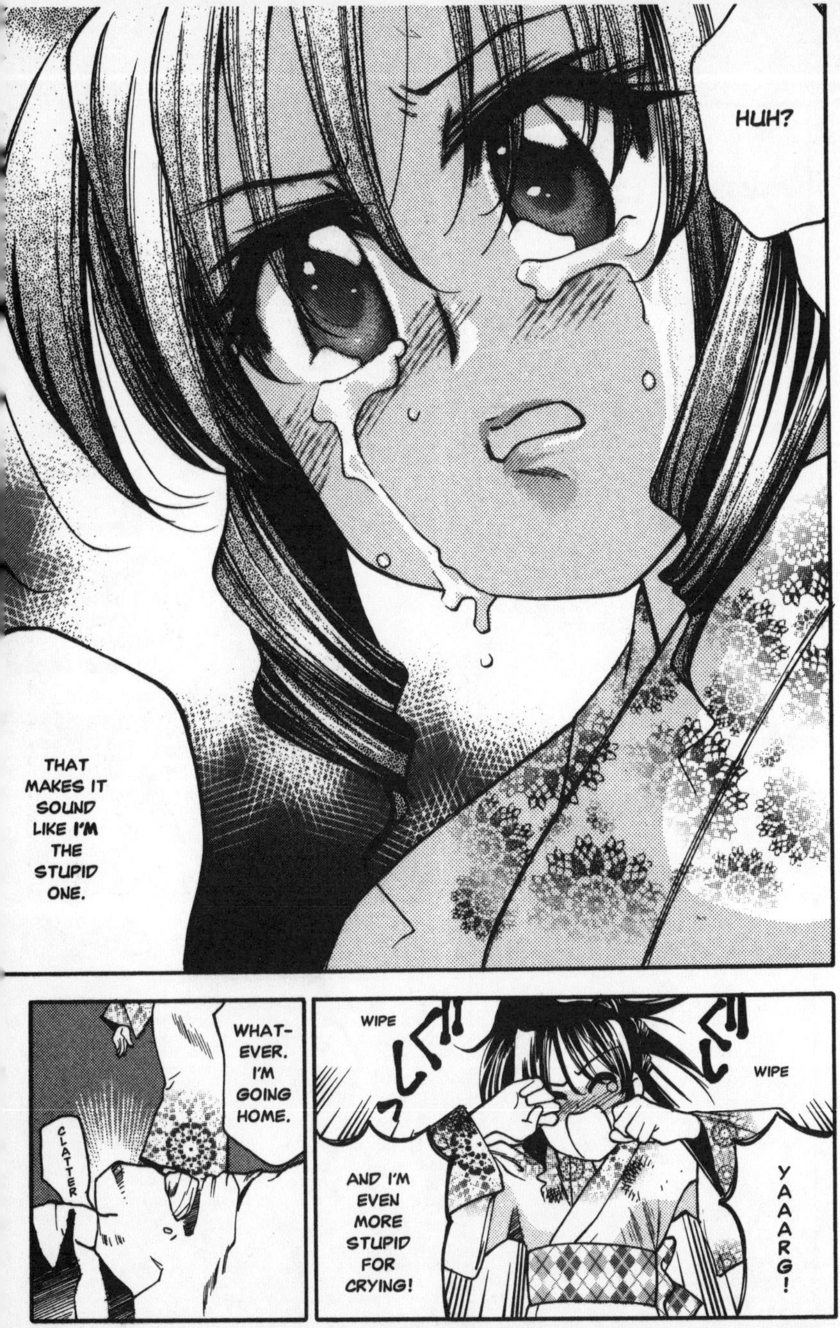
HUH?
THAT MAKES IT SOUND LIKE I'M THE STUPID ONE.
WIPE
WIPE
YAAARG!
AND I'M EVEN MORE STUPID FOR CRYING!
WHAT-EVER. I'M GOING HOME.
CLATTER

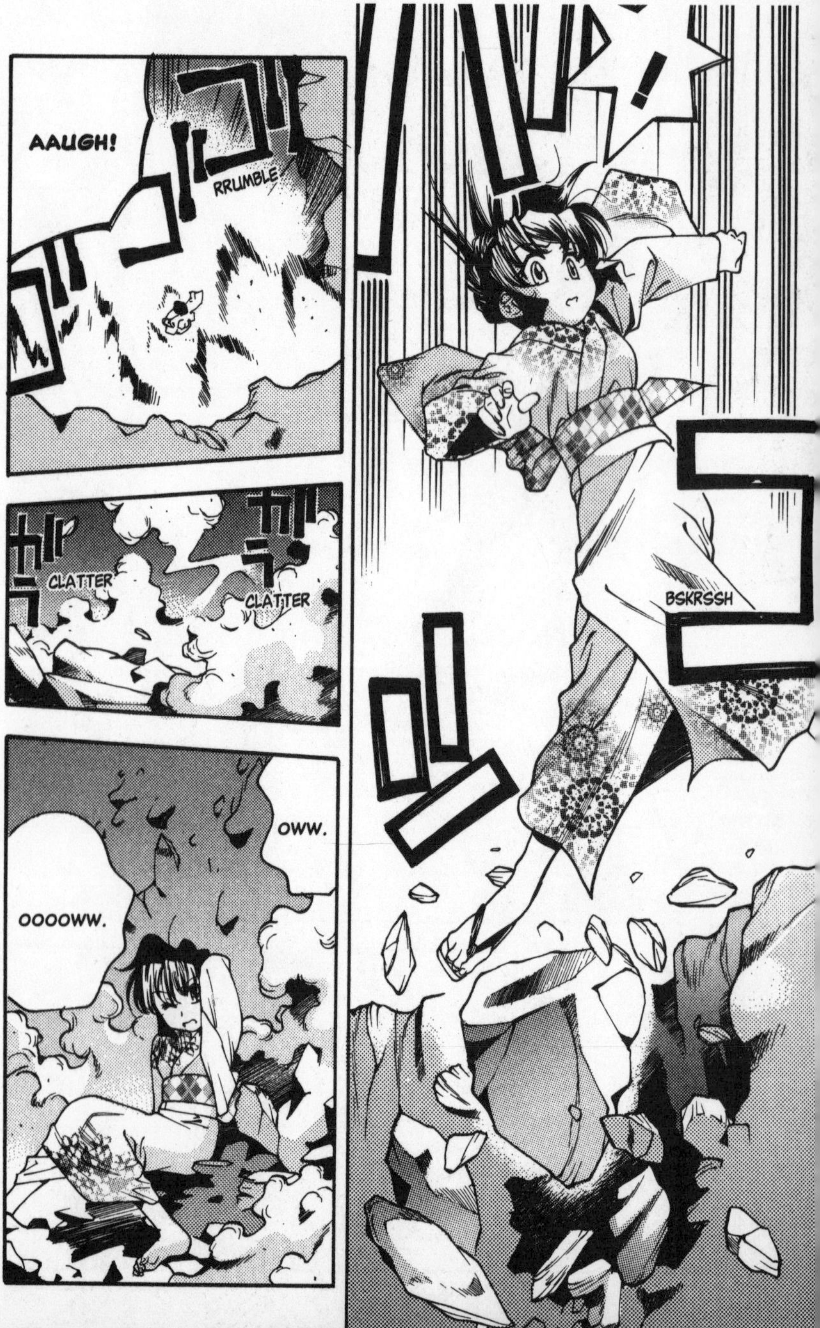
BSKRSSH
AAUGH!
RRUMBLE
CLATTER
CLATTER
OWW.
OOOOWW.

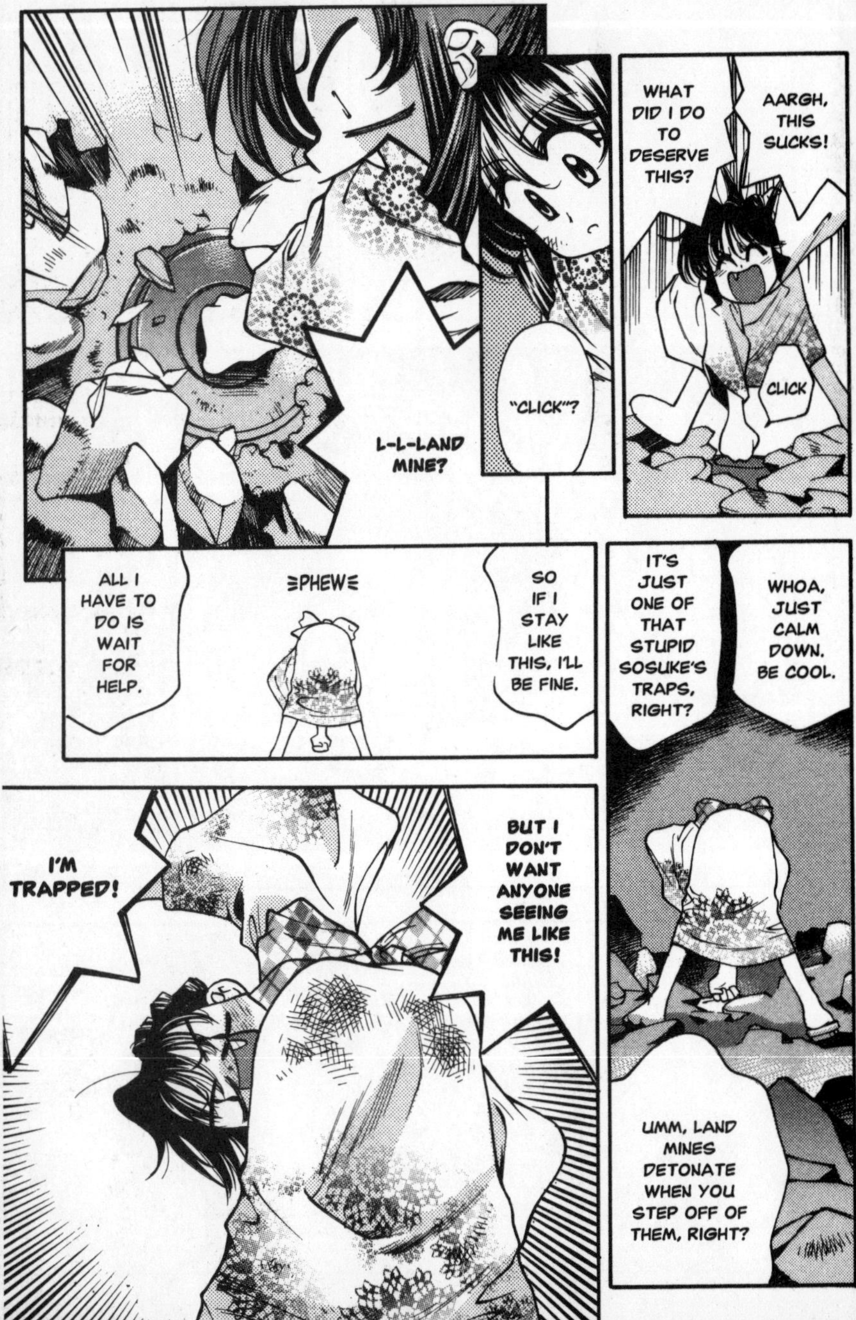
AARGH, THIS SUCKS!
WHAT DID I DO TO DESERVE THIS?
CLICK
"CLICK"?
L-L-LAND MINE?
WHOA, JUST CALM DOWN. BE COOL.
IT'S JUST ONE OF THAT STUPID SOSUKE'S TRAPS, RIGHT?
SO IF I STAY LIKE THIS, I'LL BE FINE.
PHEW
ALL I HAVE TO DO IS WAIT FOR HELP.
UMM, LAND MINES DETONATE WHEN YOU STEP OFF OF THEM, RIGHT?
I'M TRAPPED!
BUT I DON'T WANT ANYONE SEEING ME LIKE THIS!

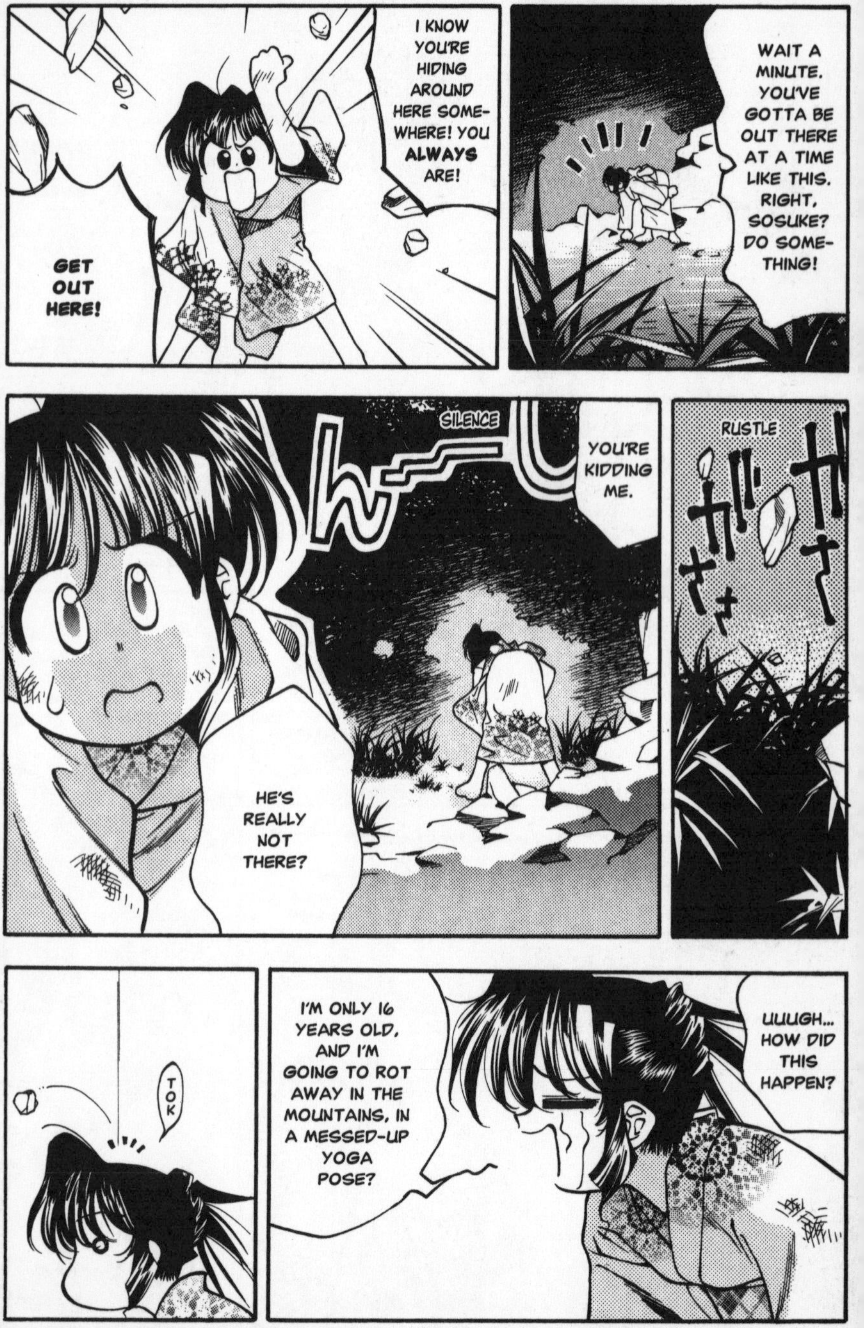
WAIT A MINUTE. YOU'VE GOTTA BE OUT THERE AT A TIME LIKE THIS. RIGHT, SOSUKE? DO SOME-THING!
I KNOW YOU'RE HIDING AROUND HERE SOME-WHERE! YOU ALWAYS ARE!
GET OUT HERE!
RUSTLE
ガサ
ガサ
YOU'RE KIDDING ME.
SILENCE
HE'S REALLY NOT THERE?
UUUGH... HOW DID THIS HAPPEN?
I'M ONLY 16 YEARS OLD, AND I'M GOING TO ROT AWAY IN THE MOUNTAINS, IN A MESSED-UP YOGA POSE?
TOK

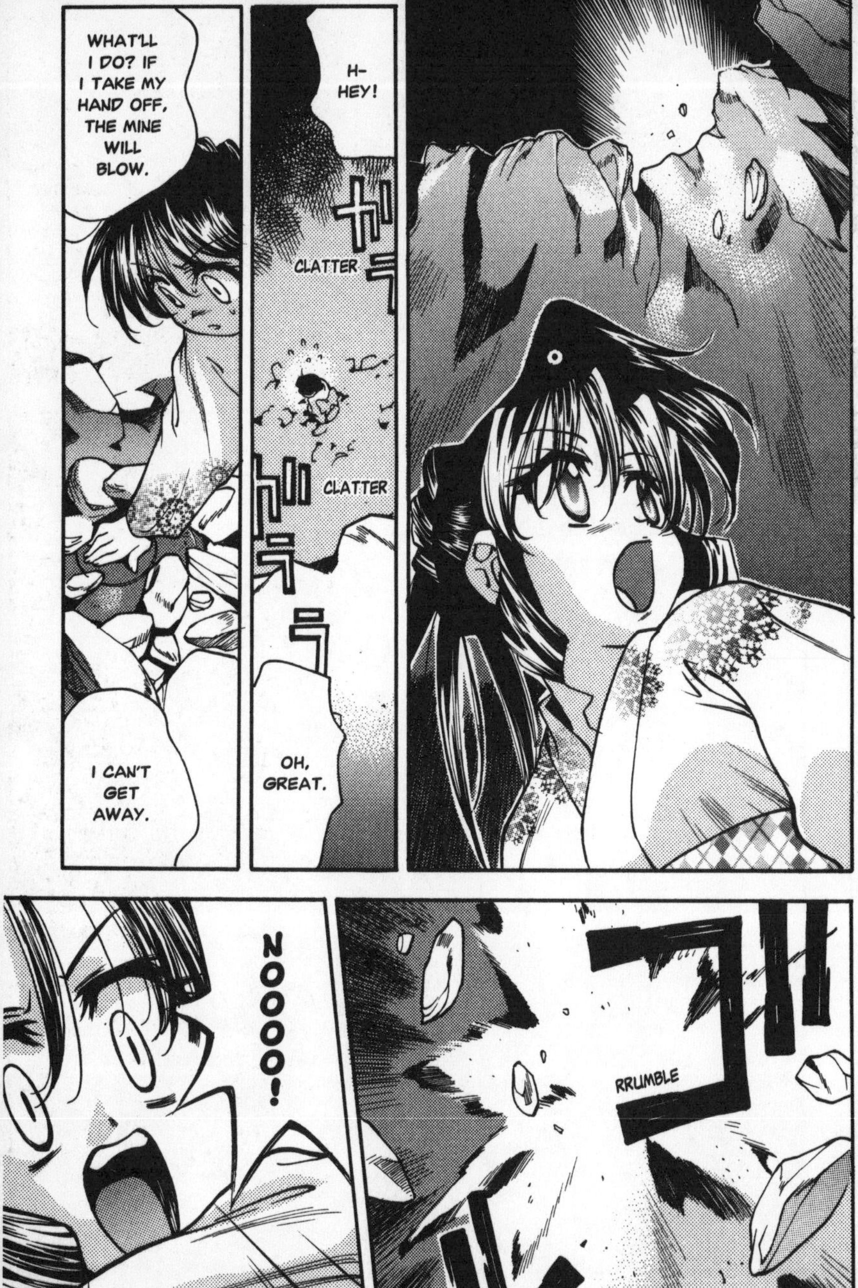
H-
HEY!
CLATTER
CLATTER
OH, GREAT.
WHAT'LL I DO? IF I TAKE MY HAND OFF, THE MINE WILL BLOW.
I CAN'T GET AWAY.
RRUMBLE
NOOOOO!

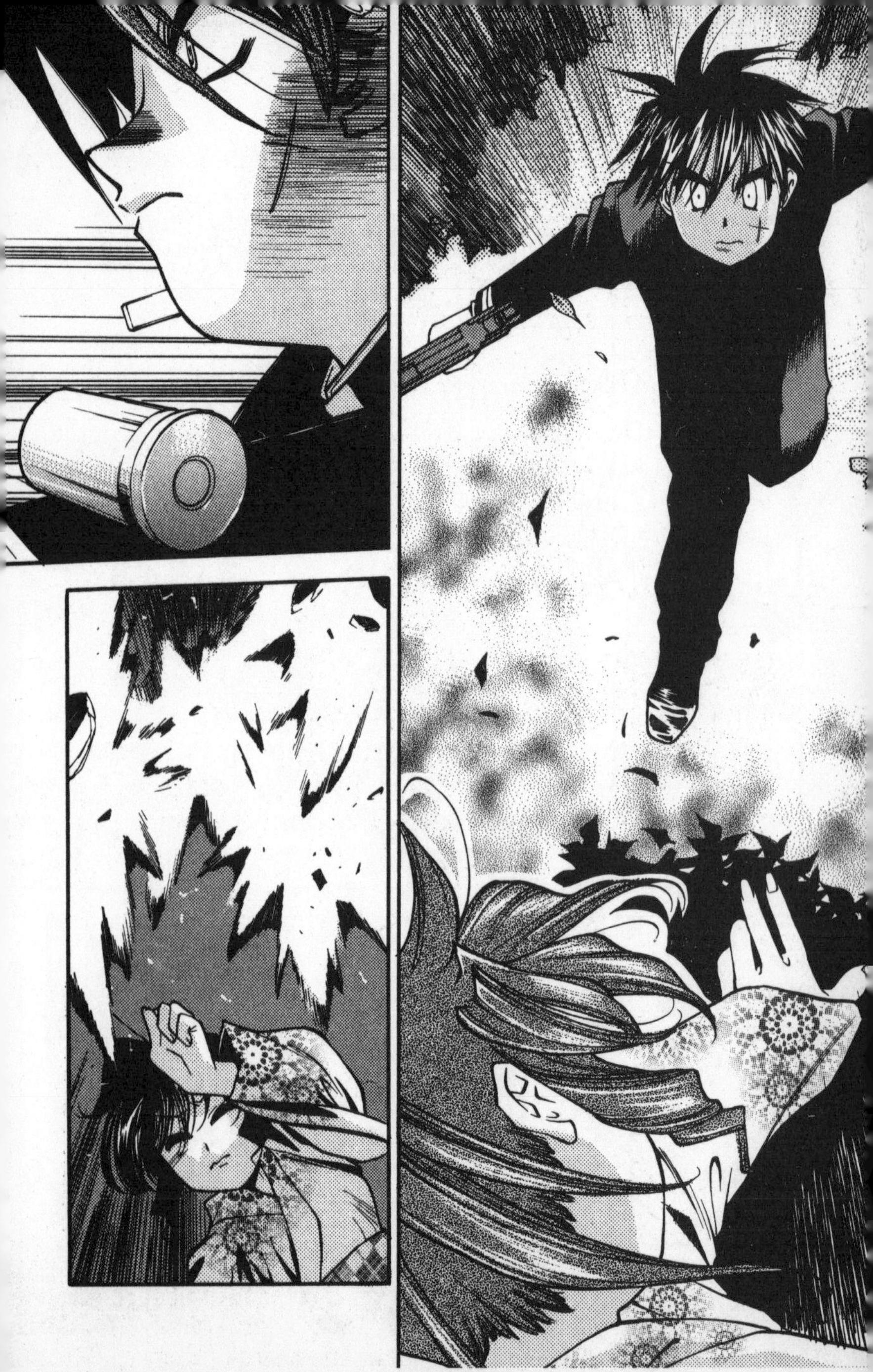

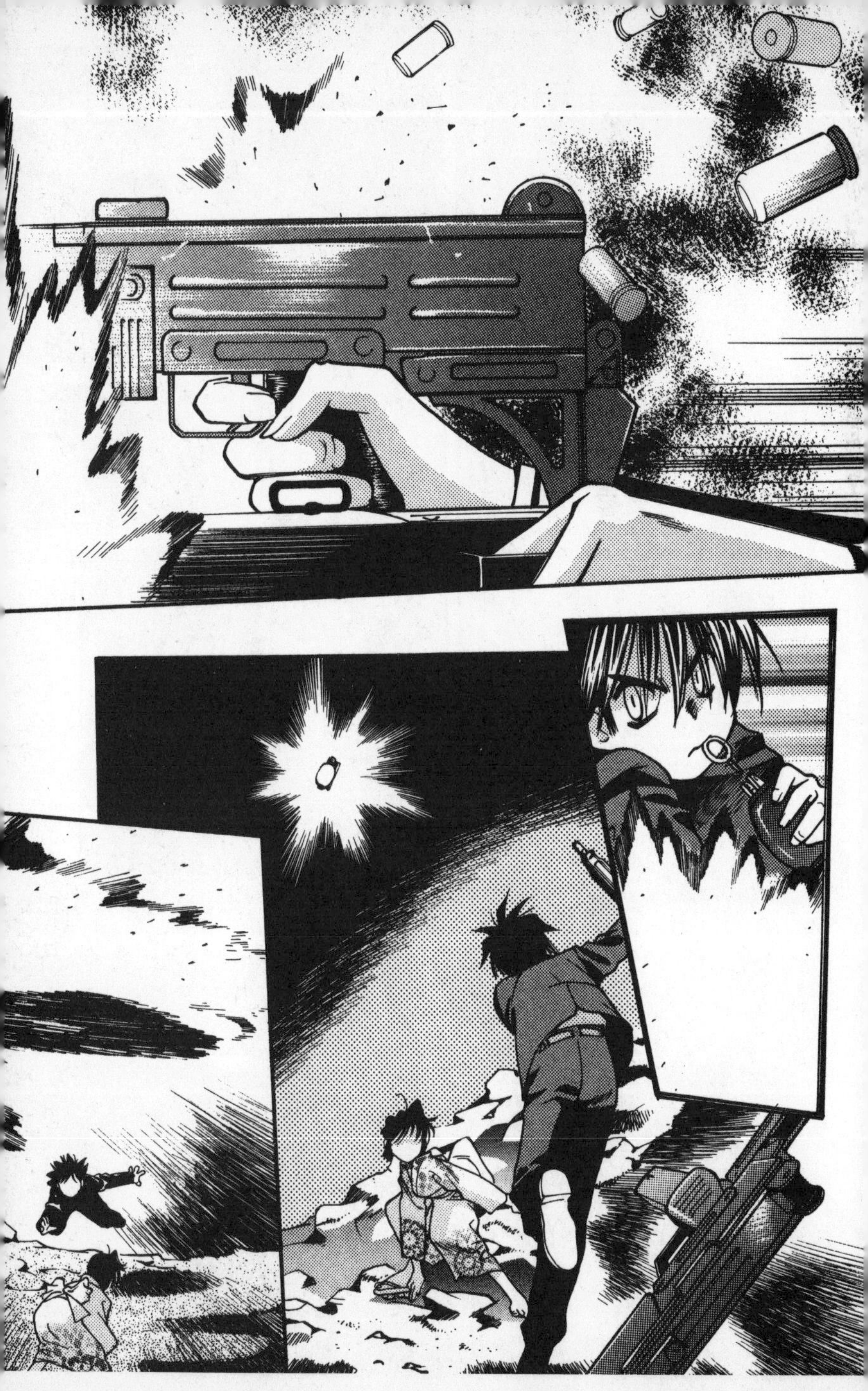

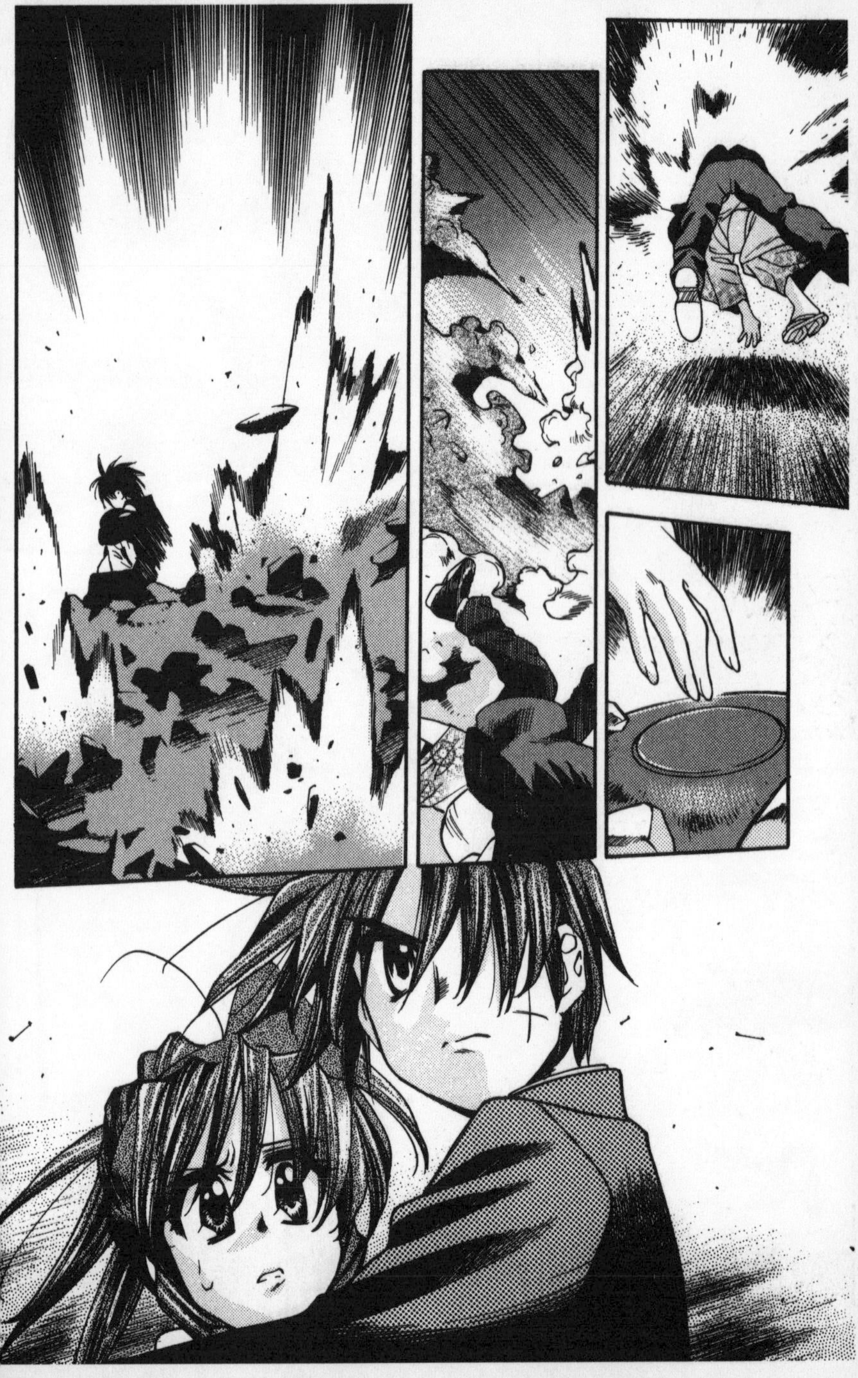

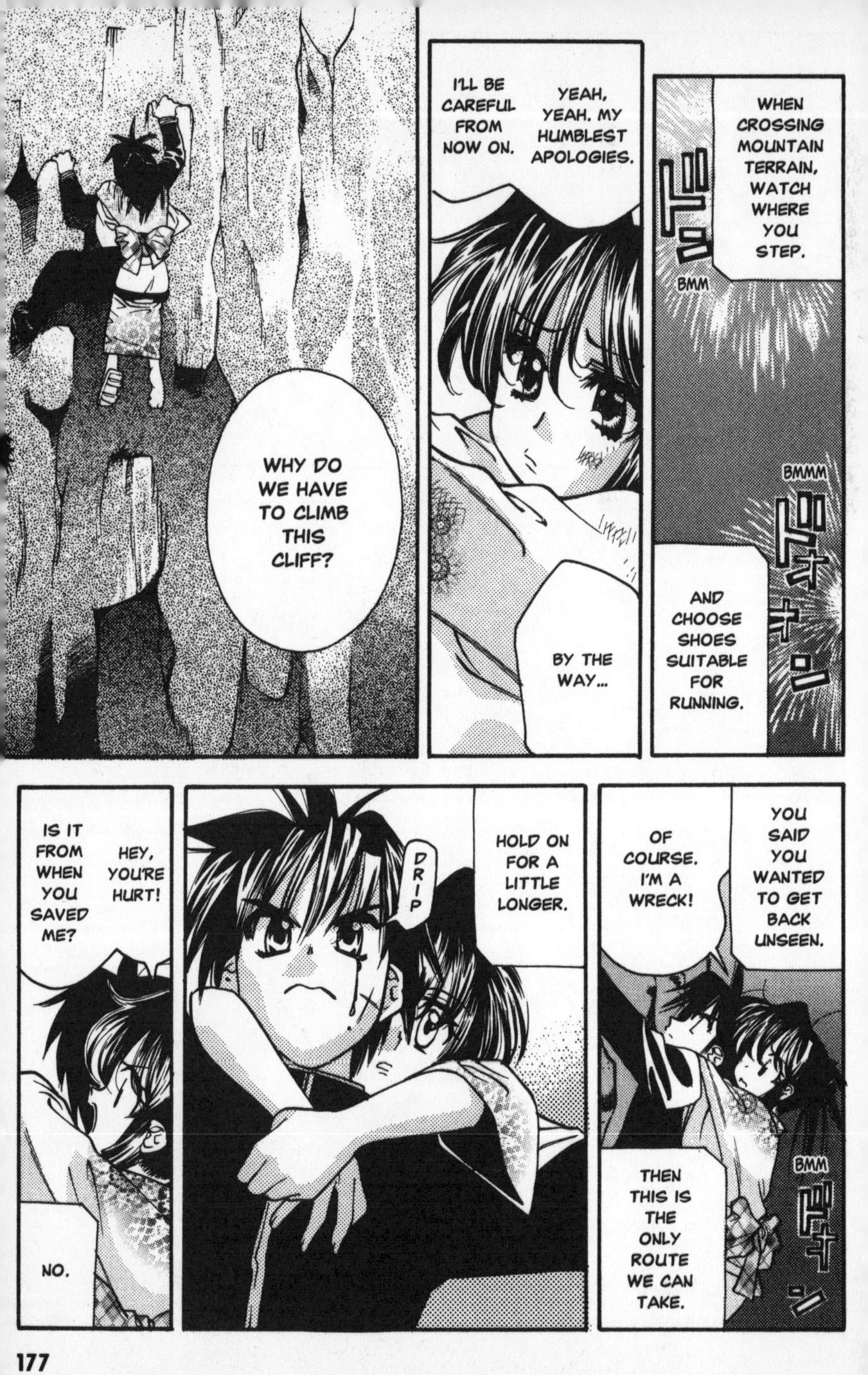

WHEN CROSSING MOUNTAIN TERRAIN, WATCH WHERE YOU STEP.
BMM
AND CHOOSE SHOES SUITABLE FOR RUNNING.
BMMM
YEAH, YEAH. MY HUMBLEST APOLOGIES.
I'LL BE CAREFUL FROM NOW ON.
BY THE WAY...
WHY DO WE HAVE TO CLIMB THIS CLIFF?
YOU SAID YOU WANTED TO GET BACK UNSEEN.
OF COURSE. I'M A WRECK!
THEN THIS IS THE ONLY ROUTE WE CAN TAKE.
BMM
HOLD ON FOR A LITTLE LONGER.
DRIP
HEY, YOU'RE HURT!
IS IT FROM WHEN YOU SAVED ME?
NO.

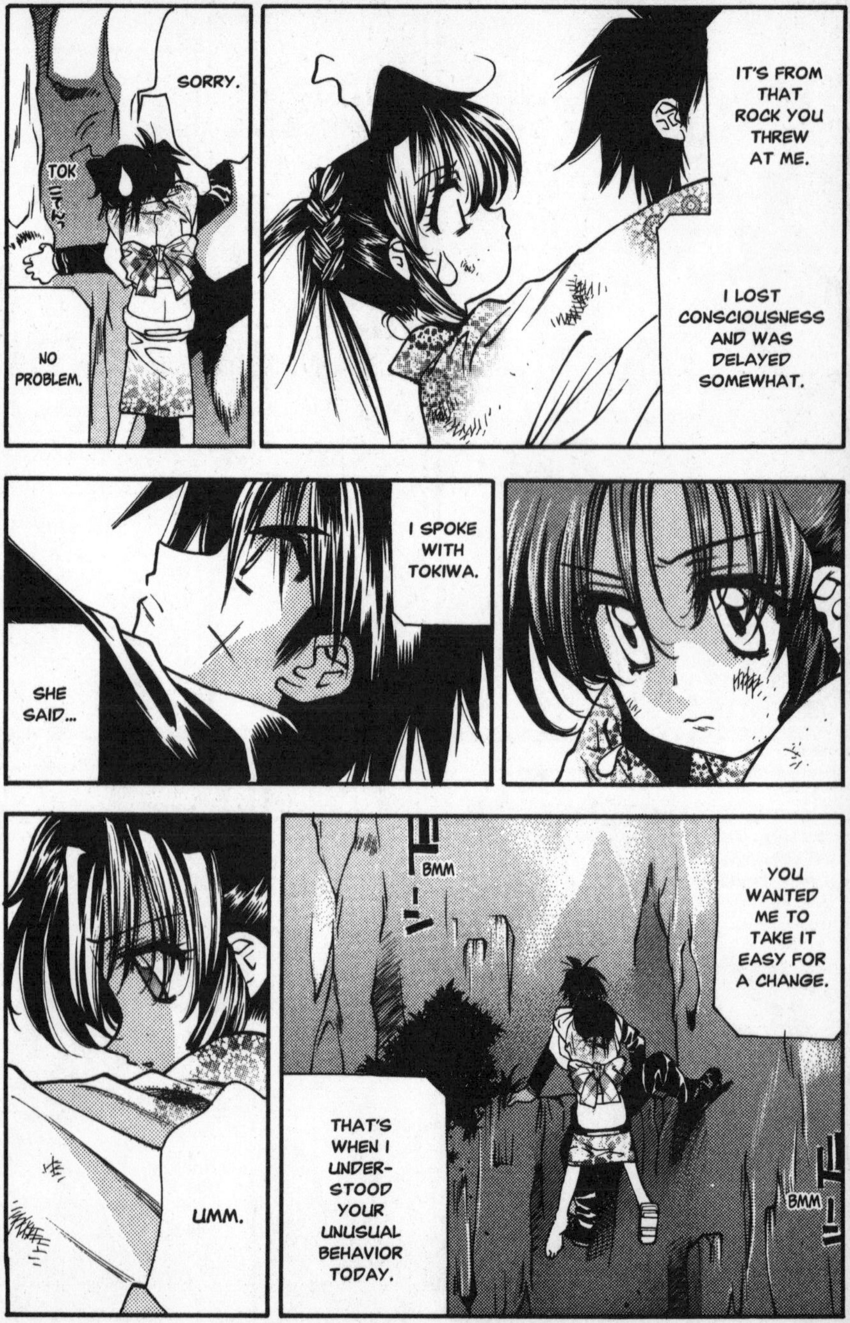
IT'S FROM THAT ROCK YOU THREW AT ME.
I LOST CONSCIOUSNESS AND WAS DELAYED SOMEWHAT.
SORRY.
TOK
NO PROBLEM.
I SPOKE WITH TOKIWA.
SHE SAID...
YOU WANTED ME TO TAKE IT EASY FOR A CHANGE.
BMM
THAT'S WHEN I UNDER-STOOD YOUR UNUSUAL BEHAVIOR TODAY.
BMM
UMM.

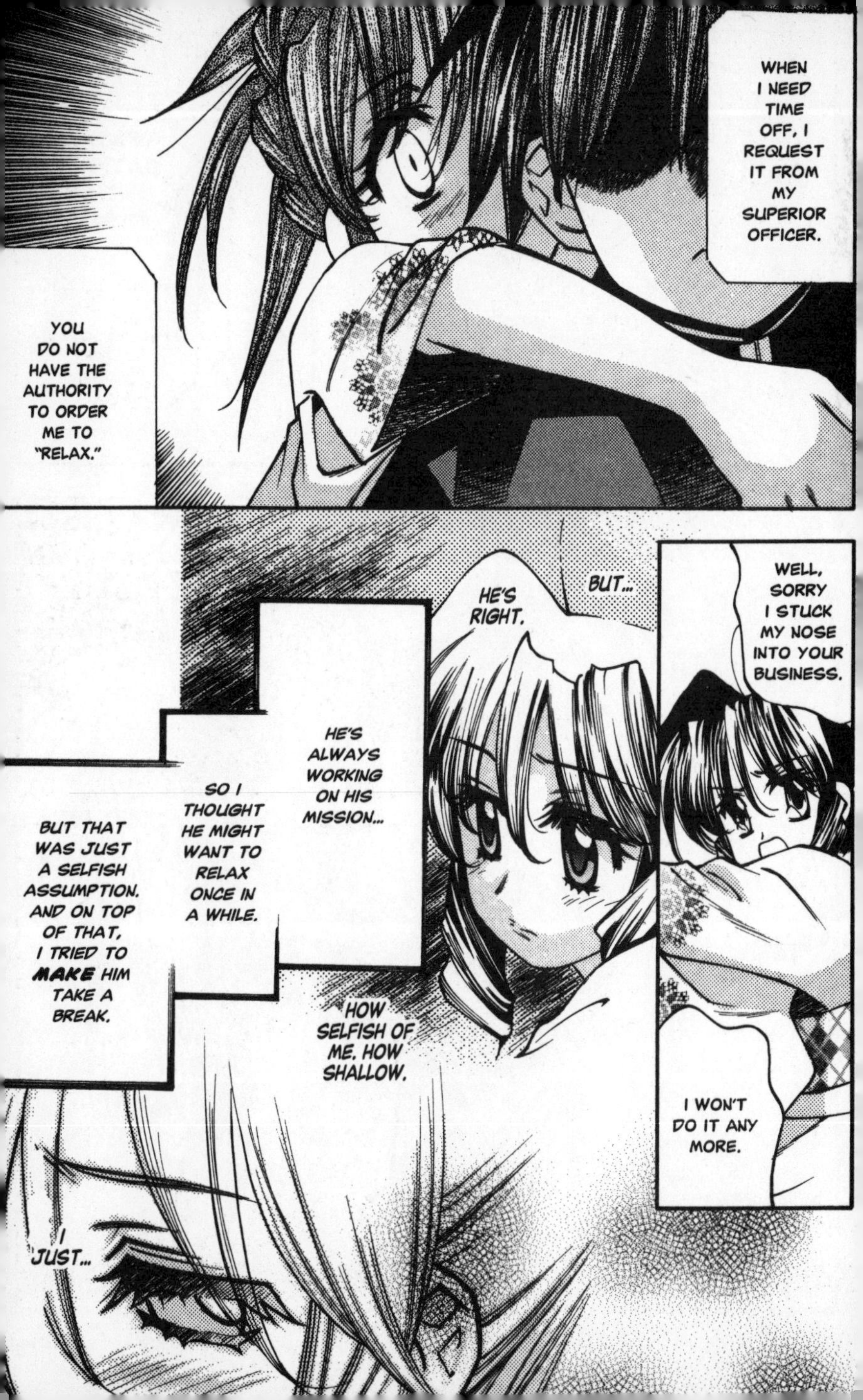
WHEN I NEED TIME OFF, I REQUEST IT FROM MY SUPERIOR OFFICER.
YOU DO NOT HAVE THE AUTHORITY TO ORDER ME TO "RELAX."
WELL, SORRY I STUCK MY NOSE INTO YOUR BUSINESS.
BUT...
HE'S RIGHT.
HE'S ALWAYS WORKING ON HIS MISSION...
SO I THOUGHT HE MIGHT WANT TO RELAX ONCE IN A WHILE.
BUT THAT WAS JUST A SELFISH ASSUMPTION. AND ON TOP OF THAT, I TRIED TO MAKE HIM TAKE A BREAK.
HOW SELFISH OF ME. HOW SHALLOW.
I WON'T DO IT ANY MORE.
I JUST...

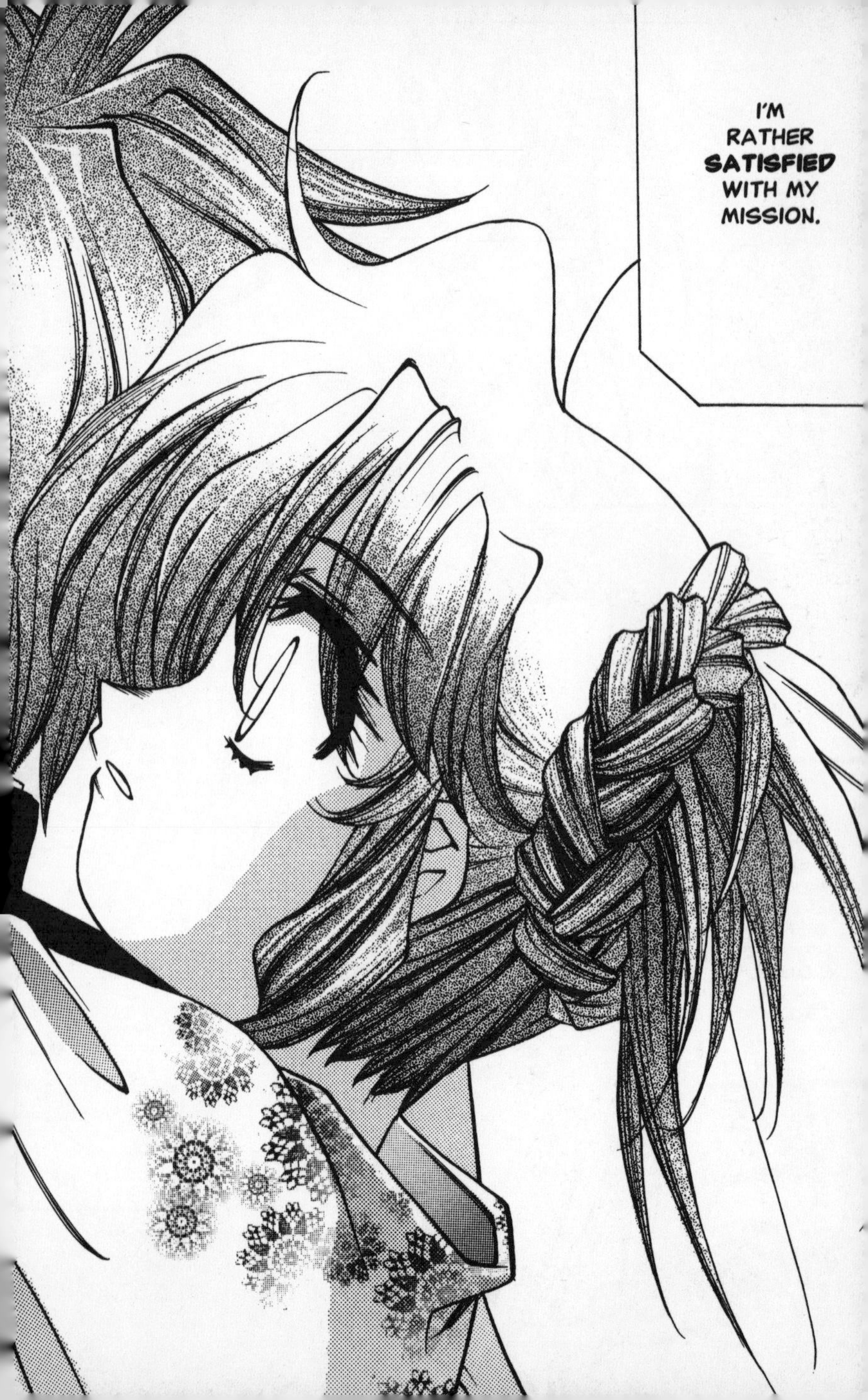
I'M RATHER **SATISFIED** WITH MY MISSION.

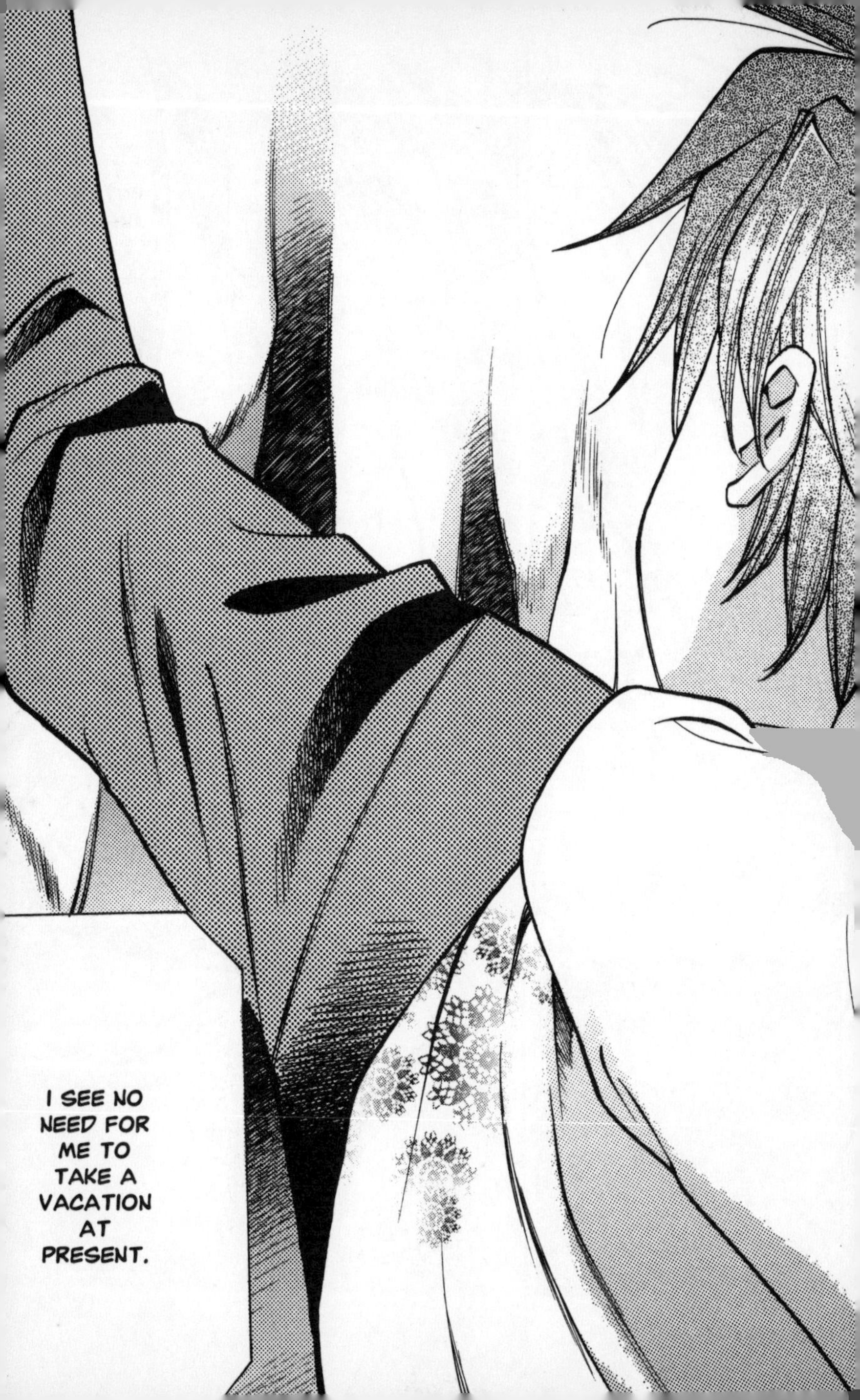
I SEE NO NEED FOR ME TO TAKE A VACATION AT PRESENT.

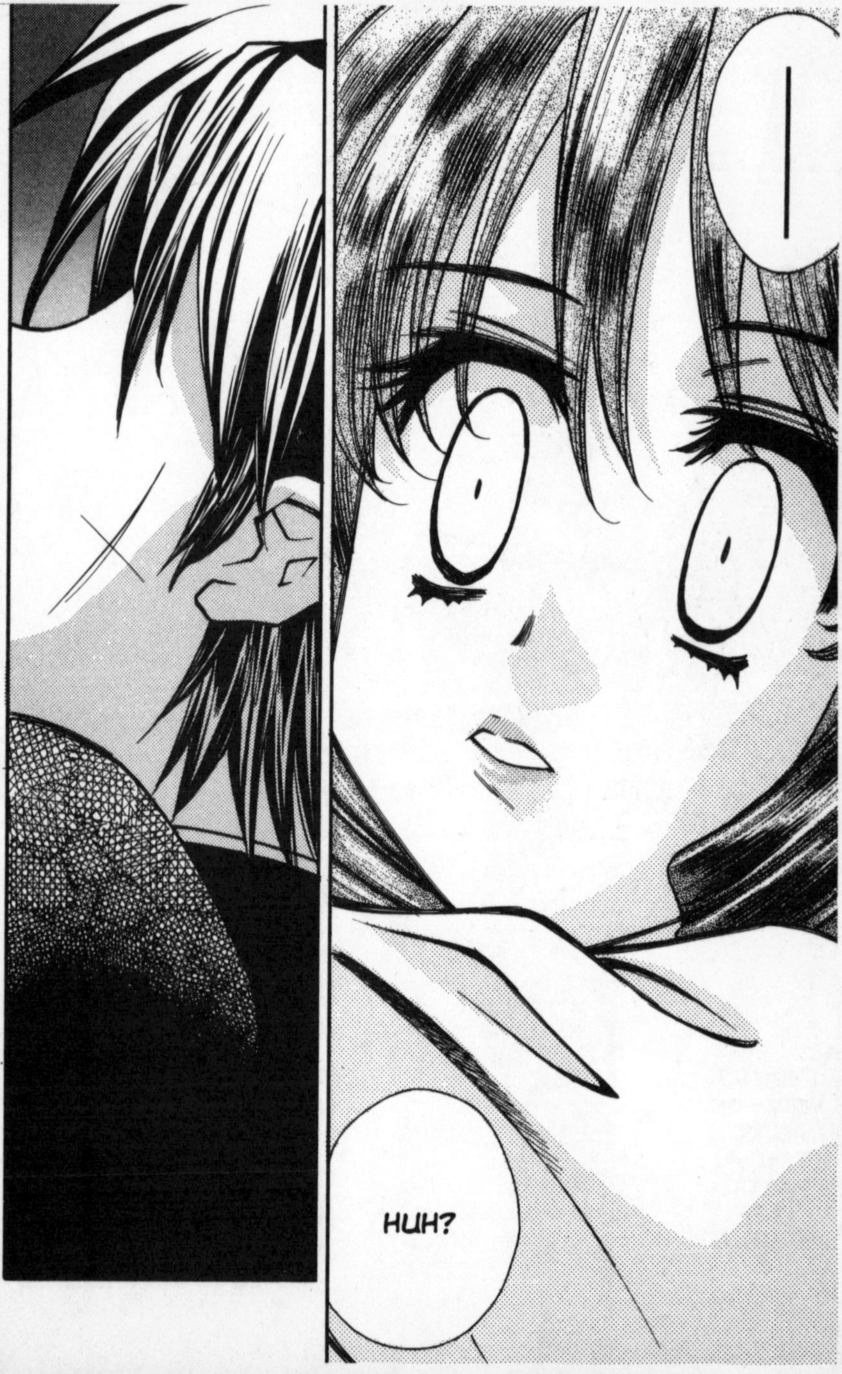

!
HUH?

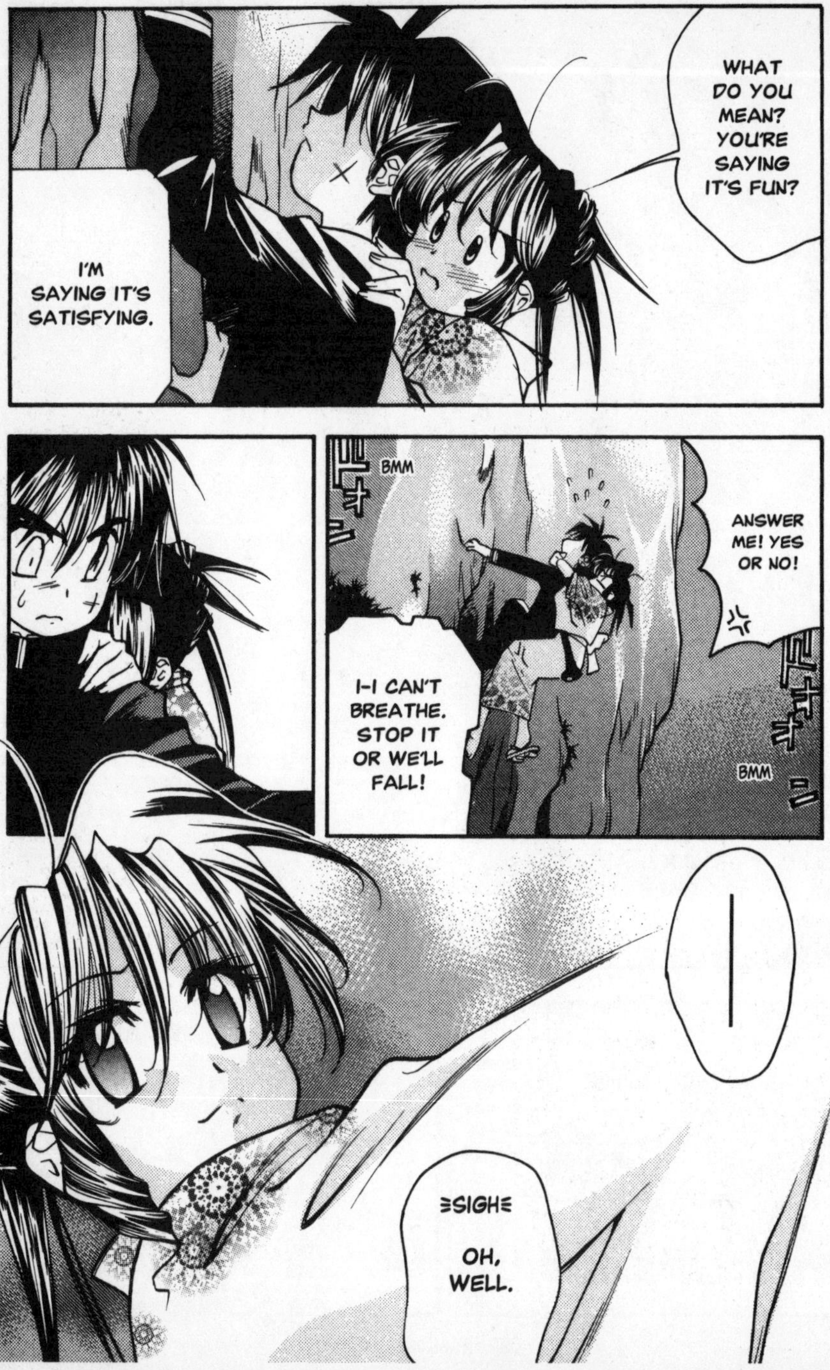
WHAT DO YOU MEAN? YOU'RE SAYING IT'S FUN?
I'M SAYING IT'S SATISFYING.
BMM
ANSWER ME! YES OR NO!
I-I CAN'T BREATHE. STOP IT OR WE'LL FALL!
BMM
≡SIGH≡
OH, WELL.

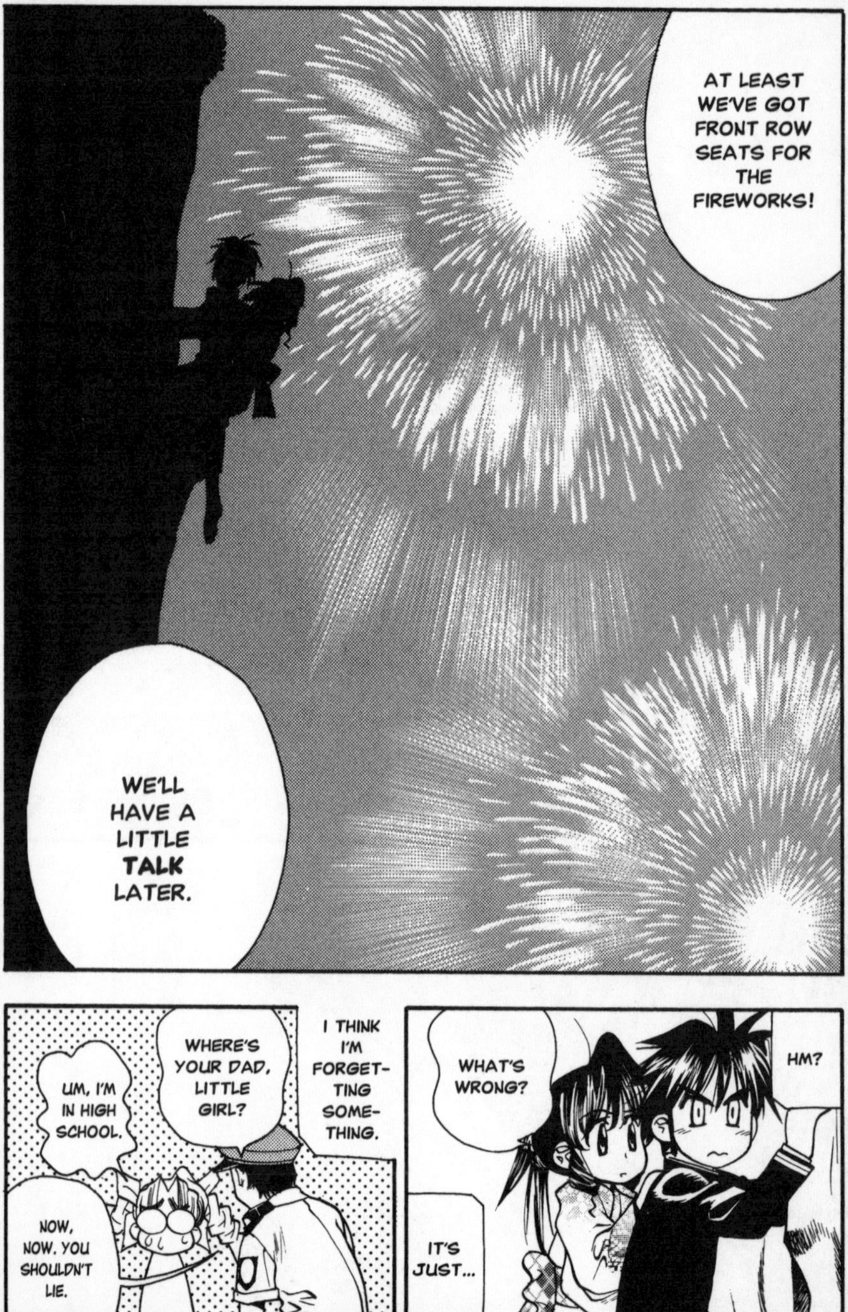
AT LEAST WE'VE GOT FRONT ROW SEATS FOR THE FIREWORKS!
WE'LL HAVE A LITTLE **TALK** LATER.
HM?
WHAT'S WRONG?
IT'S JUST...
I THINK I'M FORGET-TING SOME-THING.
WHERE'S YOUR DAD, LITTLE GIRL?
UM, I'M IN HIGH SCHOOL.
NOW, NOW. YOU SHOULDN'T LIE.

CONTINUED IN VOLUME 2

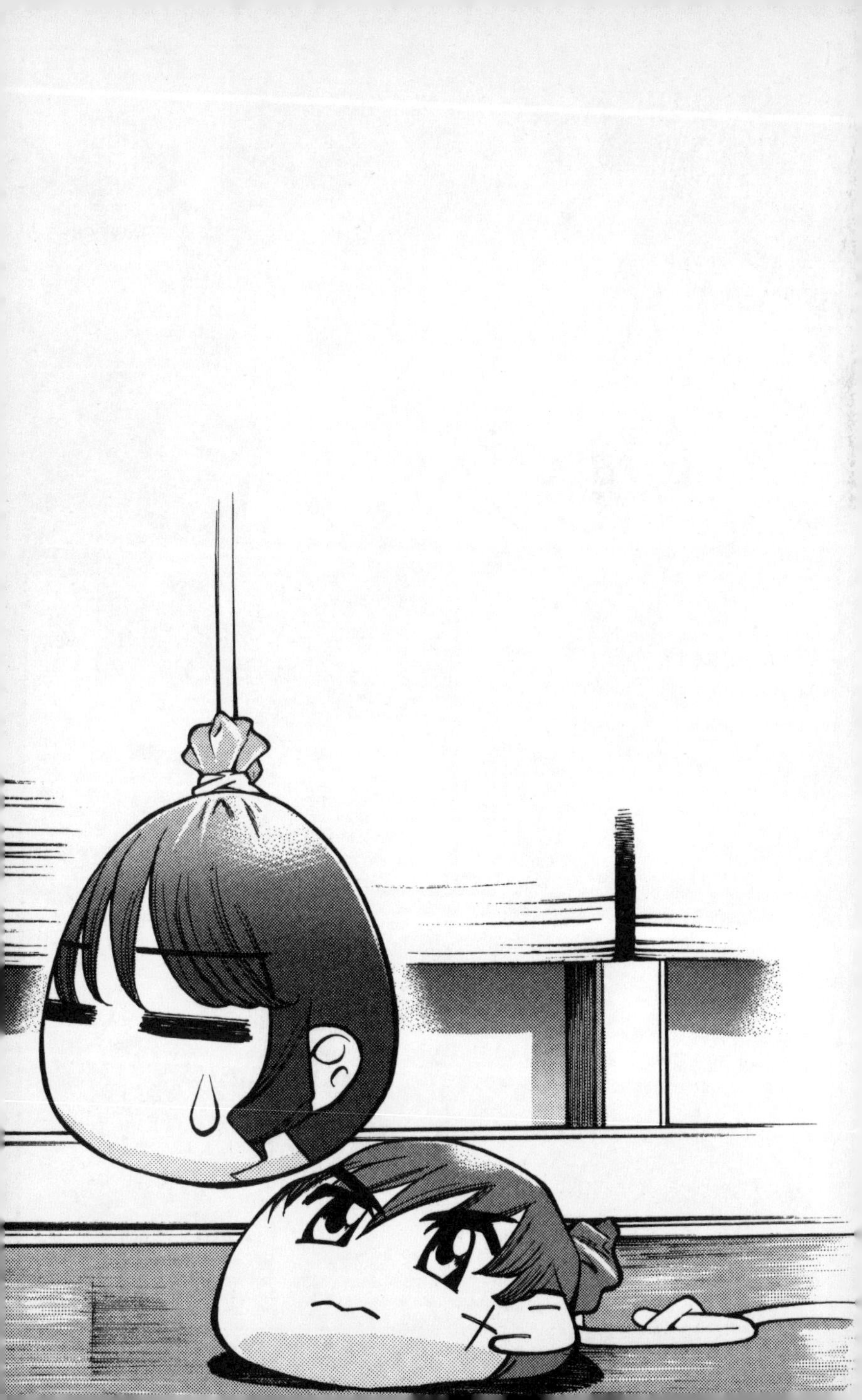

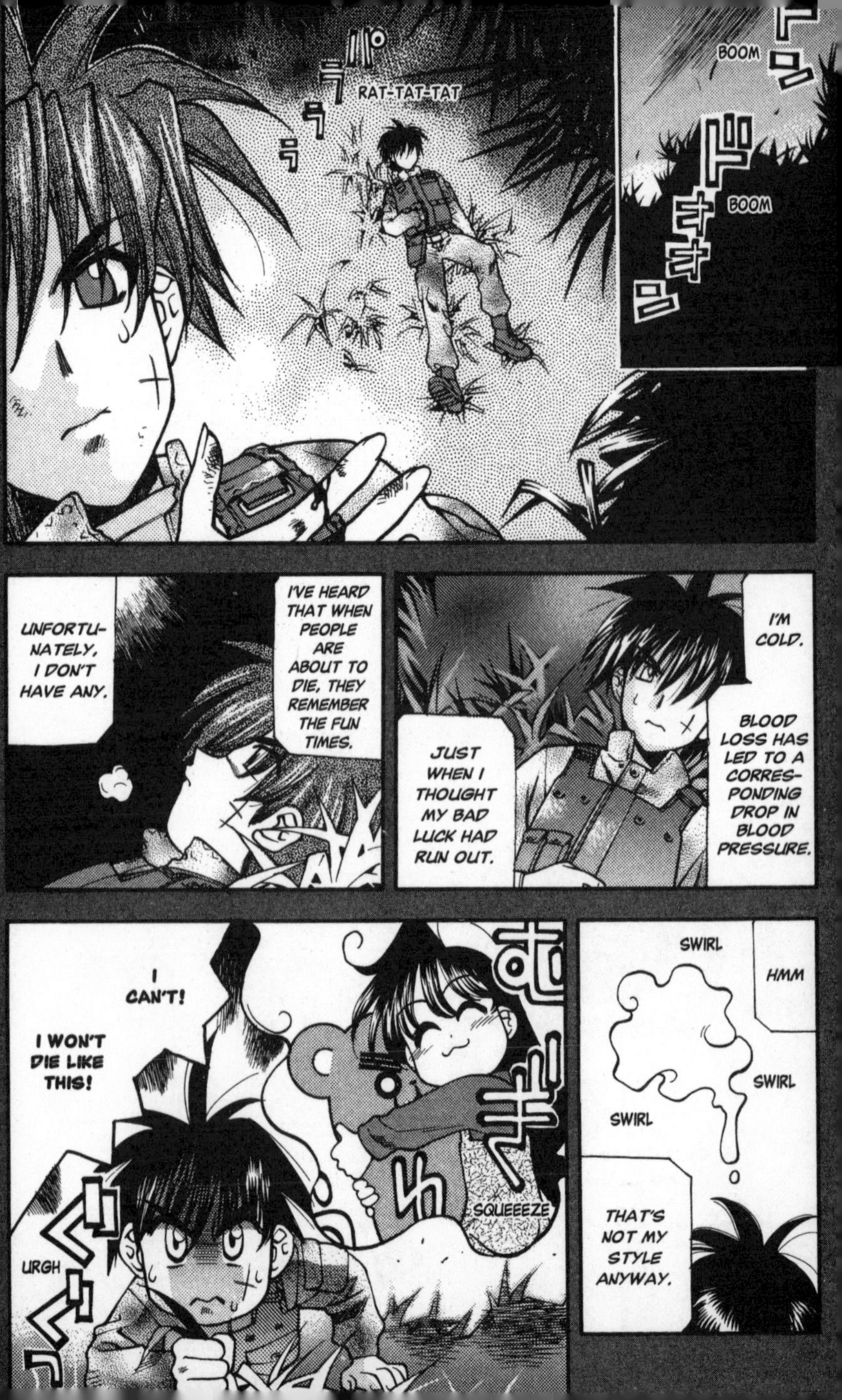
BOOM
BOOM
RAT-TAT-TAT
I'M COLD.
BLOOD LOSS HAS LED TO A CORRESPONDING DROP IN BLOOD PRESSURE.
JUST WHEN I THOUGHT MY BAD LUCK HAD RUN OUT.
I'VE HEARD THAT WHEN PEOPLE ARE ABOUT TO DIE, THEY REMEMBER THE FUN TIMES.
UNFORTUNATELY, I DON'T HAVE ANY.
HMM
SWIRL
SWIRL
SWIRL
THAT'S NOT MY STYLE ANYWAY.
I CAN'T!
I WON'T DIE LIKE THIS!
SQUEEEZE
URGH

FULL METAL PANIC! OVERLOAD! VOLUME ONE

© 2001 Tomohiro NAGAI · Shouji GATOU
© 2001 Shikidouji
Originally published in Japan in 2001 by
KADOKAWA SHOTEN PUBLISHING CO., LTD., Tokyo.
English translation rights arranged with
KADOKAWA SHOTEN PUBLISHING CO., LTD., Tokyo.

Translator **AMY FORSYTH**
Translation Staff **KAY BERTRAND AND BRENDAN FRAYNE**
Editor **JAVIER LOPEZ**
Assistant Editor **SHERIDAN JACOBS**
Graphic Artists **NATALIA REYNOLDS AND HEATHER GARY**
Intern **MARK MEZA**

Editorial Director **GARY STEINMAN**
Creative Director **JASON BABLER**
Sales and Marketing **CHRIS OARR**
Print Production Manager **BRIDGETT JANOTA**

International Coordinators **TORU IWAKAMI, MIYUKI KAMIYA,
KYOKO DRUMHELLER AND AI TAKAI**

President, CEO & Publisher **JOHN LEDFORD**

Email: editor@adv-manga.com
www.adv-manga.com
www.advfilms.com

For sales and distribution inquiries please call 1.800.282.7202

ADV MANGA™ is a division of A.D. Vision, Inc.
10114 W. Sam Houston Parkway, Suite 200, Houston, Texas 77099

ISBN: 1-4139-0315-0
First printing, June 2005
10 9 8 7 6 5 4 3 2 1
Printed in Canada

Full Metal Panic! Overload! Vol. 1

pg. 05

Don't be late without it
In anime and manga, it is a cliché that whenever a student is late for school, he or she is shown running down the street with a piece of toast dangling from the mouth, yelling "I'M LATE!" It's also very common for this person to trip or to bump into someone (especially a cute member of the opposite sex).

pg. 18

Like something out of a novel or a manga
The joke here is that *Full Metal Panic!* began as a series of novels, and is (of course) also a manga.

pg. 20

Irritability is a sign of low calcium
This is actually true. Other symptoms include hyperactivity, nervousness, high blood pressure, muscle spasms, and brittle bones.

pg. 54

Striker
"Striker" is a term for a forward on a soccer team. The joke is that "stalker" and "striker" sound fairly similar.

pg. 66

The *Wakadaisho* Series and Yuzo Kayama
Yuzo Kayama was a highly popular actor and singer in the 1960s. He had roles in Akira Kurosawa's movies *Sanjuro* and *Red Beard*, but he is probably best known for his starring role in the *Wakadaisho* series of films.

pg. 100

Koppepan
Koppepan is a kind of bread. It's shaped somewhat like a hotdog bun, sometimes slit down the middle, with a sort of cream filling.

pg. 129

Splitting the watermelon
The first panel shows Kaname using a stick to split a watermelon over Sosuke's head. This is a reference to *suikawari*, a typical summertime game in Japan wherein players are blindfolded and attempt to crack open a watermelon with a stick. Needless to say, the watermelon isn't usually put on top of someone's head!

pg. 150

Obanyaki
This is like a small, round, but very thick pancake stuffed with sweet red bean paste. The same thing made in the shape of a fish is called *taiyaki*.

pg. 151

Takoyaki
Originally created in Osaka, this simple dish consisting of a piece of octopus dropped into a small amount of batter and shaped into small, gooey balls has since spread all over Japan. *Takoyaki* is commonly sold by street vendors, but there are also sit-down restaurants such as Osaka's famous "Takomasa."

pg. 161

Mask
The mask the boy pulls over his face looks like Ultraman, the hero of a popular series of live-action superhero shows.

FULL METAL PANIC! OVERLOAD! 2

When Sosuke's old military rival worms his way into the halls of Jindai High and into the hearts of his female classmates, it's all-out war on the toughest battlefield of them all...the classroom!

Sosuke will set his studies aside to dish out a few lessons in the art of combat, but another invasion interrupts his assignment. He'll have to ward off the evil that threatens Kaname with the most lethal weapon he can find—cold medicine!

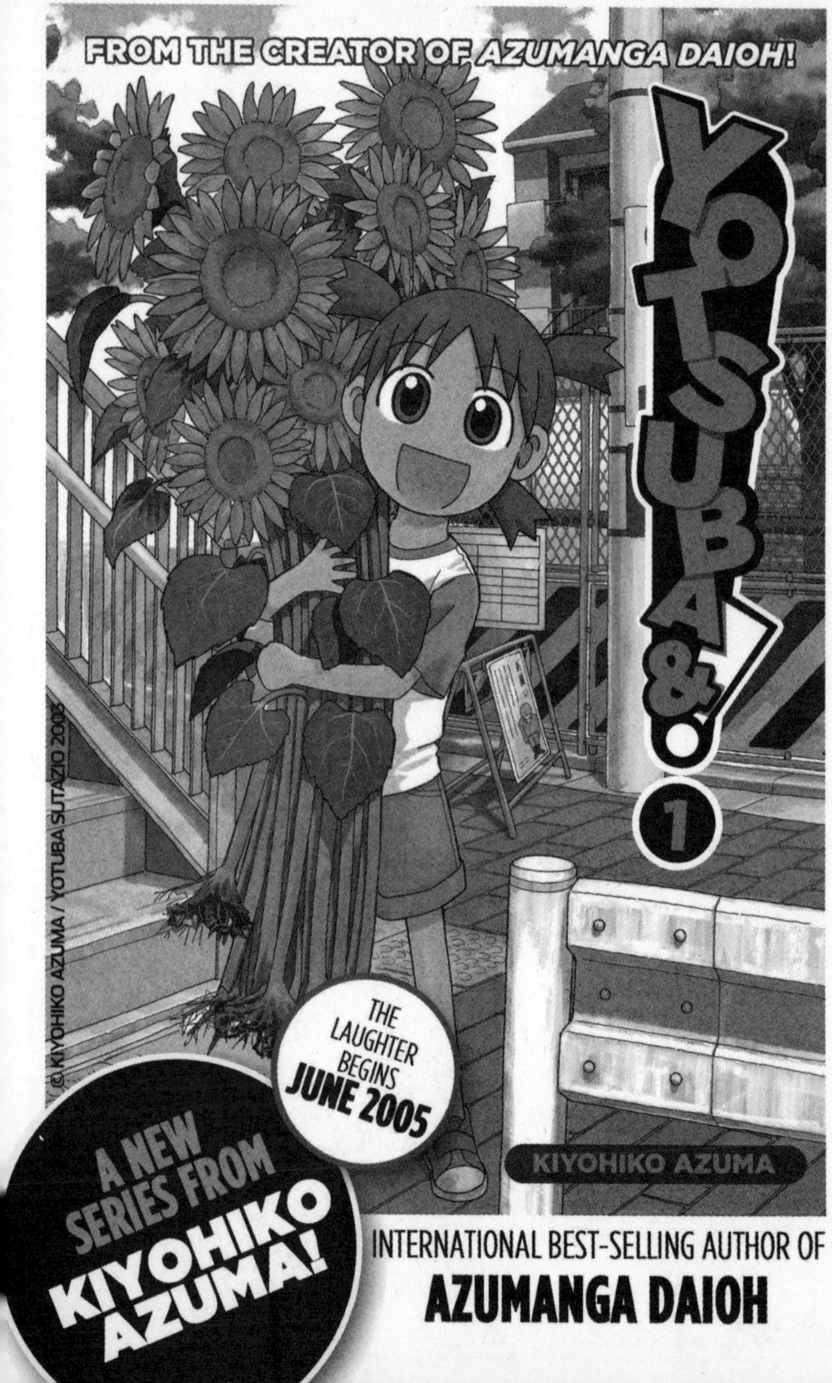
FROM THE CREATOR OF AZUMANGA DAIOH!
YOTSUBA&!
1
KIYOHIKO AZUMA
© KIYOHIKO AZUMA / YOTUBA SUTAZIO 2003
THE LAUGHTER BEGINS JUNE 2005
A NEW SERIES FROM KIYOHIKO AZUMA!
INTERNATIONAL BEST-SELLING AUTHOR OF
AZUMANGA DAIOH

DO YOU HAVE WHAT IT TAKES TO MAKE IT IN CROMARTIE HIGH?

Do you have a tough nickname?

❑ Yes ❑ No

How many fights have you been in?

❑ None ❑ More than 100

❑ 5-10 ❑ None – no one ever had the stones to challenge me

What's in your bookbag?

❑ My homework ❑ Porn ❑ A metal plate

How tough do you look? Check all that apply.

❑ Pompadour ❑ Handlebar mustache ❑ Shaved eyebrows

❑ Carpet of chest hair ❑ Lazy swagger ❑ Menacing glare

Say you checked out eleven adult videos. Three of those were new releases, so you had to return them the next day. How many videos do you have left?

❑ 3 ❑ 8 ❑ 11 – I would never give them back.

How did you rate?

10 points or less	**Errand Boy**
10 – 15	**Wannabe Punk**
30 – 40	**One Badass Dude**
More than 100	**Champ by Default**

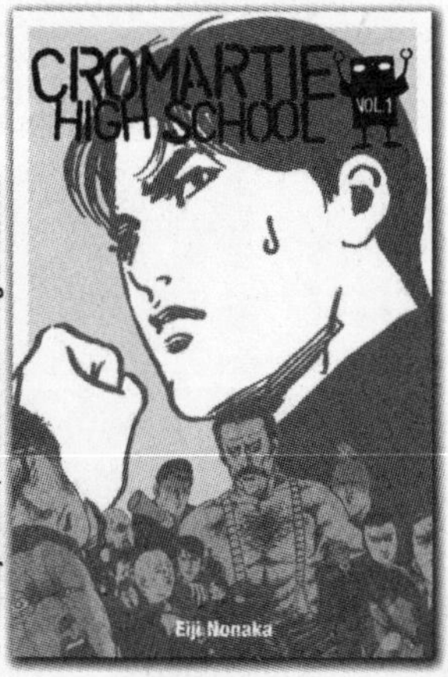
CROMARTIE HIGH SCHOOL
VOL.1
Eiji Nonaka

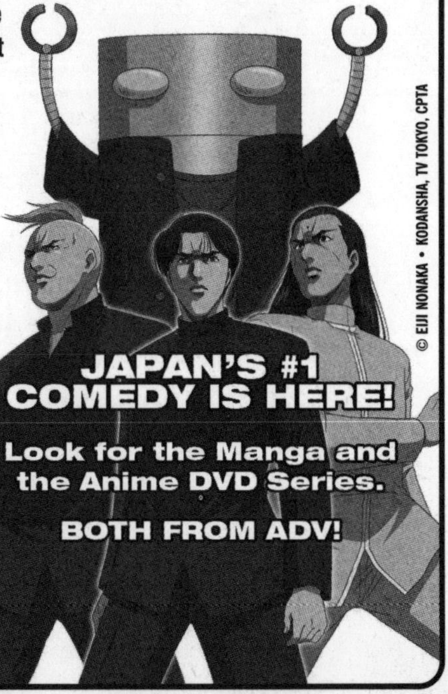
JAPAN'S #1 COMEDY IS HERE!
Look for the Manga and the Anime DVD Series.
BOTH FROM ADV!

ADV Manga™

www.adv-manga.com